SELLING THE SACRED

There's religion in my marketing! There's marketing in my religion! *Selling the Sacred* explores the religio-cultural and media implications of a two-sided phenomenon: marketing religion as a product and marketing products as religion. What do various forms of religion/marketing collaboration look like in the twenty-first century, and what does this tell us about American culture and society?

Social and technological changes rapidly and continuously reframe religious and marketing landscapes. Crossfit is a "cult." Televangelists use psychographics and data marketing. QAnon is a religion *and* big business. These are some of the examples highlighted in this collection, which engages themes related to capitalist narratives, issues related to gender and race, and the intersection of religion, politics, and marketing, among other key issues.

The innovative contributors examine the phenomenon of selling the sacred, providing a better understanding of how marketing tactics, married with religious content, influence our thinking and everyday lives. These scholars bring to light how political, economic, and ideological agendas infuse the construction and presentation of the "sacred," via more traditional religious institutions or consumer-product marketing. By examining religion and marketing broadly, this book offers engaging tools to recognize and unpack what gets sold as "sacred," what's at stake, and the consequences.

A go-to resource for those working in marketing studies, religious studies, and media studies, *Selling the Sacred* is also a must-read for religious and marketing professionals.

Mara Einstein is an internationally recognized expert on deceptive marketing tactics, a sought-after speaker and writer, and a Professor of Media Studies at Queens College (CUNY), United States.

Sarah McFarland Taylor is an award-winning author and Associate Professor of Religious Studies and Environmental Policy and Culture at Northwestern University, United States.

SELLING THE SACRED

Religion and Marketing
from Crossfit to QAnon

Edited by Mara Einstein and
Sarah McFarland Taylor

Routledge
Taylor & Francis Group

LONDON AND NEW YORK

Designed cover image: RichLegg / Getty Images

First published 2024
by Routledge
4 Park Square, Milton Park, Abingdon, Oxon OX14 4RN

and by Routledge
605 Third Avenue, New York, NY 10158

Routledge is an imprint of the Taylor & Francis Group, an informa business

© 2024 selection and editorial matter, Mara Einstein and Sarah McFarland Taylor;
individual chapters, the contributors

The right of Mara Einstein and Sarah McFarland Taylor to be identified as the authors
of the editorial material, and of the authors for their individual chapters, has been
asserted in accordance with sections 77 and 78 of the Copyright, Designs and Patents
Act 1988.

All rights reserved. No part of this book may be reprinted or reproduced or utilised in
any form or by any electronic, mechanical, or other means, now known or hereafter
invented, including photocopying and recording, or in any information storage or
retrieval system, without permission in writing from the publishers.

Trademark notice: Product or corporate names may be trademarks or registered
trademarks, and are used only for identification and explanation without intent to
infringe.

British Library Cataloguing-in-Publication Data
A catalogue record for this book is available from the British Library

ISBN: 978-1-032-37842-8 (hbk)
ISBN: 978-1-032-37841-1 (pbk)
ISBN: 978-1-003-34222-9 (ebk)

DOI: 10.4324/9781003342229

Typeset in Times New Roman
by KnowledgeWorks Global Ltd.

CONTENTS

FIGURES

CONTRIBUTORS

James S. Bielo is an Associate Professor of Religious Studies at Northwestern University. He is the author of five books, most recently *Materializing the Bible: Scripture, Sensation, Place* (2021).

Susannah Crockford is a Lecturer in anthropology at the University of Exeter in the United Kingdom. Her first monograph, *Ripples of the Universe: Spirituality in Sedona, Arizona*, was published in 2021 by the University of Chicago Press. With research interests at the intersection of religion, medicine, and environment, she has published widely in peer-reviewed journals using ethnographic material from fieldwork in Arizona, Missouri, and Louisiana in the United States, and the United Kingdom, Belgium, and Sweden in Northern Europe. She received her Ph.D. in 2017 from the London School of Economics.

Sarah Dees is an Assistant Professor in the Department of Philosophy and Religious Studies at Iowa State University. She is a scholar of American and Indigenous religions, with a focus on the history of the study and representation of Native North American religious traditions. Her published work has examined U.S. federal Indian policy, the U.S. government-funded anthropological study of Native American religions, and the historical appropriation of Native American traditions.

Mara Einstein is a Professor of media studies at the City University of New York (CUNY) and the author of six books, including *Black Ops Advertising: Native Ads, Content Marketing, and the Covert World of the Digital Sell, Compassion, Inc.*, and *Brands of Faith*. Prior to becoming an academic, she worked as a marketing executive at numerous advertising agencies as well as MTV and NBC. She is an internationally recognized expert on marketing criticism and is regularly quoted in major publications, like *The New York Times*, the *Wall Street Journal*, and *The Washington Post*. Her current research is on how brands use cult marketing tactics in the age of digital media.

Justin W. Henry is currently the Bhagwan Padma Prabhu Endowed Assistant Professor in the Department of Religious Studies at the University of South Florida. He earned his Ph.D. in the History of Religions from the University of Chicago Divinity School in 2017 and has published on aspects of Sanskrit, Pali, Sinhala, and Tamil literature in Sri Lanka and South India. His first book, *Ravana's Kingdom: The Ramayana and Sri Lankan History from Below*, was released in 2022. He is currently working on a general audience book on the "many Ramayanas" of Asia as well as a monograph project on Jain, Hindu, and Buddhist attitudes toward wealth acquisition, philanthropy, and business ethics, historically.

Brian Hughes is a Research Assistant Professor in the American University School of Public Affairs, program of Justice, Law, and Criminology. He is also the co-founder and Associate Director of the Polarization and Extremism Research and Innovation Lab (PERIL), an applied research lab that develops studies and interventions to build community resilience and reduce the risk of radicalization to extremism. PERIL is the only academic research group named in the U.S. National Strategy to Counter Antisemitism. Dr. Hughes's scholarly research explores the impact of communication technology on political and religious extremism, terrorism, conspiracy, and fringe culture. His writing has appeared in the CTC Sentinel at West Point, the International Journal of Communication, Lawfare, and the Center for Analysis of the Radical Right. His expert statement on the role of social media in the January 6th Insurrection is included in the Select January 6th Committee's record. Dr. Hughes is a Draper Richards Kaplan Foundation Entrepreneur.

Corrina Laughlin teaches media studies at Loyola Marymount University. She received her B.A. in English and Religious Studies from the University of California, Santa Barbara, and she holds an M.A. in English from New York University and a Ph.D. in Communication from the Annenberg School for Communication at the University of Pennsylvania. She is the author of the award-winning book, *Redeem All: How Digital Life is Changing Evangelical Culture*.

Eric Michael Mazur is the Gloria & David Furman Professor of Judaic Studies, professor of religious studies, and Religion, Law, & Politics Fellow of the Robert Nusbaum Center at Virginia Wesleyan University, where he teaches courses on Judaism, religion in American culture, and the academic study of religion. He is the author, editor, and co-editor of numerous works on religion and popular culture, including *The Encyclopedia of Religion & Film* (2011), *God in the Details* (with Kate McCarthy, 2001/2010), *The Routledge Companion of Religion & Popular Culture* (with John Lyden, 2015), *The Bloomsbury Reader in the Study of Religion &*

Popular Culture (with Lisle Dalton and Richard Callahan, Jr., 2022), and *Religion & Outer Space* (with Sarah McFarland Taylor, 2023), as well as shorter pieces on religion in American culture and history, the arts/literature/film, law, politics, race/ethnicity, and the sociology of religion.

John Modern is Arthur and Katherine Shadek Professor of the Humanities and Religious studies at Franklin & Marshall College. Modern co-founded and co-edits Class 200: New Studies in Religion (with Kathryn Lofton) at the University of Chicago Press. Modern is the author of *Secularism in Antebellum America* (2011) and *The Bop Apocalypse: The Religious Visions of Kerouac, Ginsberg, and Burroughs* (2001). His *Neuromatic: Or, A Particular History of Religion and the Brain* (2021) received the best book award from the International Society of Science and Religion. Modern produced the multi-media project, Machines in Between (2021–23), and is currently working on *The Book of Akron*, a project that explores the end(s) of techno-modernity through the global history of rubber. Modern is a former member of the School of Social Science at the Institute for Advanced Study and an ACLS Frederick Burkhardt fellow at the McNeil Center for Early American Studies.

David Morgan is Professor of Religious Studies at Duke University. His research has focused on the visual and material culture of religion. He was co-founder and co-editor of the journal *Material Religion*, and he co-edits a book series on the material culture of religion published by Bloomsbury. Morgan is an elected member of Clare Hall, Cambridge University, and has been supported by fellowships from the National Endowment for the Humanities, the Getty Foundation, Pew Program in Religion and American History at Yale, and the American Philosophical Society. He is the author of several books, including *Visual Piety* (1998), *The Sacred Gaze* (2005), *The Forge of Vision* (2015), *Images at Work: The Material Culture of Enchantment* (2018), and *The Thing about Religion: An Introduction to the Material Study of Religions* (2021). Morgan is currently at work on a book project that explores the history of the visual culture of revelation.

Cody Musselman is a Postdoctoral Research Associate at the John C. Danforth Center on Religion and Politics at Washington University in St. Louis. She earned a Ph.D. in Religious Studies from Yale University and has degrees in religion from Harvard Divinity School and Kalamazoo College. She is an Ethnographer of contemporary American religion, focusing on the intersections of religion, capitalism, and health. She is working on a book, "Spiritual Exercises: Fitness and Religion in Modern America."

John Durham Peters teaches and writes on media history and philosophy. He is the María Rosa Menocal Professor of English and of Film & Media Studies at Yale University. He taught at the University of Iowa between 1986 and 2016. He is the author of *Speaking into the Air: A History of the Idea of Communication, Courting* *the Abyss, The Marvelous Clouds: Toward a Philosophy of Elemental Media*, and most recently, *Promiscuous Knowledge*, with the late Kenneth Cmiel.

Kristin M. Peterson is an Assistant Professor in the Department of Communication at Boston College, teaching courses related to the intersections of media and religion. Her book, *Unruly Souls: The Digital Activism of Muslim and Christian Feminists* (2022), examines how digital spaces facilitate intersectional feminist activism within Evangelical Christian and Muslim American communities. She has published articles and book chapters on Muslim Instagram influencers, podcasts, and grief, the digital mourning after the murder of three Muslim college students in Chapel Hill, the #ChurchToo and #MosqueMeToo movements, and the Ms. Marvel comic series.

John Schmalzbauer is a Sociologist who teaches in the Department of Languages, Cultures, and Religions at Missouri State University, where he holds the Blanche Gorman Strong Chair in Protestant Studies. He currently serves as principal investigator on the Landscape Study of Chaplaincy and Campus Ministry in the United States, a five-year project funded by Lilly Endowment Inc. His research and teaching focus on religion and American culture. Schmalzbauer is the co-author with Kathleen Mahoney of *The Resilience of Religion in American Higher Education* (2018). His first book, *People of Faith: Religious Conviction in American Journalism and Higher Education* (2003), explores the role of religion in the careers of 40 prominent journalists and scholars, including Cokie Roberts, E. J. Dionne, Andrew Greeley, and George Marsden. His reviews and commentary have appeared in Religion Dispatches, the *Wall Street Journal, Sojourners*, the *Immanent Frame*, and the *PBS NewsHour's Patchwork Nation*.

Chad E. Seales is Associate Professor of Religious Studies at the University of Texas at Austin. His research addresses the cultural relationship between religion and secularism in American life, focusing on the historical development of evangelical Protestantism, workplace chaplaincy, corporate management, and industrial agriculture as entangled in the salvific promises of neoliberal capitalism. He is the author of *Religion Around Bono: Evangelical Enchantment and Neoliberal Capitalism* (2019), and *The Secular Spectacle: Performing Religion in a Southern Town* (2013), as well as articles on industrial religion, corporate chaplaincy, religion and film, and secularism and secularization in the United States.

Sarah McFarland Taylor is the award-winning author of *Green Sisters: A Spiritual Ecology* and *Ecopiety: Green Media and the Dilemma of Environmental Virtue*. She is also the co-editor with Eric Mazur of *Religion & Outer Space* (Routledge). An Associate Professor of Religious Studies, American Studies, and Environmental Policy and Culture at Northwestern University, she specializes in the study of media, religion, environment, and public moral engagement. Taylor works with students, academic professionals in both the sciences and humanities, and with entertainment industry mediamakers to teach and promote effective climate communication that engages both climate deniers and climate fatalists in productive ways. Taylor's research makes the case for fostering evidence-based climate hope as fuel for collective climate action.

Deborah Whitehead is Associate Professor and chair of the Department of Religious Studies and associate director of the Center for Media, Religion, and Culture at the University of Colorado Boulder. Her research focuses on intersections between religion and gender, popular culture, and media in U.S. history. She is the author of *William James, Pragmatism, and American Culture* (2015), and her current book project is a study of contemporary U.S. evangelical media.

ACKNOWLEDGMENTS

As co-editors for this project, we have experienced myriad points of connection and synergy. Mara is a "product" of Northwestern University's Kellogg School of Management. Sarah, as a professor at Northwestern, is a product of and enthusiastic "evangelist" for Northwestern's "AND Model," which promotes the kind of research that transcends discipline-specific approaches in order to tackle pressing collective problems. In the marketing world, "cross-functional teams," which traverse isolated silos to combine different skill sets, are the gold standard. In academia, when cross-functional collaboration works best, it fosters shared comprehension of the team's knowledge, broader thinking, strengthening of core arguments, and the capacity to generate innovative results stemming from unique perspectives. When illustrators attempt to visually represent these sorts of cross-functional collaborations, they often do so by depicting interlocking puzzle pieces. The publication of *Selling the Sacred* has been made possible by many such intersections, creating a picture that is so much larger than the sum of its parts.

First, we co-editors likely would not have met and struck up conversation had we not both been participants in research meetings hosted by the ardently (and unapologetically) interdisciplinary International Society for Media, Religion, and Culture. We owe a debt of credit to the co-founders of this guild and to the co-creators of this subfield, who have made the kind of intersecting scholarly work we do possible by cultivating a ripe ecology for novel ideas/connections to bubble to the surface.

I (Sarah) wish, most of all, to thank my co-editor Mara, who has been amazing to work with every step of the way, but especially when I fractured my arm shortly before our manuscript deadline! I feel truly blessed to have worked with such a great collaborator and to have made a good friend along the way. I also want to thank the Luce Foundation-funded multi-year "Public Religion and Public

Scholarship in the Digital Age" working scholars' group, launched and run by CU Boulder's Center for the Study of Media, Religion, and Culture. Stewart Hoover, Nabil Echchaibi, and Deborah Whitehead have been enormously supportive of my research over the years, while their leadership has modeled excellence in adapting to unforeseen circumstances (the global pandemic), fostering team cultures of mutuality and respect, and creating scholarly environments in practices and processes that are conducive to taking risks, testing, learning, and collaborating. As Stewart retires this year, I especially want to express my gratitude to him for the senior mentoring role he has so generously played in my academic life. I will also forever be grateful to Walter Capps, Clark Roof, Catherine Albanese, and Henry Jenkins for their unflagging wisdom, guidance, and good will.

I would also like to thank "The Bobs" at Northwestern, Religious Studies Professor Robert Orsi and Professor of Rhetoric and Public Culture Robert Hariman, for graciously reading and commenting on a previous draft of my PragerU chapter in this volume, as well as other work I have produced over the years. I greatly value your incisive perspectives and am perennially grateful for your time and feedback. My husband, John, also a Kellogg MBA, a growth strategy consultant with years of experience in marketing analytics, stepped up as beta reader for my chapter contribution, offering an extra set of eyes. Having been raised in the world of media and broadcasting from a young age, I am appreciative to my parents, who concertedly trained my critical eye for media analysis by having my sisters and me review television pilots at home from as early as I can remember. I have continued that media legacy in a way that no one may have imagined at the time, but it has been an enormously fulfilling way to engage in and contribute to important public conversations (especially vis-à-vis climate change), and I owe that to them.

I (Mara) would like to thank Sarah for her tireless work on this project. You could have no better collaborator. I am grateful to Gregory Epstein for taking the time to chat with me and to Jamie Cohen, who graciously made this connection.

As always, I am grateful for my husband, David, who, as a lawyer, brings analytical insights to my musings that other academics might not (again—getting out of our silos). I would never have stepped into the world of TikTok if it was not for my daughter, Cayla Einstein. She helped me imagine a place where a "mature scholar" might have something to say in that digital space. I am grateful to the many religious and ex-religious influencers I have met there. You teach me every day.

Finally, collectively, we want to make sure to express our heartfelt gratitude to all the wonderful contributors to this volume, who surmounted all sorts of challenges to deliver their chapters and images to us. There would be no volume without your creativity, thoughtfulness, hard work, dedication, and scholarly acumen. Thank you for entrusting your work to us. Editorial Assistant Phillip Davis went above and beyond, offering granular and sophisticated analysis of evangelical materials just when we needed it most. Phil, we are both impressed with your work ethic and professionalism and look forward to reading your own future co-edited volumes. Thank you to Religious Studies and Philosophy Professor Myev Rees, who was a hero, stepping in on short notice when we most needed her to lend her expertise. Myev, you are a true pro and model of grace under pressure. Last but not least, we are tremendously grateful to Rebecca Clintworth, Manas Roy, and Iman Hakimi at Routledge for their continuous enthusiasm, support, and patience in bringing this project to light. And to our anonymous reviewers and to many others who informally commented and provided sounding platforms for this project, we thank you and hope you enjoy the book.

INTRODUCTION

Mara Einstein and Sarah McFarland Taylor

At the very moment when polls show a decreasing number of Americans expressing a religious preference and church attendance is in free fall (Jones, 2023; Nortey and Rotolo, 2023), millions engage with online content or in secular spaces that act to fill a void of community and spiritual engagement. This is occurring because the tools of marketing and religion have effectively coalesced to attract consumers to products viewed as secular, sacred, and/or that span a spectrum in between.

Selling the Sacred is the first scholarly work to explore the religio-cultural and media implications of what we see as a two-sided phenomenon: marketing religion as a product and marketing products as religion. Its chapters reflect how social and technological changes are reframing the religious and spiritual landscape. At the same time, the work engages themes related to capitalist narratives, gender and race, and the intersections of religion, politics, and marketing, among other issues. Some of the key questions we address include: How does marketing concertedly engage religious ideas, rhetorics, sensibilities, aesthetics, and practices? And, what might various forms of religion/marketing collaboration tell us about 21st-century American culture and society?

In these chapters, scholars examine the phenomenon of selling the sacred, providing readers with a better understanding of how marketing tactics married with religious content influence their thinking and their everyday lives. The importance of this cannot be overstated; what we call religio-marketing is far-reaching and has worked to reduce both consumer and congregant agency. Our contributors bring to light myriad ways that political, economic, and ideological agendas infuse the construction and presentation of the "sacred," whether via more traditional religious institutions or consumer-product marketing. By examining religion and marketing broadly in this way, we provide citizens with tools to recognize and unpack what gets sold as "sacred" and with what outcomes and interests in mind.

DOI: 10.4324/9781003342229-1

The religio-marketing nexus has existed as a serious field of research for almost two decades. As interdisciplinarity has called for more integration across key areas of the academy, this work is an example of where integrating scholarship can bring important new insights to topics such as politics, late capitalism, race, and gender. No existing work looks at marketing and religion as a single entity and its impact on culture and society.

There's Religion in My Marketing; There's Marketing in My Religion

Religion and marketing have a long, intertwined history. Marketing historian Eric H. Shaw has argued that pre-historic precursors to marketing practices can be identified and traced back as far as 40,000 years (Shaw, 1995; Shaw and Jones, 2005), and other marketing scholars have made the case for marketing dating back to ancient world (Brown, Hirschman and Maclaren, 2001). In 2018, a team of Egyptologists from the German University of Tübingen uncovered a sophisticated mummification workshop on the banks of the Nile in Saqqara. Ramadan Hussein, the team's lead archeologist, has said the artifacts found point to "Priest-embalmers [having been] professional entrepreneurs who offered burial packages for every budget." Papyrus documents recovered from the area more than a century prior to the 2018 discovery show that the market-minded preparers of the dead also offered and advertised "spiritual upkeep plans," in which priests would "shepherd wayward spirits and maintain their tombs" (Curry, 2020; Wu, 2020). The Marketing Museum, a digital collection of marketing artifacts, curates items ranging from popular signed ("branded") pottery from (600–700 BC), depicting athletes participating in the sacred ritualistic games of Ancient Greece, event advertising "merch" in the form of souvenir cups from gladiator battles in Ancient Rome (50–100 AD), and bronze printed posters from Song Dynasty China, advertising the unique offerings of local merchants and services providers.[1] A tour through the ancient city of Pompeii, preserved by the volcanic ash eruption of Mount Vesuvius nearly 2000 years ago, reveals erotic frescos on the walls of many dwellings, but especially so in and around the local brothel. Those practicing the "oldest profession" (prostitution), or at least their managers, were also savvy marketers (another old profession), crafting an ambiance to whet potential customers' appetites to consume a variety of sex acts by evoking imaginative possibilities, and by deploying a visual rhetoric suggestive of Venus, Pompeii's patron goddess of sex and love and a powerful "influencer" (Levin-Richardson, 2019).

"Church merch" dates back at least to the Middle Ages and spans the marketing and purchase of saint relics and reliquaries, vials of holy water and saint's blood, prayer beads, painted miniatures, religious artwork, and pilgrimage "swag" (Dyer, 1989; McDannell, 1995; Robinson, 2010; Bell and Dale, 2011). In "The Medieval Pilgrimage Business," economic historians Bell and Dale observe, "our medieval forebears were very much aware of what we describe today as 'brand management.' Shrine managers targeted their clientele, promoted their advantages over competitors, and provided supporting evidence for miraculous claims with story collections." These practices continued throughout the ages, gaining more traction at the turn of the last century.

With the invention of Gutenberg's printing press (c. 1455), marking the start of the early modern era, the speed, scope, and scale of marketing accelerated drastically, as advertising handbills were used to promote newly mass-produced Bibles (Lamal et al, 2021). Fast forward several hundred years and we see religious organizations using local newspapers and roadside billboards to announce their services (Kotler and Wrenn, 1992; Moore, 1994; Einstein, 2008). With the introduction of broadcast media—first radio and then television—sermons and religious services became staples of programming that were required by law (Hoover, 1988; Ferré, 1990; Hangen, 2002). While not outright advertising as we might think of it, these programs marketed the notion that religion was fundamental to American life (Kruse, 2016; Brehm, 2021). By the 1980s, televangelists were a staple on broadcast television, especially in Sunday morning time slots, and more broadly on the newly emerging cable networks. Channels, like Eternal Word Television Network (EWTN), The Inspiration Network (INSP), Jesus Christ TV (JCTV), and the Trinity Broadcast Network, were solely devoted to religious content.[2] Whether on a dedicated network or not, these shows promoted not only faith but also the televangelist, their congregation, and a plethora of books and tie-in merchandise. More recently, with the advent of digitization, a growing number of religious and spiritual groups use increasingly sophisticated marketing techniques—from online influencers to free streaming services to mobile software applications—to promote their content. While televangelists unapologetically marketed themselves, making themselves fabulously wealthy in the process, more traditional institutions have been seemingly more demure, casting a critical eye on the crassness of their marketing-savvy neighbors, even while envying their successes. Ambivalence about contemporary religious marketing plans belies a history of business-minded mainline churches and their self-promotion tactics dating back to at least the 19th century.

Today, however, when everyone has become a media outlet and self-marketer (Shirky, 2008), religious institutions are not only following suit but also in many cases are leading the way. As religions borrow marketing tools from the world of business, marketers reciprocally embed powerful religious ideas, images, mythologies, and resonances into their work. In the late 1800s, Philadelphia's iconic Wanamaker's department store famously built a church organ and altar right into the main selling floor (Kirk, 2018). Making purchasing feel like a sacred experience drove financial success and the store thrived. In early 2002, "True Religion, Clothing Company" similarly invoked notions of authenticity, devotion, and faith to attract consumers and build brand loyalty. Women's fashion brand Altar'd State continues in this tradition, combining an Anthropologie-like retail environment, dotted with spiritual fare such as prayer request books, and touting their "mission to change the world." Beyond retail, and in light of the proliferation of digital media, religious ideas have been further enmeshed with marketing practice. "Marketing evangelists," a term coined by an Apple executive (Kawasaki, 2015), are consumers who believe so fervently in a product that their word-of-mouth promotion on social media outlets drives sales. In doing so, these social media evangelists provide free marketing for companies and can be effective in "converting" others. The designation of so-called brand cults invokes more religious idiom in order to communicate the un-questioning or sometimes blind consumer followings that certain symbol-intensive brands command (Ragas and Bueno, 2002). These brand cults inspire community and ritual practices, which are facilitated by brands in online spaces. Cult brands such as Coke, Harley Davidson, or Apple, also engender "in" and "out" dynamics and rivalries. A biker who forgoes pushing a mechanically finicky "Hog" in order to ride a more reliable Honda may be seen as a heretic or apostate. One of the latest promotional trends is "mindful marketing." This strategy emphasizes Buddhist values of compassion, empathy, and staying "present," while advising marketers to "listen to learn" from consumers as they consciously show them more generosity—all with the underlying goal of improving customer relationships and corporate profit (Wilson, 2014; Gelles, 2016).

As market logics and digital technologies have come to dominate our cultural space, religious marketing (broadly defined) has grown exponentially not only in terms of speed, scope, and scale but also in terms of becoming more fully en-cumbered, whereby religions employ marketing techniques, and marketing prac-titioners use and exploit religious symbols and psychology. In a growing number of social spaces, we are seeing the impact of this explosive cross-pollination. Gyms brand their services as places for community and fellowship on the path to a potentially perfected body. Exercise trends such as CrossFit (see Cody Mus-selman's chapter in this volume) or Soul Cycle steep their product in messages of an achieved transcendent ultimacy via ritualistic performances. Businesses use "Capitalist mindfulness," not for spiritual enlightenment but to extract additional labor from their workers (Chen, 2022).[3] Multi-level marketing (MLM) is used as a tool to grow new religious movements, while providing an opportunity for "job creation" for faith groups that frown on women working outside the home.

Previous Scholarship

The body of scholarship on the intersection of religion and marketing is growing. Works have examined religion/spirituality and marketing broadly (Moore, 1994; Carrette and King, 2004; Miller, 2005; Sheffield, 2006; Einstein, 2008; Rinallo, Scott and Maclaren, 2012; Lofton, 2017) and in more specific ways such as mar-keting black churches (McGee, 2017), marketing evangelicals (Lee and Sinitiere, 2009; Vaca, 2019), the sacred marketing of raw materials and consumer goods (Callahan, Lofton and Seales, 2010), marketing ecopiety and environmental virtue

(Taylor, 2019), the religious marketing of beauty pageants (McMichael, 2020), and even the religious marketing of drugs (Laderman, 2021). Journals have dedicated special issues to the topic, including the *Journal of Management, Spirituality and Religion* (v 16, 2019) and *Religion, Media, and Digital Culture* (2022). A growing number of works are finding the realms of religion and marketing to be mutually embedded and, in many cases, inextricable from one another. This volume builds upon these insights and extends them into new unexplored areas of research.

Traditionally, discomfort in dealing with the intertwined dynamics of religion and marketing has been rooted in a cultural assumption that commodified or transactional religion is somehow "inauthentic" religion, as this represents a transgression of a perceived binary between the "sacred" and the "secular." In the case of marketing scholarship, this misreading and misperception can largely be traced back to a seminal article published in the 1970s by Norwegian Marketing Professor Johan Arndt. In the *Journal of Marketing*, Arndt famously asked the question, "How Broad Should the Marketing Concept Be?" (Arndt, 1978). His response was that the term "marketing" could only legitimately be applied to exchanges in "economic" areas. Conversely, applying the term "marketing" to "non-economic" areas was an overly broad misuse of the term and a fundamental confusion of categories. What was one of Arndt's prime examples of a "non-economic" area? Churches. Run that line of reasoning by any Religious Studies scholar, and they are almost sure to reply, "Churches are 'non-economic'? Since when? Ever?"

In 1911, Shailer Matthews, the Dean of the Chicago Divinity School, extolled the virtues of running churches like "a business establishment" (p. 213). Francis H. Case, a Presbyterian who worked in youth ministry, published the 1921 *Handbook of Church Advertising*, which contended that "mixing faith and business" was a necessity if "civilization is to endure" (213). In 1925, one of the best-selling non-fiction books of the era was *The Man Nobody Knows*. Written by adman Bruce Barton, the son of a Congregational minister, the book touted Jesus' superb advertising instincts and acumen.

But scholars today have perpetuated a historically tone-deaf division that approaches the confluence of religion and marketing as a kind miscegenation of otherwise pure categories. Gauthier and Martikainen's work on the "marketization of religion" in the United States (2020), for instance, contends that the drive to run churches "like a business," while utilizing marketing strategies, is an operational framework that only co-arises with the advent of neoliberal politics in the 1970s and 1980s. This "marketization," the argument goes, first infiltrates evangelical churches and then, only more recently in the 21st century, do mainline churches succumb to its influence. On the contrary, pre-dating the megachurches of today by a good century, mainline Christian churches developed the "original recipe" for marketing and consumer approaches to institutional growth and financial gain—a template that evangelical churches adopted and made their own (Moore, 1994).

The Wide, Wide World of Religio-Marketing

In a wide-ranging collection of essays, scholars explore (1) the history of religion and marketing; (2) the interconnections among politics, religion, and marketing; (3) the growth of religious influencers who sell religious ideas as well as religious goods; (4) the rise of multi-level marketing programs and their connection to religious groups and ideologies; (5) the introduction of marketing lifestyle branding to services that transform into "brand cults" and purpose marketing; and (6) how religion fuels capitalism and even, perhaps, the idea to step away from it.

To date, the typical reaction to examining the interaction between religion and marketing has run the gamut from shocked and scandalized to dismissive. The reality is that religious organizations are strategically deploying marketing tactics while marketers blatantly use religious idiom, iconographies, and narratives as branding tools to sell consumer products and services. And yet, too often the conventional wisdom defines "religion" and "marketing" as discrete categories that are only problematically merged.

This volume is about taking another tack. Responding to the query of what religion could *possibly* have to do with marketing, the scholarly contributions in this volume point to a more incisive question: Socially and historically, where can we point to instances where religion and marketing are *not* intertwined? Rather than being tangential to studies of religion and studies of marketing, the religion and marketing interface is, more often than not, integral, if not co-constituting. The peripheral attention paid to religion and marketing in academia largely ignores the very real alliances ongoing among industry professionals and religious communities, both today and historically.

What's Ahead ...

Religion, Branding, and Promotion—Past and Present

In "From Logos to Logo and Back Again: Images as Transactional Objects in the History of Christian Devotion," David Morgan proposes that images operate as transactional objects, connecting viewers to visual nodes within networks of images. To explore this, he examines the history of images of Saint Sebastian, a figure who has enjoyed veneration as a late Roman martyr down to the present. The image circulates as a logo, a visual brand. The motif's proliferation may not only change the image's meaning but it also remembers and sometimes intensifies it.

The appropriation of spiritual and medical practices has become a significant topic among scholars and practitioners of Native American religions. In "Spiritual Healing for Sale: Medical Pluralism and the Commodification of Native American Healing Traditions," Sarah Dees examines scholarly focus on New Age religion as the primary realm in which the commodification and appropriation of Indigenous religious beliefs, practices, and objects have occurred. Since the 1960s, practitioners of New Age religion have drawn on an eclectic array of spiritual practices, including those originating in Native American communities, for inspiration. Dees' chapter examines the commodification and appropriation of Native American healing traditions within a context of medical pluralism. Cultural outsiders interested in natural medicine may seek out Indigenous healing traditions as one of many choices in the marketplace of Complementary and Alternative Medicine (CAM). However, practitioners of Indigenous spiritual and healing traditions view acts of appropriation as materially and spiritually harmful. Dees delves into the troubling use and exploitation of Native American tropes in the popular imagination for the marketing and branding of native-themed alternative products and services.

In a historical examination of religion and marketing ("Rex Humbard, Psychographics, and the Hard Sell"), John Modern provides a fascinating window into the religious-business empire of famed televangelist Rex Humbard. Modern shows us how Humbard, in his brew of hard love and the hard sell, was a pious actor within a secular order defined by "old-time" religion and new psychographic marketing techniques. Humbard's data-driven mission, Modern argues, was nothing less than an attempt to enfold the interior lives of his largely female flock into a system of benevolent self-organization. In examining the marketing strategies of Rex Humbard Ministries, Inc., contends Modern, we bear witness to a primitive mechanics of our increasingly algorithmic life.

Politics and Religio-Marketing

John Durham Peters provides a thought piece on Sharpiegate—the famous press event where then-President Trump rewrote a weather forecast with a large black marker. Peters argues that imagining the weather to be free of marketing is just as big a delusion as imagining it free of religion or politics. With a stroke of the pen, Trump stepped up, like a meteorological magus, to try to control the weather himself. In one way, he obviously failed to guide the storm, but in another, he succeeded in becoming the ever-changing, constant topic of discussion and observation, usurping the spot once uniquely held by the weather.

In "Two Truths and a Lie: Unpacking PragerU's Hostile Rebrand of Climate Action in *Religion of Green*," Sarah McFarland Taylor dives into the dark world of climate denial mediamaking. Specifically, she analyzes the strategic instrumentalizing of "religion" to discredit climate action efforts. She argues that, in merely turning away from and tuning out right-wing climate disinformation marketing campaigns like those produced by (faux university) PragerU, we miss out on gleaning some valuable takeaways. Those takeaways, she contends, can assist not only in countering the likes of PragerU but can significantly aid in crafting more effective, resonant, and engaging climate communication moving forward.

In "A Head for Politics: *Yarmulkes,* Presidential Politics, and the Marketing of (Jewish) America," Eric Michael Mazur's chapter on the campaign-related yarmulke examines the use of the Jewish skullcap as a new location for presidential campaigning. After examining the origins of the campaign-related yarmulke, Mazur carefully examines its "markets" and determines that the popularity of the item has less to do with presidential politics and more to do with what the item itself communicates. Concluding that it is a possible connection to Judaism for those who may never wear it and a possible connection to non-Jewish fellow partisans for those who do, Mazur argues that the campaign of the campaign-related yarmulke is less about who gets elected than it is an admission ticket into larger American society for those who wear them.

Brian Hughes takes on the task of exploring the intersections of QAnon, magic, and the market. In "First Thoughts on a Second Qoming: Reading QAnon's Occult Economy Through the Works of Jean and John Comaroff," he explores the QAnon subculture's relationship with magic and witchcraft on one hand, and markets and finance on the other. Using the Comaroff's model of "occult economy" as a guide, this chapter describes how QAnon interprets wealth in our age of speculation and rackets as the outcome of occult forces. This interpretation has both a positive valence (as in the case of Donald Trump's dubious fortune) and a negative, even violent one, as in the case of conspiracy theories which accuse politicians and businesses of human trafficking and worse.

Old Marketing in New Media

In "Faith-centric TikToks: Promoting religion through personalized experience and engagement," Mara Einstein draws insights from practitioner "best practices" and social capital theory, in conversation with Religious Studies. The chapter uses content analysis to examine how influencers leverage resources (followers, personal branding, content, engagement) to enhance religious content on this platform. Importantly, TikTok's algorithm is "hyperpersonalized," increasing opportunities for parasocial relationships and word-of-mouth marketing on a level not seen elsewhere. This chapter compares and contrasts how this platform can be used for interpersonal "selling" by analyzing Orthodox Jewish TikTokers as well as a broad-based promotional tool by examining the Christian revival at Asbury University.

Kristin M. Peterson's "Selling to 'Smarties': The Marketing Strategies of a Social Justice Influencer" focuses on the work of Blair Imani Ali, who has developed a significant following as a "social justice influencer." She centers her account on her intersectional identity as Black, bisexual, and Muslim. Imani Ali has developed a novel influencer approach of educating her followers, who she terms "Smarties," about the historical background behind current social justice issues through videos, image carousels, and captioned photos. Despite her distinct educational content, Imani Ali still incorporates typical influencer posts like fashion styles, reflections on her relationship with her romantic partner, skincare routines, and sponsored content. This chapter focuses on Imani Ali's sponsored posts in order to evaluate how an influencer who often posts about deconstructing capitalistic systems of power is framing content about consumption.

Sociologist of religion John Schmalzbauer offers us a case study of a progressive Lutheran campus ministry at a Midwestern public university. This chapter looks at how mainline Protestants promote their organization in a crowded campus religious marketplace. Drawing on field visits, media accounts, and interviews with ten students and two staff members, it looks at how a mainline ministry utilizes social media and material culture (sidewalk chalk, a gothic church, and a rainbow flag) to market itself. Utilizing a rhetoric of hospitality and inclusion, it has recruited students dissatisfied with more conservative campus ministries. Located in the city of George Floyd's murder, the ministry has sponsored programming on racial justice and systemic racism. Despite these initiatives, diversity remains an ongoing challenge, reflecting the overwhelmingly white composition of the ministry's parent denomination.

In "Inventing a digital evangelical audience," Corrina Laughlin explores myriad ways evangelical identities are being negotiated in and through digital new media. Drawing from interviews with faith-tech entrepreneurs to look at how Christian mobile applications are marketed on the digital landscape with the intent of creating an evangelical audience of tech users, Laughlin analyzes the normative assumptions and concerns of this nascent digital public.

These apps, Laughlin argues, engender adversarial themes that activate an evangelical audience in ways that fuel the rise of Christian nationalism, a dangerous trend for American evangelicalism and for American democracy. Though these marketing strategies may be effective tools for creating a digital evangelical audience, Laughlin cautions, they may also have disastrous consequences.

Spirituality and Multi-level Marketing (MLM)

"Live Your Best Life Now: Wellness, Spirituality and Multi-Level Marketing in the Health Freedom Movement" by Susannah Crockford explores the interconnections among wellness ideologies, spirituality, religion, and MLM schemes in the U.S. South. The Health Freedom movement provides a crystallization of seemingly disparate politics—drawing from both left and right-wing—in opposition to orthodox medicine and in support of alternative, unregulated supplements and treatments, handily supplied by MLMs. Crockford brings to light and problematizes the troubling ways that those in the Health Freedom Movement have rebranded themselves using a label that invokes the civil rights movement, thus positioning themselves as an oppressed minority fighting against the "privileged" majority.

Deborah Whitehead digs further into MLMs through a case study of LuLaRoe, a women's clothing company made notorious in the Amazon docuseries, *LuLaRich*. This chapter explores how religion, nationalism, capitalism, and gender intersect in 21st-century U.S.-based MLM and direct sales companies that primarily market to and recruit women, such as LuLaRoe. Whitehead shows how the language of freedom, empowerment, and abundance is employed to sell products and also to recruit, appealing particularly to women in conservative religious communities.

Cult Branding, Purpose Marketing, and the Body Politic

In "Drinking the CrossFit Kool-Aid: Cult Marketing Meets Functional Fitness," Cody Musselman draws us into the high-intensity world of CrossFit and situates the emergence of CrossFit as a cult brand within the early 21st-century trend of cult-marketing. Separated into two sections, the first section of this chapter traces popular attitude toward cults in the latter half of the 20th century and shows how religious fanaticism inspired a new approach to brand marketing. The second section introduces CrossFit as a cult brand. CrossFit burst onto the global fitness scene while brand strategists and marketing specialists were codifying what it meant to be a cult brand. With CrossFit serving as a paradigmatic cult brand, this chapter demonstrates how religion and economy mixed and mingled in the early 21st century to produce cultlike market offerings and to remake the cult designation into an economic category.

Chad Seales's chapter on evangelical marketing and conscious capitalism provides us a fascinating window into the marketing development of "purpose driven food" that emerged around the biblical-based diet plan, known as *The Daniel Plan*, promoted by evangelical celebrity pastor Rick Warren. The chapter argues that *The Daniel Plan* offered a cultural evangelical marketing strategy for an ongoing consumer movement against industrial agriculture and the factory farming of animals as the prevailing mode of food production in the United States. For the study of religion, the significance of this marketing trend, known as purpose-driven marketing, is that it promoted a brand of cultural evangelicalism that was also a secularism, in the sense that it made evangelical and secular identities interchangeable for the consumer by transcending congregational particularity and political affiliation and subsuming them into a spiritual lifestyle of personal choice. After outlining the marketing development of purpose-driven food as a consumer critique of industrial agriculture in *The Daniel Plan*, the chapter considers the limits of cultural evangelicalism and consumer politics by showing how biotech corporations rebranded the term to capture new markets for healthy eating.

Religion, Marketing, and the Spirit of Capitalism

Justin Henry's innovative chapter on "Hinduism and the New Spirit of Capitalism" considers 21st-century self-improvement literature promising both financial success and spiritual fulfillment in relation to Luc Boltanski and Eve Chiapello's definition of the "new spirit of capitalism." To this end, he probes the religious dimensions of Deepak Chopra and Vishen Lakhiani's recent media output, including intersections with well-established theological schools of thought, continuities with "New Age" literature, and gestures to classical Hindu theology. Henry highlights the overlap between the worldviews of these two figures and those of Friedrich Taylor and Mark Parker Follett, formative early 20th-centuries thinkers in the field of scientific management, specifically their shared insistence that free-market, corporate modernity offers a portal to the most equitable, most peaceful, and most humane future world. The chapter concludes with critical reflections on the precarious labor culture which the "vocational theologies" of Chopra and Lakhiani are intended to underwrite, as well as an argument in support of Boltanski and Chiappello's historical view of an emerging "new spirit of capitalism," which departs in fundamental ways from the early modern "Protestant work ethic" as envisioned by Max Weber.

James S. Bielo demonstrates how material Christianity has evolved in "Vintage not Retro: The secondhand social life of Christian material culture." This chapter explores the marketing and sale of Christian material culture through the networked assemblage of estate sales, thrift stores, flea markets, antique booths, auction houses, eBay, and Instagram. The ethnographic focus is on resellers who scavenge second-hand venues in search of donated, discarded, and passed-over items. The analysis centers on the terms that resellers use and refuse in classifying their inventory: from "kitsch" and "junk" to "treasure," "collectible," "curiosity," "oddity," "upcycled art," "vintage," "antique," and "retro." The diverse array of terms and their divergent, inconsistent uses reveals the unregulated, centripetal character of this economic assemblage. In the context of material religion scholarship, this analysis examines the power of classification (Morgan 2017) in a system where meaning and performative function are unfixed and constantly negotiated.

In "(Not) Marketing Atheism," co-editor Mara Einstein interviews Gregory Epstein, humanist chaplain at Harvard and MIT and author of the bestselling book *Good Without God.* The two discuss the growing number of religious "nones," especially among younger demographics, and the ways that religious marketing tends to manipulate this target group. Epstein shares his thoughts on the ethics of marketing humanism, making the case that religious (or non-religious) groups should not be marketing. He questions the capitalist logics of a growth-for-growth sake model, though his views go beyond traditional arguments against the use of self-promotion, recruitment strategies, and marketing tactics. Along the way there are some surprises.

Finally, we hope that you the reader learn as much from reading this book as we ourselves have from working with one another. *Selling the Sacred* is somewhat uniquely edited by two scholars whose expertise spans both marketing studies *and* religious studies. Mara Einstein has an MBA in marketing and strategic planning from the Kellogg Graduate School of Management at Northwestern University as well as over a decade of corporate marketing experience. With a doctorate in Media Ecology (NYU), and a specialization in advertising and marketing criticism, Mara's book, *Brands of Faith* (Routledge, 2008), was the first book to examine critically the intersection of religion and marketing. Sarah McFarland Taylor is a professor of Religious Studies at Northwestern University with a doctorate in American

Religion and Culture, but she also earned an MA in Media History, Philosophy, and Criticism, focusing her research on "green marketing" and the promotion of eco-products. One of the most enjoyable aspects of this project has been having a trusted scholarly partner to fill in the things we didn't know we didn't know. This enabled us the freedom to experiment to a greater degree than we might ordinarily have felt comfortable and to play with a variety of frameworks, knowing we could fill in the blanks for each other as needed.

Indeed, in many respects, this kind of joint covering of bases is the larger purpose of the book. Marketing students, researchers, and professionals have an opportunity with this volume to fill in a lot of what they may not have known about religion, religious dynamics, and the history of religion and marketing. By the same token, most religion scholars have not spent their formative academic training steeped in marketing courses. This volume, then, seeks to create a series of bridges, or at least elevated walkways, for better "foot traffic" between our two disciplines, and consequently more opportunities for productive fraternization and cross-fertilization. With this goal in mind, we have tapped a broad range of contributors who speak to popular as well as neglected topics that intersect with religion and marketing. It is often said in marketing that smart collaborative teams do not merely ride trend shifts, they start them. With this in mind, may *Selling the Sacred* be the first of many such religio-marketing collaborations to come.

Notes

1 See "Milestones in Marketing History," The Marketing Museum: https://marketing. museum/marketing-history/.
2 Today, this list includes the National Christian Network, CBN, PTL, Trinity Broadcasting Network, National Jewish Television, BYU Channel, and The Church Channel, among others.
3 https://medium.com/@theleaderoftomo/part-3-capitalist-mindfulness-how-mindfulness-is-exploited-by-business-66f8d9369797

Works Cited

Arndt, J. (1978). How broad should the marketing concept be? Should it be developed into a full-fledged behavioral science? *Journal of Marketing*, *42*(1), 101–103.
Bell, A., and Dale, R. (2011). The medieval pilgrimage business? *Enterprise & Society*, *12*(3) (Sept): 601–627.
Brehm, S. (2021). *America's Most Famous Catholic (According to Himself): Stephen Colbert and American Religion in the Twenty-First Century*. New York: Fordham University Press.
Brown, S, Hirschman, E., and Maclaren, P. (2001). Always historicize! Researching marketing history in a post-historical Epoch? *Marketing Theory*, *1*(1), 49–90.
Callahan, R. J., Jr, Lofton, K., and Seales, C. E. (2010). Allegories of progress: industrial religion in the United States? *Journal of the American Academy of Religion*, *78*(1), 1–39.
Carrette, J., and King, R. (2004). *Selling Spirituality: The Silent Takeover of Religion*. London: Routledge.

Chen, C. (2022). *Work, Pray, Code: When Work Becomes Religion in Silicon Valley*. Princeton: Princeton University.

Curry, A. (2020). Ancient Egyptian 'Funeral Home' Was One-Stop Shop for the Afterlife. *National Geographic*. May 3: www.nationalgeographic.com.

Dyer, C. (1989). The consumer and the market in the later middle ages? *Economic History Review*, *42*(3) (Aug), 305–327.

Einstein, M. (2008). *Brands of Faith: Marketing Religion in a Commercial Age*. London: Routledge.

Ferré, J. (1990). *Channels of Belief: Religion and American Commercial Television*. Ames: Iowa State University Press.

Gauthier, F., and Martikainen, T., eds. (2020). *The Marketization of Religion*. London: Routledge.

Gelles, D. (2016). The Hidden Price of Mindfulness Inc. *New York Times*. March 19: www.nytimes.com.

Hangen, T. (2002). *Redeeming the Dial: Radio, Religion, and Popular Culture in America*. Raleigh: University of North Carolina.

Hoover, S. (1988). *Mass Media and Religion: The Social Sources of the Electronic Church*. Thousand Oaks: SAGE Publications.

Jones, J. (2023). U.S. Church Attendance Still Lower Than Pre-Pandemic. *Gallup*. June 26: www.newsgallup.com.

Kawasaki, G. (2015). The Art of Evangelism. *Harvard Business Review*. (May): www.hbr.org.

Kirk, N. (2018). *Wanamaker's Temple: The Business of Religion in an Iconic Department Store*. New York: NYU Press.

Kotler, P., and Wrenn, B. (1992). *Marketing for Congregations: Choosing to Serve People More Effectively*. Nashville: Abington Press.

Kruse, K. M. (2016). *One Nation Under God: How Corporate America Invented Christian America*. New York: Basic Books.

Laderman, G. (2021). Just Say Yes: In Drugs We Trust. *Sacred Matters Magazine*. Retrieved July 21, 2023 from https://sacredmattersmagazine.com/just-say-yes-in-drugs-we-trust/.

Lamal, N., et al. (2021). *Print and Power in Early Modern Europe (1500–1800)*. Boston: Brill Publishing.

Lee, S., and Sinitiere, P. (2009). *Holy Mavericks: Evangelical Innovators and the Spiritual Marketplace*. New York: NYU Press.

Levin-Richardson, S. (2019). *The Brothel of Pompeii: Sex, Class, and Gender at the Margins of Roman Society*. Cambridge, UK: Cambridge University Press.

Lofton, K. (2017). *Consuming Religion*. Chicago: The University Of Chicago Press.

McDannell, C. (1995). *Material Christianity: Religion and Popular Culture in America*. New Haven: Yale University Press.

McGee, P. L. (2017). *Brand® New Theology: The Wal-Martization of TD Jakes and the New Black Church*. Maryknoll, New York: Orbis Books.

McMichael, M. (2020). How beautiful are those who bring good news: Baptist theology and the making of miss America? *Baptist History and Heritage*, *55*(3), 52–68.

Miller, Vincent J. (2005). *Consuming Religion: Christian Faith and Practice in a Consumer Culture*. New York Bloomsbury Publishing USA.

Moore, R. L. (1994). *Selling God: American Religion in the Marketplace of Culture*. New York: Oxford University Press.

Morgan, David. (2017). "Material Analysis and the Study of Religion," pp. 14–32, in Materiality and the Study of Religion: The Stuff of the Sacred, ed. Tim Hutchings and Joanne McKenzie. London: Routledge.

Nortey, J., and Rotolo, M. (2023). How the Pandemic Has Affected Attendance at U.S. Religious Services. *Pew Research Center*. March 28: www.pewresearch.org.

Ragas, M., and Bueno, B. (2002). *The Power of Cult Branding: How 9 Magnetic Brands Turned Customers Into Loyal Followers*. New York: Crown Business.

Rinallo, D., Scott, L., and Maclaren, P., eds. (2012). *Consumption and Spirituality*. New York: Routledge.

Robinson, J. (2010). "From Altar to Amulet: Relics, Portability, and Devotion." In M. Bagnoli, H. A. Klein, C. G. Mann, and J. Robinson, eds. *Treasures of Heaven: Saints, Relics, and Devotion in Medieval Europe*, New Haven: Yale University Press, pp. 111–116.

Shaw, E. H. (1995). The first dialogue on macromarketing? *Journal of Macromarketing, 15* (Spring), 7–20.

Shaw, E. H., and Jones, D. G. B. (2005). A history of schools of marketing thought? *Marketing Theory, 5*(3), 239–281.

Sheffield, T. (2006). *The Religious Dimensions of Advertising*. New York, NY :Palgrave Macmillan.

Shirky, C. (2008). *Here Comes Everybody: The Power of Organizing Without Organizations*. New York: Penguin Books.

Taylor, S. M. (2019). *Eco-Piety: Green Media and the Dilemma of Environmental Virtue*. New York: NYU Press.

Vaca, D. (2019). *Evangelicals Incorporated: Books and the Business of Religion in America*. Cambridge, MA: Harvard University Press.

Wilson, J. (2014). *Mindful America: The Mutual Transformation of Buddhist Meditation and American Culture*. New York: Oxford University Press.

Wu, K. (2020). Ancient Egyptian Funeral Home Reveals Embalmers Had a Knack for Business: Funeral Parlors' Enterprising Staff Offered Burial Packages to Suit Every Social Strata and Budget. *Smithsonian Magazine*. May 7: www.smithsonianmag.com.

PART I

Branding, Promotion, and Religious Media—Past and Present

1

FROM LOGOS TO LOGO AND BACK AGAIN

Images as Transactional Objects in the History of Christian Devotion

David Morgan

The history of Christianity offers robust evidence of the diverse use of images. Promoting the faith and nurturing devotion to saints, the practice of pilgrimage, teaching children and converts, and proclaiming the religion in public settings have all relied on imagery and visual symbols. This chapter will focus on how the history of Christian imagery as a primary means of giving the religion a presence in daily life relies on the visual dynamics of replication, which have made marketing the faith a process bearing fundamental features of visual communication.

Images made for altars were designed to be the focal point of ritual, prayer, and pious contemplation. This ecology of the image put it to work as an interface, the medium for connecting to several other actors—saints, Mary, or Jesus, and such terrestrial actors as priests, friars, nuns, other pilgrims, and a variety of material actors such as relics, reliquaries, the sacramental Host, rosaries, incense, chant, and, importantly, *other images*. A devotee could recognize a saint like Sebastian because his images bore a family resemblance. It was important for devotees to know whom they were looking at because recognizing the saint meant that the image could then operate as access to a larger web, bringing pious viewers into a community of interacting agents. In gazing upon the image, the devotee encountered a portal to other connections. I want to argue that this web of connections relies on the reproduction of images for its proliferation. Images operate as a kind of traffic, a flow or current generated by the repetition of their features in new images. This flow of images issues from nodes such as altar paintings in the form of copies that link viewers to the node, toward which the current ebbs in return in memory and acts of devotion. But even as images undergo reproduction, they do so in new settings. Replication therefore maintains connections to the past but also introduces change, pressing the traffic of images in new directions.

DOI: 10.4324/9781003342229-3

Images as Transactional Objects

To understand these visual dynamics of ebb and flow, it is helpful to begin with two examples that show how this traffic of images has worked in religious life. Both show how replication is the medium of visual connection, the means by which images link far-flung components into a network that allows viewers to interface with distant and even invisible parties such as saints. In 1642, in the midst of the bloody Thirty Years War, which ravished Western Europe, including the area around the village of Kevelaer situated a few kilometers east of the Rhein, an image of Our Lady was displayed in a chapel at the gates of the city of Luxembourg and shortly later was credited with miraculously ending a bout of the plague. The image became a pilgrimage destination, and reproductions of it quickly proliferated. Two soldiers passing through a town near Kevelaer offered to sell a copy of the image to Mechel Busmann, wife of a local tradesman, Hendrik Busmann.[1] She could not afford the print but soon had a vision of the image of Our Lady enthroned in a small shrine. When she told her husband about the image in the vision, he sent her to track down the print since he himself had recently heard a voice instructing him to build a "small chapel," a roadside shrine or *Bildstock*, which answered his private query about the voice and whom it would honor.[2] Mechel did so, finding the print in the possession of an imperial officer imprisoned after a battle against German forces in the region. She purchased the print, and in 1642, she and her husband built the small shrine she had envisioned, then installed the engraving of Our Lady of Consolation in it (Figure 1.1).[3] This "small chapel" was consecrated and quickly became a popular destination for pilgrims who came to venerate the image as a Marian apparition. The structure was rebuilt in 1654 as the chapel that stands today, where the image remains. The object of veneration in this case is not an original, one-of-a-kind image, but a multiple, a printed engraving of the image at Luxembourg. And the engraving has proliferated on prayer cards and on postcards such as one from the 1930s reproduced here (Figure 1.2), in which the engraving appears above the chapel and basilica.

The Veil of Veronica is another fascinating case of an image that lives in reproduction. It was said that the image of Christ's face appeared on a cloth that was given to him by a young woman as he approached Calvary. Jesus touched the cloth to his face, and his features were miraculously transposed to it. By the early thirteenth century, what was thought by some to be the original Veronica had come to be housed in St. Peter's in Rome. Figure 1.3 is said to be a nineteenth-century rendition of the original in St. Peter's, which had been lost during the pillaging of Rome in 1527, then rediscovered in the seventeenth century.[4] In the past, pilgrims who came to Rome to see the Veronica sewed small representations of it to their hats as pilgrimage badges. Painters were officially licensed to produce reproductions of the Veronica as were merchants authorized to sell them.[5] After the image in Rome was seen to glow in 1849, replicas engraved on linen such as Figure 1.3 were sold in large numbers to pilgrims, each one bearing a wax seal as the mark of

FIGURE 1.1   Our Lady of Consolation in the Chapel of Mercy, Kevelaer (Courtesy Paul Hermans, Creative Commons Attribution-Share Alike 4.0 International)

https://commons.wikimedia.org/wiki/File:Genadekapel_met_Genadebeeld_Kevelaer_24-04-2019_11-44-21.jpg

FIGURE 1.2   Postcard, Chapel of Mercy and Basilica, Kevelaer, Germany, 1930s
(Collection of the author)

Vero Effigies Sacri Vultus Domini Nostri Jesu Christi

qua Roma in Sacrosancta Basilica S. Petri in Vaticano religiosissime observatur et colitur

FIGURE 1.3 Veil of Veronica, lithograph on linen with wax seal, second half of the nineteenth century (Collection of the author)

authenticity (visible in the lower left corner). The image bears the following text in Latin: "True Effigy of the Holy Face of Our Lord Jesus Christ."

These two examples suggest that the power of images resides in their ability to transmit motifs by reproduction without losing the power to inspire veneration, convey information, or connect devotees to the object of their affection. Their reproductions such as Figures 1.2 and 1.3 are examples of what I will call *transactional objects*, by which I mean media that connect people to nodes within networks. In the dynamics of a network, transactional objects are links to a node. These two operate in tandem: the node converges a number of actors and produces links to itself and thereby to the network. In the form of images, the links extend access to the node as replications of it.[6] Thus, the postcard of the engraving of Our Lady of Consolation (see Figure 1.2) is a link to the node at Kevelaer (Figure 1.1); or the lithographed image the Veronica on linen (see Figure 1.3) is a link to the nodal image in Rome. At one time, the image in Figure 1.1 was a link to the statue of Our Lady of Luxembourg, but when the engraving became the subject of an apparition and the object of pilgrimage at Kevelaer, the link became a node and generated links of its own such as Figure 1.2.

The relationship of node and link is important for understanding the historical basis of commodifying and marketing brand identity. Pilgrims and tourists alike are compelled to take things with them to remember their trip—relics or souvenirs. Both may be propelled by a pledge or vow—to visit a sacred site or to see a wonder of nature. Of course, the two go about their visit very differently. Pilgrims may undertake an arduous, demanding trek as part of what they offer the saint whose shrine they visit. Tourists, by contrast, commonly travel in bubbles of convenience. But both return home with important things—objects that document their journey and pictures, photographic traces of the places they saw, all of which will be the means for narrating their journey to friends and family. The node that attracts visitors generates a host of links that will continue to connect the pilgrim/tourist to it. What they take away are transactional objects.

A remarkable instance of this happens in the Louvre whenever a crowd of tourists clamors before the *Mona Lisa* (Figure 1.4). Many of them hold their cameras overhead to snap a picture of Leonardo's vaunted painting. They might have simply purchased a postcard in the museum gift shop. But that would have failed to do what even a blurry snapshot can accomplish: to demonstrate that they were there, in the presence of *the thing*—the node of a vast network of pulsing, charismatic energy that connects the pilgrim/tourist to something that matters. What is that network? In the case of *Mona Lisa*, it is an assemblage of Leonardo, genius, the Renaissance, the Louvre, Paris, Western civilization—and the pilgrim, who gets to take the picture away as a relic of the day the link and node met. *Mona Lisa* is not a religious picture, but we might easily substitute for it images that are and exert a comparable effect. For example, Michelangelo's *Pieta* in St. Peter's Basilica in Rome has been reproduced in untold numbers as souvenirs, collectibles, emblazoned on medals, and as a 10 Euro coin issued by the Vatican in 2020.

FIGURE 1.4   Tourists taking photographs of Mona Lisa in the Louvre (Courtesy Alamy)

The images of Our Lady of Consolation at Kevelaer and the Veronica in Rome generate copies of themselves, which can be described as transactional in the sense that they become the enduring manner in which devotees maintain a link to the nodal image. They leave with copies that help sustain an ongoing relationship with the saint. The same process takes place with other sorts of artifacts such as contact relics, samples of oil, sand, water, or grain that pilgrims to the Holy Land take away with them or rosaries or prayer cards that visitors to the Vatican take home. Transactional objects are media of communication because they move from one person or place to the next by different means such as the contagion of touch or in the case of images by replication. Whether image or artifact (vials of oil, bottles of holy water, decoupaged icons, pebbles, canisters of soil), transactional objects act as relays that engage devotees in communication with one another, with saints, with God, and distant others such as the sacred past and sacred sites, doing so by proliferation, partition, and circulation.

Reproduction does not destroy the node's aura but rather packages and redeploys it. The aura of the original, as Walter Benjamin famously noted, is an expression of an object's uniqueness and its ritual function.[7] Mechanical reproduction certainly interposes an image between a viewer and the original, which means that the original is no longer encountered in its unique setting but as a reproduction set within a new context of viewing. Inasmuch as an image serves to bring its original to mind, to excite desire for it, to promise its eventual return, or to narrate encounter with the node, we may say that reproductions direct the viewer to the original, serving as links that do not dissipate aura but ultimately preserve it by extending and enhancing allure of the original.

The history of Christian devotion to saints provides ample evidence for this and shows how images and objects spawn the very means of marketing the faith. A robust sense of the visual proliferation of links is found in the career of a single devotion. For that, I will turn to examine a stream of objects arising from the early Roman Catholic cult of Saint Sebastian, a late antique devotion with a long life in which reproducibility has been key. This chapter closes with consideration of images of Saint Sebastian at the edge and just beyond Christian tradition in order to consider how images evolve in step with shifting webs of connection.

Saint Sebastian: Cultus and the Proliferation of Images

Hagiography is not about verisimilitude. Writing the life of saints and martyrs was the business of devotees with an agenda. The *passio* of Saint Sebastian, which has been securely dated to the early fifth century, has remarkably little to say about the saint's suffering, and much more about his long speeches as a zealous "soldier of Christ."[8] The longest passio to have survived the early Christian era, Sebastian's account is largely composed of a series of oratorical scenes, exorcisms, and miraculous healings that tell little of his actual life and much about the theology of martyrdom and its authoritative anchoring in the senatorial elite of Rome's early Christians. Sebastian, as revealed in the hagiographical glow of his passio, was a vindication of the faith as an early fifth-century devotee understood it.

But the ages have remembered Saint Sebastian in a different way. Whereas the portrayal of the saint's demise takes place in a few lines at the end of the long narrative, visual depictions of the martyr since the thirteenth century have often focused on the bound and penetrated body of the saint. According to the passio, the emperor Diocletian ordered that Sebastian be used as target practice. The saint was shot so full of arrows that he "bristled with arrow-shots almost like a hedgehog."[9] This is the scene that was lifted from the passio for special treatment, but not until after Sebastian became associated with delivery from the bubonic plague during the fourteenth century. He had been credited with the power to do so as far back as 680, when the plague raged in Rome and Pavia. In his life of Sebastian in the thirteenth-century *Golden Legend*, Jacobus de Voragine also drew on Paul the Deacon's eighth-century *History of the Lombards* to relate that it had been "divinely revealed that the plague [in Lombardy] would never cease until an altar was raised in [the capital city of] Pavia in honor of Saint Sebastian."[10] Dedicating one in the church of St. Peter in Chains in Pavia accomplished this when, it is said, the saint's relics were translated there from Rome.

But the scene of Sebastian being shot with arrows only emerged as the signal image of his cult in connection with his intercessory role in the recurring history of pestilence.[11] An example of this is a fourteenth-century Italian altarpiece that features Sebastian riddled with arrows in its center panel (Figure 1.5). The image is flanked on both sides by other scenes from the saint's life as narrated in the *Golden Legend*, including the actual moment of his death in the center panel on the right side: when he failed to die from the archers' arrows, Diocletian ordered him to be bludgeoned to death. Figure 1.5 reveals an important reason why the image of the impaled saint was experienced as powerful. The passio makes no mention of Sebastian being lashed to a tree or column or cross, but the *Golden Legend* has Diocletian tell his soldiers "to tie him to a post in the center of the camp, and … to shoot him full of arrows."[12] Jacobus de Voragine's account of the life of Sebastian was the source for what became a standard feature of Sebastian's representation in the later

FIGURE 1.5   Giovanni del Biondo, Martyrdom of St. Sebastian and Scenes from his life, triptych, late fourteenth century (Courtesy Scala/Art Resource, NY)

Middle Ages and after. Neither the passio nor the *Golden Legend* makes any mention of his being clad only in a loincloth. A late seventh-century mosaic in Rome includes an image of Sebastian as a bearded old man, not a beardless young one.[13]

It is noteworthy, then, that these features of the early Renaissance cult image of Sebastian signal his similarity to the crucified Jesus. The loincloth and the vertical structure (sometimes a tree, a column, or another architectural element) are also standard characteristics of Crucifixion scenes. Figure 1.5 places the saint on a post that resembles the vertical member of Christ's cross. The reference to Christ is a key link, and it was repeated in many depictions of Sebastian from the fifteenth to the seventeenth century. To invoke Sebastian was to invoke, in turn, the mediating power of Christ. Saintly intercession was understood as a rising chain of links that moved from the saint through a hierarchy of celestial figures that might include John the Baptist, the Virgin, to Christ and ending at the throne of God the Father. The vertical structure of intercession was the upper portion of a hierarchy that extended downward through the shrine or church building, to the altar and its relics, the devotional image, possibly accompanied by additional images of local patron saints.

In the late Middle Ages and Renaissance, altarpieces operated as primary nodes within a visual piety of intercession. They were the site at which the Eucharist was celebrated and cult imagery displayed for prayer and contemplation. Altar images were primary means of interface with the saints, Mary, or Christ, the place where divine presence was literally understood to manifest in the sacrament, and devotion was addressed directly to the figure portrayed and honored at the altar. Altars were commonly the destination of pilgrims since relics and cult imagery were located there. Originally focused in Rome, records show that Sebastian's relics were housed in no fewer than twenty-six churches in Rome.[14] But Saint Sebastian's relics spread from Italy to France during the Carolingian era as his cult grew, spreading nodes northward through Italy into western Europe. One scholar has argued that Sebastian's status as plague saint did not occur until his relics came to an abbey near Paris in 1348. In this fateful year of the Black Death, the bishop of Paris issued an indulgence of forty days to those who visited the altar and prayed there.[15] Altars dedicated to the saint acquired cult images that honored the saint, who was present in his relic and was invoked in prayers and masses performed at the altar. Such nodes generated links for maintaining connection to it. For pilgrims and devotees, this consists of what they take away with them. Those who are devoted to a saint display these transactional objects in their homes or carry them on their person as badges, emblems, insignia, mementos, or medals that keep the saint close to them in daily life. The traffic of images conducts devotion through an extensive series of links over space and time to the life of the saint and his presence in heaven. Understood in this way, the links and the nodes are part of a far-ranging network that produces the presence and relationship that nurture the life of belief in material practices. This traffic captures the dynamic character of representation: the power of images to connect viewers through a cloud or assemblage of linkages to other images, to what they portray, and to fellow devotees.

Fundamental to this process of representation is the production of links, which may be ephemeral or mass-produced. This is apparent in the print culture of engravings and lithographs and in medals, pendants bearing the saint's image that are carried on one's person. Figure 1.6 is an amulet displayed domestically to protect the household or carried on one's person to safeguard one from the plague. Printed in Catalonia in 1854, the print features two saints long revered for the protection they offered: St. Roch and St. Sebastian. Lashed to a cruciform tree that echoes the "form of the cross" beside him, the figure of Sebastian appears Christ-like. Produced en masse and purchased from peddlers or in printer's shops, the print was hung in the home or carried on one's person to provide comfort as well as protection by invoking the aid the saints. The invocation was purely visual as well as vocal and performative. The cross in the center of the page consists of a series of repeating letters that correspond to prayerful invocations listed below. One way of using the amulet was to assign one person or a chorus of people to each utterance cued to the letters forming the cross. By speaking in turn, the assembled group would collectively beseech the aid of God and his two saints for deliverance from the plague threatening the community. The inexpensive print could be distributed among the participants, who then might keep their copy as a relic of the communal invitation of divine assistance. As a transactional object, the amulet page connected the owner to a long tradition of patronage, on the one hand, and, on the other, to the community with which one shared the hope for blessing of protection. The printed, ephemeral image of the saint in Figure 1.6 brought him and his deeds described in the passio (and its endless stream of devotional texts, sermons, and catechetical uses) into the immediate world of the present. This mere piece of paper, fortified by the conjoined prayers of a community, plugged everyone using it into both a textual and pictorial assemblage and operated as a continuous link.

The power of the logo, the visual brand, was what linked the devotee to the larger apparatus of the piety. This is particularly clear in the popular use of medals among Catholics. Medals bearing the imagery of a saint are often the gift of a family member, godparent, teacher, nun, or priest, so their invocation of a saint's aid comes with the added value of a link to someone within one's trusted circle. Since the early sixteenth century, medals have been indulgenced by popes, meaning that wearing them and praying to the saint to whom a medal is dedicated reduces the time in purgatory awaiting the individual. One scholar of Catholic medals has suggested that this practice of indulgencing medals helped create the devotional medal of post-Reformation Catholic piety.[16] Medals are very often available as gift or purchase at pilgrimage sites and churches, in particular the Vatican, where, like other sacred objects such as rosaries, they may be blessed by priests, bishops, or even the pope. Medals of St. Sebastian are often based on paintings of the saint. Figure 1.6, for example, recalls a number of different pictures by Renaissance artists—Antonella da Messina, Pietro Perugino, and Marco Basaiti, among others that once graced altars, and likely those with relics of the saint.

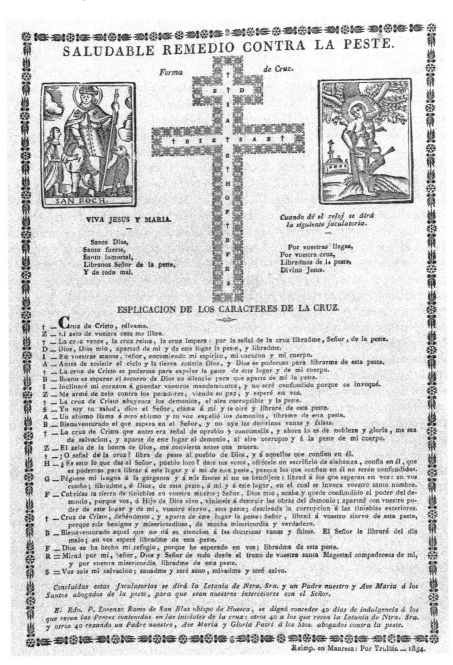

FIGURE 1.6 Healthy remedy against the plague, Saints Roch and Sebastian with the Cross and invocations, 1854, printed in Manresa, Catalonia (Courtesy Alamy)

Medals are created for a variety of reasons—commemoration, recognition for achievement, gifts, ex-votos, and for invoking patron saints. The Catholic cult of saints exhibits an adaptability that keeps devotion alive. For example, Figure 1.7, a twentieth-century medal of Saint Sebastian, documents the saint's ongoing development as the patron of athletes. His link to Jesus is repeated here with the appearance of the Sacred Heart of Jesus above him. But the added layer of patronage to athletes is signaled by the military gear behind the figure (shield, helmet, and chest armor), extending Sebastian the military officer in the Praetorian Guard to patron of those who don the equipment of the Christian athlete. Military gear rarely if ever appears in altar paintings of St. Sebastian. Its inclusion would have complicated the saint's resemblance to Jesus. (Perhaps that is why the Sacred Heart

FIGURE 1.7 Medal of St. Sebastian, Patron of Athletes, twentieth century, one inch high (Collection of the author)

is added to this medal.) And the story, as his passio and Jacobus' Life portrayed it, turned on renouncing his secular status in Rome for the sake of his faith. But the modern use of the saint as patron of Christian athletes activates the equipment to remodel his relevance. The verso of Figure 1.7 reads: "St. Sebastian, Martyr, Athlete, Soldier," and adds a tiny image of Our Lady of Carmel, who is the source of the scapular, a traditional amulet that protects the wearer, and suggests the amuletic function of the St. Sebastian metal for those engaged in athletic combat. In an age when the threat of a plague like the Black Death has significantly diminished, the relevance of St. Sebastian shifts to other domains of importance such as athletics. Since Catholic schools in the United States promote the practice of sports among youth, and the tendency to characterize athletic competition in military terms is keyed to fostering character development, the application of Sebastian's patronage found a new relevance in modern Catholic life. The nude male figure in Figure 1.6 references the long visual tradition of the heroic nude Sebastian but adds to it the modern ideal of male beauty associated with athletic prowess.

The traffic of images bears a cultural logic of appropriation and redeployment for any group in search of a totem, icon, logo, or visual branding that will conduct its public representation. Badges, insignia, and crests are all signs of membership that define the social body of the group, serving to differentiate it from others by limning its boundaries. There are countless examples of such totemic imagery deployed as collective representations. Processional banners hail the Saint as the patron of parish and congregation. Catholic high schools around the world named for Saint Sebastian display school heraldry that deploys on the saint's iconography. Clip art issued by Catholic educational websites provide images of Saint Sebastian for children to color as aids in learning about the saint.[17] The contour imagery of these websites is either traced from original works of art or derived from it, thereby maintaining a connection to the visual tradition of saintly devotion. The market for such imagery is such that even non-religious image vendors such as Shutterstock offer clip art to members for various uses. The dizzying variety of media and forms of reproduction issued by religious producers and organizations as well as laic sources tempers any notion of secularization. Secular vendors cater to the religious demand because there is a market for it, but there is nothing new about that relationship.[18] Religious organizations have always worked with artists, printers, artisans, metalworkers, architects, and designers to produce the range of images, buildings, books, and artifacts that are the material culture of religion.

Saint Sebastian Outside the Church

Images are not static. They move, evolve, decay, fall into oblivion, and then resurface. The traffic of images means they are always in motion, and that reproduction is both the means of survival and the assurance of change. That means that the salience of sacred imagery depends on the setting in which the work is viewed as well as the forms of reproduction that circulate the imagery far beyond its original ritual setting. Museums are where most people today encounter religious artifacts of artistic stature. As Figure 1.4 shows, the museum is a space made for spectators to marvel at rare works of art carefully installed in marble halls that recall palaces, shrines, or temples. Many museum visitors devote part of their visit to museum gift shops, which often commoditize paintings by reproducing them on pendants, bracelet charms, posters, tote-bags, and postcards, as symbols or logos of the museum experience, serving to advertise the institution. Such reproductions are not intended to vulgarize the original imagery, but they do transform it into commodities as souvenirs to take away from pilgrimage to the museum's collection. The financial benefits that gift shops provide museums are substantial. Yet for the customers, the souvenirs are infused with a salience that surpasses financial transaction. Logo finds its way back to logos. Taking something away from the visit is compelling for those who sense that the artifacts make a claim on their attention. For many museum visitors, when it is allowed, taking pictures is irresistible. Consider Figure 1.4 once again: an enthusiastic crowd of art pilgrims clamors before Leonardo's picture to capture in their snapshots a visual record of their presence before it. As transactional objects, the photographs bear a link to the pilgrims' presence before the work of art that figures in the narratives about the visit that pilgrims share with others and use to remember the trip for themselves. Because it acts as a link to an absent or a past referent, the transactional object acquires a charisma or aura of its own. It serves as a kind of double medium: as a portal to the original event and as the means for sharing with others what continues to matter to the pilgrim.

Seen in this way, veneration of works of art and the purchase of their representations in museum gifts shops is not entirely "secular." Objects taken from churches such as reliquaries, icons, altar paintings, and devotional artifacts are re-installed in the rarefied space of museums, where they are enthroned, carefully lit, and closely guarded. This constructs a manner of seeing that replaces religious ritual engagement with aesthetic contemplation. The aura of ritual function gives way to the aura of artistic uniqueness. That makes museum souvenirs something more than secular commodities since they take with them something of the mystique of the aestheticized cult object. If pious pilgrims were meant to gaze devotedly on the saint's image above an altar because it would deliver them from tribulation, museum visitors are intended to gaze on works of art for the edifying pleasure of appreciating craft, genius, and cultural achievement. In both instances, looking intently at the object is understood to produce a useful benefit, and reproduction is a way of channeling the benefit into everyday life. In the process, however, the object's aura changes and with it the object's meaning. This should not be uniformly categorized as de-sacralization, but various forms of re-sacralization. The posters of paintings by Leonardo, Fra Angelico, or Monet bought at museum gift shops are often expensively framed by owners and proudly displayed in their homes. The aura of the original does not "wither," as Benjamin wrote, so much as take a new form.

But change can also be the occasion for obscuring the religious significance of images. An example can be found in the municipality of São Sebastião do Paraíso, a city in southeastern Brazil. The city was founded as a village in 1821 when a family of cattle ranchers devoted to Saint Sebastian built a small chapel dedicated to the saint. The present church was constructed between 1937 and 1952 on the site of the chapel (Figure 1.8) and has since served as the iconic center of the

FIGURE 1.8   Church of St. Sebastian, 1952, with monument in foreground, 1971, São Sebastião do Paraíso, Brazil (Courtesy Larissa Carneiro)

community, forming one side of a large public square.[19] In 1971, on the occasion of the city's 150th anniversary, a monument was erected and topped by a bronze figure of the Saint, who is lashed to a tree and pierced by arrows. Below Sebastian appears a heraldic crest in which two angels hold swords downward beneath a looming Roman helmet with two arrows crossed behind him (Figure 1.9). The helmet and arrows refer to the saint. The angels may recall a detail from the story of Sebastian in the *Golden Legend*, where Jacobus de Voragine mentioned a good and a bad angel associated with the plague, but only the latter carried a "hunting spear" (*venabulum*), not a sword, with which he struck dead victims of the plague

FIGURE 1.9   Seal of São Sebastião do Paraíso, 1971 (Courtesy Larissa Carneiro)

at the instruction of the good angel.[20] It seems quite likely, therefore, that this was not the source of the crest's imagery. In 2017, a flag and seal for São Sebastião do Paraíso were posted on Wikipedia that modify the bronze crest, re-drawing the Roman headgear as an ancient Greek helmet and replacing the arrows with spears (Figure 1.10). The seal includes an explanatory if confusing text: "A Roman military helmet, two arrows; a fitting homage to the city's patron, the fearless, the

FIGURE 1.10 Seal of São Sebastião do Paraíso, 2017 (Wiki-commons, public domain)

Source: https://pt.m.wikipedia.org/wiki/Ficheiro:Bras%C3%A3o_de_S%C3%A3o_Sebasti%C3%A3o_do_Para%C3%ADso_-_MG.svg

intrepid, Captain Sebastian, Chief of the Imperial Guard of Diocletian, killed as a ritual offering for his faith. Two archangels, an allusion to the biblical figures of the earthly Paradise."[21] The (Greek) helmet and spears falter in recalling the cult of Saint Sebastian. No less confusing is the indication that the pair of "archangels" refer to the angel that guarded the entrance to Eden (= Paraíso) whence Adam and Eve were expelled. The hold of the imagery on the religious referent has clearly loosened. The Wikipedia description indicates that the design of the flag and seal are conceived in the language of heraldry. If that is so, it comes at the expense of remembering the religious past.

A citizen of Paraíso since the 1950s posted the following commentary on the church and square in 2021: "the Square was always welcoming, and as such, social, artistic, political, religious, cultural, and folkloric events were experienced there, notably for having in its space the Mother Church of Saint Sebastian, a postcard of Paraíso, which, by extension, dignifies the other religious denominations, since in this Christian universe, all paths aim to tune in and walk towards our Creator."[22] His characterization of the church as a "postcard" of the city captures the role of images to convey the charisma of a nodal site like the Church of Saint Sebastian. But one wonders about the author's adoption of other religions to "this Christian universe" overseen by the saint. In fact, the 2010 census showed that only 46.5% of the city's 72,000 residents declared they were Catholic.[23] Thus, for the majority of the city's citizens, the historical reference to Saint Sebastian may be insignificant. The vagueness of the digital versions of the seal and flag further loosens the link to the religious referent and presses the images into the realm of municipal booster-ism in a city that is much less Catholic than it once was.

However much the original meaning has dimmed, it must be said that the Saint remains perched on the monument, participating in an iconic setting. As the com-munity has grown and diversified, the public square, the church edifice, and the monument have continued to limn the center of municipal consciousness, bearing a significance that is less sectarian, but more inclusive for being so. Yet tradition pushes back sometimes. In May, an entourage of horse- and mule-mounted farm-ers helped open the annual agricultural fair in São Sebastião do Paraíso by riding through the streets of the city, carrying a banner that featured a colorful picture of the Saint bound to a tree and pierced with arrows. The past does not give up when the present won't let it.

Notes

1 Theodor Bergmann, *Der Wallfahrtsort Kevelaer* (Kevelaer: Verlag Butzon & Bercker, 1949), 12, 14.
2 Johannes Oomen, *Kevelaer: Entstehung und Geschichte der Wallfahrt und ihrer Heiligtümer* (Kevelaer: Butzon & Bercker, 1971), 5.
3 For the story, see https://tomperna.org/2018/12/03/mondays-with-mary-our-lady-of-kevelaer-germany/. For the statue in Luxembourg Cathedral, see https://en.wikipedia.org/wiki/Our_Lady_of_Luxembourg

4 Hans Belting has summarized the history of the Veronica in *Likeness and Presence: A History of the Image before the Era of Art*, tr. Edmund Jephcott (Chicago: University of Chicago Press, 1994), 219–24.
5 Belting, *Likeness and Presence*, 221.
6 For further consideration of how images work in this way, see David Morgan, *Images at Work: The Material Culture of Enchantment* (New York: Oxford University Press, 2018).
7 Walter Benjamin, "The Work of Art in the Age of Mechanical Reproduction," in *Illuminations: Essays and Reflections*, ed. Hannah Arendt, tr. Harry Zohn (New York: Schocken Books, 1968), 217–51, esp. 220–24.
8 "St. Sebastian and Companions," in Michael Lapidge, *The Roman Martyrs: Introduction, Translations, and Commentary* (Oxford: Oxford University Press, 2017).
9 "St. Sebastian and Companions," 135.
10 Jacobus de Voragine, *The Golden Legend: Readings on the Saints*, tr. William Granger Ryan, 2 vols. (Princeton: Princeton University Press, 1993), vol. 2, 101; see Paul the Deacon, *History of the Lombards*, ed. Edward Peters, tr. William Dudley Foulke (Philadelphia: University of Pennsylvania Press, 1907), bk VI, ch. 5, 254–55.
11 Scholarship on Saint Sebastian is extensive. Two excellent essays are: Sheila Barker, "The Making of a Plague Saint: Saint Sebastian's Imagery and Cult Before the Counter-Reformation," in *Piety and Plague from Byzantium to the Baroque*, ed. Franco Mormando and Thomas Worcester (Kirksville: Truman State University Press, 2007), 90–127; and Ottó Gecser, "Intercession and Specialization: St Sebastian and St Roche as Plague Saints and their Cult in Medieval Hungary," in *Les saints et leur culte en Europe centrale au Moyen Âge (xie - début du xvie siècle)*, ed. Marie-Madeleine de Cevins and Olivier Marin (Tournhout: Brepols, 2017), 77–108.
12 Jacobus de Voragine, *Golden Legend*, vol. 2, 100.
13 Barker, "The Making of a Plague Saint," 93.
14 See the early fifteenth-century *Descriptio Urbis Romae*, which documented relics in Roman churches—transcribed by Martin Bauch, "The Relics of Roman Churches in Nicolò Signorili's Descriptio Urbis Romae," in *Relics, Identity, and Memory in Medieval Europe*, ed. Marika Räsänen, Gritje Hartmann, and Early Jeffrey Richards (Turnhout: Brepols, 2016), 115–84.
15 Ottó Gecser, "Sermons on St. Sebastian after the Black Death (1348-ca. 1500)," in *Promoting the Saints: Cults and Their Contexts from Late Antiquity until the Early Modern Period*, ed. Ottó Gecser et al. (Budapest and New York: Central European University Press, 2011), 264.
16 Eli Heldaas Seland, "19th Century Devotional Medals," in *Instruments of Devotion: The Practices and Objects of Religious Piety from the Late Middle Ages to the 20th Century*, ed. Hennig Laugerud and Laura Katrine Skinnebach (Aarhus: Aarhus University Press, 2007), 165–66.
17 See for instance: https://www.thecatholickid.com/saint-sebastian-coloring-page/ and http://www.biblekids.eu/index.html
18 See David Morgan, "Mediation or Mediatisation: The History of Media in the Study of Religion," *Culture and Religion* 12, no. 2 (June 2011): 137–52.
19 https://www.ipatrimonio.org/sao-sebastiao-do-paraiso-igreja-matriz-de-sao-sebastiao/#!/map=38329&loc=-20.917250304287204,-46.991861322548154,17
20 Jacobus de Voragine, *Golden Legend*, vol. 1, p. 101; for the Latin, Jacobus de Voragine, *Legenda Aurea/Goldene Legende*, ed. and tr. Bruno W. Häuptli (Freiburg: Herder, 2014), 390.
21 "Um capacete militar romano, duas setas; justa homenagem ao patrono da cidade, o destemido, o intrépido, Capitão Sebastião, Chefe da Guarda Imperial de Deocleciano, morto em holocausto à sua fé. Dois Arcanjos; alusão às bíblicas figuras do 'Paraíso Terrestre'…" https://pt.m.wikipedia.org/wiki/Ficheiro:Bras%C3%A3o_de_S%C3%A3o_Sebasti%C3%A3o_

do_Para%C3%ADso_-_MG.svg. The flag is at: https://commons.wikimedia.org/wiki/
File:Bandeira_de_S%C3%A3o_Sebasti%C3%A3o_do_Para%C3%ADso_-_MG.svg
22 Roberto Noguiera, "Praça Comendador José Honório uma história à parte no bicen-
tenário," posted October 25, 2021, http://www.jornaldosudoeste.com.br/noticia.php?
codigo=210569: "a Praça sempre foi acolhedora, e como tal nela se vivenciou momen-
tos sociais, artísticos, manifestações políticas, religiosas, culturais e folclóricas, notada-
mente por ter em seu espaço a Igreja Matriz de São Sebastião, cartão postal de Paraíso,
que por extensão dignifica as demais denominações religiosas, de vez que nesse universo
cristão, todos os caminhos objetivam a sintonia e caminhar rumo ao nosso Criador."
23 https://cidades.ibge.gov.br/brasil/mg/sao-sebastiao-do-paraiso/pesquisa/23/22107?detal
hes=true

2

SPIRITUAL HEALING FOR SALE

Medical Pluralism and the Commodification of Native American Healing Traditions

Sarah Dees
Iowa State University

On October 9, 2009, James Arthur Ray, a professional speaker and "self-help guru," hosted a sweat lodge ceremony in Sedona, Arizona. The ceremony was part of a "Spiritual Warrior" retreat in which participants would, among other things, learn how to "carve out [their] own destiny and quickly develop the strength and determination to live it." Participants in the event paid nearly $10,000 each for this "heroic quest for higher consciousness" (Ray, "Spiritual Warrior"). Ray's version of the sweat lodge, based on an Indigenous spiritual and healing ceremony, was carried out in a haphazard fashion. After fasting, around fifty participants entered a short, wide lodge covered with a plastic tarp—rather than natural materials, such as branches, that are generally used in culturally authorized versions of the tradition. The lodge was heated to an extremely high temperature, and the participants were expected to remain in the lodge for successive rounds of "sweating." Many participants fell ill during the ceremony but were encouraged to stay in the sweltering lodge as part of their "quest." According to witnesses, Ray goaded participants into remaining, despite their concerns, and refused to allow struggling participants to leave (Dougherty, 2009). As a result of the ceremony, three participants died, and over twenty were hospitalized or medically treated ("Third Arizona 'Sweat Lodge Death'," 2009).

The disaster at Sedona reignited debates about the commodification and appropriation of Indigenous spiritual and healing traditions; these debates have only become more pronounced in the ensuing years. From expensive healing retreats based on Indigenous practices and principles, to the selling of medicinal sage and sacred bundles in mainstream shopping outlets, examples abound of culturally specific Indigenous healing traditions that are marketed to non-Native consumers. Practitioners of Indigenous traditions have argued that acts of appropriation encroach on their ability to engage in their own self-determined spiritual and medical traditions,

DOI: 10.4324/9781003342229-4

and many activists have spoken out about these harms for decades (Deloria, 1999; Deloria, 2023; Rose, 1992). Yet, the cultural appropriation and marketing-for-profit of Native spirituality and medicine continues.

Medical pluralism—the presence within a modern society of a wide array of medical systems, from standard to unorthodox (Baer, 2004a)—has become more mainstream in the United States. Patients and consumers are increasingly open to drawing on a wide array of healing options, including those that fall under the rubric of complementary and alternative medicine (CAM). While CAM practices are marketed as universal, some have their origin in culturally specific traditions. And, for some practitioners of these culturally specific traditions, including Native North Americans, the adoption of their healing practices constitutes an act of spiritual and medical appropriation. Through processes of commodification, Indigenous healing practices have been extracted from their communities of origin and marketed as broadly relevant. During this extractive process, culturally specific elements—including spiritual and historical components—are erased in order to create a more universal medical commodity. While outsiders may understand themselves to be drawing on Indigenous practices as one of many CAM options, for cultural insiders, these acts of commodification are not "authentic" and perpetuate serious harms. This chapter explores the non-Native adoption of Native North American healing practices and its consequences—social, physical, and spiritual.

The Ongoing Harms of Religious Appropriation

In *Stealing My Religion* (2022), religious studies scholar Liz Bucar suggests that a key distinguishing feature of religious appropriation—as opposed to religious borrowing—involves harms, ranging from offense and spiritual exploitation to cultural genocide—that befall those whose religion is targeted. According to scholar of religion Julianne Cordero-Lamb (2005), healing practices are often singled out by outsiders who appropriate Indigenous cultural practices. She argues that "few areas more exploited, inappropriately co-opted, and misinterpreted by non-Indian scholars, as well as by non-Indian individuals seeking a spiritual path that they believe will harness for them the power of Native ceremonies" (367). Practitioners, activists, and scholars have identified a number of overarching harms that occur through the ongoing appropriation of Indigenous spirituality: the dissemination of sacred or secret tribal information, the romanticization of Native people and communities, the erasure of histories of violence against Native people, and the obfuscation of current social and economic struggles Native communities face (Aldred, 2000; Crawford O'Brien and Talamantez, 2020; Deloria, 1999; Deloria, 2023; Dees, 2023; Jenkins, 2004; Jocks, 2000). As evidenced by the deaths at Sedona, physical harm can befall those who engage in improperly conducted ceremonies. Further, spiritual leaders warn that appropriation can cause metaphysical harm. Sarah McFarland Taylor, a student of the leading scholar of Native American religions Inés Talamantez, relayed to me her teachings: the inappropriate use of Indigenous ceremonies can result in tangible spiritual threats to practitioners, including angering spiritual entities, polluting sacred places, and weakening the efficacy of specific practices.

At the economic, transactional level, a fundamental harm of appropriation results from religious outsiders benefitting materially from the knowledge and traditions of another community, which occurred in the Sedona tragedy (Looking Horse, 2009). This is especially egregious when considering the many challenges Indigenous communities have faced—in the United States and around the world—to safely and legally engage in their own traditions. Religious appropriation is one area of focus for the Great Plains Action Society, a grassroots, Indigenous-led organization based in Iowa. It was founded by Sikowis (Christine) Nobiss, a Plains Cree and Salteaux citizen of the George Gordon First Nation. As she explained in a 2023 interview, Indigenous people find it disrespectful for others to access and benefit from sacred knowledge that religious insiders have struggled to maintain themselves (Kieffer, 2023).

From the earliest instances of European contact with Indigenous Americans, efforts have been underway to forcibly convert Native peoples to Christianity (Niezen, 2000). In the United States, federal policies banned Native people from engaging in traditional ceremonies (Graber, 2018; Wenger, 2009). Native children were forcibly sent to boarding schools to strip them of their traditions (Child, 2018). Legislation protecting the free exercise of Native American religions was only passed in 1978 with the American Indian Religious Freedom Act—which offered only conditional protection (Dees, 2021). Legal struggles continue to this day, especially regarding the use of sacred lands (Lloyd, 2023; McNally, 2020).

In the aftermath of the Sedona disaster, many practitioners, religious leaders, and activists condemned members of the New Age tradition for the appropriation of Indigenous spiritual and healing traditions. James Arthur Ray, a New Age leader, was featured in the wildly popular 2006 New Age book and DVD *The Secret* (Sancho and Brown, 2010). Ray's affiliation with the New Age was highlighted in critical responses to the tragedy (Flynn, 2009). The "New Age movement" refers to a wide variety of beliefs and practices, often involving spirituality drawn from many cultural sources (Sutcliffe, 2003). Although it is an umbrella term for a large movement rather than a canonical set of beliefs and ideas, Paul Heelas (1996) suggests that a common factor among New Age adherents is a form of "self-spirituality," in which a practitioner adopts an eclectic mix of beliefs and practices. Many critiques have been directed at participants in the New Age movement for engaging in systematic and continued forms of commodification—packaging and selling a practice, object, or tradition—and appropriation—taking practices/traditions out of their normal context and benefitting from it (Carrette and King, 2005; Einstein, 2008; Owen, 2008).

Medical Pluralism: A Landscape of Healing Alternatives

The New Age, however, is not the only factor to blame for the appropriation of Indigenous religion and healing practices. Our contemporary healthcare landscape, characterized by medical pluralism, creates an atmosphere that encourages cultural borrowing of healing practices originating from a diverse array of cultures. Diverse approaches to medicine and health have been popularized by well-known personalities, including Jon-Kabat Zinn, Deepak Chopra, Andrew Weil, and Christine Northrup. Seekers of health are increasingly interested in accessing healing by whatever means necessary, including "alternative" practices (Brown, 2013). This represents a shift, as mainstream Western medicine has long maintained medical hegemony (Baer, 2004b). Medical professionals have sought to distinguish their field—variously known as conventional, standard, allopathic, Western, mainstream, scientific, orthodox, and bio-medicine—from alternative medical practices. Yet, increasingly, even conventionally trained doctors and their patients are seeking non-conventional forms of healing (Coulter and Willis, 2004).

Non-conventional healing traditions take many forms and have varying relationships with the "standard treatments" pursued in conventional medicine. A strict definition of *alternative medicine* is a non-standard healing practice that is used *instead of* conventional medicine. *Complementary medicine* is a type of practice that blends non-standard traditions with conventional medical practices. *Integrative medicine* refers to a practice based on standard care that selectively incorporates non-standard practices that research has shown to be effective. The philosophy behind integrative medicine stresses a holistic approach to health, integrating a patient's physical, emotional, and spiritual well-being. The label CAM itself is a broad descriptor that encompasses a wide array of practices (National Cancer Institute, 2023).

Numerous healthcare practices fall under the CAM umbrella. According to U.S. federal agencies devoted to CAM research, these include biologically based practices (taking vitamins and supplements, following special diets, and plant medicine, including the use of cannabis products), body-based practices (massage and chiropractic therapy, reflexology), mind-body practices (yoga, tai chi, deep breathing, meditation, biofeedback, hypnosis), and energy healing (reiki, therapeutic touch) (National Cancer Institute, 2023; National Center for Complementary and Integrative Health, n.d.). According to a study by the Pew Research Center (2017), "about half of Americans report having tried some form of alternative medicine, such as herbal remedies, acupuncture, chiropractic treatment, or energy therapies, at some point during their lifetime"—either instead of or in addition to standard medicine practices.

In addition to these examples of individual therapies (many of which may be combined), some alternative medical healing practices are considered "whole medical systems." These include culturally specific practices such as Traditional Chinese Medicine (TCM); Ayurvedic medicine, an Indian system which incorporates a variety of practices; and "folk medicines," a generic term for longstanding culturally specific medical traditions (National Cancer Institute, 2023; National Center for Complementary and Integrative Health, n.d.). While they are not frequently spotlighted in the National Institutes of Health (NIH) resources, we might also consider religiously specific traditions, such as Christian Science, to be whole medical systems.

While CAM is intended to be universal, many facets grew out of culturally specific practices. This includes Reiki and qigong, two forms of healing that originated in Asian healing practices. Other professionalized systems of healing, including chiropractic and acupuncture, similarly grew out of religious systems (Albanese, 2008; Brown, 2013). Although many forms of CAM originated in spiritual practices, alternative healthcare practitioners open their services to clients and patients with diverse backgrounds. Those who practice CAM see universal value, and the potential for universal efficacy, for all who wish to participate. This leads to a key question with regard to "Native American Healing:" whether the ceremonies should benefit the community from which they originated, or religious outsiders.

Native American healing systems—those practiced by Indigenous practitioners—are best understood as "whole medical systems." "Native American healing" is a general term used to refer to Indigenous healing practices in what is now the United States; it is important to note, however, that there is not one cohesive set of healing practices used by all Indigenous communities. There are 574 federally recognized Native American nations in the United States—sovereign nations with their unique laws, cultures, languages, religious practices, and healing traditions. Native American healing systems involve specific healing practices as well as overall philosophies about physical and spiritual well-being. These practices are not static; they have changed before and after contact with Europeans. Many Native people use modern biomedicine as well as forms of CAM. For many practitioners of Indigenous traditions, healing and medicine are closely intertwined with religion and spirituality (Crawford O'Brien, 2008).

The process of commodification, when applied to Indigenous healing traditions, involves the packaging and selling of a practice, object, or insight that promises some form of healing potentiality to outsiders. Through the course of this process, elements that usually have cultural specificity are detached from their cultural foundations. The result is a more universalized product that appeals to a broader consumer base. In this way, the term "Native American healing" may actually refer to two constellations of beliefs and practices associated with two distinct populations. The first constellation involves an ethnically delineated system of beliefs and rituals used by Indigenous people in North America, as described above. This taxonomy may include what is known as "ethno-medicine," "religious healing," and "folk medicine." Ethno-medicine is culturally specific, rooted in the traditions and worldviews of particular religious and cultural groups. For this group of people, healing practices constitute a significant subset of spiritual practices, more generally, which are themselves often closely associated with everyday beliefs and practices (Crawford O'Brien, 2008). While medical practices help to heal individuals, the family and community play important roles in the ceremonies, which help to reinforce relationships. Well-being involves the entire nation (Cordero-Lamb, 2005, 362). The second constellation involves the practices of non-Native people who utilize healing elements derived from the Indigenous healing practices, in a non-Native cultural context. For this group, "Native American healing" may best be understood as a form of CAM, often used along with other forms of healing which may include chiropractic, Reiki, acupuncture, and other therapeutic approaches. These practices are generally focused on one individual.

Healthcare and Healing in Native North America

Due to centuries of attacks and settler colonial policies meant to diminish the well-being of Indigenous communities, healthcare and healing are important issues in Native America. Against a historical backdrop of violence in cultural contact situations, changes of lifestyle due to confinement of tribal nations on reservations, and U.S. government attempts at forced assimilation and acculturation, many Native Americans face pressing health concerns (Jones, 2006). As Lakota physician and scholar Donald Warne outlines:

> Unfortunately, American Indians suffer among the worst health disparities in the nation with alarming gaps in life expectancy. Death rates from preventable causes such as diabetes and alcoholism are dramatically higher in American Indians than in the rest of the population. Nearly a third of our people live in poverty as compared to approximately 12 percent of the rest of the country. In Arizona, the average age at death is 72.2 years for the general population, but it is 54.7 years for American Indians.
>
> *2009, 7*

Other studies, including those sponsored by the U.S. government, confirm that Native Americans have greater health concerns than the general population. Native people have a higher risk of dying from alcoholism and tuberculosis, and their life expectancy is generally lower. Scholars have linked physical problems directly to this history of colonialism and a current lack of resources on the reservations. Suzanne Crawford O'Brien has argued that "health and wellness concerns are the most pressing issues facing Native communities today, issues arising directly from the experience of colonialism, racism, and systemic oppression" (2008, 2). The lived experience of illness in Native America, then, is deeply intertwined with the history of contact with Europeans (Reff, 2004). In addition, cultural histories of individual tribal nations are filled with traumatic events such as forced removals and massacres (Trafzer and Hyer, 1999). The events are not only in the distant past, but fairly recent. In the nineteenth and twentieth centuries, Indigenous family structures were attacked when children were sent to government boarding schools and when adults were relocated to urban centers during the "relocation era." These events continue to affect Indigenous cultural memories. In addition to individual medical problems that Native people face, entire Native communities and nations are in need of healing.

Indigenous healing methods, then, must reflect the unique needs of Native American people living on and off reservations and take into account the widely recognized need for psychological and cultural healing. In addition to being sensitive to cultural contexts, the methods must resonate with Native understandings of the world. As a result, these healing methods are often closely associated with religious and spiritual practices (Talamantez, 2006). Unlike proponents of modern biomedicine who place a distinction between medicine, health, science against religion and spirituality, Indigenous people living in the United States today often understand their healing practices as part of religious rituals. Crawford O'Brien explains that "the ways in which contemporary Native individuals, communities, families, and tribal nations are making sense of illness and constructing approaches to healing are vastly important; it points toward these peoples' fundamental value systems, worldviews, and spiritual beliefs" (2008, 2). Healing fits into larger religious systems, which are closely linked, and even inseparable from, cultural systems. These cultural systems draw on pre-contact traditions but are always adaptive and adapting, consciously reflecting histories of contact with European populations.

Whereas, for Native Americans, traditional healing practices are located within an ethnic cultural context, many non-Natives who participate in Native healing practices view it as one of many forms of "complementary and alternative medicine." Physicians Kaptchuk and Eisenberg explain, "Occasionally, a culture-bound medical system ventures outside its historical sphere of influence and becomes another option available to the general U.S. population .... Partly because of New Age affinities, this may also happen with Tibetan medicine and Native American ceremonies." As the authors note, "as a general taxonomic statement, consistent with stubborn racist prejudices, one could say that medical practices of ethnic communities are described as ethno-medicine while the 'ethno-medicine' of mainstream white Americans is generally classified as CAM" (2001, 200). Thus, these two populations are at odds: although non-Natives see this form of healing as one of many paths to good health, from an Indigenous perspective, "Native American healing" is a set of special practices proper to a culturally defined group.

The differences between insider and outsider use of Indigenous healing systems reflect the conversion of ethnic outsiders to a religious tradition historically associated with another ethnic or cultural group. In her article "Multiple Meanings of Chinese Healing in the United States" (2005), Linda Barnes describes two broad categories of participants in Chinese healing in the United States—ethnic Chinese and non-Chinese converts. Since the 1970s, many non-Asians have converted to religious systems extracted from a Chinese cultural setting: Buddhism, Confucianism, and Taoism. For instance, the form of Taoism adopted by a non-Asian is strikingly different from ethnic Chinese forms, and converts selectively choose elements of the tradition that appeal to them (Barnes, 2005, 327). They may adopt Taoist philosophical tenets and systems of physical exercise but ignore traditions of ancestor worship common to Chinese Taoist practices. Barnes describes the uneasiness of this situation, including lingering questions about the totality of a convert's conversion: "This process of invention entered the borderlands between conversion and appropriation, sometimes residing more on one side or the other, sometimes sitting awkwardly on the fence" (2008, 317). A non-Asian person cannot choose their ancestors or change their ethnic identity, but due to the widely held understanding that spiritual Asian cultures have universal benefits, non-Asians can participate in Asian practices. As Barnes illustrates, an Americanized form of Buddhism has developed that creates a space for non-Asians to practice these traditions. Similar issues exist in the appropriation of Native traditions, as the following case study will illustrate.

The Cultural Specificity of Indigenous vs. Asian Healing Practices

A case study involving a healer trained in both Indigenous and Asian practices helps to probe some of the intricacies of the broad use of these traditions, as they are marketed to non-Native consumers. Author and educator Kenneth Cohen describes himself as a traditional healer and qigong master of Russian Jewish heritage. Cohen's 2003 book *Honoring the Medicine: The Essential Guide to Native American Healing* has been a popular source on Native American healing practices. The book won the "Best Spiritual Books" award from *Spirituality and Health Magazine*, and the "National Health and Wellness Book Award" from Books for a Better Life and the National Multiple Sclerosis Society. Cohen self-consciously distances his work on Indigenous healing from New Age healing practices, and his articles, books, and websites indicate a critical awareness of the debates about non-Native practices of Native healing. Reflecting culturally specific practices, Cohen's distinct presentations of Native American healing and qigong indicate efforts to distinguish between culturally specific and universal healing systems, yet some questions remain about who these traditions are meant to heal.

Cohen maintains a pair of websites that provide consumers with information on the different types of healing services and educational opportunities he offers: *The Way of Qigong: The Teachings of Kenneth S. Cohen* (https://www.qigonghealing.com), and *Honoring the Medicine: Native American & First Nations Health and Cultural Education* (https://www.sacredearthcircle.com). The websites show compartmentalization, or even "code switching," to strategically market two types of healing to the consumer. Each website provides a professional profile, an explanation of the systems of healing he uses, his training and credentials, and his writings on healing. He also markets his services on each site. On *The Way of Qigong* website, the "Products" page includes his 2018 book *The Way of Qigong* and links to a secondary audiobook shop with a variety of qigong-related products. Cohen offers educational opportunities, including in-person and online workshops, consultations, and trainings. Cohen's *Honoring the Medicine* site primarily highlights educational offerings related to Native American religion rather than selling healing practices. His presentation of each system reveals distinct conceptions of universal vs. culturally specific practices.

Cohen's own image and identity are constructed differently in the two websites. When I first visited the *Sacred Earth Circle* site in 2009, he introduced himself as

Kenneth "Bear Hawk" Cohen. Currently, he introduces himself as Kenneth Cohen, Lᴺᵇ· ᕁᵇ·ᶢᶜᒧᵒ, reflecting his adoption into a Western Cree family. The name "Bear Hawk" is now absent from the site, and he clarifies that while he is connected to a Cree family, he is *not* a member of an Indigenous nation. In a photograph of Cohen posted on *Sacred Earth Circle*, he wears a jacket with colors recognized to be sacred in a number of Native communities—black, red, yellow, and white. This is different from the way he presents himself on the *Qigong Research and Practice Center* website, in which he shares his Chinese name "Gao Han" and wears a Chinese robe in photographs. He presents his identity differently on each of these websites. In Sarah McFarland Taylor's analysis, this can be interpreted as "changing his 'brand' to appeal to different target audiences and consumers" (2023).

In the biography on each of the websites, he cites different sets of teachers, trainers, and experiences. On *Sacred Earth Circle*, his biography describes him as "a traditional healer and health and cultural educator who has lived and practiced indigenous ways for most of his 70+ years." Among his influences and mentors, he lists a number of Native North American healers from different tribal nations, as well as Indigenous healers from the Philippines and Nigeria. On *Qigong Research and Practice Center*, Cohen is presented as "a world-renowned health educator, China scholar, and Qigong Grandmaster with more than fifty years experience." Although he by no means hides his experience with both traditions—each website contains a prominent link to the other, and he briefly mentions his additional experiences on each website—he clearly presents different identities on each. In order to be viewed as a legitimate healer for each system, it is necessary to "market" himself in distinct manners. As a healer and educator following different paths, he must identify a discrete set of mentors, credentials, and publications in order to demonstrate his authority. This can be interpreted as a strategic form of branding.

In a phone interview on October 9, 2009, I spoke with Cohen to better understand the different ways he views these healing traditions. According to Cohen, a primary difference lies in who may access each tradition. Cohen understands qigong as a universal practice and Native American healing as culturally specific. As an outsider to these tribal nations, Cohen explained that he may access and lead some forms of Native American healing because he follows the proper protocol and is respectful of those who share their tradition with him. However, he believes that he needs no permission to access qigong, because it is a universal energy system. He suggested that widespread use of qigong does not constitute an appropriation of Eastern traditions.

In his writings on Native healing practices, Cohen points to the debates about the appropriation of Native spirituality, and the interconnectedness of healing with spirituality. He writes, "from the Native American viewpoints, healing, quality of life, and spiritual development cannot be separated from politics and economics" (Cohen, 2006, 3). His understanding of Indigenous healing reflects cultural insiders' ideas. When describing Indigenous medicine systems, Cohen writes, "from the Native American perspective, medicine belongs more to the realm of healing than curing. These two concepts are not identical. Physicians aim to cure disease, to vanquish it, and to make it go away. Traditional indigenous healers emphasize healing, in the sense of 'making whole' by establishing, enhancing, or restoring well-being and harmony" (2006, 1). Cohen's discussions of Native American healing correspond with the ways professional scholars of Native American healing describe healing—healing practices involve physical and mental healing on the individual level, as well as greater cultural healing at the level of community and tribal nation.

In addition to careful self-reflection used in his descriptions of Native understandings of religion and healing, Cohen makes moves to distance himself from New Age understandings and appropriations of Native spiritual traditions. Clearly aware of the critiques made by those who have studied appropriations, Cohen articulates the ways in which he is distinct from leaders like James Ray, whose healing practices were clearly derived from Native practices for Ray's own gain. When describing the services he provides to others on his webpage "Healing, Counseling, Consultation," he cautions potential clients: "Please do not confuse traditional indigenous 'doctoring' with either Shamanism or New Age dabbling." In his book, he discredits New Age writings as "frequently overtly imaginative, based on channeling from 'higher' extraterrestrial sources, 'memories' from past lives, or the unrestrained fantasies of self-styled experts" (2006, 7). In educational lectures about Native healing practices, Cohen includes segments on the appropriation of Native healing practices, demonstrating an awareness of the issues at stake.

Cohen's website indicates that he does not intend to profit off Indigenous healing ceremonies, one of the main problems scholars cite regarding the appropriation of New Age practices. On a page describing the public presentations he gives, he explains,

In keeping with traditional Native American/First Nations protocols, I do not and have never charged money for healing treatments or ceremony. A healer only facilitates the connection between the "patient" and the sacred healing forces. And because healing is a gift from Creator, we are not allowed to attach a monetary value, turning healing into a commodity. Yet, this does not mean that healing is free. Some sacrifice, some offering must be made by the patient. A traditional offering of tobacco shows respect for the healer. The patient may also need to provide travel expenses for the healer and his or her helpers. I generally recommend that a client also make a donation to a Native American organization (such as the Native American Rights Fund) to demonstrate generosity and good will. In the old days, a patient might give horses and blankets; today a patient might offer personal gifts or a monetary donation. But I personally feel that it is wrong to charge a fee for traditional healing.

Lectures, Workshops, and Courses

By noting the problems with sharing sensitive cultural knowledge, Cohen distinguishes himself from white and Native "plastic shamans" who make money by divulging secrets to non-Native people.

In addition, Cohen heeds the strict forms of protocol. When discussing the forms of healing he can do, he explains, "Traditional healing requires following cultural protocols, including how one asks for a healing ('offering tobacco'), when during the cycle of the month it might be more appropriate or inappropriate to ask for healing, the meaning of 'reciprocity', proper ways to show respect through style of dress and speech, and so on" ("Healing, Counseling, Consultation"). In his book, he includes lengthy discussions of protocol (2006, 151–66). His discussion includes when and how one may attend a ceremony, ceremonial etiquette, proper handling of ceremonial materials, and more pieces of information that would be of value to a cultural outsider wishing to partake in a Native ceremony. The care he takes to describe protocol indicates that Cohen has a deep respect for Indigenous cultures, religions, and methods of healing.

For these reasons, it appears as though Cohen has avoided many of the pitfalls associated with non-Native involvement in Indigenous healing practices. However, there are still elements in his presentation of Indigenous healing, in general, and his own role in healing, that could be controversial. Even though Cohen maintains that Native practices are cultural, he seems to value a universal element in them. His book opens with a prayer by a Cree elder: "I pray that [this book's] knowledge be spread throughout the land. May it be helpful to many people, not only Native people but also Europeans, Africans, Chinese, and All Nations" (2006, xviii). Cohen appeals to Native elders who believe Indigenous healing practices should be available for wider usage. Citing Native people who advocate the sharing of their traditions with outsiders, Cohen seeks to legitimate his decision to publish a book about these practices. Religious Studies scholar Christina Welch observes that "not every American Indian is totally against the dissemination of indigenous practices" (2002, 29). However, not all traditional healers agree. Some, including noted Lakota scholar and activist Vine Deloria, believe this practice is "contrary to every known tenet of any tribal tradition" (Welch, 2002, 29). While most Native people would likely be against the widespread adoption of their practices, it is impossible to follow a universal set of standards because there are many perspectives on this issue.

Although Cohen contends that Indigenous healing practices are culturally specific, he does point out that "at the level of roots and breath, at the level of our humanness, there are only small differences among us" (Cohen, 2006, 1). This statement can be interpreted in multiple ways; it draws connections between diverse cultures and societies but can also serve to erase important, unique features of Native societies and casually gloss over centuries of settler colonialism (Todorov, 1999). In addition, he seems to romanticize Native religion and healing systems when he writes that "Native American healing takes us to these roots because it is an expression of the ancient wisdom of humanity. Indigenous spirituality is the world's oldest religion" (1). Here, he seems to suggest that all religions can be traced to—and therefore claim—Indigenous traditions, a point that scholars critique as a form of continuing cultural imperialism in the guise of comparative religion (Kelley, 2014).

In addition, his materials seem to be primarily directed to a non-Native audience for the purpose of self-healing. In the introduction to his book *Honoring the Medicine* (2003), he explains that the book was written for a wide popular audience as well as physicians. "In Native American communities, certain individuals are born with a gift of healing or possess a particular ability to receive and carry back to us messages from the Creator or helping spirits. Nevertheless, we all have latent healing abilities that can be awakened" (3). This focus on individual spiritual awakening is strongly reminiscent of the New Age healing practices Cohen criticizes.

Finally, while Cohen points to connections between the current social issues faced by Native people, at times he extracts Indigenous religious and spiritual elements out of their cultural and political contexts. On his website, Cohen mentions the relation of religion and healing to political and economic systems, but only in passing. In his book, he does briefly describe the history of colonialism that orients Native health problems and solutions. However, after introducing the political stakes of Native American healing, he quickly shifts to a less-politicized topic.

> Finally, it must be said that from the Native American viewpoint, healing, quality of life, and spiritual development cannot be separated from politics and economics. Native American healing emphasizes harmony with the earth as an essential ingredient in personal health .... We cannot preserve original healing traditions without recognizing the rights of the original people of North America to autonomy and control over their own lives and lands. The elders say that plants, swimmers, crawlers, four-leggeds, and those who fly are also "people," with God-given rights to the food, shelter, and happiness that nature provides.
> *This is in _Honoring the Medicine_ (pg. 3).*

Cohen mentions tribal autonomy and discusses the very real, pressing issue of Indigenous land rights. While speaking about the significance of animals, plants, and land is in keeping with many Indigenous ways of knowing and being, focusing on non-human persons can also move the conversation away from Native claims to their own lands and universalize environmental issues. The tension of universality vs. cultural specificity still lingers when non-Native healers present their services, teachings, and insights to non-Native audiences seeking their own personal, individual healing.

Conclusion

The incident at Sedona aroused the public's interest in non-Native appropriation of Native healing practices. In the midst of debate about the authenticity of these religious practices and in the face of human deaths resulting from what most agree was an ill-planned sweat lodge ceremony, a number of questions have emerged about the authenticity of healing practices. The rise of CAM and medical pluralism help to explain the continuing commodification and appropriation of Native American healing practices, despite protests from Indigenous leaders, healers, and scholars. Even healers like Ken Cohen, who reflect on the harms of New Age appropriation, may still perpetuate distorted pictures of Indigenous healing systems as universal practices by marketing their potential benefits for non-Native individuals. Non-Natives interested in these practices assume that they are universally useful.

Indigenous healing methods practiced for and by their communities of origin and Native American healing as an alternative therapy are best understood *not* as two sides of the same coin but as two separate sets of practices. Although much of the language is similar, they appeal to different audiences. Indigenous alternative healing practices are culturally specific, reflecting the histories and needs of particular communities. While there may be instances in which religious outsiders may participate with the agreement of insiders, the decision about who may participate generally lies in the hands of the insiders. For non-Natives who participate in Native healing practices, following protocol, it seems, may earn the respect of some elders; however, not all practitioners are in agreement that outsiders should be able to access particular traditions. While non-Natives may seek to learn about Indigenous healing systems, it is essential for non-Native seekers of health and well-being to realize the many physical and metaphysical injuries that commodification and appropriation can perpetuate.

Bibliography

Albanese, Catherine (2008). *A Republic of Mind and Spirit: A Cultural History of American Metaphysical Religion*. New Haven: Yale.

Aldred, Lisa (2000). "Plastic Shamans and Astroturf Sun Dances: New Age Commercialization of Native American Spirituality." *The American Indian Quarterly* 24.3: 329–52.

Baer, Hans A. (2004a). "Medical Pluralism," in *Encyclopedia of Medical Anthropology: Health and Illness in the World's Cultures*, edited by Carol R. Ember and Melvin Ember. New York, NY: Springer.

Baer, Hans A. (2004b). *Toward an Integrative Medicine: Merging Alternative Theories with Biomedicine*. Walnut Creek: AltaMira Press.

Barnes, Linda (2005). "Multiple Meanings of Chinese Healing in the United States," in *Religion and Healing in America*, edited by Linda Barnes and Susan Sered. Oxford: Oxford University Press, 307–31.

BBC (October 18, 2009). "Third Arizona 'Sweat Lodge' Death." *BBC*. http://news.bbc.co.uk/2/hi/americas/8312954.stm (accessed July 19, 2023).

Brown, Candy Gunther (2013). *The Healing Gods: Complementary and Alternative Medicine in Christian America*. Oxford: Oxford University Press.

Bucar, Liz (2022). *Stealing My Religion: Not Just Any Cultural Appropriation*. Cambridge: Harvard University Press.

Carrette, Jeremy and Richard King (2005). *Selling Spirituality: The Silent Takeover of Religion*. London: Routledge.

Child, Brenda (2018). "The Boarding Schools as Metaphor." *Journal of American Indian Education* 57.1: 37–57.

Cohen, Kenneth. (2017). *Honoring the Medicine: Native American and First Nations Health and Cultural Education*. [Website]. https://www.sacredearthcircle.com

Cohen, Kenneth. (ND). *The Way of Qigong: The Teachings of Kenneth S. Cohen*. [Website]. www.qigonghealing.com.

Cohen, Kenneth (2006). *Honoring the Medicine: The Essential Guide to Native American Healing*. New York: Ballantine Books.

Cordero-Lamb, Julianne (2005). "Healing Traditions, California," in *American Indian Religious Traditions: The Encyclopedia*, edited by Suzanne Crawford and Dennis Kelley. Santa Barbara: ABC-CLIO, 361–8.

Coulter, Ian D. and Evan M. Willis (2004). "The Rise of Complementary and Alternative Medicine: A Sociological Perspective." *Medical Journal of Australia* 180: 587–9.

Crawford O'Brien, Suzanne J. (ed.) (2008). *Religion and Healing in Native America: Pathways for Renewal*. Westport: Praeger.

Crawford O'Brien, Suzanne J. and Inés Talamantez (2020). *Religion and Culture in Native America*. Lanham: Rowman and Littlefield.

Dees, Sarah (2021). "Religion and U.S. Federal Indian Policy," in *A Companion to American Religious History*, edited by Benjamin E. Park. New York: Wiley, 276–86.

Dees, Sarah (2023). "Before and Beyond the New Age: Historical Appropriation of Native American Medicine and Spirituality." *American Religion* 4.2: 17–44.

Deloria, Phil (1999). *Playing Indian*. New Haven: Yale University Press.

Deloria, Vine (2023). *God Is Red: A Native View of Religion (50th Anniversary Edition)*. Wheat Ridge: Fulcrum Publishing.

Dougherty, John (October 21, 2009). "For Some Seeking Rebirth, Sweat Lodge Was End." *New York Times*. https://www.nytimes.com/2009/10/22/us/22sweat.html

Einstein, Mara (2008). *Brands of Faith: Marketing Religion in a Commercial Age*. New York: Routledge.

Flynn, Johnny (October 15, 2009). "A New Age Tragedy in Sedona." *The Guardian*. https://www.theguardian.com/commentisfree/belief/2009/oct/15/sedona-sweat-lodge-native-american (last accessed July 22, 2023).

Graber, Jennifer (2018). *The Gods of Indian Country: Religion and the Struggle for the American West*. Oxford: Oxford University Press.

Heelas, Paul (1996). *The New Age Movement*. Oxford: Blackwell.

Jenkins, Philip (2004). *Dream Catchers: How Mainstream America Discovered Native Spirituality*. Oxford: Oxford University Press.

Jocks, Christopher Ronwanièn:te (2000). "Spirituality for Sale: Sacred Knowledge in the Consumer Age," in *Native American Spirituality: A Critical Reader*, edited by Lee Irwin. Lincoln: University of Nebraska Press, 61–77.

Jones, David S. (2006). "The Persistence of American Indian Health Disparities." *American Journal of Public Health* 96.12: 2122–34.

Kaptchuk, Ted and David Eisenberg (2001). "Varieties of Healing 2: A Taxonomy of Unconventional Healing Practices." *Annals of Internal Medicine* 135.3: 196–204.

Kelley, Dennis (2014). *Tradition, Performance, and Religion in Native America: Ancestral Ways, Modern Selves*. New York: Routledge.

Kieffer, Ben (Host) (2023, June 27). "Non-Natives Have Commodified 'Indian Remedies' and Indigenous Spirituality Since the 19th Century." [Radio broadcast]. *River to River*. Iowa Public Radio. https://www.iowapublicradio.org/podcast/river-to-river/2023-06-27/non-natives-have-commodified-indian-remedies-and-indigenous-spirituality-since-the-19th-century

Lloyd, Dana (2023). *Land Is Kin: Sovereignty, Religious Freedom, and Indigenous Sacred Sites*. Lawrence: University Press of Kansas.

Looking Horse, Arvol (October 16, 2009). "Concerning the Deaths in Sedona." *Indian Country Today*.

McNally, Michael (2020). *Defend the Sacred: Native American Religious Freedom beyond the First Amendment*. Princeton: Princeton University Press.

National Cancer Institute (June 2, 2023). *Complementary and Alternative Medicine*. https://www.cancer.gov/about-cancer/treatment/cam (last accessed July 20, 2023).

National Center for Complementary and Integrative Health (n.d.). *Terms Related to Complementary and Integrative Health*. https://www.nccih.nih.gov/health/providers/terms-related-to-complementary-and-integrative-health

Niezen, Ronald (2000). *Spirit Wars: Native North American Religions in the Age of Nation Building*.

Owen, Suzanne (2008). *The Appropriation of Native American Spirituality*. London: Continuum.

Pew Research Center (February 2017). *Vast Majority of Americans Say Benefits of Childhood Vaccines Outweigh Risks*. https://www.pewresearch.org/science/2017/02/02/vast-majority-of-americans-say-benefits-of-childhood-vaccines-outweigh-risks/.

Ray, James Arthur (n.d.). *Spiritual Warrior*. James Ray International, Inc. http://jamesray.com/events/spiritual-warrior.php [As of July 19, 2023, this page has been unpublished, but is still viewable via waybackmachine.com.]

Reff, Daniel (2004). *Plagues, Priests, and Demons: Sacred Narratives and the Rise of Christianity in the Old World and the New*. Cambridge: Cambridge University Press.

Rose, Wendy (1992). "The Great Pretenders: Further Reflections on Whiteshamanism," in *The State of Native America: Genocide, Colonization and Resistance*, edited by M. Annettee Jaimes. Boston: South End Press, 403–21.

Sancho, Miguel and Kimberly Brown (2010). "Arizona Sweat Lodge: The Inside Story of James Ray's Fatal Retreat." *ABC News*. https://abcnews.go.com/Primetime/james-arthur-ray-arizona-sweat-lodge/story?id=11016900

Sutcliffe, Steven J. (2003). *Children of the New Age: A History of Spiritual Practices*. London: Routledge.

Talamantez, Inés (2006). "Teaching Native American Religious Traditions and Healing," in *Teaching Religion and Healing*, edited by Linda Barnes and Inés Talamantez. Oxford: Oxford University Press, 113–26.

Todorov, Tzvetan (1999). *The Conquest of America: The Question of the Other*. Oxford: Oxford University Press.

Trafzer, Clifford and Joel Hyer (eds.) (1999) *Exterminate Them: Written Accounts of the Murder, Rape, and Enslavement of Native Americans During the California Gold Rush*. East Lansing: Michigan State University Press.

Warne, Donald (2009). "Ten Indian Health Policy Challenges for the New Administration in 2009." *Wicazo Sa Review* 24.1: 7–23.

Welch, Christina (2002). "Appropriating the Didjeridu and the Sweat Lodge: New Age Baddies and Indigenous Victims?" *Journal of Contemporary Religion* 1: 21–38.

Wenger, Tisa (2009). *We Have a Religion: The 1920s Pueblo Indian Dance Controversy and American Religious Freedom*.

3

REX HUMBARD, PSYCHOGRAPHICS, AND THE HARD SELL

John Modern

Dear Pastor Rex: I really have enjoyed hearing you on television. I can never thank the Lord enough for what He has done for me through your ministry.

When I first began to listen to your services on TV, my husband would go outside and not come back in until it was over, but I just kept on turning you on every Sunday morning. After a few Sundays went by, he would come through the room a few times while the program was on. Then one Sunday morning, he turned on the TV and said to me, "Aren't you going to listen to Rex this morning?" I answered him, "I sure am." So he sat down and listened to the singing and your sermon. Then one Sunday when you asked all who wanted to be prayed for to come up and you would pray for them, he stood up by his chair and said, I want you to pray for me.

I was so happy I cried. He was just fine for two months, then he dropped dead with a heart attack.

So that is why I am so glad to have you for my TV pastor. I shall always be so very grateful for you and the Cathedral of Tomorrow. I know that God is with me and will never let me down.

Mrs. F.C., California ("How Prayers are Answered," 9)

You Are Loved

Rex Humbard pitched his tent just outside Akron, Ohio, during his 1952 summer "Gospel Big Top" tour. Humbard, an ordained Pentecostal minister, heralded from Little Rock, Arkansas, and had grown up in a traveling gospel ministry led by his parents. When Humbard arrived in this midwestern industrial hub, he was the patriarch of his own traveling music ministry (with his wife, Maude Aimee, and eventually with his children, Rex Jr., Don, Elizabeth, and Charles). During his summer Akron stint, Humbard took a trip downtown. As Humbard recalled, he was walking

DOI: 10.4324/9781003342229-5

down the street one night when he noticed a crowd gathered outside a department store window. He had a revelation right then and there, an insight into the future of crowds, his destiny, and a world increasingly tied to screens. God, claimed Humbard, had given us the gift of television. "Even more remarkable [than] the TV medium's unique person-to-person intimacy [was] the undeniable power of the picture tube [...] to hold on to the newly attracted attention of the listener until he begins to realize in his mind and heart the truth of what he is hearing" ("To Tell the World," 165).

Months after the "Gospel Big Top Tour," Humbard purchased the Ohio Theater in Cuyahoga Falls, a suburb of Akron, rechristened it the Cavalry Church, and contacted WAKR, a local television affiliate, where he secured a weekly slot to broadcast his religious services. Before long, he found himself leading a vibrant congregation that hosted movie nights on Saturday, evening bible study classes, and Dial-a-Prayer, a number that, when phone called, would play the prayer of the day. Humbard had had a vision in which technology would not only aid and abet his mission but also become the very medium through which he enacted "person-to-person intimacy" with his flock.

In 1958, Humbard built from a scratch a spectacular structure in Cuyahoga Falls, one which housed a broadcast television station and a domed theater that could hold 5,400 people. He named it the Cathedral of Tomorrow and immediately had a 32-ton illuminated cross hung from the ceiling. It is still ranked among the largest interior crosses in the world. The experiential ground of Humbard's Pentecostal context—the sensual demand to submit to the Holy Spirit—had become something more invasive within the walls of the Cathedral, something more precise. Specifically, Rex Humbard Ministry, Inc. assumed the presence of a public sensorium *in order to* take the measure of and to engage *that public* for particular purposes.

Over the course of the 1960s and early 1970s, Rex Humbard Ministries grew from a regional radio broadcast into a corporation with a global reach. The Cathedral of Tomorrow became the center of a media-business-entertainment-missionary complex with many different moving parts and services available to the parishioners and the general public. There was a Sunday school, a music program revolving around the nationally recognized Cathedral Quartet, retirement apartments, and weekly worship services—and a global reach. "In just the first half of 1972, nearly 53,000 people from 38 countries and all 50 states came to Akron to see the Cathedral of Tomorrow complex [....] By comparison one of the major rubber company tours drew 30,000 persons for *12 months*" ("World/Scan" 1973, 5). By the mid-1970s, Humbard's signature program, *You are Loved*, was broadcast on television weekly and had an audience of over 1.5 million Americans (or more precisely, 175 stations across the United States with an average audience of 9,589 households per station) (Hadden). Such impressive ratings were not unrelated to the fact that Humbard Ministries had a lean business model that thrived, internally, on the presence of algorithms. Humbard himself monitored revenue reports about each station that carried his program. Computers were used to survey each station to record the viewer mail and donations it generated for Humbard Ministries. In the spirit of optimization, stations that failed to reach predetermined revenue standards were dropped as outlets[1] (Ellens, 79).

The hour-long *You Are Loved* was, first and foremost, a genre that followed a template. The order, arc, and rhythm remained the same from week to week as did the scene, the faces, and the set pieces. And so did the pre-recorded testimonies and songs and close-ups and camera pans and cuts to audience members in attentive rapture. While small elements like the content of the banter between Rex and his wife, for example, may have changed from week to week along with the topic of the sermon and the lineup of special guests—Johnny Cash, James Cleveland, Kathryn Kuhlman, and Chuck Woolery—the rote repetition of Humbard's performance suggested a lurking systematicity emanating from the altar. In the figure of Rex Humbard, one witnessed a man sincerely touched by and overflowing with something akin to divinity. In the figure of Rex Humbard, one witnessed the institutional strategy to saturate the entire world with an all-but-anonymous technical expertise.[2]

The Sphere of God's Grace

During each broadcast of *You Are Loved*, around the 20-minute mark, Humbard would take center stage alongside an altar, his hair close-cropped and gray, his suit brown banker tweed. He was into the business of prosperity. He would kneel on one knee. He would then put one arm on an altar, piled up and overflowing with envelopes and hand-written notes, and he would extend his other arm upward and toward his audience. His head was bowed and his eyes closed, and beads of sweat would become visible on his brow.

The camera would pan slowly back from an altar draped with lonely paper missives. The screen would reveal an audience of thousands who were themselves focused intently on the man at the altar. Humbard would then issue a prayer: "I want every one of you, beyond these walls listening by radio or television, I want you to pray with us. I want every person that is standing here […] I want you to pray with us, right out loud." Humbard, here, was offering a gentle invitation to those within the Cathedral of Tomorrow, to join him in a massive act of incorporation:

> *You see those there in their homes, beyond the walls of the Cathedral of Tomorrow. You know their need [... .] And heal each of those who said in an act of faith, "pray for me." And now we call our Prayer Key Family together to prayer over the needs of every person who's written in [... .] And this altar represents every person's who has written this week [... .] Lord we give our prayers to every person who has written us this week. Each one this week who has written we believe that their need will be met.*[3]

In order for your prayer to be answered, you must contact Humbard Ministries by either mail or telephone. Needs were met in direct proportion to your willingness to reveal them to Rex and to have them incorporated. In becoming a member of his "Prayer Key Family," your prayer request would be placed upon the altar and your name would be "entered into a beautiful leather-bound Prayer Key Family Membership Book." As Humbard promised, you would then become part of a vast familial network, a system of sympathetic energy. "This book is placed every Sunday on the Prayer Altar during the televised services, when all members join in prayer for each other" ("Rex Humbard Prayer Key Family" 1974, 9).

Deciding to become a member of the Prayer Key Family represented a moment of biopolitical intensification—a transparent choice in which you subjected your conscience and moral will to Humbard's gaze and the workings of his enterprise. All prayers were collected for free and for a small monthly contribution you would receive the following: a *You Are Loved* pin or an ornamented prayer key locket indicating your membership in the Prayer Key Family; a membership card; *The Prayer Key Book* by Rex Humbard; and a 24-Hour Prayer Group telephone reminder sticker to put on your telephone.[4]

The circulation of prayer between audience members and Humbard involved many steps. There was the act of making prayer requests and then submitting them. But there were also the leaps of TV-addled faith: imagining those very same requests piled onto an altar when you are watching Rex put his hand on that very same altar, reading—from your living room—the prayer requests and testimonials of others, and experiencing the anticipation of your request or testimonial being chosen to be addressed on air or published in Humbard's monthly publication, *The Answer*.

As a virtual patriarch, Humbard was composed and well-coiffed. He was a slightly miscast Hollywood leading man—square-jawed and humble but with sublimated, sexy goodness. ("If you need a prayer.... Call 216–929–8691.") He was a preacher prone to embrace the aesthetics of banking. In personal appearance, he was hyper-normal, an epitome of mid-century masculinity (Humbard 1977). In terms of theology, he made explicit promises that faith would be rewarded in this life. He evoked confidence in his fine-tuned cultivation of a successful business sheen.

Humbard's appeal was self-consciously gendered; he was well aware that significantly more women than men watched *You Are Loved*. Indeed, at the dawn of data profiling and consumer lifestyle statistical research, Humbard's pitch was often tailored to women, specifically to "older, female Protestants with relatively low socioeconomic status" (Buddenbaum, 272). Indeed, Humbard was explicit in inviting his audience to imagine Prayer Key Family schwag as part of a gendered economy—women receiving a locket and booklet from Humbard, women cherishing those items, and women giving these items to other women and creating a common media space. And the gendered dynamic of the pitch carried through off stage—to his robust publishing house and beyond—as Humbard Ministries turned the traumas, ambitions, and fears of working-class women into fodder for a machine of benevolent design. Every piece of datum gathered lifted burdens and served to save both *You Are Loved* and the souls of its audience from cancellation. "As one of the Prayer Key Family" assures the anonymous ad copy in a direct address, "you will be sending prayer requests in letter form, and you will, in any emergency, call the Prayer Group which originates from the Cathedral of Tomorrow." As is often the case with missionary endeavors, the voice of ethical imperative is stern and instrumental: "You will invite others to share their burdens with members of the Prayer Key Family, perhaps thus leading them to know, accept, and love the Lord" ("What Holy Scripture Tells Us," 9).

Humbard's computational capacities were a measure of his gendered sincerity as he signed off every broadcast—"so that you may truly know that *you are* loved." For such love was premised upon his capacity to store and sort and distribute information about his largely female audience. In such storing and sorting and redistributing, Humbard created an unprecedented data set even as he imagined a network of surveillance that pales in comparison to contemporary marketing practices. His strategy was sincere, however, in that it aligned with his espousal of a new kind of divinity, a God whose mediated presence and algorithmic inference sought to modulate identity in the most subtle of ways (Foucault, de Certeau).[5]

The Elementary Forms of Psychographic Life

> It is not God who is on trial, but you and I. The trouble is not God's fault. He laid down the pattern for us to follow ....
>
> *Humbard (1974a)*

You Are Loved utilized one of the most powerful IBM mainframe computer systems in Ohio. Leased from the First National Bank of Akron, Humbard employed punch card operators to encode data from each and every piece of mail. The data was "mainly requests for prayers, which are sorted out according to a data processing code—'Loved One in Service,' 'Broken Home'—and answered by form letter." With its Common Business Oriented Language (COBOL) platform, Humbard's IBM mainframe assembled a most impressive data bank. The selling point of COBOL was that it could provide "a significant degree of machine independence in the description of data and the specification of algorithms" (Terry; Brown, 47). Humbard was at the cutting edge, at least in terms of a statistical way of seeing. In his capacity to utilize computers as an integral component of his religious mission, Humbard made sure that the anxious habitations of his audience became usable data—they were not merely collected but collated and connected with other sources of demographic information and parsed for patterns. Although the effects are hard to measure, Humbard's computers were always calibrating, to the best of their ability, the target of future appeals (Horsfield, 268–69).

Humbard's strategies were plentiful and included the psychographic arts of audience targeting, predictive potentials, and building and deploying lists of potential consumers with dot matrix sheen. The better the computer the more malleable these lists could become. There was the way in which the name had a buzzing life behind it that intersected with other names, other lives. Each name, among millions, became potentially personalized, known outside of itself for this data point or that one. The name could then be scattered automatically throughout the letter. The name would then, ideally, gather more data from the recipient. Prayer requests mined for the personality and lifestyle behind them. The name could then be scattered, again, automatically, throughout a new letter that was even more precise in its appeal (ibid). And so on and so forth. Through immense feats of faith-driven computation, the burdens, ambitions, and fears of Humbard's largely female audience were collected, inflected, and fed back to them. With its masculinist pitch aimed at securing the interiority of a feminine piety, Humbard was a spectacle of patriarchal authority. Humbard was generating an ideological fortress inside of which the kingdom of the heterosexual body was built, and in doing so, he secured religion "deep" within a sexualized body and its taken-for-granted gender hierarchies.

Humbard and his creation stand as a rather luminous example of secularism in the 1970s, exemplary of how religion becomes *proprietized* as an interior matter, and how it dovetails with the regulation of sexuality and gender as private matters. As has been pointed out in previous studies of the secular, this trend was long-standing within Western modernity.[6] With the advent of psychographic marketing and its particularization of demographic aggregates, long-standing markers of interiority—values, attitudes, beliefs—became algorithmic phenomena (Baier).[7] Rather than argue that religious experience was becoming commodified or feminized here—"churches serv[ing] church members in their acquisition of religious experience," I want to highlight what was made possible by Humbard's technical apparatus, what Saba Mahmood calls "the pernicious symbiosis created between religion and sexuality under modern secularism" (Kotler, 47; Culliton; Mahmood, 114).

Secularism, here, refers to those conditions and processes that generate religion. These conditions are not immediately available to consciousness, and these processes structure more—much more—than matters of religious adherence. This point, of course, does not sit well in a narrative of modernity as a process of secularization. Rather than posit a thing called religion that recedes or becomes re-entrenched or undergoes a revision to its essential nature, scholars must appreciate the massive undertaking involved in the making of the religious and its antitheses. In what follows, I am interested in attending to the practices and ideas of self that contribute to new concepts of religion—in this case, the religion of Humbard Ministries—*and* how those concepts simultaneously intersect with practices and imaginaries of self that are part of the so-called secular world (Modern 2011).

Working Feverishly for the Control of the Whole World

> Of the vast number of Satan's agents, two thirds of them are women. The Holy Word of God strictly forbids our having anything to do with this satanic religion.
> *Humbard (1974a)*

In his productions of intimacy, Humbard relied heavily upon the prophetic plea—fire and brimstone filtered through a Zenith console and independent cable channels of the 1970s. In the hands of Humbard, prophecy became a matter of technical application. It was fine-tuned. It followed a narrative mechanics and involved incorporation. Prophecy's goal was to create a closed loop with extreme purpose, outside of which one could not think without assuming incredible risk (Hughey, 39).

For these were dangerous times. Things were falling apart according to Humbard's pre-millennial blueprint. In his prophetic conviction, Humbard offered a storied frame that grounded and certified his interpretation of the present precisely because it had already been deemed inevitable. The world was ending, "scheduled," he claimed, "to become a disaster area." Humbard knew this because he could read the data. "Prophecy is history written in advance," he wrote. "When the Word of God states that an event will take place, it is as sure to happen as if it has already happened" (Terry; Humbard 1979, 5). According to Humbard, we were living in the last days. Satan was everywhere. Satan's armies were not simply amassing for the final cosmic battle. They were already waging it. Indeed, the satanic atmosphere was so thick as to obscure its mechanics and source for unbelievers—Satan came through the TV, sex, rock music, and even "church members who are not saved." But Humbard was calm and clear-eyed in facing this crisis: "This great invasion of demon spirits into the world comes as no surprise to us who belong to Jesus. We know these forces of evil are working feverishly for the control of the whole world" (Humbard 1974a, 12, 41, 12, 35, 36).

Given the pervasiveness of Satan, Humbard's approach to his largely female audience was not only benevolent but necessary—it represented a desire to regulate their nature in the name of their salvation and a redeemed humanity. Humbard modeled his actions on Jesus who exorcized the seven demons from Mary Magdalene and "set her free." The population in general, according to Humbard, was at cosmic risk, subject to demon possession and all manner of ungodly influence. Women, however, were not only at risk; they were also the primary vehicle of such influence and primary source of that risk. "Of the vast number of Satan's agents," concluded Humbard, "two thirds of them are women." Demons "enter into [those] whose house [is] empty."

As the source of addiction, "nervous disorders" and criminality were agents of Satan that "take people under their control and, as it were, move into your body and mind and spirit" (Ibid., 14, 40, 11–12). Because such afflictions corrupt by way of penetration and seepage, women could queer the very division that makes a category meaningful to itself and other categories. The feminine, the very thing Humbard did so much to define, target, and manage, was forever putting everybody else at risk. In other words, the prophetic component of Humbard Ministries served, in part, to justify the psychographic approach to women as a living, and therefore malleable, category that necessitated data penetration. This was Humbard's mechanics of seduction (van Geuns).

Humbard was versed in generating a sense of urgency—a sexual panic of apocalyptic proportions—to which he, alone, could respond. The divine normalcy of his body would provide shelter from the storms of modernity. While generating a sense of crisis, Humbard concomitantly provided a safe haven in which the crisis could be resolved. Here, the tight boundaries around sexual identity could be reinscribed through technological means, that is, through a single prayer request. For there was praying and healing, and praying and the reception of data, and the analysis and rearrangement of data on more and more punchcards of unique data sets. The horizon of precision went on forever. And it was enveloping. Mathematical security becoming cosmic in the figure of Rex Humbard. For Rex and his audience both. So while Humbard's secularism was absolutely technological in its character, the machines themselves—computers, automation, operations research—were not determinative but rather fed the "collective apparatus" by which a dominant mode of power moved ever outward and in… (See Gilles Deleuze, "Postscript on Control Societies," in Negotiations, 1972–1990, trans. Martin Joughin (1990), 177–82.).

By the end of the 1970s, the name Rex was being uttered more than twice per minute on *You Are Loved*, slightly above the rate for God. Behind such self-regard on Humbard's part was an apparatus skilled in the strategic dissemination of messages. Feedback loops between input and output served to reinforce particular habituations of femininity that were seemingly under threat. Humbard, for example, provided a thirty-point list of characteristics to his audience to help them identify demons in their midst. The list of characteristics served both as a means of defense and also as evidence for the demonic as part of an everyday feminine: "They have feelings … They have power of choice … They have lustful desires and allure … They are quite religious and go to church … they are worldly and fashion minded" (Humbard 1974a, 14–15; Kess and Schmidt, 101; Schmidt and Kess 1986).

So while prayers could be answered and demons identified, women were also being taught to be suspicious of their own sexual energies—most of these demons that would be identified, after all, would be women. This lesson in gendered self-surveillance was subliminal, of course, coded as it was into the seamlessness of the technological seduction and engineered affects of the psychographically accurate teletype.

Given his theological commitment to gendered separation and a public order that depended upon it, Humbard managed an elaborate strategy of containment. It was executed, in part, to control the threat of women's interior energies spilling over into that order. For Humbard, the interior space of women was precisely the site at which religion took hold. Piety and sexual difference were to be mutually constituted through a moral code that would find its practical and public pathways. Here was a strategy that modeled a future in which "business organizations gather continuous information about changes in the environment and about their own performance" (Kotler and Levy, 14).

The Buffered Self in the Age of the Algorithm

The goal of Rex Humbard Ministry, Inc. was to target, with God-given precision, the hearts, minds, and money of its largely female audience. In crafting its pitch in relation to the real-time lives of their audience, Rex Humbard Ministry, Inc. enacted an algorithmic plan of secular governance. I am interested, here, in how Humbard's religious reform both fueled and reflected orders of political persuasion that were bound up in the consumer marketplace. Humbard deployed an elaborate strategy by which his audience could cultivate a self that could "see itself as invulnerable, as master of the meanings of things for it" (Taylor, 38). This was, of course, the very same kind of self that was idealized in civic, economic, and legal spheres.

The incentives of the buffered self are key to the co-constitution of the religious and the secular within modernity. But rather than place a definitive value and ontology upon the buffered self, as philosopher Charles Taylor does in his use of the term, I am more interested in exploring the making of the buffer, both its strength and its vulnerabilities as they have played out in history. For the buffered self, I contend, is an advertisement, more a ritual representation than ontology (Modern 2013). Indeed, earnest celebrations of the buffer make it incredibly difficult to sustain conversations about the ways in which the self is subject to the agencies of the object world, to history, to strangers and expertly branded institutions, and to forces that do not announce themselves as such. There is fullness and pleasure to be had in such relays, for better or for worse. As an advertisement that has been wildly successful, the buffered self occludes from consideration the complex conditions of its own possibility. And finally, theoretically, a buffered self leaves little room for the experience of dread, for insight into the plurality of worlds we inhabit together, and for consideration of the range of agents within those worlds.

In the age of algorithms, the buffered self is, by definition, impossible. Yet the advertisements continue apace. Consequently, there is a nagging contradiction in the spectacle of Humbard—the strategic and social construction of a self who sees itself as wholly natural, as heroically removed from history, potentially immune from even Satan himself. In *Devils*, for example, Humbard hints at, but does not name, the paradox of inhabiting both a violable and an inviolable subjectivity: "You, too, can have complete mastery and power over demons in Jesus's name. Just be sure you understand the spiritual requirements of God's word to have this unlimited power. There are conditions to be met" (Humbard 1974a, 30). These conditions were a matter of becoming suffused with the Holy Spirit, filling their minds and hearts with God rather than Satan. And they must be met—religious freedom was executed in choosing one form of submission over another. For it is only in the correct submission that one can then don the "shield of faith" ("Testimonies from our TV Partners," 6–7).

For on the one hand, the legacy of Protestant volunteerism is pronounced in Humbard, so much so that prayer becomes wholly intercessory, a technique like any other in extending the will of the wielder. Indeed, the entire apparatus that is Humbard Ministries was predicated on the fact that prayer was a strategy for "living a vital and exciting life of faith" and a "potent" instrument to move past the agents of Satan and "the problems of life" (Humbard 1973, 10). On the other hand, Humbard did not hesitate in calling for a "spiritual invasion" ("TV Rally Scan" 1973, 5). He called on his audience to "bring your prayer requests, and specifically to bring the names of unsaved loved ones with you" ("TV Rally Scan" 1975, 12). Conversions, in other words, could be forced by way of a divine triangulation. Even still, it was precisely the disconnect between principle and desired effect that made Humbard's strategy so viable. The incredible confidence conveyed in describing your interior powers is precisely what makes the corruption of that interior possible. You have the power. You are vulnerable. You are prone to making the wrong choice. "Moral people," wrote Humbard, "give to charities, and give to all kinds of things, but they still find themselves prone to do evil, to sin, to have bad habits." And you must submit properly—not to the powers of Satan but to the "Power of God within" (Humbard 1974b, 4). The right choice, in other words, was divinely decreed—the choice to let Rex's love in.

Humbard Ministries distills the structural paradoxes that haunt the secular project. Such paradoxes, in turn, beget contradictions that are "generative." These contradictions, in other words, not only constitute the norm; they normalize the norm by way of its transgression. Secular orders of governance—of which Humbard's persuasive appeal to "true religion" was a formation—often depend upon the violation of their first principles to maintain their authority. In Humbard's case, the principle in question was the inviolability of conscience. The relegation of the religious to the private sphere—as a matter of belief and conscience—in and around the Cathedral of Tomorrow was a typical Protestant celebration of a notion of religious freedom. But the conscience of Humbard's audience was not inviolable. Nor should it have been, given how many souls there were to be saved. Humbard's violation of his own principles, then, served to re-establish them. The "inescapable quality" of his secularism was bound up in the problems it created and the solutions that it offered (Mahmood, 4, 11).

Conclusion

Rex Humbard, in his brew of hard love and the hard sell, was a pious actor within a secular order. His data-driven mission was nothing less than an attempt to enfold the interior lives of his largely female flock into a more encompassing system of benevolent self-organization. "In our age of guided missiles and misguided men," argued Humbard, "we need more than ever the touch, the glory of the Lord" (Humbard 1973, 58). Humbard's performative effects speak to the buffered self as a masculinist ideal within the secular age as well as one born of a certain desperation. In the end, Humbard's patriarchal charisma depended upon all manner of strategies to buffer other selves, to manage and manipulate them in order to maintain the semblance of his own ontic strength and institutional legitimacy. Humbard's efforts were consistent and strategic, if not always successful.

Which is to say that coursing through Humbard was a form of power that does not follow a linear trajectory but rather helps create the conditions of its own viability. It was secularism suffused with algorithmic application. It was a secularism that served systematic ends yet defied systematic explanation. To account for the generative force of this secularism is to approach it as not simply self-regulating—in the sense that mere ideology conserves its power—but rather as self-organizing; its generative force arises in those points and moments of boundary maintenance, where and when an outside is necessarily maintained. The discursive dynamism of this secularism owes to its feedback qualities, that is, how it conserves a private/public distinction by perpetually disrupting it and then providing the ideological resources for renewing its very stability. This secularism, in other words, depended upon the production of the excesses that it could then domesticate. In this system, the production of the abject was a necessary condition, as was the maintenance of its invisibility. This is how it generated seamless experiential forms despite its logical internal contradictions.

In this short report from Akron, Ohio, in the 1970s, we witness a secular imaginary renewing itself—in the case of Humbard Ministries, bringing sexual identity under the sway of missionary technique, conjuring a gendered division, and using that division as a market advantage.

In light of the accelerating network density of surveillance that you, dear reader, are right now experiencing, the visionary moves executed by Rex Humbard Ministries seem rather quaint. Perhaps even primitive. An era of naïve ideological appeal, pre-cable television, and a relatively stable and attentive demographic. But as Durkheim put the question to a different, yet seemingly savage archive of the Arunta in 1912, there was still an opportunity to glimpse "the fundamental states characteristic of the religious mentality" in the weird mirror of the Australian outback, despite the so-called advances of civilization and increasing "clash of theologies, the variations of ritual, the multiplicity of groupings, and the diversity of the individual" at the time of (t)his writing (Durkheim 5).

Notes

1 Since the evangelical surges of the 19th century, evangelicals have often been on the cutting edge of using new media technologies for purposes of mass mobilization. See, for example, Modern (2008), Supp-Montgomerie (2021), and Hangen (2002).
2 See *You Are Loved* (Akron, Ohio: Rex Humbard Foundation & Ministry, 2014), 32 videodisc set available at Shadek Fackenthal Library, Franklin & Marshall College.
3 The promotional documentary "You Are Loved" provides a basic introduction to Humbard's ministry, particularly its global reach in TV specials in places like Manila, Hawaii, Australia, and more remote parts of Africa, and in syndication across Asian markets. http://www.godtube.com/watch/?v=FBC9C1NU

4 As Sarah McFarland Taylor brilliantly pointed out in her comments, the Prayer Key Family was contemporaneous with the phenomenon of Playboy Club Keys in which male members would present to a "Door Bunny" and use like a credit card while inside. See the Playboy Online Museum here: http://www.playboymuseum.com/keys/. The Prayer Key Family was also an early instance of membership marketing, loyalty marketing, and personal branding that have only intensified since the 1970s. There is, of course, an erotic charge to all of this. Which is to say that the "psychographic turn" in marketing was one of many innovations that was not strictly ideological but empowered the individual by celebrating their submission. The biopolitical intensification is marked not just by a media virality but also what one might call an ontic virality (Maheshwari 2023).

5 For contemporary and disturbing examples of pastoral systematicity, see Woollacott and Baker-White.

6 On sex and the regulation of religion as an interior matter—legal, categorical, affective— see Pellegrini and Jakobsen; Scott; Fernando; Mahmood.

7 In the "move from demographic to psychographic categorizations [] clusters of consumer types were created to better understand the non-essentialist character of demographic based consumption patterns" (Cheney-Lippold, 167).

Bibliography

"How Prayers are Answered". (February 1974). *The Answer*, 9.

"The Rex Humbard Prayer Key Family". (June 1974) *The Answer*, 9.

"TV Rally Scan". (February 1975). *The Answer*, 12.

"TV Rally Scan". (May 1973). *The Answer*. 5.

"What Holy Scripture Tells Us About Prayer". (November 1973). *The Answer*, 9.

"World/Scan". (April 1973). *The Answer*, 5.

Baier, M. (February 1971). "Psychographics: New Key to Segmenting Market Lists." *Direct Marketing*, 33, 35–39.

Baker-White, E. (January 24, 2022). "Nothing Sacred: These Apps Reserve the Right to Sell Your Prayers." *Buzzfeednews.com*. https://www.buzzfeednews.com/article/emilybakerwhite/apps-selling-your-prayers

Brown, W.R. (1976). "COBOL," in *Encyclopedia of Computer Science and Technology*, eds. J. Belzer, A.G. Holzman, A. Kent, Vol. 5. New York: Marcel Dekker, 47–71.

Buddenbaum, M. (June 1981). "Characteristics and Media-Related Needs of the Audience For Religious TV." *Journalism and Mass Communication Quarterly*, 58, 266–72.

Cheney-Lippold, J. (2011). "A New Algorithmic Identity: Soft Biopolitics and the Modulation of Control." *Theory, Culture & Society*, 28, 164–81.

Culliton, J.W. (1959). "A Marketing Analysis of Religion: Can Businesslike Methods Improve the 'Sales' of Religion?" *Business Horizons*, 2(1959), 85–92.

de Certeau, M. (1988). "Believing and Making People Believe," in *The Practice of Everyday Life*, trans. S. Rendell. Berkeley: University of California Press, 177–89.

Deleuze, G. (1990). "Postscript on Control Societies," in *Negotiations, 1972–1990*, ed. M. Joughin. New York: Columbia University Press, 177–82.

Durkheim, E. (1912/1995). *The Elementary Forms of Religious Life*, trans. Karen E. Fields. New York: Free Press.

Ellens, J.H. (1974). *Models of Religious Broadcasting*. Grand Rapids, MI: Eerdmans Publishing.

Fernando, M.L. (2014). "Intimacy Surveilled: Religion, Sex, and Secular Cunning." *Signs*, 39, 685–708.

Foucault, M. (1983). "The Subject and Power," in *Michel Foucault: Beyond Structuralism and Hermeneutics*, 2nd ed., eds. H.L. Dreyfus and P. Rabinow. Chicago: University of Chicago Press, 208–26.

Hadden, J.K. (1993). "The Rise and Fall of American Televangelism." *The Annals of the American Academy of Political and Social Science*, 527, 113–30.

Hangen, T.J. (2002). *Redeeming the Dial: Radio, Religion, and Popular Culture in* America. Chapel Hill: University of North Carolina Press.

Horsfield, P.G. (October 1981). "'And Now a Word from Our Sponsor': Religious Programs on American Television." *Revue francaise d'études américaines*, 12, 268–69.

"How Prayers are Answered". (February 1974). *The Answer*, 9.

Hughey, M.W. (1990). "Internal Contradictions of Televangelism: Ethical Quandries of That Old Time Religion in a Brave New World." *International Journal of Politics, Culture, and Society*, 4, 31–47.

Humbard, R. (1973). *The Prayer Key Book* (1973). Akron, OH: Rex Humbard Television Ministry.

Humbard, R. (1974a). *Devils: Who, What, When, Where, Why*. Akron, OH: Rex Humbard Ministry.

Humbard, R. (July 1974b). "Three Powers." *The Answer*, 4.

Humbard, R. (1975). *To Tell the World*. Englewood Cliffs, NJ: Prentice-Hall.

Humbard, R. (1977). *Your Key to God's Bank*. Akron, OH: Rex Humbard Foundation.

Humbard, R. (1979). *The Rex Humbard Prophecy Bible*. Akron, OH: Rex Humbard Foundation.

Kess, J.F., & Schmidt, R. (1984). "Persuasive Language in Advertising and Televangelism." *Working Papers of the Linguistics Circle*, 4(1), 91–113.

Kotler, P. (April 1972). "A Generic Concept of Marketing." *Journal of Marketing*, 36, 46–54.

Kotler, P., & Levy, S.J. (1969). "Broadening the Concept of Marketing." *Journal of Marketing*, 33(1), 10–15.

Maheshwari, S. (2023). "For Gen Z, Playing an Influencer Comes Naturally." *New York Times*.

Mahmood, S. (2015). *Religious Difference in a Secular Age: A Minority Report*. Princeton: Princeton University Press.

Modern, J.L. (2008). "Evangelical Secularism and the Measure of Leviathan." *Church History*, 77(4), 801–76.

Modern, J.L. (2011). *Secularism in Antebellum America*. Chicago: University of Chicago Press.

Modern, J.L. (4 Mar. 2013). "Confused Parchments, Infinite Socialities." *The Immanent Frame*. Accessed 5 June 2023. http://blogs.ssrc.org/tif/2013/03/04/confusedparchments-infinite-socialities/.

Pellegrini, A., & Jakobsen, J. (2003). *Love the Sin: Sexual Regulation and the Limits of Religious Tolerance*,

Rex Humbard Foundation & Ministry. (2014). *You Are Loved*. 32 videodisc set available at Shadek Fackenthal Library. Lancaster, PA: Franklin & Marshall College.

Schmidt, R., & Kess, J.F. (1986). *Television Advertising and Televangelism: Discourse Analysis of Persuasive Language*. Amsterdam/Philadelphia: John Benjamins Publishing.

Scott, J.W. (2017). *Sex and Secularism*. Princeton: Princeton University Press.

Supp-Montgomerie, J. (2021). *When the Medium Was the Mission: The Atlantic Telegraph and the Religious Origins of Network Culture*. New York: New York University Press.

Taylor, C. (2006). *A Secular Age*. Cambridge, MA: Belknap Press.

Terry, C. (Oct. 2–8, 1971). "It's a Far Cry From the Church in the Wildwood." TV Guide, 38–42.

"Testimonies from Our TV Partners Whom God Has Blessed with a Special Shield of Faith." (September 1973). *The Answer*, 6–7.

"The Rex Humbard Prayer Key Family". (June 1974) *The Answer*, 9.

"TV Rally Scan". (May 1973). *The Answer*. 5.

"TV Rally Scan". (February 1975). *The Answer*, 12.

van Geuns, S. (forthcoming). *Seductive Methods: Success and the Computational Imagination*. Chicago: University of Chicago Press.

"What Holy Scripture Tells Us About Prayer". (November 1973). *The Answer*, 9.

Woollacott, E. (May 3, 2022). "Creepy' Mental Health And Prayer Apps Are Sharing Your Personal Data." *Forbes.com*. https://www.forbes.com/sites/emmawoollacott/2022/05/03/creepy-mental-health-and-prayer-apps-are-sharing-your-personal-data/?sh=757bdcb54672

"World/Scan". (April 1973). *The Answer*, 5.

PART II
Politics and Religio-Marketing

4

SHARPIEGATE

John Durham Peters

"We can never tell weather from the gods" quipped media theorist Friedrich Kittler. To the gods, he might have added kings and prophets. A spell of catastrophic weather could expose a Chinese emperor as having lost "the mandate of heaven." Typhoons in 1274 and 1281 spared Japan from Mongol invasion and gave us the word "kamikaze," meaning "divine wind." In 1588, the Elizabethans similarly thanked a "Protestant wind" for turning back the Spanish armada from the shores of England. In the Bible, Moses, Elijah, and Jesus all exercised shamanistic control over the weather for political gain, moral rebuke, and faith-promoting thaumaturgy (the art of performing miracles).

We moderns sometimes like to congratulate ourselves on having left behind such meteorological statecraft and stagecraft for enlightened science. Not so! A recent episode shows why not.

One of the many bits of flotsam produced by the Trump White House in its ongoing grabbing of public attention was the episode soon dubbed Sharpiegate, which, on the whole, was a relatively minor item in the catalog of Mr. Trump's adventures with truth. When he first tweeted on Saturday 31 August 2019 that Hurricane Dorian would hit Alabama, he received online pushback from meteorologists and mockery from trolls. It was a simple and forgivable mistake, but the criticism got under his skin. During the approach and then landfall of the storm, he repeatedly tweeted that he was correct that the storm would touch Alabama. If only, as the late-night comics quipped, Dorian had destroyed a few buildings in Alabama, Mr. Trump would have been much happier. Like Jonah looking down on Nineveh, Trump clung to the outdated forecast, preferring disaster wrought on others to being wrong himself.

At an Oval Office briefing a few days later on Wednesday 4 September, Trump showed an earlier weather map of the storm's trajectory on which someone—an unnamed White House official said it was the President himself—had drawn a

DOI: 10.4324/9781003342229-7

FIGURE 4.1   Mr. Trump Makes the Rain (AP Photo, used by permission)

crescent-shaped line with a Sharpie pen (a writing implement Trump is known to prefer) extending the storm's reach to include a small section of Alabama (Figure 4.1). The Sharpie stroke was vaguely in the tradition of weather forecasters on postwar live TV who directly hand-drew weather patterns on maps, paper, or Plexiglas, typically using a crayon or grease pencil.[1] Thus Vladimir Nabokov in 1962 described a TV forecast: "A male hand traced from Florida to Maine/The curving arrows of Aeolian wars."[2]

Perhaps an even more alarming doctoring came in an unsigned statement from the National Oceanic and Atmospheric Administration supporting Trump's claim, apparently in response to pressure from the White House.[3] The statement was issued without approval of NOAA scientists and went contrary to their projections; NOAA's acting director, Neil Jacobs, was later found to have violated the agency's code of ethics.[4] NOAA's acting chief scientist, using an apt meteorological metaphor, was "flabbergasted to leave our forecasters hanging in the wind."[5] As usual, Trump was toying with knowledge institutions, melding fact with whim, and testing the outer limits of his trust- and truth-shaking cunning. Shakespeare's King Lear was helpless before the storm, but Trump had somehow gotten someone inside the agency to change not the weather but the report. Cartoonists were not the only ones to pick up on the fact that even the weather had become topic for political polarization (Figure 4.2).

The Sharpie stroke—and if Trump's hand did not draw it, he clearly willed it (sovereigns like to outsource manual labor)—was only one item in a vast collection

*"That was Brad with the Democratic weather.
Now here's Tammy with the Republican weather."*

FIGURE 4.2   Weather Divides (Conde Nast, used by permission)

of temporizing and self-justification. And yet in this case, it may have been a crime. U.S. law outlaws false weather reports. The statute dates to the 1890s and was originally aimed at speculators, hoaxers, bookies, advertisers, and others who stood to gain from counterfeit forecasts.[6] The weather report is a tempting target for hi-jackers. The law protects the accuracy of forecasts and the credibility of weather data against those with incentives to warp them.[7] The state, in other words, has a monopoly not only on the legitimate use of violence (as Max Weber would re-mind us) but the legitimate forecasting of weather. (The state's vigilance over epis-temic accuracy in other domains is obviously and necessarily much more tenuous!) Weather reports are strategic intelligence, and during World War II, for instance, there were essentially no weather reports on American radio due to wartime cen-sorship; even sports announcers couldn't state that a baseball game had been rained out without risking sanction.[8]

Sovereignty rules with a stroke of the pen: it can put laws into effect or sign off on a death sentence. Drawing lines on maps is what power does, as when the pope in 1494 divided the known world between the Portuguese and the Spanish by one single sovereign stroke. Yet a weather map is quite a different thing from a political map: it is a map of variables rather than constants, of the ever changing atmosphere rather than the relatively constant geosphere. It's easier to decree a political boundary than a climate condition into being. By looping into Alabama, Trump put himself in a long lineage of tyrants who rage against adverse nature, like Xerxes whipping the sea for wrecking his bridges or Captain Ahab chasing the white whale. Weather is one thing the sovereign cannot alter, though he may be held responsible for it. The tyrant's writ has met its match. Weather, compared to public attention, was hardly putty in Trump's hands. Media may be ontological operators, but weather forms one stark challenge to their reach.

Online wits had a field day with Trump's drawing as wish-fulfillment, tweeting Sharpie-altered pictures of a completely built Mexican border wall, Trump's apocryphal bone spur that had exempted him from service in Vietnam, a vast inauguration crowd, his wife Melania reaching out her hand to him, his newly buff physique, and a map extending the US border to surround Greenland, which Trump earlier in the summer, in a sudden flare-up of real-estate chutzpah, had tried to buy from Denmark. The Danes, as it happened, were as impervious as the weather to his will.

Ultimately Sharpiegate shows something even creepier: Trump's rivalry with the weather as something unpredictable and dominating public attention on a daily basis. The belief that weather is a zone immune to all marketing is a belief in which we kid ourselves just as much as supposing it free of religion and politics. Trump didn't have to listen to scientists or worry about accuracy: he could become a meteorological magus himself. Modern TV weather forecasters still activate ancient traditions of augury and divine intervention; Trump wanted a piece of the action. During his presidency, most of the people I knew did not talk about the weather for their daily chit-chat: they talked about Trump. For four long years, Trump *was* the weather.

Notes

1 Robert Henson, *Weather on the Air: A History of Broadcast Meteorology* (Boston: American Meteorological Society, 2010), 68, 87–9.
2 Vladimir Nabokov, *Pale Fire* (1962; New York: Vintage, 1989), 47.
3 Andrew Freedman and Jason Samenow, "'Help!!!' Emails show how Trump roiled NOAA during Hurricane Dorian," *Washington Post*, 1 Feb 2020.
4 Christopher Flavelle, "NOAA Chief Violated Ethics Code in Furor over Trump Tweet, Agency Says," *New York Times*, 15 June 2020.
5 Freedman and Samenow, 'Help!!!'
6 18 US Code §2074: "Whoever knowingly issues or publishes any counterfeit weather forecast or warning of weather conditions falsely representing such forecast or warning to have been issued or published by the Weather Bureau, United States Signal Service, or other branch of the Government service, shall be fined under this title or imprisoned not more than ninety days, or both."
7 Jamie Pietruska, "Why President Trump's Sharpied weather map was likely a crime–and should be," *Washington Post* online, 6 Sept 2019.
8 Henson, *Weather on the Air*, 48.

5

TWO TRUTHS AND A LIE

Unpacking PragerU's Hostile Rebrand of Climate Action in *Religion of Green*

Sarah McFarland Taylor

> By mixing a little truth with it they had made their lie far stronger.
>
> *The Chronicles of Narnia (Lewis, 2001 [1956], p. 723)*

In the ad world, it can be tricky to attack a competitor and successfully execute a "hostile rebrand" of the rival's profile and/or product. Marketing strategists back in the 1980s and 1990s famously touted "frontal attacks," "flank attacks," and "guerilla attacks" to the competitor, literally delving into military history and literature to develop these strategies (Kotler and Singh, 1981; Kotler, 1999). Kotler and Singh (quoting Albert Emery) characterize marketing as being "merely a civilized form of warfare in which most battles are won with words, ideas, and disciplined thinking" (p. 30). But such attacks are risky and can backfire, compromising the aggressor's own reputation (Deeran, 2009; Godin, 2009, p. 125–130). One victorious execution of the "hostile rebrand" tactic, however, has achieved iconic status. In 1984, via a team at Madison Avenue ad agency Dancer Fitzgerald Sample (now part of Saatchi & Saatchi), the Wendy's fast food chain campaign, "Where's the beef?", managed to amplify its own product by rebranding its staunch rivals (McDonald's and Burger King) as selling a whole lot of bread to camouflage their serving up essentially a "nothing burger."[1] This was no small feat, especially considering that most Americans at the time could easily sing from memory the McDonald's jingle, "Two all-beef patties, special sauce, lettuce, cheese, etc." Without ever naming a "Big Mac" or a "Whopper," the Wendy's ad presented an ostensible truthteller/ skeptic in the form of crotchety octogenarian Clara Peller, who in one line deflated the colossal-sounding names of the competition's products. Peller stared down Wendy's rivals, demanding to know "Where's the beef?" Wendy's subsequently executed a hostile rebrand of the Big Mac into the "Big Bun." Follow-up ads then

DOI: 10.4324/9781003342229-8

featured spoof (but damning) scenes of the CEO of "Big Bun" (McDonald's) out of touch on his yacht, the "S.S. Big Bun." Wendy's sales jumped 31 percent and increased their global sales to $945 million in just one year. Though this was in pre-Internet days, the "Where's the beef?" slogan went viral in a big way, giving rise to a pop song, countless merchandise items, and even made an appearance in the 1984 Presidential debates, in which Walter Mondale infamously and aggressively asked Gary Hart, "Where's the beef?" (Logie, 2020).

Watching conservative advocacy media machine PragerU's 2020 climate disinformation docushort, *Religion of Green*, which has 2.3 million views on one YouTube posting alone, brings to mind the tactics of Wendy's hostile rebrand. Wendy's "Where the beef?" campaign conveyed two truths: (1) Wendy's burger patties were actually larger than the competition, and (2) Wendy's buns were also indeed smaller than those of its competitors. Coupled with these two truths was a lie and a powerful one – that the meat content in rival sandwiches was either miniscule, or by implication, non-existent – essentially a "rip off." The first two truths made the third point, a fabrication, more believable and resonant. Both Peller and the "Where's the beef?" slogan became synonymous with "telling it like it *really is*." The emperors at Burger King and McDonald's effectively had no clothes, and their buns had no beef. That was not true, but the lie mingled with truth made the ad's 30-second "Big Bun" hostile rebrand more digestible.

In its 18-minute streamed video, *Religion of Green*, PragerU similarly and routinely weaves lies together with truths, ascribing each lie a veneer of credibility via association. In so doing, PragerU's video characterizes the climate movement as all bluster and bun, ultimately serving up a "nothing burger" under the auspices of a fabricated "climate crisis."[2] But PragerU also goes a step further. By instrumentalizing the category of "religion" and, at the conclusion of the docushort, deploying the fear-inducing pejorative term "cult," PragerU seeks to execute a hostile rebrand of environmentalism. The video's narrative specifically restories climate action as a kind of hysterical apocalyptic "cult" and, concomitantly, environmentalism as its undergirding and totalizing "religion."[3] At the video's conclusion, Prager's host emphasizes the final take-home point: "Doomsday cultists have predicted the imminent end of the world for all of recorded history. They have always been wrong. Just as wrong as the environmental alarmists are today."

Though *Religion of Green* is not an advertisement in the conventional sense, it is a media vehicle for marketing climate denialism more widely, making climate denialist converts, and it does so with considerable scope of social media circulation and influence. PragerU's rebranding of environmentalism as a kind of "religion" is made more complicated by the fact that Religious Studies scholars themselves, albeit with different objectives in mind, have argued that environmentalism bears strong family resemblances to religion, or even in one case, that radical environmental activist movements constitute a kind of "dark green religion" (Albanese, 1991; Taylor, 2009).

This chapter begins by briefly situating *Religion of Green* within the context of PragerU's media mission, politics, and precipitous ascent as a significant influencer in the digital streaming world. It then outlines some of the key marketing tactics PragerU utilizes to promote climate denialism, particularly in ways that target younger demographics. We then delve into the framework and positioning of "religion" in this particular video and the kind of rhetorical "work" the category of religion performs in Prager's efforts to discredit the growing call for climate action. At this point, the easy thing to do would be simply to point out the internal contradictions, misleading content, or out-and-out fabrications in the PragerU video. There is no shortage of these. And I do some of this in analyzing *Religion of Green*, but a full debunk would far exceed the space limits of this chapter. Multiple YouTube videos do address PragerU's climate disinformation videos in point-by-point corrections[4] and news agencies such as Reuters have published rejoinders to PragerU climate propaganda, as have media-watch organizations (Molloy, 2019).[5] These media interventions are warranted, and I direct the reader to them. However, rather than simply dismissing *Religion of Green* as mere right-wing propaganda (which, to be clear, it *is*) and moving on, my aim is to listen and learn from the areas where PragerU strategically exploits certain vulnerabilities in climate communications. *Religion of Green* provides an ideal case study for that project. Ultimately, this chapter argues that, in merely turning away from and tuning out right-wing climate disinformation marketing campaigns like those produced and transmediated by PragerU, we miss out on gleaning some valuable takeaways. Those takeaways can not only assist in countering the likes of PragerU but can also significantly aid in crafting more effective, resonant, engaging climate communication moving forward.

What Is PragerU and Why Should We Care?

The first and foremost order of business to get out of the way is that PragerU, also known as "Prager University," is *not* a university. The Vicks Formula 44's TV ad "spokesdoctor" famously used to say that he was "not a real doctor" but "plays one on TV." This kind of roleplay applies to PragerU. The right-wing advocacy mediamaking platform performs a dramatic rendition of "academic scholarship" for video streaming audiences. In so doing, PragerU leverages the public *perception* of university branding and exploits the presumption of scholarly legitimacy in order to lend its content supposed intellectual weight and public credibility (Molloy, 2019). PragerU self-describes as a "digital marketing campaign" and does include a disclaimer (for liability purposes) that it is not an accredited university.[6] But the optics and visual rhetoric of PragerU's YouTube videos tell a different story. Hard to miss is PragerU's university-like logo tactically posted in the corner of every video. For younger audiences, who are more accustomed to online learning entities, especially those who became steeped in virtual learning curricula at home during the pandemic, PragerU's bite-sized, portable, digestible videos, complete with cartoon animations and bright friendly edu-graphics, serve as a kind of communication "cosplay," mimicking digital learning platforms like Khan Academy or the PBS Digital Studios/Green Brothers' educational partnership YouTube channel, CrashCourse.[7] The merchandising section of PragerU's web site cleverly sells all sorts of look-alike campus gear, emblazoned with the Prager University logo.

All of it looks uncannily similar to sweatshirts and T-shirts from (the real accredited) Purdue University and advances the PragerU brand, especially to college or high school students – typical consumers of college gear and more tuned into the campus scene. PragerU's affected scholarly respectability has been critical to the success and efficacy of the PragerU multimedia franchise (podcasts, streaming video, social media sites, film shorts, books, school curricula, etc.) and has helped to establish its campus presence at both the college and secondary-school level (Oppenheimer, 2018; Molloy 2019).

PragerU was co-founded in 2009 by right-wing radio talk show host Dennis Prager and screenwriter Allen Estrin, best known for his work on the fantasy drama TV series, *Touched by an Angel* (1994–2003). The original idea for PragerU was to establish a physical university along the lines of something like conservative Patrick Henry College in Virginia. As such, Prager University would ideally fill the halls of Congress and pack the clerkships of the Supreme Court with its newly minted right-wing young ideologues, who would take charge of the direction and leadership of the nation (Bowles, 2020). Though PragerU co-founders and executives are Jewish, the organization is heavily funded by conservative evangelicals, and its mission bears similarity to the conservative Christian objective of installing a "Joshua Generation" (sometimes called "GenJ") of young Christian fundamentalists (largely homeschooled) into major seats of power to rule the nation (Farris, 2005; Jones, 2023; Sutton, 2017).[8] This resemblance is fitting, since PragerU also markets itself as a valued and trusted source for homeschoolers and produces multiple videos championing homeschooling, including one called "Homeschooling Saved My Kids from Indoctrination," which is part of a video series hosted by evangelical actor Kirk Cameron.[9] Unlike much of conservative homeschooling fare, however, PragerU has excelled in producing snackable videos that are like eating potato chips out of the bag. Its main slogan is "Short Videos. BIG ideas." It is even easier to go down the proverbial "rabbit hole" of PragerU's shorter and snappier TikToks. Many of my students have told me that if they watch one, they watch 15, and some have spoken about having been devoted PragerU followers in middle and high school. When it was widely reported in July of 2023 that the well-respected annual "Monitoring the Future Survey" (an ongoing national study of adolescent attitudes, behaviors, and values since 1975, conducted by the University of Michigan, and funded in part by the National Institutes of Health) found that "Twelfth-grade boys are [now] nearly twice as likely to identify as conservative versus liberal," marking a "rightward drift of high school boys," I was not surprised (De Vise, 2023). Some of my environmental policy students have related that they were climate deniers in their pre-college years, a position they attribute to a steady diet of PragerU anti-environmental videos such as "Fossil Fuels: The Greenest Energy."[10]

Among PragerU's most robust funders are fossil-fuel industry fracking billionaires Dan and Ferris Wilks, who are colloquially known as "the Koch brothers of the Christian right" (Bowles, 2020; Dembiki, 2022; Oppenheimer, 2018). Ferris Wilks pastors a fundamentalist church in Texas that his parents founded. Along with The Daily Wire (co-founded by Ben Shapiro), PragerU is among the biggest and loudest sources of climate disinformation (Dembiki, 2022) with propaganda video fare such as: "Why You Should Love Fossil Fuel" and "What's Wrong with Wind and Solar?" (spoiler alert: apparently, *everything*). In the wake of the 2016 election of Donald Trump to the White House, PragerU's donation revenue boomed. In just two years, it tripled from 5.42 million to 18.6 million (Wiener, 2020) gratis of those throwing their support behind the PragerU mission to advance "the Judeo-Christian values on which America is founded: free speech, free enterprise, a moral foreign policy, and the rational case for God's existence," while supporting its aim to take down and supplant "the leftist indoctrination imposed by schools and universities" (Wiener, 2020).

In 2018, YouTube analytics pointed to PragerU having clocked over a billion views of their streamed videos, with viewers under 35 making up more than 60 percent of their audience (Oppenheimer, 2018). By 2021, PragerU claimed more than 5 billion views of its streamed videos, and 58 percent of viewers had changed their mind on a policy issue after viewing 11-to-50 videos.[11] In addition to being well-funded, much of its success can also be attributed to the savvy ways that PragerU optimizes its videos specifically for YouTube, adapts on the fly to breaking news developments, and how it shrewdly times and targets ads on both YouTube and social media platforms that are most frequented by younger viewers, such as Instagram and TikTok (Rozsa, 2020). Journalist Mark Oppenheimer delves into the success of PragerU's tactical youth marketing strategies and other means of targeting younger demographics in his sobering feature, "Inside the Right-Wing YouTube Empire That's Quietly Turning Millennials Into Conservatives" (2018).

PragerU partners with thousands of high school and college PragerU brand ambassador/influencers, called "PragerForce," which self-describes in its Instagram (IG) profile as "The Official Student & Young Professionals Program of PragerU." PragerForce's IG postings show photos of an ethnically diverse group of hip-looking students who are "pushing back against woke culture." PragerU also markets to primary and secondary-school teachers, providing them ready-made materials along with "PragerU's 5-Minute Ideas" videos (Bowles, 2020). And for the elementary school set, PragerU markets its children's books, which profile American Presidents and a collection of "great heroes," such as Ayn Rand, who is featured in their *Women of Valor* book series.[12] Unlike a lot of right-wing mediamaking outlets and pundits (think Sean Hannity, Alex Jones [*Infowars*], and the late Rush Limbaugh), PragerU's tone is even, measured, and concertedly assumes a stance of "civil discourse," making the content even more attractive to often overwhelmed and underpaid teachers in search of ready-made lesson plans and "educational" content (Shea, 2015). In the summer of 2023, the Florida Board of Education approved the use of PragerU Kids videos in grades K-12 across the state's public schools, giving individual teachers the power to incorporate PragerU-produced materials into their classrooms even when their own school does not recommend their use (Archie, 2023).

In a university course I teach on media and the environment, I assign students to watch PragerU's *Religion of Green* for homework, and then we analyze it in the classroom. It has been instructive to learn from class discussions how the few students (many well-read in environmental policy), not yet familiar with PragerU, initially thought *Religion of Green* was a pro-environmental and pro-climate video, until at some point in watching they did a doubletake and experienced a "WTF?" head-scratching moment. But the initial look-alike features were convincing. Learning what specific parts of the video led to students' initial assumptions and the parts of the video that seemed to ring true has provided valuable insights, which I share below.

How the Game Is Played: Tools, Techniques, and Tactics

If you ever went to summer camp or participated in family game night, you've probably played the game, "Two Truths and a Lie." As the name suggests, this is a game in which players present three statements – two are true, one is a lie, and then the other players have to guess which is which. A feature in *Parade Magazine* provides tips for winning: "Don't say a lie last. Don't over explain the lie. Don't let your facial expression give you away" (Liles, 2022). These strategy tips could come straight from the PragerU playbook. By far, though, the most effective camouflage for the lie is that it is mingled together with two truths. As psychological researchers Verigin et al. (2020) demonstrate, weaving lies into a set of truths makes them more credible to the point of increasing the chances of evading lie detection tools. In their psychology, crime, and law study of the interaction of truthful and deceptive information, the researchers conclude:

> … our exploratory tests revealed that lies become more detailed when they are flanked by truthful information relative to when they are flanked by other deceptive information. The finding that truthful and deceptive information interacts to influence detail richness provides insight into liars' strategic manipulation of information when statements contain a mixture of truths and lies. Strategic manipulations of this kind could potentially threaten the reliability of commonly used verbal lie detection tools
>
> *2020*

This effective strategy is also a key reason why crafting aliases, alibis, and other cover stories with as many elements of truth interjected as possible makes them more likely to be believed and less likely to get tripped up by the facts. Similarly, popular marketing guru Seth Godin, in his classic *All Marketers Are Liars* (2005), which he more recently retitled *All Marketers Tell Stories* (2012), explains, "Marketers are a special kind of liar. Marketers lie to consumers because consumers demand it. Marketers tell the stories, and consumers believe them" (2005, p. 3). PragerU's snackable, easily spreadable videos come to mind, as Godin advises,

"Either you're going to tell stories that spread, or you will become irrelevant" (p. 1), advice that is echoed by media researchers Jenkins, et al. in their research on media spreadability (2018). If you are good enough at marketing, says Godin, facts or no facts, you can "create a story that can become true," arguing that "once we believe something, it becomes a self-fulfilling truth" (p. xv–xvii).

Godin says the idea for his liars' book came to him during the lead-up to the 2004 U.S. Presidential election, which the Democrats lost. Both candidates had told lies, Godin noticed, but Republicans had told more "authentic" and thus more "believable" lies, which American citizens/consumers had subsequently "bought" (Bloom, 2005). Back in 2004, when Godin was writing the book, the search engine Google was not as ubiquitous as it would become in the years that followed. By 2011, Google was managing 3 billion searches a day and had to construct 11 additional data centers (Redding, 2018). In the preface to the 2012 revised edition of the book, Godin changed the title of the book and issued an updated caveat for the (by then) ubiquitous digital search engine age. "Lying does not pay off anymore," he cautions, because now, "when you fabricate a story that just does not hold up to scrutiny, you get caught. Fast" (2012, p. xvii). Granted, Godin wrote that bit of advice in pre-QAnon days and before major trusted news sources were repeatedly maligned as "fake news" by Republican nominee and then President Trump, but Godin does urge marketers to find a way to tell an "authentic" story about their brand or product without the kind of fabrication that can get them caught and compromise the brand's reputation.

One strategy for how to do this is called "paltering" and PragerU could teach a masterclass. Paltering is defined as "the devious art of lying by telling the truth" (Hogenboom, 2017). That is, one uses selective or edited truthful statements in order to mislead. One reason that paltering is so effective is that it is "difficult to spot a misleading 'fact' when we hear something that on the face of it, sounds true" (Hogenboom, 2017). To be clear, at various points in *Religion of Green*, PragerU out-and-out lies, as when pundits in the video claim that climate change is made-up. But they also combine false statements with aspects of the truth in a misleading way, often withholding the larger story or context, or omitting key components. A cited example of this in marketing is Colgate's 2007 claim in its advertising that "More Than 80% of Dentists Recommend Colgate!" This statement was true – sort of. What the ad did not say is that dentists in the survey were asked, in general, what toothpastes they would recommend to patients, and Colgate popped up in responses about 80 percent of the time, but not to the exclusion of other brands. The toothpaste brand was merely one of a list of brands dentists checked off, but the slogan made it sound like dentists were recommending Colgate above the competition 80 percent of the time. After complaints from competitors, the ad campaign was banned, and Colgate-Palmolive censured by the British Advertising Standards Authority (Sharp, 2019).[13]

Similarly, supposed "climate expert" Michael Shellenberger, a public relations specialist for the nuclear and shale gas industry and frequent guest on FOX

News' now-defunct "Tucker Carlson Tonight," points out in *Religion of Green* that "Damage [from storms] to property has increased over time, but it's entirely explained by the fact that we're just much wealthier than we were." The video underscores this stance by showing a photo comparison of how many more buildings there are today in Miami Beach than there were in 1920. So, yes, there are more buildings now to damage, but that does not mean that, at the same time, storms are not also intensifying and increasing in frequency. Shellenberger also completely leaves out the fact of rising sea levels and the serious threat flooding and storm surges are already posing to the area of Miami Beach (Cusick, 2020; Harvey, 2023). The fact that Miami is one of the most vulnerable cities to climate-induced rising sea levels is not exactly a "minority report" (Ramirez 2021; Shetty, 2021; Irfan 2023). In paltering, Shellenberger offers a truth – Miami has experienced a lot more development since 1920, so there is now more property to damage and offers this as evidence of climate alarmists having completely fabricated a non-existent crisis.[14]

One thing to note in the featured interview with Shellenberger and others in the video is that PragerU has stacked the deck with supposed "climate experts" without actually revealing who these talking heads are, who they work for, or their investments.[15] Prager's talking heads on climate are effectively shills or "beards" for various fossil-fuel industry lobbying and front groups. This adds yet another level to PragerU's fakery and deception. Michael Shellenberger has written a climate-denial book called *Apocalypse Never*, which is plugged at the end of the video. ClimateFeedback.org, a non-partisan climate fact-checking site, published the conclusions of seven academic reviewers who reviewed Shellenberger's claims. The reviewers conclude that Shellenberger "mixes accurate and inaccurate claims in support of a misleading and overly simplistic argumentation about climate change."[16] In *Religion of Green*, he raises paltering and the game of "Two truths and a lie" to an artform.

Other climate "experts" featured in the video include Jacki Deason, who is a right-wing radio talk show host and "Senior Fellow" for the Texas Public Policy Foundation (TPPF). TPPF, according to SourceWatch.org, is a conservative think tank, a member of the right-wing State Policy Network, the funders of which are a "Who's Who of Texas polluters, giant utilities, and big insurance companies."[17] Alex Epstein, who appears in a number of PragerU climate denial videos, touting how wonderfully "green" fossil fuels are, is the author of *Fossil Fuel Future* (also plugged at the end of the video). Epstein is the Libertarian founder of the Center for Industrial Progress, which is funded by the Koch brothers and promotes fossil fuels. The final talking head is Charles McConnell, who was a former assistant secretary in the U.S. Department of Energy for three years but is also a member of the National Coal Council, has served on subcommittees for the National Petroleum Council, served as vice president at Praxair, an industrial gas company, and he was an executive for 30 years at Union Carbide chemical company, the same company infamous for the 1984 Bhopal pesticide chemical massacre in India.

Viewers may not have the media or scientific literacy to discern who is a credible climate expert and who is not. Again, PragerU self-identifies on its web site as a "digital marketing campaign," but were PragerU climate-denial videos classified as "infomercials," there would be Federal Trade Commission rules about this. The Federal Trade Commission, which is charged with protecting consumers, instructs advertisers that experts should be actual experts, warning:

> A person who speaks as an expert should be an expert, and what your expert endorser says about your product should be based on an evaluation or tests that other experts in the field generally would find sufficient to support your expert's conclusions.[18]

But here the "product" being marketed is climate denial, and PragerU's strategies appear to be effective not simply with a growing number of Gen Zs and Millennials but with many adult viewers as well. Overwhelmingly, the nearly 3,000 *Religion of Green* viewer comments on YouTube are laudatory, enthusing that the video is "brilliant," a "real eye opener," and that PragerU is "doing God's work." Far and fewer between are the comments of viewers who notice that the experts on climate and environment are not experts. A lone post by @alexander-r observes wryly: "I like the part when they didn't use a single credible study and just took the word of people who work for think tanks that are funded by oil and gas companies."[19]

But again, why give climate denial propaganda like this any time at all? This is a good time for a reminder that school teachers across the nation are partnering with and becoming "members" of PragerU's "PragerForce," and that its mediamaking influence is only growing, especially among younger viewers. As @toddbowles8201 posts in the viewer comments, amidst other teachers, "Well done. I'm a teacher and this religion [environmentalism] is taught in schools." It behooves those who care about climate change communication, its efficacy, and impact to watch what Gen Zs and Millennials are watching and glean what insights we can into the sorts of political realignment tactics outlets like PragerU use to rebrand climate change, at best, as a "nothing burger;" and climate action, at worst, as something sinister, scary, and "cultish."

With that setup, let's dig into the actual content of *Religion of Green*. The video is divided into five sections dealing with a different characteristic of "religion": (1) Fear, (2) Doctrine, (3) Superstition, (4) Apocalypse, and (5) Priesthood. In each of these categories, religion is operationalized almost as a funhouse mirror for PragerU's own anxieties and psychological projections, while ginning up the very fear it accuses the climate movement of exploiting.

Rebranding and Restorying via Religious Frames

To host *Religion of Green*, PragerU astutely does not select some Liberty University graduate who looks like a buttoned-up Republican Congressional page.

Instead, PragerU assigns this job to Will Witt, the platform's good-looking, twentysomething, sandy, surfer-haired host, who is a University of Colorado, Boulder dropout and exudes cool kid vibes.[20] In marketing materials, PragerU shows photos of Witt at PragerU headquarters in L.A., hanging out with a gaggle of hip-looking, ethnically diverse Millennials, who are portrayed as "young Turks" rebelliously bucking the tyranny of the "woke." Witt is known in the "Pragerverse" for his "man-on-the-street" interviews, which feature quick snippets of "campus liberals" often sounding absurd and hair-brained. In a comedy routine popularized as "JayWalking" on *The Tonight Show with Jay Leno* (2010–2014), Leno would often head out into the streets of L.A. to test Americans on things like their geography. Responses were predictably idiotic, but as with Witt's man-on-the-street segments, audiences were not privy to any serious or thoughtful responses, only seeing what the video producers curated with specific objectives (in Leno's case, comedic ones) in mind. Witt borrows this tactic to discredit those concerned about climate change.

The advertisements for *Religion of Green* all feature a photo of Will Witt's head enveloped by a shady dark background. Superimposed over Witt's head to look like a halo is a glowing, green-arrowed recycling symbol, the internationally recognized symbol of (and shorthand for) the environmental movement. Witt's eyes are cast upward, as though in reverence to a higher power, and yet we also see his eyes filled with what looks like fear. In the video's introduction, the title "RELIGION OF GREEN" rises out of a dark scene of flickering votive candles on some sort of religious altar, as scary organ music reaches a crescendo.

In Part 1, the word "FEAR" appears on screen in all caps against a background of desolate smoking ground that appears to be the aftermath of a destructive fire. This section of the video asserts that environmentalism more broadly and the climate movement more specifically constitute a religion (read: an extreme/sinister religion) because this religion uses fear to control people. By implication, legitimate/biblical religion sends the message to its followers, "fear not," and reassures the faithful that God is on the throne and in charge. That implicit message is echoed in the stream of viewer reaction comments posted on YouTube, especially from those reacting to the opening night live screening premier of *Religion of Green* simultaneously streamed online and at a special event hosted by evangelical megachurch Calvary Chapel's Chino Hills, California location. A common theme in the comments is that God will do everything in His own time, and if he wants to keep the polar ice caps from melting, He will. Nothing to see. Nothing to fear.

In an interview with the right-wing outlet Newsmax following the video premiere, Witt again emphasized this theme of fear, contending that "The Left controls people by making them afraid."[21] The ruse of climate change has thus been concocted by "the Left" as a sinister political and psychological tool of control and manipulation. The irony here is palpable since PragerU in this very video aggressively stokes fears in viewers that a "Religion of Green" wants to control their children, who are being alarmingly indoctrinated into the "religion" of environmentalism in their public-school curriculums (yet another reason to homeschool, as PragerU's other videos promote). By rebranding environmentalism as a "religion," the video also riles up PragerU's conservative audience by pushing a hot button: the perceived hypocrisy that separation of church and state (in the Establishment Clause of the First Amendment) has been used by "leftists" to prevent children from collectively praying in school, and yet environmental curricula (also by PragerU' rebranded as "religious") can be taught from an early age. PragerU proceeds to supply its own homeschool videos and children's books as an antidote to what it characterizes as a corrupt infiltration of public schools by environmental religion. No distinction of course is made between an environmental science curriculum, or natural science and ecological studies curricula, and environmental activism, as all of these are lumped together as essentially "religion." It is worth noting here that evangelical parents have made a very similar argument about the inclusion of yoga workouts in public school gym classes, bringing parental lawsuits against local school boards (Ramey, 2017), and illustrating how legally complicated, and politically fraught, definitions of religion can be.

Religious Studies scholars know that the definition of "religion" can be highly tricky, hotly debated, and is always intertwined with political investments and power relations (Chidester, 2005; McCutcheon and Hughes, 2021; Orsi, 2012, p. 1–11; 84–101; Smith, 1998). Within this definitional ambiguity in mind, PragerU's rhetorical application of the term "religion" to characterize, if not rebrand, the environmental movement is not beyond the pale.

Throughout the video, Michael Shellenberger (MS) outlines why the environmental movement constitutes a "religion" and why viewers should be deeply concerned about this.

MS: "Most of us want something to believe in. Most of us need some kind of faith, some sort of belief in a higher power. And so that shifted for many educated people from a belief in God to nature. So, nature became sort of the new God." Later in the video, MS paints with a breathtakingly large brush as he cautions viewers to remember that the "elites" – examples include the people who run *The New York Times*, the Democratic politicians, elite university scientists, and well-educated activists – are all very "secular" people. "They really don't have a traditional religion, so they have constructed this new religion."

Shellenberger's wording and arguments bear a strong resemblance to both Jonathan Tobin's article in *The National Review*, "The Religion of Environmental Alarmism" (2018), and the writings of the late Robert Nelson, an economist and Professor of Public Policy at the University of Maryland, a fellow at the libertarian Independent Institute, and author of *The New Holy Wars: Economic Religion Versus Environmental Religion in Contemporary America* (2010). Nelson argued that, whereas economics had once been the dominant "secular religion" of our society, "environmental religion" as a secular religion has now taken over that top spot, fundamentally serving as our most prominent public theology. Nelson's definition of religion borrows from William James and Paul Tillich:

> Some argue that a religion must have a God, disqualifying environmentalism. Yet, as the great American psychologist and philosopher William James observed in his 1902 classic, *The Varieties of Religious Experience*, it is not necessary to "positively assume a God" in order to have a religion. James insisted that "godless or quasi-godless creeds" also can qualify as religions, which – given its devout belief system and the fervor of its adherents – clearly would include today's environmentalism ... Paul Tillich, the greatest American theologian of the 20th century, similarly defined religion as a comprehensive belief system that seeks to answer questions of "ultimate concern" to human existence. For Tillich, it was characteristic of our time that "the most important religious movements are developing outside of (official) religion."
>
> *Nelson (2012)*

Though not necessarily referencing James and Tillich, similar arguments have been made by Religious Studies scholars, such as American religious historian Catherine Albanese, author of *Nature Religion in America* (1991), and ethicist/religious ethnographer Bron Taylor. In *Dark Green Religion* (2010), published the same year as Nelson's book, Taylor traces the rise of "green religions" in North America, which he depicts as ranging from radical environmental activist groups like Earth First! to bioregional lifestyle groups, to New Agers espousing "ecopsychology." Although Bron Taylor's work is never explicitly mentioned in the PragerU video, due to YouTube's algorithm dynamics, his mention in Prager's video is likely not even needed to form associations. The numerous times that I have viewed PragerU's *Religion of Green* (from a variety of computers and different IP addresses and locations), the list of suggested videos subsequently generated by the YouTube algorithm, after the Calvary Church video premier and the docushort trailer, included the following: (1) "Dark Green Religion with Prof Bron Taylor" (an interview with Taylor about the growing landscape of "green religions" worldwide); (2) an episode of "Nature Revisited," a podcast interview with Taylor on the evolution of nature-centered religions; and (3) a Christian group's exposé video called "Dark Green Religion Explained."[22] This last posting is a compilation of video footage of scholars at academic conferences referencing Bron Taylor's work on "naturalistic Gaianism," "spiritualistic animism," and "biocentric green religion," or videos of Bron Taylor himself, making the case for the emergence of "dark green religion" and its ties to radical environmental groups. In the video notes, the group outlines the main points of Taylor's academic book for easy viewer reference. Thus, viewers of PragerU's *Religion of Green* who may question the credibility of its claims that environmentalism is a "religion" immediately are presented with videos popping up on their screen that appear to confirm, or at least validate, Prager's fear-inducing themes of environmentalism as a "dark green religion."[23]

Bundled together with videos from a reputable university scholar, who specializes in the study of religion and environment, and who seemingly makes the same argument as Shellenberger, *Religion of Green* gains greater credibility. To be clear, Bron Taylor is a tireless advocate for climate action and does not consider the emergence of what he calls "dark green religion" to be a negative or scary social development. In fact, he expresses sympathy with "green religions" and their adherents, but in the algorithmic association of his videos, digitally right next door to *Religion of Green*, Taylor's scholarship inadvertently buttresses PragerU's argument.[24]

In the "Doctrine" section of PragerU's video, MS goes on to trace the roots of the "religion of green" back to the nineteenth-century German philosopher Friedrich Nietzsche. On a popular level, many young conservative Christian PragerU followers will recognize Nietzsche as the ideological villain of the popular evangelical Christian film *God's Not Dead* (2014), one of the most successful independent films of its decade, streamed on multiple platforms, and shown in church youth groups across the U.S. and the world (Wilkinson, 2019).

MS: "Nietzsche pointed out that as belief in God and the afterlife declined, people would create new religions. And that's what happened in the early part of the twentieth century. The rise of fascism and the rise of communism … basically acted as two new religions … they were both apocalyptic in their own way. After communism was discredited in the United States and around the world in the 1950s, environmentalism took over that role on the Left."

While MS argues that environmentalism is a successor and stand-in for a gap left by the secularizing forces of communism and/or fascism, Bron Taylor argues that with the statistical rise of the "nones" (the religiously unaffiliated), and with the decline of traditional religious institutions, "green religions" have gained ground to fill the gap. Again, Taylor's work does not portray this phenomenon as constituting a bad thing, but PragerU poses an uncannily similar argument. Jacki Deason (JD) goes on to articulate a similar "secularization thesis," in which green religion has arisen as a consequence of a decline of belief and faith in Western civilization.

JD: "Traditional faiths are declining in America and Europe and around the world, and so this [the environmental movement] is kind of taking the place. People have to have something to believe in. They need something bigger than themselves. And so this is just a convenient, I think, substitute." YouTube viewers' comments equate this substitution with deception and idolatry. As @yourmomwenttocollege25 observes: "They exchanged the truth about God for a lie and worshipped and served created things rather than the Creator – who is forever praised. Amen. – Romans 1:25."

Alex Epstein (AE) adds a dimension of theodicy to the argument: "A common narrative in religions is that if you violate the god's commandments, then you're going to be punished with some sort of hell. And you can see there's an enormous parallel between this and what you could call the modern environmentalist commandment that we shouldn't impact the earth. There's just this assumption that if we have any impact on climate or if we consume resources, or if we put more plastics into the world, then it must just be a total catastrophe."

Here again, we see PragerU's strategy of paltering – misleading by telling an incomplete truth in order to rebrand its opposition. Do the environmental and climate movements have "religious" sensibilities and commitments? It depends upon one's definition of religion and one's investments. But no distinction is made here between climate activism and actual climate science. Nor is there acknowledgment that there are moral, ethical, spiritual commitments, and religious aspects endemic to any number of movements, such as the Civil Rights Movement, for example. Possessing these qualities does not necessarily make those movements "religions." But, so what if it did? The point is that Prager's "experts" portray the "belief" in global climate change as a kind of radical theology, a "false religion," and indeed one that is dangerous, blasphemous, and bent on world control.

In the "APOCALYPSE" section of the video, MS further argues that climate activism espouses and promotes a kind of arrogant, narcissistic "superhero fantasy." He contends that the climate movement particularly wants us to believe in "something that threatens the end of the world and we as individuals will save the world. I mean, it is like a Marvel comic strip … What has happened with the rise of 'secular religion' is that individuals adopt a kind of messianic, you know, story where they are themselves the Messiah – something that is rejected by most traditional religions."

DS adds: "Well, unfortunately, I think the number one principle for the environmental movement is submission." [Background music: scary and suspenseful synthesized organ music, sounding like it was composed for the horror films *The Omen* or *Rosemary's Baby*] "What it requires is submission to the agenda. I absolutely think that people who are leading this movement [visuals of Al Gore, Bill McKibben, and Jeff Bezos] – and not just the environmental movement but the fringe catastrophic climate change sector of that movement – are using fear."

Religion scholar Jason Bivins' *Religion of Fear: The Politics of Horror in Conservative Evangelicalism* (2008) unpacks just how pervasive (and traumatizing) fear culture is for many evangelicals who are steeped in it – from gruesome Halloween "Hell Houses" to terrifying apocalyptic Christian media. Since viewers such as those at the Calvary Chapel film premier are likely no strangers to notions of "biblical authority," "umbrellas of authority," and godly submission, nor to the deep elements of fear endemic to premillennial dispensationalist apocalyptic theology, if not the terrorizing notion of the impending "Rapture," deploying the rhetoric of "fear" and "submission" throughout *Religion of Green* is a fascinating example of what psychologists call "projection," a well-known tactic used in propaganda communication.

In his now classic work analyzing Nazi propaganda, *Conquering the man in the street: A Psychological Analysis of Propaganda, in War, Fascism, and Politics* (1940), social psychologist Ellis Freeman famously demonstrated the ways that projecting onto an opponent your own misdeeds functions as a powerful propaganda suasion tactic, deflecting blame from the accuser and placing it on to the accused. Applying this projection tactic beyond the context of fascist politics to see how it might operate in the world of marketing, or what they call "the effects of the pot calling the kettle black," Derek Rucker (Northwestern Professor of Marketing, specializing in advertising strategy and methods of suasion) and Anthony Pratkanis (emeritus professor of Psychology at UC Santa Cruz, specializing in the study of propaganda) found in four separate experiments that projection is "effective in (a) increasing the blame placed on the target of the projection and (b) decreasing the culpability of the accuser (or projectionist). These effects occurred despite (a) raising suspicions about the motives of the projectionist, (b) providing evidence that the projectionist is guilty of the deed, and (c) timing the projection so that it occurred after the misdeeds came to light" (Rucker and Pratkanis, 2001).

At several points in Prager's video, Will Witt (WW) interviews people on the street in San Francisco, asking them what their biggest fears are. The footage is shot during 2020 with the pandemic in full swing, so interviewees are masked, even WW is wearing a bandana, and there is an apocalyptic feel to the footage. A middle-aged woman responds to Witt's question: "Trump, Coronavirus, and the climate." Two college-aged young women respond: "The planet withering away to the point where we can't live on it anymore. Like, where you just don't have a life." The first woman adds, "I think it may be the end of our civilization." This is followed by a clip of Greta Thunberg's emotional speech to world leaders at the UN climate action summit in New York that went viral in 2019, in which she says, "You have stolen my dreams and my childhood with your empty words." Commenting on the clip, WW interprets her words as indicative of a doomsday cult: "So when Greta Thunberg says 'You've ruined my childhood. You've stolen my childhood,' she's talking about the end of the world."

A snippet follows of Congresswoman Alexandra Ocasio-Cortez (AOC), taken out of context, in which she says, "The world is going to end in 12 years if we don't address climate change." In the full speech, AOC was referring to the absurdity that young people are hearing the message that "the world is going to end in 12 years," but they then are being told that the world is too expensive to fix.[25] This is a reference to reports issued by the Intergovernmental Panel on Climate Change (IPCC), the United Nations' scientific group charged with assessing the science of climate change. What the authors of the IPCC report have actually said is that we have a certain window to cut emissions and address climate change substantively, or the cascading effects of climate change could act as a runaway train that will be much harder to curb, let alone reverse. A number of climate scientists push back against this "12-year window" rhetoric, arguing both that climate change impacts are already here, and that the rhetoric of a "closing window" to act is actually counterproductive to inspiring action (Freedman, 2019).

Compounding the apocalyptic soundbites from Thunberg and AOC, the video then shows a clip from Al Gore commenting, "Every night on the TV news is like a nature hike through the book of revelation." On the heels of Gore, WW lobs a softball at MS, asking, "What are some of the negative consequences of telling people that this is apocalyptic and the world's going to end?"

MS: "I think we have seen some very significant mental health impacts of this apocalyptic environmental discourse, particularly on climate change. So, we now know there have been surveys that one out of five children in Britain suffer nightmares from climate change. I think that the numbers are probably very similar in the United States. I suspect that they're even higher." An interview sequence follows, asking college-aged women on the street about how many years they think humanity has left before it goes extinct. The answers range from the more optimistic 200–400 years to the more sobering estimation of just 20 years. The apocalypse portion concludes with a clip of Science Guy Bill Nye setting a globe ablaze and shouting, "The planet is on effing fire!"

It is important to note here that PragerU mixes the lie that climate change is not happening, and/or is no big deal, together with a truth that a number of climate scientists, media strategists, and popular culture critics agree on (Gross and Giles, 2012a; Hess, 2023), though for different reasons. That is, promoting apocalyptic thinking, can be tragically counterproductive, as it tends to foster inaction. Climatologist Michael Mann, director of the University of Pennsylvania's Center for Science, Sustainability, and Media, for instance, cautions,

> Doom-mongering has overtaken denial as a threat and as a tactic. Inactivists know that if people believe there is nothing you can do, they are led down a path of disengagement. They unwittingly do the bidding of fossil fuel interests by giving up
>
> *Watts (2021)*

New media strategist Matthew Barrett Gross similarly argues that popular mediations of apocalypse too often frame the end of the world as an inevitably approaching event that cannot be stopped, not a trend of crises that we humans can pull together to avert. We "paralyze ourselves with inaction – or the wrong course of action" (Gross and Giles, 2012b). Rather than apocalyptic prognostications inspiring our better natures and prompting us to care collectively for our communities, more often it merely triggers packing "bugout packs for a quick escape or stocking up on gold, guns, and canned food" (2012b). It also triggers feelings of depression, helplessness, anxiety, despondency, and emotional paralysis (Marks et al., 2021; Ray, 2020). This cocktail of desperation is not exactly the recipe we need to move the world into action, and is it any wonder that, for younger generations experiencing apocalypse fatigue (Hess, 2022; Wray, 2023), setting down that cocktail to imbibe PragerU's propaganda brew holds great appeal?

Uncomfortable Insights for Better Climate Action Marketing and Communication

There is so much more to unpack in *Religion of Green*, but this is a good place to pause and take a good hard, if uncomfortable, look at how PragerU effectively addresses some of the climate movement's vulnerabilities and how current climate communication falls short or sometimes shoots itself in the foot. Without vindicating PragerU and its climate-denialist propaganda, it is important for us to take cognizance of certain failures in current climate messaging and do better. For instance, when the IPCC declares we have "12 years left," or 8 years, or 6, and the "climate clock" in New York's Union Square very publicly counts down the minutes and seconds of that doomsday "closing window," that messaging has been misheard (innocently or purposefully) in popular understanding as there being 12 years left until "we're all going to die." As I have argued in greater depth elsewhere (McFarland Taylor, 2024), this message actually fuels climate fatalism and doomerism, which shuts down climate action and thereby benefits the fossil-fuel industry's interests. The "falling off a cliff" narrative of climate irreversibility, post the closing of a narrow IPCC-defined time window, not only inculcates panic paralysis but also despair and crippling anxiety in those who otherwise support climate action. This anxiety is particularly acute in children (Kelsey, 2020, Marks et al, 2021; McFarland Taylor, 2024; Ray, 2020). In *Hope Matters* (2020), Elin Kelsey, who studies the impact of "doomerist" climate narratives on children, recounts being called to consult after an incident with a young student at a Toronto school who came home deeply distraught because she learned at school that "we are all going to die in eight years." Kelsey recounts,

> The girl had attended a climate change presentation at school that featured Greta Thunberg's emotional speech to the UN Climate Action Summit … "You have stolen my dreams and my childhood," Greta said. "People are suffering. People are dying. Entire ecosystems are collapsing. We are in the beginning of a mass extinction, and all you can talk about is money and fairy tales of eternal economic growth." After watching the video of the speech, the children were shown the climate change doomsday clock as it rapidly counts down the years, days, and seconds we have left. Imagine being a kid seeing this and believing we are literally moments from the end of the world. When teachers and other trusted adults take on the role of telling kids just how wrecked the world is, in the name of *telling them the facts so they will be inspired to act*, they fuel the cycle of fear, anxiety, and hopelessness.
>
> *Kelsey (2020), p. 64–65*

So, when PragerU rebrands the climate movement as a "doom cult," and that reading is resonating with Gen Z and Millennial viewers, who are sick of being told they have no future, nothing to look forward to, and the world's going to end (in the case of my college students, many have vowed not to have children because they regard it as cruel to bring new humans onto a dying planet), we overlook or ignore the real role mediated doom messaging plays in shutting down climate action by evoking deep despair and mental health crises. So, what's the alternative?

In the list of steps marketing specialists advise when dealing with attacks from a competitor (in this case, a competitor in the mediated marketplace of ideas, public discussion, and policy action), one of those steps is to change the narrative, and the other is to actually "listen and learn" from the attack. Curious Marketing Agency, a digital marketing agency based in London, in its guide, "When Brands Fight Back," offers several points of advice to its clients when attacked by a rival. Under the heading "Listen and Learn," they advise dropping immediate defensiveness and instead to get curious:

> Take note and acknowledge that the area of the business that's under fire is potentially falling short. This is in fact the perfect moment to take a step back, reevaluate the business' offering/position in the market and regroup. From here, it's about developing these problem areas and turning them into strengths that can be publicized and offered to consumers.[26]

Curious Agency issues sound marketing advice to its clients, reassuring them, as many agencies would: "If you come under fire from a competitor then they feel threatened by you. Keep this in mind at all times, and while it's crucial you don't sink to their level, your response will shape how strongly you come out of the encounter."[27] This is certainly true for PragerU and its fossil-fuel industry shills, who on some level, *do* recognize that climate denial is becoming harder to make a case for. The fact that the climate movement warrants an attack like *Religion of Green* (and PragerU's growing list of climate denial videos) in many ways speaks volumes to the inroads the climate movement has made (Aronczyk and Espinoza, 2022). At the same time, it can be useful to take a clear-eyed look at attacks for ways to strengthen climate-action mediamaking and messaging.

Changing the narrative of climate doomerism does not mean advocating Pollyanna-like wishful thinking and naivete. It does mean cultivating what Elin Kelsey calls fact-based hope and highlighting wins as well as losses. Climate scientist Katharine Hayhoe, Director of the Climate Science Center at Texas Tech, author of *Saving Us: A Climate Scientist's Case for Hope and Healing in a Divided World* (2021), and host of PBS's climate series *Global Weirding* (now on YouTube), offers a template for truth-telling about climate without inducing apocalyptic fatalism, paralysis, and despair. I feature Hayhoe's monthly newsletter in my media and environment course as an example of an effective approach. The structure of Hayhoe's communication is consistent, inviting, and accessible. Each month, she starts off with a section designated, "Good News," which features inspiring news about real progress being made on climate action and adaptation. After this, she moves to "Not-So-Good News." Note that this section is not about "horror" or "existential doom." The "Not-So-Good" modifier makes these topics more digestible, so the reader is more receptive to the content and does not simply shut down or turn away. Hayhoe often features stories in this section about how we are not moving nearly fast enough on climate action and how we need to ramp up our response, working together to effect systemic changes. In the final section, "What You Can Do," Hayhoe always includes actionable steps and clickable hyperlink buttons to make it ridiculously easy for the reader to get connected and take action. Her newsletter communicates climate hope, without sugarcoating climate realities; it is solutions-based, and it empowers the reader to move from mere concern into concrete action. The communication is quick, bite-sized, and informs in a manageable way that does not overwhelm. Upscaling this approach, making it more "spreadable" (Jenkins, Ford and Green, 2018) across social media platforms like TikTok, while crafting compelling stories about climate that inspire hope and action, would be even more productive.

Already Gen Z is getting on board with this anti-doomerist approach, spreading climate hope to boost collective action. Both Gen Z climate writers Leah Thomas (founder of the Intersectional Environmentalist climate justice collective) and Zahra Biabani, author of *Climate Optimism: Celebrating Systemic Change Around the World* (2023), drive home the message that hope and love are by far more powerful motivators than doomerism and fear (with the significant added benefit of not inducing counterproductive states of terror and paralysis in their generation).[28] Biabani even makes climate TikToks that include viral dances and partners with other climate TikTokers to inspire and spur Gen Zs into action via social media.

Though Jacki Deason repeats in the PragerU video that "fear is a powerful motivator," it can also backfire and cause people to freeze (Heglar, 2019). Striking a balance, as Hayhoe, Thomas, and Biabani do, not only avoids the crippling effect of climate anxiety but also invites younger generations out of despair and into a community of action. Without such options readily available in a digital mediasphere, where climate doomerism too often prevails (Kelsey, 2020; Ray, 2020), PragerU's climate denial can appear to climate-weary Gen Zs, in particular, like the only way to set down the heavy existential burdens imposed on their generation. Of course, the most obvious remedy for youth anxiety about climate change would be to take serious, swift, and impactful global measures to draw down carbon to safer levels, while also transitioning our infrastructure to cope with a rapidly heating world. More than likely, though, achieving this will take more time. In the meantime, we have got to stop pickling our youth in terror and apocalypticism. PragerU's *Religion of Green* very purposely touches this nerve; it is effective, and it points to a very real climate movement messaging vulnerability, if not failing. And though Prager plays the game of "Two Truths and a Lie" well, the stakes are no game at all.

Finally, but not insignificantly, scholars of both religion and media need to take sober cognizance of how our theorizing of the category of "religion," "implicit religion," "cultural religion," or "secular religion" can be instrumentalized by entities and platforms like PragerU and used to rebrand, discredit, and undermine public perceptions of climate science and thus thwart climate action. As we become more consciously aware of how our scholarship can be potentially weaponized to ends we have not intended, developing an interdisciplinary depth, as this volume promotes, in both the study of religion and in the understanding of marketing principles, tactics, and strategies, is critical to anticipating, countering, and learning from climate-denial hostile rebranding maneuvers.

Notes

1 See Wendy's original "Where's the Beef?" television ad here: https://www.youtube.com/watch?v=1FZNYXKHwNw.
2 Readers familiar with Naomi Oreskes and Erik Conway's *Merchants of Doubt* (2010) will recognize these as similar tactics used by the tobacco industry to cast doubt on the science linking cigarettes to lung cancer and the ways the fossil-fuel industry subsequently poached these tactics to plant and then fuel public doubts about climate science.
3 For a fuller discussion of the mechanisms and power of "restorying" tactics in media and marketing, especially vis-à-vis climate and environmental messaging, see Chapter 1 in my book, Ecopiety: Green Media and the Dilemma of Environmental Virtue (McFarland Taylor, 2019).
4 See the compiled playlist, "How PragerU Lies to You: Good PragerU Debunks": https://www.youtube.com/playlist?list=PLdjtfnD9syhEAPCNxy3ABBO1CZV3tjqvq. Particularly concise but incisive is the video posted by Current Affairs, "Conservatives Are Wrong About Climate," which takes PragerU's chronically unlabeled and unsourced creatively improvised "graphs" to task. See https://www.youtube.com/watch?v=gSQpskL-O-w.
5 See, for example, Reuters' "Fact Check: Video Presents Climate Change Statements That Lack Key Context" (2020): https://www.reuters.com/article/uk-factcheck-prageru-missing-context-cli/fact-check-video-presents-climate-change-statements-that-lack-key-context-idUSKBN2712EY.
6 See PragerU's mission here: "Our comprehensive digital marketing campaign promotes the ideas that have made America and the West the source of so much liberty and wealth. These values are Judeo-Christian at their core and include the concepts of freedom of speech, free markets and love for our country—The United States of America." https://www.politicon.com/speaker/prager-u/.
7 See www.khanacademy.org; www. https://www.youtube.com/@crashcourse; and www.thegreatcourses.com.
8 The term "Joshua Generation" was coined by Michael Farris, who founded the Homeschool Legal Defense Foundation to fight against any kind of government regulation imposed on homeschoolers.
9 See Kirk Cameron's homeschooling advocacy video here: https://www.facebook.com/watch/?v=1095573451228057.
10 See PragerU's Alex Epstein-hosted video here: https://www.youtube.com/watch?v=BJWq1FeGpCw.
11 See "10 years and 5 billion views: PragerU is the undeniable conservative media leader of the next generation": https://www.prageru.com/press/10-years-and-5-billion-views-prageru-is-the-undeniable-conservative-media.
12 See https://www.prageru.com/kids/read.
13 See also "Colgate Censured Over Advert": https://www.reuters.com/article/uk-britain-colgate/colgate-censured-over-advert-idUKL1654835620070117.
14 See also the World Health Organization, "Climate Change and Health: Climate Change – the biggest health threat facing humanity": https://www.who.int/news-room/fact-sheets/detail/climate-change-and-health.
15 For a guide to more tactics like this, see Melissa Aronczyk and Maria Espinoza's, *A Strategic Nature: Public Relations and the Politics of American Environmentalism* (2022).
16 See https://climatefeedback.org/evaluation/article-by-michael-shellenberger-mixes-accurate-and-inaccurate-claims-in-support-of-a-misleading-and-overly-simplistic-argumentation-about-climate-change/.
17 See SourceWatch.org's report here: https://www.sourcewatch.org/index.php/Texas_Public_Policy_Foundation.
18 See at Federal Trade Commission web site: https://www.ftc.gov/news-events/news/speeches/myths-half-truths-about-deceptive-advertising.
19 See comments at: https://www.youtube.com/watch?v=UTgNtvTuYRU.

20 On Witt's Prager bio page, he relates his own kind of cult escape narrative, explaining how he dropped out of CU Boulder in order to flee "the Left's relentless indoctrination of students." See https://www.prageru.com/presenters/will-witt.

21 See Chris Salcedo's October 2020 interview with Will Witt posted on Newsmax's Facebook site: https://www.facebook.com/watch/?v=1779566055541940.

22 See "Dark Green Religion with Bron Taylor," https://www.youtube.com/watch?v=9R4matNOK0c&list=PLtEH6WWbRSNS6wEAajYmGtoZraa4j7zyH&index=17; "Episode 63: Bron Taylor – The Sacred in Nature": https://www.youtube.com/watch?v=vMLomxCIGrU&list=PLtEH6WWbRSNS6wEAajYmGtoZraa4j7zyH&index=18; and "Dark Green Religion Explained": https://www.youtube.com/watch?v=924SziTX7NE&list=PLtEH6WWbRSNS6wEAajYmGtoZraa4j7zyH&index=22.

23 For more analysis of the disturbing and potentially politically radicalizing effects of AI algorithms, see techno-sociologist Zeynep Tufekci's 2017 TedX talk, "We're Building a Dystopia Just to Make People Click on Ads": www.ted.com.

24 My gratitude to both Bron Taylor and Evan Berry for offering their insights into this thorny issue.

25 See streaming video of AOC's full conversation with Ta-Nehisi Coates at the 2019 "MLK Now" event: https://www.facebook.com/watch/?v=581651792309581.

26 Ibid.

27 https://curiouslondon.com/when-brands-fight-back-how-to-counter-a-rival-brand-attack-in-style/

28 See Leah Thomas's environmental justice collective here: https://www.intersectionalenvironmentalist.com/.

References

Albanese, C. (1991). *Nature Religion in America: From the Algonkian Indians to the New Age*. Chicago: University of Chicago Press.

Archie, A. (2023). "A Lot Is Happening in Florida Education. These Are Some of the Changes Kids Will See." National Public Radio. (August 14): www.npr.org.

Aronczyk, M. and Espinoza, M. (2022). *A Strategic Nature: Public Relations and the Politics of American Environmentalism*. New York: Oxford University Press.

Bivens, J. (2008). *Religion of Fear: The Politics of Horror in Conservative Evangelicalism*. New York: Oxford University Press.

Bloom, J. (2005). "Authenticity, Not Perfection, Is the Key to Reaching Consumers." *Advertising Age*. March 21: www.adage.com.

Bowles, N. (2020). "Right-Wing View for Generation Z, Five Minutes at a Time." *New York Times*. January 4: www.nytimes.com.

Chidester, D. (2005). *Authentic Fakes: Religion and American Popular Culture*. Berkeley: University of California Press, pp. 269–284.

Cusick, D. (2020). "Miami Is the Most Vulnerable Coastal City Worldwide." *Scientific American*. February 4: www.scientificamerican.com.

Deeran, S. (2009). "Attack Ad Mistakes." *CBS News Money Watch*. January 4: www.cbsnews.com.

Dembiki, G. (2022). "How Fracking Billionaires, Ben Shapiro, and PragerU Built a Climate Crisis-Denial Empire." *Vice News*. August 25: www.vice.com.

De Vise, D. (2023). "High School Boys Are Trending Conservative." The Hill. (July 31): www.thehill.com.

Farris, M. (2005). *The Joshua Generation: Restoring the Heritage of Christian Leadership*. Nashville: B&H Publishing Group.

Freedman, A. (2019). "Scientists Refute Twelve-Year Deadline to Curb Global Warming." *Axios*. January 22: www.axios.com.

Freeman, E. (1940). *Conquering the Man in the Street: A Psychological Analysis of Propaganda, in War, Fascism, and Politics*. New York: Vanguard.

Godin, S. (2009). *All Marketers Are Liars Tell Stories*. New York: Penguin.

Gross, M.B. and Giles, M. (2012a). *The Last Myth: What the Rise of Apocalyptic Thinking Tells Us About America*. Amherst: Prometheus Books.

———. (2012b). "How Apocalyptic Thinking Prevents Us From Taking Political Action." *The Atlantic*. April 23: www.theatlantic.com.

Harvey, C. (2023). "Southeastern U.S. Seas Are Rising at Triple the Global Average." *Scientific American*. April 11: www.scientificamerican.com.

Hayhoe, K. (2021). *Saving Us: A Climate Scientist's Case for Hope and Healing in a Divided World*. New York: One Signal Publishers.

Heglar, M.A. (2019). "Home Is Always Worth It." *Medium.com*. September 12: https://medium.com/@maryheglar/home-is-always-worth-it-d2821634dcd9.

Hess, A. (2022). "Apocalypse When? Global Warming's Endless Scroll." *New York Times*. February 3: www.nytimes.com.

Hess, R. (2023). "The Dangers of Apocalyptic Thinking." *Education Week*. March 23: https://www.edweek.org/policy-politics/opinion-the-dangers-of-apocalyptic-thinking/2023/03

Hogenboom, M. (2017). "The Devious Art of Telling the Truth." *BBC News*. November 15: www.bbcnews.com.

Irfan, U. (2023). "The Ocean Is Rising and So Is Miami's Skyline." (September 18): www.vox.com.

Jenkins, H., Ford, S. and Green, J., eds. (2018). *Spreadable Media: Creating Value and Meaning in a Networked Culture*. New York: NYU Press.

Jones, S. (2023). "A Generation Moves On." *New York Magazine*. May 30: https://nymag.com.

Kelsey, E. (2020). *Hope Matters: Why Changing the Way We Think Is Critical to Solving the Environmental Crisis*. Berkeley: Greystone Books.

Kotler, P. (1999). *Kotler on Marketing: How to Create, Win, and Dominate Markets*. New York: The Free Press.

Kotler, P. and Singh, R. (1981). "Marketing Warfare in the 1980s." *Journal of Business Strategy*. 1(3), 30–41.

Lewis, C.S. (2001). *The Chronicles of Narnia [1956]*. New York: Harper Collins.

Liles, M. (2022). "Two Truths and a Lie: How to Play, the Sneakiest Tips & Tricks, Plus 100 of the Best Lie Ideas We've Ever Hear." Parade Magazine. (September 29): www.parade.com.

Logie, J. (2020). "'Where's the Beef?' The Story of the Most Famous Slogan Ever: How One Line Changed Pop Culture and Even an Election." *Better Marketing*. September 15: https://bettermarketing.pub/wheres-the-beef-the-story-of-the-most-famous-slogan-ever-550d3f0c48c.

Marks, E. et al. (2021) "Young People's Voices on Climate Anxiety, Government Betrayal, and Moral Injury: A Global Phenomenon." *The Lancet*. September 7: https://papers.ssrn.com/sol3/papers.cfm?abstract_id=3918955.

McCutcheon, R. And Hughes, A., eds. (2021). *What Is Religion?: Debating the Academic Study of Religion*. New York: Oxford University Press.

McFarland Taylor, S. (2019). *Ecopiety: Green Media and the Dilemma of Environmental Virtue*. New York: New York University Press.

———. (2024). "Canceling the Apocalypse: Defiant Hope as a Call to Action in the Climate Era," in W. Bauman, R. Bohannon, and K. O'Brien, eds. *Grounding Religion: A Field Guide to the Study of Religion and Ecology*. New York: Routledge.

Molloy, P. (2019). "PragerU Relies on a Veneer of Respectability to Obscure Its Propagandist Mission." *Media Matters for America*. September 9: www.mediamatters.org.

Nelson, R.H. (2010). *The New Holy Wars: Economic Religion Versus Environmental Religion in Contemporary America*. Pittsburgh: Penn State Press.

———. (2012). "Environmentalism Is Secular Religion." *Athens Banner-Herald*. April 19: www.athensonline.com.

Oppenheimer, M. (2018). "Inside the Right-Wing YouTube Empire That's Quietly Turning Millennials into Conservatives." *Mother Jones*. March/April: www.motherjones.com.

Oreskes, N. and Conway, E. (2010). *Merchants of Doubt: How a Handful of Scientists Obscured the Truth on Issues From Tobacco Smoke to Global Warming*. London: Bloomsbury Press.

Orsi, R. (2012). "Introduction" and "The Problem of the Holy," in R. Orsi, ed. *The Cambridge Companion to Religious Studies*. New York: Cambridge University Press.

Ramey, S. (2017). "Is Yoga Religious?" in A. Hughes and R. McCutcheon, eds. Religion in 5 Minutes. Sheffield: Equinox Publishing, p. 204–206.

Ramirez, R. (2021). "Climate Scientists Say Building Collapse Is a 'Wake-Up Call' About the Potential Impact of Rising Seas." CNN (June 30): www.cnn.com.

Ray, S.J. (2020). *A Field Guide to Climate Anxiety: How to Keep Your Cool on a Warming Planet*. Oakland: University of California Press.

Redding, A.C. (2018). *Google It: A History of Google*. New York: Feiwel and Friends.

Rozsa, M. (2020). "The Internet Has Become Captured by the Right. The Gravel Institute Is Trying to Take It Back." *Salon.com*. November 29: www.salon.com.

Rucker, D. and Pratkanis, A. (2001). "Projection as Interpersonal Influence Tactic: The Effects of the Pot Calling the Kettle Black." *Personality and Social Psychology Bulletin*. 27(11), 1494–1507.

Sharp, D. (2019). "The Truth About Misleading Numbers in Advertising." *Medium*. February 26: www.medium.com.

Shea, B. (2015). "Fracking Titans Spend Millions Proselytizing School Children." *Rewire News Group*. April 30: www.rewirenewsgroup.com.

Shetty, D. (2021). "Climate Change Would Cause 83 Million Excessive Deaths by 2100." *Forbes*. July 30: www.forbes.com.

Sharp, D. (2019). "The Truth About Misleading Numbers in Advertising." Medium. February 26: www.medium.com.

Smith, J.Z. (1998). "Religion, Religions, Religious," in M. Taylor, ed. *Critical Terms for Religious Studies*. Chicago: University of Chicago Press.

Sutton, M. (2017). *American Apocalypse: A History of American Evangelicalism*. Cambridge, MA: Harvard University Press.

Taylor, B. (2009). *Dark Green Religion: Nature Spirituality and the Planetary Future*. Berkeley: University of California Press.

Tobin, J. (2018). "The Religion of Environmental Alarmism." *The National Review*. December 20: www.nationalreview.com.

Verigin, B., Maijer, E., Vrij, A. and Zauzig, L. (2020). "The Interaction of Truthful and Deceptive Information." *Psychology, Crime, and Law*. 4(September), 367–83.

Watts, J. (2021) "Climatologist Michael E. Mann: 'Good People Fall Victim to Doomism. I Do too, Sometimes' [Interview]," *The Guardian*, February 27: www.theguardian.com.

Wray, B. (2023). *Generation Dread: Finding Purpose in an Age of Climate Anxiety*. New York: The Experiment Publishing.

Wiener, D. (2020). "Right-Wing PragerU Triples Revenue in Two Years." *Center for Media and Democracy's PR Watch*. January 16: www.prwatch.org.

Wilkinson, A. (2019). "How the 2014 Christian Film *God's Not Dead* Became a Hit and Spawned and Ideological Empire." *Vox*. December 18: www.vox.com.

6

A HEAD FOR POLITICS

Yarmulkes, Presidential Politics, and the Marketing of (Jewish) America

Eric Michael Mazur[1]

In the months leading up to the 2000 U.S. presidential election, a campaign item appeared unlike any that had been available before: a manufactured yarmulke onto which had been imprinted an endorsement for a political candidate.[2] Technically residing somewhere between commanded and traditional, the yarmulke has, over the past century, become a central symbol of Judaism, both within and beyond the Jewish community, a sign that communicates different messages to different audiences. In the non-Jewish world, it is the *sine qua non* of the "Jew in the midst," a marker of an outsider in the Christian dominant culture. In the Jewish world, it can be a map, locating the wearer by practice, ethnicity, and identity politics.[3] It is an object worn by all Orthodox Jewish males (men and boys), by any Conservative Jew (male or female), and by some Reform Jews: small and suede or large and velvet for regular wearers, large and polyester for occasional wearers, and knit for religious Zionists (see Goldberger 2015).[4]

For the past quarter century, however, while the yarmulke has remained a marker of Jewish identity, the "campaign-related" yarmulke has added a new layer of meaning. Not only does it locate the wearer in terms of Jewish identity, but it also locates the wearer in terms of secular American politics. This is not to suggest that American Jews have not participated in secular American politics; of course, they have. But the promotion of a secular American political message—and more to the point, the endorsement of a single political candidate on the most common marker of Jewish identity in a way that is shielded by the presumed sacrality of the object and the piety of the wearer—is a significant shift in the way American electoral politics is promoted. No other item so closely associated with religious ritual practice—Jewish or not—has been the locus of such political marketing and messaging. But the significance of the campaign-related yarmulke lies not in its inspiration, design, or production—or even its mere existence—but in the way that it

DOI: 10.4324/9781003342229-9

signals to both fellow Jews and non-Jews a secular political message that, in many ways, has little to do with the candidate being endorsed. Even as it narrowcasts to fellow Jews the political preference of the wearer, it broadcasts to non-Jews a message more profound than simply the presence of the stranger in their midst; it articulates a declaration of the wearer's belonging in the newly reorganized political world.[5] On any other surface, such a message would be just another political statement for all to see. But on the yarmulke, the message becomes a strong statement not only of political preference but also of a new expression of Jewish identity, both within the Jewish world and in the broader American political culture.

Heads and Tales

The yarmulke is borne of the Jewish sense that one should cover the head during prayer. Some trace this sense to the high priests at the Holy Temple in Jerusalem, others to *khukkot ha'goy* (the expectation that Jews distinguish themselves from non-Jews; see Leviticus 20:24). Some identify the "vestimentary apartheid" practices of Catholic Europe, others the post-Expulsion interactions of Sephardi Jews (whose Muslim neighbors covered their heads) and Ashkenazi Jews (whose Christian neighbors did not), and still others the increased importance of the medieval *Shulkhan Arukh* (an authoritative compendium on Jewish practice) as partially responsible for the elevation of the habit of covering the head from ethno-cultural pattern to broadly applicable expectation. It also may have been augmented by pietistic "one-upmanship" (Grossman 2010; Silverman 2013b).

In early twentieth-century America, the debate over how Jewish men should cover their heads shifted to the question of when (and whether) they should do so. Experiencing a higher level of cultural interaction with non-Jews, many American Jewish men felt compelled to remove their hats indoors (as was the custom of the dominant culture), going bareheaded when in secular public settings. The yarmulke—often but not always tolerated in non-Jewish settings—enabled the more observant of these men to keep their heads covered but still seem sensitive to the dominant culture's disapproval of hats indoors (see Joselit 1990:21; Grossman 2010). Cultural anthropologist Eric Silverman argues that it was only when the secular style of men wearing hats outdoors fell out of favor—particularly in the years following World War II—that the yarmulke became the "vestimentary token of Jewishness" that it is today (Silverman 2013b:189).[6]

Initially, the yarmulke may not have seemed out of place in an America where brimless, close-fitting head coverings were already common. One can find media accounts of Christian American political figures wearing these secular skullcaps as early as 1884 ("Bad Blood" 1884; "Politics in Connecticut" 1884). Presidential candidate Woodrow Wilson refused to wear one to cover a head injury because he thought it made him look old ("Gov. Wilson's Head" 1912); Governor Charles Bryan "nearly always" wore one indoors (Osnes 1967:51n12). Even Supreme Court Justices wore them, often as outdoor adjuncts to their judicial regalia ("Cap Revives

FIGURE 6.1   Campaign "beanie": James Cox, 1920 (Division of Political History, National Museum of American History, Smithsonian Institution)

Court Custom" 1989).[7] Head coverings (identified as "beanies") were also part of the brick-a-brac connected to both state and federal political campaigns (see Figure 6.1).

Reports of politicians wearing skullcaps identified specifically as yarmulkes began to appear in the 1920s (see "Bryan Tells Jews" 1923; "Walker Defends" 1927).[8] News coverage tended to cluster in areas with large Jewish populations (see "Mayor Urges U.S. Jews" 1946; "'Stalling' on Jews" 1946). By the 1960s, politicians of all levels—including former, current, and aspiring presidents—were being reported (and photographed) wearing yarmulkes regularly in Jewish settings (for example, see "Jews Honor Eisenhower" 1965; van Gelder 1968).[9] They also were keeping them handy—or being told to do so by their staff—just in case they needed one (for example, "How the Candidates Go" 1970). Starting in the late 1970s, non-Jewish politicians could be found wearing yarmulkes during visits to overseas locations of Jewish significance (see Claiborne 1978) and in traditionally non-Jewish governmental ceremonial spaces such as Camp David (Hoagland 1978), the U.S. Capitol building (Clines and Rosellini 1982), and the White House (Freda 1993), where they might be attending an activity related to Judaism. Reflecting the frequency with which both he and other politicians wore yarmulkes, Rudolph Giuliani joked during his 1989 New York mayoral campaign that, rather than a toupee, "[t]he only transplant I've had lately is the yarmulke built onto the back of my head" (Roberts 1989).

By the 1960s, accounts (and photographs) of non-Jewish politicians wearing personalized yarmulkes began appearing in the media. The roots for this phenomenon, however, are found not in American politics but in Jewish American marketing and popular culture. In the years just after World War II, members of newly affluent Jewish communities were able to spend more on celebrations that accompanied life-cycle events, particularly weddings and bar mitzvah ceremonies. One increasingly common

FIGURE 6.2   Wedding yarmulke (interior) (collection of the author)

expense was on "personalized" yarmulkes that included (on the interior) the celebrant's name and the date of the event, which guests could wear during the ceremony and then take home as mementos (Silverman 2013b:188–189) (see Figure 6.2). A do-it-yourself movement in the 1970s Judaism (as reflected in the *Jewish Catalog*; Siegel et al. 1973), combined with the growth of Jewish day schools in the 1980s and 1990s, meant that more was being done with yarmulkes just as more students were wearing them more often (Heilman 2000:3). Manufacturers marketed yarmulkes adorned with popular imagery, largely in response to demand created by parents and teachers trying to keep young Jewish boys interested in wearing them all day every day ("The Yarmulke is Now" 1990). While this resulted in a few notable brushes with the law as corporations sought to protect their brands, as the trend became more popular, rights were secured and offerings expanded (Rovell 2013).[10]

Although often a gift from an admirer, the appearance of a personalized yarmulke on a politician's head came to signal his advancing political ambitions. Hubert Humphrey, for example, received one bearing his monogram during his

1972 presidential campaign (Reeves 1972). George Pataki had one bearing his first name during his 1994 gubernatorial campaign, as did Alphonse D'Amato in his 1998 re-election campaign (Brand 1998; Sack 1994). An admirer crocheted one for Joseph Lieberman after the Senator was named the 2000 Democratic vice-presidential nominee (Shameer 2000). Chris Christie was seen wearing a personalized yarmulke in Jerusalem in 2012, three years before he officially launched his 2016 presidential campaign (Chung 2012); Ron DeSantis was photographed wearing one at the same location seven years later, four years before officially launching his own 2024 presidential campaign ("Photo Release" 2019).

Message on the Medium

The 1952 presidential campaign seems to be the first in which yarmulkes were produced not as gifts to the candidate but as part of a larger marketing strategy for the campaign (for example, see "Eisenhower I Like Ike Foreign Language Buttons" 2023) (see Figures 6.3 and 6.4). Campaign-related yarmulkes were not reported again until 1984, when members of Ronald Reagan's staff produced and distributed yarmulkes, ostensibly as mementos of his visit to a Conservative synagogue one

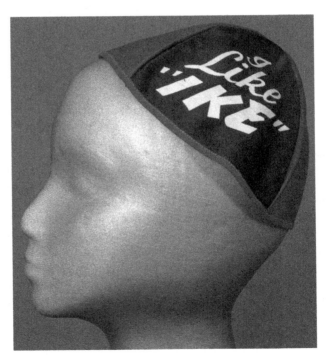

FIGURE 6.3 Eisenhower "I Like Ike" beanie, 1952 (the Susan H. Douglas Political Americana Collection, Division of Rare and Manuscript Collections, Cornell University Library)

FIGURE 6.4   Eisenhower "I Like Ike" yarmulke, 1952 (photograph by Jon Grinspan, National Museum of American History, Smithsonian Institution, and is used with permission)

week before Election Day (Weisman 1984) (see Figure 6.5). Both the Eisenhower and Reagan yarmulkes, however, were not sold but given away by staffers. The first campaign-related yarmulkes to be manufactured, marketed, and sold were those endorsing Lieberman for vice-president in 2000. Reports of these items—which were neither "official campaign material" nor initiated by the campaign—started appearing in September of that year ("On the Trail" 2000). Some identified both Gore and Lieberman; some mentioned only Lieberman. Similar yarmulkes were produced for the 2004 election cycle (Weiss 2003) (see Figure 6.6).

FIGURE 6.5   Yarmulke commemorating Pres. Reagan's trip to synagogue (the image is from the Website of RonWadeButtons.com, and is used with permission)

FIGURE 6.6   Lieberman yarmulkes, 2000 and 2004 (from the collection of the author)

The 2008 election was the first for which yarmulkes were manufactured and sold endorsing the nominees of both major parties. Initially, a small-run batch of "Obama '08" yarmulkes—dubbed "Obama-kahs"—was produced before the primaries by volunteers associated with an organization not officially connected to the Obama campaign ("Obama's Yarmulke" 2007) (see Figure 6.7). By the summer of 2008, one could find manufactured yarmulkes endorsing (or opposing) both the Obama and McCain campaigns (now identified as the "Obamica"/"Obamulke" and the "McKippah," respectively), as well as versions

FIGURE 6.7   The original "Obama-kah" (collection of the author)

FIGURE 6.8   Playful use of Yiddish, 2008 (collection of the author)

endorsing Republican Vice-Presidential candidate Sarah Palin or expressing admiration for John McCain's wife Cindy and Barack Obama's wife Michelle. A number of these yarmulkes used Yiddish and Hebrew words or phrases transliterated into English; others used Hebrew letters (Philologos 2008)[11] (see Figure 6.8).

There was a considerably smaller selection of campaign yarmulkes for the 2012 election cycle, with those endorsing the incumbent mostly replicating designs of the previous election. Fewer of them used Hebrew or Yiddish, even in transliteration, while at least one created a word to fit the circumstance (see Figure 6.9).

FIGURE 6.9   Newt Gingrich campaign yarmulke, 2012 (collection of the author)

FIGURE 6.10   Romney/Ryan campaign yarmulke, 2012 (collection of the author)

However, while those endorsing the Romney/Ryan campaign—identified as "yarMITTkahs," "Romneykas," and (by one writer) "Rom-ulkes" (see Heil 2011; Kamen 2011)—bore the candidates' logo only (see Figure 6.10), some yarmulkes endorsing Obama/Biden incorporated a *mogen David* into the familiar Obama "O."

The 2016 election cycle began early; campaign-related yarmulkes endorsing Hillary Clinton were available by the beginning of the summer, 2014 (Walker and Cannon 2014) (see Figure 6.11). Others followed within the year. Those endorsing Bernie Sanders—dubbed the "Bernika" (see Figure 6.12)—appeared shortly

FIGURE 6.11   Early Clinton yarmulke, 2016 (collection of the author)

FIGURE 6.12   The "Bernika," 2016 (collection of the author)

before the first primaries (Zaltzman 2016a), while those supporting other candidates followed as their fortunes rose and fell throughout the primaries. In late July 2016 a new line of campaign-related yarmulkes became available endorsing both Clinton and Donald Trump (see Figure 6.13).

Although "inauguration" yarmulkes were available before Trump was sworn in (see Figure 6.14), official "Trump 2020" campaign-related yarmulkes were available by 2018, and those endorsing Joseph Biden hit the market by July 2019

FIGURE 6.13   Later 2016 yarmulkes for (from left to right) Clinton, Cruz, and Trump (collection of the author)

FIGURE 6.14   Trump inauguration yarmulke, 2017 (collection of the author)

(Schoenburg 2019). By the height of the primary season, yarmulkes could be purchased endorsing most of the Democratic hopefuls (Richman 2019).[12]

Yarmulkes for the Trump 2024 campaign were available by the 2022 mid-term elections, with Biden yarmulkes appearing the following year.

Parsing the Data

There is no doubt that sales of the 2000 Lieberman yarmulke were aided both by novelty and a lack of competition.[13] The original version sold well online as well as at "brick-and-mortar" establishments, with one vendor reporting that they were "selling like hotcakes, or latkes" (Verdon 2000; Needleman 2008; see also Kennedy 2000). Lieberman's early exit from the 2004 campaign cut into both production and sales; no campaign-related yarmulkes were reported for other candidates.

For the 2008 election cycle, the original "Obama-kahs" sold out in the weeks before Election Day (Walters 2008). The later "Obamicas" and "McKippahs" also sold well, both online and at stores, with sales for the two nominees seeming to be evenly distributed (Needleman 2008). (No sales data for the 2012 election cycle could be located.) In the 2016 cycle, Sanders yarmulkes did well early, while Clinton and Trump versions caught up by mid-March (Kampeas 2016), and sales for these three candidates remained approximately even through Election Day (Yellin 2016). Sales of yarmulkes endorsing other candidates trailed significantly (Kampeas 2016). A new line of yarmulkes became available after the parties' nominating conventions in July and August, with the designer reporting that Trump yarmulkes were outselling his Clinton yarmulkes two to one, expanding to five to one in the last weeks of the campaign ("Kippa Election Tracker" 2016; Oryszczuk 2016).[14]

Early in the 2020 cycle, one vendor reported that Sanders yarmulkes were "what's most in demand" (Richman 2019), while another noted that he was "inundated by requests for the Trump yarmulke" (Yellin 2020). One designer reported in late February that, since 2016, he had sold "roughly 10,000" Trump-related yarmulkes, but that those endorsing Sanders had "picked up in the past few weeks" (Yellin 2020).

While it is almost certain that the initial production and sale of campaign-related yarmulkes was directly related to the nomination of the first Jewish vice-presidential candidate on a major party ticket, there seems to be little relationship between the existence and sales of subsequent yarmulkes and the Jewishness of the candidates. McCain was an Episcopalian-turned-Baptist, Mitt Romney a Mormon. Clinton was raised as a Methodist, Trump was raised as a Presbyterian, Biden a Catholic, and until the summer before he was elected, Obama was a member of the United Church of Christ.[15] Clinton and Romney running mate Paul Ryan had Jewish ancestors, although Clinton's was by marriage and Ryan's was unknown to him until after the election ("Hillary has Jewish Roots" 1999; Chiu 2018).[16] All of the Jewish candidates downplayed their religious identity, and none regularly wore a yarmulke in non-religious circumstances.[17]

As with the candidates, the Jewishness of the designers, while certainly related to the origin of campaign-related yarmulkes, seems not to have been a factor in their sales. All were Jewish, and almost all were (or had been) directly involved with Jewish organizations in the United States or Israel (see Greenwald et al. 2016; Oryszczuk 2016). The most seemingly traditional—the son of a Lubavitcher rabbi—described himself as a "Hasidic Jew with a ton of chutzpah" and was involved in a variety of enterprises, some of them questionable, others potentially illegal (see Duin 2008; "The Royal Tennenhaus" 2009). Another had been exploring his Jewishness for a decade before selling yarmulkes primarily as a vehicle to promote *tikkun olam* ("healing of the world") through gardening (Zaltzman 2016b). Several of the designers were motivated by their desire to promote specific candidates (Ain 2016; Walters et al. 2007), but others did so with a desire to transform yarmulkes—any yarmulkes—into "fashion statements" (Kauffman 2000) that were "culturally significant [and] fun" (Weiss 2003) and that were something "non-Jews also can wear" (Miller 2008; ben Gedalyahu 2008). The four designers of the most popular yarmulkes produced them for both Democratic and Republican candidates.

The Conundrum

Unlike a campaign button or a yard sign, a yarmulke—any yarmulke—is not a secular item; it is unlikely to be purchased by non-Jews (regardless of what is printed on it). This means that the pattern of campaign-related yarmulke sales should not be compared to overall polling trends but to Jewish voting trends, which (as it turns out) differ dramatically from trends in both secular polling and (as we have noted) political yarmulke sales.[18] Since 1928, the estimated percentage of American Jews voting for the Democratic Party has been higher than 60% in all but two elections: 1980 and 1984. It was higher than 80% in 8 of the 17 election cycles between 1932 and 1996 ("U.S. Presidential Elections" 2023). The 2000 Gore/Lieberman ticket—the first to be accompanied by campaign-related yarmulkes—received an estimated 79% of votes cast by American Jews and might have done better had it not been for voter confusion in Florida (see Herron and Lewis 2007). In the campaign-related yarmulke era, the percentage of American Jews voting for the Democratic candidate wavered—from a high of 78% to a low of 69% (in 2008 and 2012, respectively). Between 2000 and 2016—and particularly since 2008 and the introduction of yarmulkes for both major party nominees—the percentage of Jews voting for the Democratic Party has never dropped below 68%, something that cannot be said for 6 of the 12 election cycles before campaign-related yarmulkes were available.[19] Despite this lopsided Democratic representation in the American Jewish community, sales of yarmulkes endorsing candidates from the two major parties sold in numbers that were either equal or that slightly favored Republicans, suggesting that there is more going on here than a random distribution of Jewish consumers purchasing campaign-related yarmulkes.[20]

One possible explanation may be that, because there are different patterns of yarmulke use within the Jewish world, there are also different levels of demand. In 2020, 73% of the American Jewish community identified as Jews "by religion" ("Jewish Americans" 2021:8). Of that group, only 9% identified as Orthodox; the remaining 91% consisted of those who identified as Reform (37%), Conservative (17%), or without denominational affiliation (32%; "Jewish Americans" 2021:14).[21] Of those affiliated with the Reform movement, 85% attended religious services "a few times a year or less"; of those affiliated with the Conservative movement, it was 67%; and of those who were unaffiliated, 98% ("Jewish Americans" 2021:80). Although the Reform movement's official position has shifted (see Goldman 1989), yarmulke wearing is still neither universal nor required. Most non-Orthodox Jews who do wear yarmulkes do so only while engaging in Jewish ritual (in the synagogue or at home), and because most synagogues provide yarmulkes on site, many non-Orthodox Jews who own several get them as gifts, at a Jewish function, while visiting Israel, or by accidentally returning home still wearing the one they used at the synagogue. Those who attend religious services infrequently (or not at all) have little use for a yarmulke of any design and therefore might purchase a campaign-related yarmulke as a novelty or as a statement in support of a particular candidate. However, it seems unlikely that they would feel motivated to purchase more than one, be it campaign-related or not. Of those who identify as Orthodox, 84% reported attending services "once or twice a month" or more ("Jewish Americans" 2021:80). As one vendor noted, non-Orthodox Jews might wear a yarmulke a few times a year, but Orthodox Jewish men and boys wear them all the time, meaning that they are likely not only to have more than one, but they are also more likely to buy more than one.[22]

Additionally, Orthodox Jews who are more likely to purchase multiple yarmulkes are also more likely to vote Republican. A recent survey noted that, while approximately 70% of the American Jewish community tends to favor the Democratic Party, nearly 60% of those who identify as Orthodox identify as conservative, and 75% identify as (or lean) Republican ("Jewish Americans" 2021:159). This suggests that not only are Orthodox Jews more likely to purchase more yarmulkes, but they also aremore likely to purchase those endorsing a Republican candidate over those endorsing a Democratic candidate. We might conclude that the approximately balanced sale of campaign-related yarmulkes is because, while there are many more non-Orthodox Jews than there are Orthodox Jews (who, as we noted, constitute only 9% of the 73% who identify as "Jewish by religion"), the Orthodox have a greater need for yarmulkes, buy more yarmulkes, and are more likely to buy yarmulkes endorsing Republicans than Democrats. It seems reasonable that fewer Orthodox Jews buying a plentitude of yarmulkes might equal that of many non-Orthodox Jews buying few (or no) yarmulkes. That is, the surprising volume of Republican-endorsing campaign-related yarmulkes sold (as compared to Jewish voting trends) might be due to the demands of Orthodox Jews who need and use more yarmulkes, while the volume of Democratic-endorsing yarmulkes sold was—by comparison—lower than expected because, while there are many more non-Orthodox Jews, they need, use, and therefore purchase fewer yarmulkes.

But beyond demographics and patterns of use, it is likely that some level of enthusiasm (similar to that felt by consumers purchasing specific brands) better explains the sale of political yarmulkes. As we noted earlier, Lieberman yarmulkes (though few in number) sold well because of enthusiasm for the candidate—what one Gore spokesperson called "Liebermania" (Dizikes 2000). However, there wasn't another Jewish candidate seeking a spot on a major party ticket until 2016; if the religion of the candidate is not the issue, certainly there must be some other source.

The answer may be found reflected in the curiosity one designer articulated during the 2016 cycle when he noted that yarmulkes endorsing Sanders (reputed to be secular) and Trump (reputed to be antisemitic) were his best sellers (Gerber 2016). As with any "brand-bearing" product, the choice to purchase either Sanders and Trump yarmulkes—or any of the various campaign-related yarmulkes—is likely as much about what the buyer perceives each of the candidates stands for as it is about the item itself. Sanders seemed more like the majority of the American Jewish community, "a mix of religious ambivalence and ethnic pride" (Eden 2016) and was perceived as more concerned about issues other than the State of Israel, just like most American Jews (only 45% of whom considered "caring about Israel" to be an "essential part of what being Jewish means" to them; see "Jewish Americans" 2021:66). This "Jewish Everyman" quality may explain why Sanders was particularly popular with younger Jewish voters. In 2020, 27% of American Jews thought of themselves similarly to Sanders—that is, "Jews of no religion"—a percentage that increased as the respondents got younger. Of those born between 1971 and 1990, the percentage was 33%; of those born between 1991 and 2002, it was 40% ("Jewish Americans" 2021:8). Inversely, while 52% of those born before 1955 privileged "caring about Israel," the percentages decreased with each age cohort: 49% of those born between 1956 and 1970, 43% of those born between 1971 and 1990, and 35% of those born between 1990 and 2002 ("Jewish Americans" 2021:66). In other words, as the age of the respondents lowered, "caring about Israel" became less important, while the percentage of those identifying as "Jews of no religion" increased. Not surprisingly, Sanders campaign merchandise sold well at open rallies, likely because of the enthusiasm of younger voters who attended them (see Kampeas 2016; Talbot 2015).

Initially, on the issue of Israel, Trump benefitted from Sanders's lack, and yarmulkes endorsing him also sold well at mass events, although not at campaign rallies.[23] In 2016, the best location for the sale of Republican-endorsing yarmulkes was the annual policy conference of the American Israel Public Affairs Committee (AIPAC; see Richter 2016).[24] This should come as no surprise. Historically bipartisan, over the last few election cycles, AIPAC has become decidedly more Republican (see Eisner 2022). It has long been home to Jewish "neocons," whose strong interests in foreign relations, military preparedness, and the promotion of democracy overseas have intersected with AIPAC's staunch support for Israel (High 2009). Even so, it has shifted rightward as the perception has grown that the Democratic Party is increasingly antagonistic toward the state of Israel (Saad 2023). This has brought more Jewish conservatives—who already attended AIPAC conferences—into greater view in the Republican Party. This would include some Reform Jews, but most noticeably it has included an increasing number of Orthodox and *Haredi* Jews who (as we noted earlier) already leaned Republican (see Heilman 2023), and for 53% of whom identified "care for Israel" as an "essential part of what being Jewish means"—second only to Conservative Jews (at 66%; "Jewish Americans" 2021:66). Again, not surprisingly, one journalist reported that AIPAC conference attendees bought "several thousand" Trump yarmulkes at the 2018 conference (Schoenburg 2018).

This shift did not begin with the 2016 election but followed an arc also traced by Joe Lieberman. Always a political moderate, six years after joining Gore on the Democratic ticket, Lieberman left the party and became an Independent after losing the Connecticut Democratic primary. In 2008, he endorsed McCain over Obama in a speech at the Republican Convention, criticizing the Democratic candidate for his position on Israel. Lieberman's name was floated as a potential running mate for McCain in 2008 (Enda 2017). While McCain ultimately named Sarah Palin instead, McCain was still viewed favorably within the Jewish community (Kampeas 2017), possibly explaining the strong sales of McCain/Palin yarmulkes (Needleman 2008).[25] In addition, *Haredi* Jews who once shunned national partisan politics have joined the Orthodox and become more involved politically ("The GOP Dons a Kippah" 2015; Spitzer 2022). This would seem to explain the popularity of Republican campaign-related yarmulkes in Israel, home to nearly 200,000 Americans eligible to vote in the United States (see Estrin 2020).

The Medium *IS* the Message

While we can now be a bit more confident about who might be purchasing the various campaign-related yarmulkes and why they are purchasing the particular ones when they do so, we are still left with the question of why they are doing so in the first place. On the one hand, we have yarmulkes endorsing Democratic candidates likely being purchased by Jews who are less likely to use them for religious purposes (that is, wear them in synagogue). On the other hand, we have campaign-related yarmulkes endorsing Republican candidates likely being purchased by Jews who are more likely to use them for religious purposes but are purchasing them at non-religious events and (from the lack of reports) are either wearing them in synagogue without controversy or not wearing them in synagogue but somewhere else.

The most telling evidence that the campaign-related yarmulkes are being used for political rather than religious purposes is the complete lack of evidence to the contrary. Initially, major national news outlets—including the Associated Press, *Economist*, and *Life*—provided most of the coverage, while a few regional secular and Jewish outlets covered local angles: local designers and their yarmulkes appearing at local events. By 2008, while major news and trade outlets—including the *Wall Street Journal*, *Washington Times*, *AdRants*, and *Advertising Age*—still covered the story and regional coverage still seemed motivated by local connections, Jewish news outlets based in the United States and in Israel but with international Jewish readership—including *Forward*, *Haaretz*, and the Jewish Telegraphic Agency—provided the most coverage. All took notice when figures of national prominence were spotted wearing the items (for example, see Heil and Brotherton 2008), but by the end of the 2016 cycle, national secular media coverage was completely dwarfed by coverage in Jewish media outlets.

The earliest coverage may have been broad because of the item's novelty, but it was clear that over the five election cycles between 2000 and 2020 campaign-related yarmulkes became *de rigueur*. Nonetheless, none of the Jewish media reported any controversy over the use of the political yarmulkes in synagogue—the one place where one might expect it, and where one might expect a reaction to it. Instead, responses from both liberal and conservative critics were aimed at profaning the yarmulke itself and not the space in which it was used. Liberal Michael Lerner argued that advertising and profiting from the sale of campaign-related yarmulkes was a "misuse of a religious object" (Needleman 2008), while conservative Gil Troy identified it as *avoda zara* ("idol worship"; Troy 2016). One critic, a registered Republican—apparently oblivious to non-political yarmulkes bearing commercial logos—argued that "advertising on a kippah is inconsistent with Jewish ideology" (Needleman 2008). Only former Nixon speechwriter William Safire registered a location-specific critique of turning "a religious sanctuary into the site of the most distasteful political rally of the year," and that was in response to the Reagan yarmulkes of 1984, which were neither purchased by congregants nor brought into the sanctuary by them (Safire 1984). Nonetheless, the yarmulkes were popular at public events, in attendance with non-Jews (Sanders rallies and the Republican National Convention; see Cortellessa 2016) and with mostly or exclusively Jewish participants (AIPAC and the national meeting of the Republican Jewish Coalition; see Posner 2022).

Like all religions, Judaism has its performative aspects. Lynn Neal examines the use of T-shirts as vehicles for anti-Muslim sentiments, arguing that it is the very "Americanness" of the shirt that makes its message acceptable (Neal 2014). In a parallel way, the campaign-related yarmulke seems to serve as a signal to others that the wearer belongs. When worn among Jews, any yarmulke would be a common enough sight to draw no unusual attention. In these circumstances, it is the message on the yarmulke that matters most. Just as a Nike yarmulke and a Yankee yarmulke express brand loyalty, the campaign-related yarmulke signals the preferences of the wearer, albeit political preferences. While this might be an unusual sight inside the synagogue, since a yarmulke is also worn in other circumstances, it is hardly scandalous. When worn among non-Jews, however, a yarmulke identifies the wearer as "other." In these circumstances, while a yarmulke might marginalize the wearer, the accompanying political message serves as a signal—and an assertion—of belonging in the group, either as a fellow partisan (in groups of like-minded individuals) or as a fellow American (as a citizen involved in the political debates of the day). Because it is an item associated with religious practice, it is protected as an expression of religious freedom just as its wearer is protected as a religious person. For those who purchase the political yarmulke but do not wear it—particularly those who rarely attend religious services—its meaning as a statement of political preference is marginal. For these purchasers, the yarmulkes "express the thoroughly modern values of individualism, taste, and sometimes mere amusement" (Silverman 2013b:190). Unused for its religious purpose, its political purpose is to serve as a token exchanged for a contribution, a financial or emotional commitment to the cause, but also as a seemingly religious act with no actual religious cost. For those who purchase it and wear it outside of the synagogue, it serves as a political statement, either to fellow Jews who are not distracted by the item on which the message is set or to non-Jews who may be entirely distracted by the item but reassured by the message it bears that the wearer is "one of us." Like the Nike and Yankee yarmulkes, campaign-related yarmulkes serve as "the quintessential signs of modern identity," permitting wearers to "resist, even as they embrace, acculturation" (Silverman 2013a:183). As a scholar of American Orthodox Judaism, Samuel Heilman declared shortly after Lieberman's nomination at the very beginning of the campaign-related yarmulke era, "these days one need not simply be an American Jew but rather can be a proud Jewish American, one whose religious and ethnic identity modifies his American identity rather than the other way around" (Heilman 2000).

Post Script

In response to the appearance of campaign-related yarmulkes, one shocked rabbi asked, "Would anybody put 'Vote for McCain' or 'Vote for Obama' on a cross?"

(Needleman 2008). It is a good question, revealing how unique the item is in both political marketing and religious identity formation. One wonders if it will stop here. In the Jewish world, the next obvious target would be the *tallit*, the prayer shawl worn by approximately the same demographic as the yarmulke.[26] Unlike the yarmulke, because the *tallit* bears *tzitzit* ("fringes on the corners of their garments"; see Numbers 15:38–40), the person who wears it is expected to recite a prayer before putting it on, an indication that the act is commanded by God. Nonetheless, like the yarmulke, the *tallit* has recently been insinuated into debates over Jewish identity, primarily involving sexual and gender egalitarianism (see Engber 2012; Gordan 2013; Hajdenberg 2023).[27] However, because a number of Christian groups have "long interwoven Jewish or Hebrew rituals into services while also revering Jesus Christ as the Messiah" (Kestenbaum 2016; see also Kaiser 2014), it also has entered the electoral political arena, albeit in Christian sacred space, but (so far) without campaign logos or images ("Donald Trump Dons Jewish Prayer Shawl" 2016). However, if what we have explored here is correct, there is little danger of the *tallit* following in the way of the yarmulke, at least in a Jewish context. Even though the *tallit* has come to serve as another marker of Jewishness in popular culture (for example, during the wedding reception in the pilot for *The Marvelous Mrs. Maisel*), its limitations to specific spaces and—most importantly—specific uses mean that, unlike the campaign-related yarmulke, the *tallit* will serve to mark neither secular politics to other Jews nor religio-identity politics to non-Jews.

Notes

1 An earlier version of this chapter was presented at the 2018 Association for Jewish Studies annual meeting. Special thanks to Jason Erkes, Jon Grinspan, and Matt Walters for their material assistance, and Virginia Wesleyan University for very generous research and travel support.
2 The etymology of "*yarmulke*" and "*kippah*" is uncertain (on the former, see Plaut 1955; on the latter, see Philologos 2016). Often used interchangeably, according to Philologos, "all kippot and yarmulkes are skullcaps, and every yarmulke is a kippah, not every kippah is a yarmulke." One scholar points out that a preference of terms may be generational, with *kippah* preferred by those who "tend to be younger, have at least some knowledge of Israeli Hebrew, and/or have visited or lived in Israel" (Gold 1987:183). Yarmulke, however, seems to be preferred by non-Jewish media outlets. A search of the *New York Times* (covering publication from 1851 to 2014, conducted on 16 February 2018) revealed that "yarmulke" (and variant spellings: *yarmulka/yamilke/yamulke/yarm alke*) appeared 1,128 times; "kippah" (and variant spelling *kippa* and plural form *kippot*) appeared 26 times. However, for most American Jews, it is a difference without a distinction. For simplicity, in this chapter I use "yarmulke" unless quoting a source directly.
3 For discussions of yarmulkes and gender, see Darwin (2017); Milligan (2013); Milligan (2014).
4 In this chapter, "Conservative Jews" refers to those affiliated with the Conservative movement (denomination). Jewish conservatives are Jews who may belong to any Jewish movement but are traditional in their attitudes toward secular politics and culture. "Tradition-bound" Jews (sometimes called "Torah-true" Jews) are predominantly (but not exclusively) Orthodox and *Haredi* ("ultra-Orthodox") Jews for whom the fulfillment of the *mitzvot* ("commandments") is of central personal and communal importance.

5 David Domke and Kevin Coe define "broadcasting" as the use of behaviors and rhetoric "with most audiences and in most contexts with little risk of offending moderate voters." "Narrowcasting," therefore, is the use of behaviors and rhetoric to "target a particular constituency with words and actions that are public but that fly below the radar of most Americans" (2008:73). Giving a commencement speech is broadcasting; giving a commencement speech at Notre Dame University or Bob Jones University may be narrowcasting.

6 For a discussion of the decline of men's hats, see Steinberg (2004).

7 Justice Scalia regularly wore one that was a gift from a Catholic organization and likely considered more like a *zucchetto* (see Zuckerman 2013)—a difference without much of a visual distinction.

8 This is not to suggest that politicians did not visit Jewish locations prior to this, or that they did so inappropriately adorned. Some wore hats (per synagogue custom), others attended non-liturgical events where head coverings were not expected, and still others attended events at Reform synagogues where head coverings were not required.

9 One writer suggests that a photo of Robert Kennedy wearing a yarmulke was integral in Sirhan Sirhan's decision to assassinate him two weeks later (see Schumacher 2018:269).

10 According to one report, the Children's Television Workshop prohibited one vendor from selling unlicensed *Sesame Street* yarmulkes, while others (bearing the trademark "swoosh") were confiscated as part of a larger investigation by Nike officials (who did not pursue the matter further; Kershaw 2000).

11 Examples include "My Bubby [grandmother] is voting Obama," "John McCain is Zayer Shain" [great], "Michelle [or Cindy] is my Rebbitzin [wife of a rabbi]," and "Sarah Barrajewdah Eshet Chayl" [woman of valor; see Proverbs 31:10] (Gersten 2008). Because of how Hebrew is written, Palin's name on one yarmulke could be read as "fleen."

12 One version of the Biden/Harris yarmulke transliterated the first letter of each of their last names into Hebrew, suggesting (to the creator, if not others) the phrases *baruch haShem* (colloquially translated to mean "thank…" or "praise God") and *b'ezrat haShem* (colloquially translated as "with God's help") (Zaltzman 2020).

13 The data on sales are not intended to be scientific. Overall sales numbers were low and reporting of those numbers was sporadic, incomplete, and anecdotal. As conservative pundit Ann Coulter tweeted in response to the apparent pandering of Jews by Republican candidates during a September 16, 2015, debate: "How many fucking Jews do these people think there are in the United States?"

14 Most of the designers also sold the items in person, online, or wholesale (to vendors who sold the items online or in established stores).

15 In late October 2020, Trump announced that he no longer considered himself a Presbyterian but "a non-denominational Christian" (Silliman 2020).

16 A number of the candidates have Jewish descendants: Clinton's son-in-law, Trump's daughter (by conversion) and her children, and Biden's two daughters-in-law (and their children) and son-in-law (see Savage 2010; David 2020).

17 On Lieberman, see Goodstein (2000); on Sanders, see Berger (2016). Both were criticized for the ways in which they deflected attention to the issue: Lieberman through humor (see Bronner 2003:40; Kellman 2007:50), Sanders through obfuscation (see Lieber 2016; Prager 2016). One writer argued that Sanders was "the most Christian candidate in the race" (Prothero 2016)—a comment likely meant to shame the actual Christian candidates, but which seemed to negate Sanders's Jewishness for him.

18 By comparison, between 1980 and 2008 the most reliable predictor of election outcomes was the sale of Halloween masks in the likenesses of the nominees (Cendrowski 2008:12).

19 Voting data for 2020 is not included here; traditional exit polling was not conducted that year because of the increased use of early and mail-in balloting ("U.S. Presidential Elections" 2023).

20 While there is some "traffic" in Lieberman yarmulkes (which can be found for sale online), there is little for any of the campaign-related yarmulkes produced since. While this does not rule out the possibility that at least some of the political yarmulkes were purchased by collectors (including this author), it does suggest that, since 2008, those who purchased them have held on to them (and thereby also invested them with significance beyond religious use, like this author).

21 The remaining 4% identified as affiliated with other, smaller Jewish movements—Reconstructionism, Jewish Renewal, etc.—with a rounding error of 1%.

22 Personal conversation with Daniel Levine, owner of J. Levine Books and Judaica (26 August 2018). One designer expressed optimism that Rosh Hashanah, Yom Kippur, and Sukkot—all major holidays that occur in the weeks before Election Day—would be his best opportunity to increase sales among the occasional wearers (ben Gedalyahu 2008).

23 A 2022 analysis of 300 Trump rallies before the 2016 election concluded that "Trump's political message activated attentive whites' sense of threat and prejudice toward racial, ethnic, and religious minorities and encouraged a number of people to act on that threat" (Feinberg et al. 2022:263).

24 Nearly 20,000 delegates attended the 2016 conference, at which Trump, Clinton, Cruz, and Kasich spoke, but not Sanders (Phillip and Johnson 2016).

25 It might also explain the popularity of Sarah Palin wigs ("Palin Wigs" 2008).

26 Properly called a *tallit gadol* (lit.: "large tallit"), the item is worn by those who have passed bar/bat mitzvah age (although in some Orthodox congregations, it is limited to married men.) The *tallit katan* (lit.: "small tallit") is worn by the most tradition-bound Jewish men and boys. It is available (mostly in child sizes) with images imprinted on it which—because they are on an item that is worn as an undergarment—could not communicate any kind of message in public space, be it communal or political.

27 It is worth noting that, while many non-Orthodox women wear a yarmulke, and yarmulkes have been available endorsing female non-Jewish politicians since 2016, I am unaware of any female presidential candidate being photographed wearing a yarmulke (of any design).

Works Cited

Ain, Stewart (2016). "Filling the Trump Void." *New York Jewish Week* (17 August); available online: <http://jewishweek.timesofisrael.com/filling-the-trump-void/> (accessed 8 May 2018).

"Bad Blood Stirred Up" (1884). *New York Times* (19 October): 3.

ben Gedalyahu, Tzvi (2008). "Obama, McCain Supporters Have Kippot on the Brain." *Arutz Sheva* [Israel] (28 July); available online: <https://www.israelnationalnews.com/news/126976> (accessed 17 January 2018).

Berger, Joseph (2016). "Bernie Sanders Is Jewish, but He Doesn't Like to Talk About It." *New York Times* (24 February); available online: <https://www.nytimes.com/2016/02/25/us/politics/bernie-sanders-jewish.html> (accessed 4 April 2018).

Brand, Rick (1998). "Campaign '98: Jewish Vote Likely to be Vital." [New York] *Newsday* (7 October).

Bronner, Simon J. (2003). "The Lieberman Syndrome: Public and Private Jewishness in American Political Culture." *Journal of Modern Jewish Studies* 2, 1: 35–58.

"Bryan Tells Jews of World's Needs" (1923). [Jewish Telegraphic Agency] *Daily News Bulletin* (4 December): 5.

"Cap Revives Court Custom" (1989). *New York Times* (21 January): 9.

Cendrowski, Scott (2008). "Election Tricks." *Fortune* 158, 6 (September 29): 12–13.

Chiu, Allyson (2018). "A Surprise in Paul Ryan's Ancestry." *Washington Post* (3 August); available online: <https://www.washingtonpost.com/news/morning-mix/wp/2018/08/01/a-surprise-in-paul-d-ryans-ancestry-hes-slightly-jewish/> (accessed 21 January 2022).

Chung, Jen (2012). "Chris Christie in Israel: Personalized Yarmulke, 2016 Rumors." *Gothamist* (3 April 2012); available online: <https://gothamist.com/news/chris-christie-in-israel-personalized-yarmulke-2016-rumors> (accessed 27 February 2023).

Claiborne, William (1978). "Mondale Heckled, Applauded on Visit to the Wailing Wall." *Washington Post* (1 July): A12.

Clines, Francis X., and Lynn Rosellini (1982). "Briefing." *New York Times* (11 May): A16.

Cortellessa, Eric (2016). "Outside the Republican Convention, Jews Talk Trump." *Times of Israel* (19 July); available online: <https://www.timesofisrael.com/outside-convention-jews-talk-trump/> (accessed 22 April 2018).

Darwin, Helana (2017). "Jewish Women's Kippot: Meanings and Motives." *Contemporary Jewry* 37, 1: 81–97.

David, Keren (2020). "Joe Biden's Very Jewish Family." [London] *Jewish Chronicle* (9 November); available online: <https://www.thejc.com/news/world/joe-biden-s-very-jewish-family-1.508420> (accessed 17 February 2023).

Dizikes, Peter (2000). "Lieberman First National Jewish Candidate." *ABC News* (8 August); available online: <http://abcnews.go.com/Politics/story?id=121120&page=1> (accessed 27 March 2016); "Notes and Quotes from Campaign 2000."

Domke, David, and Kevin Coe (2008). *The God Strategy: How Religion Became a Political Weapon in America*. New York, NY: Oxford University Press.

"Donald Trump Dons Jewish Prayer Shawl at Black Church in Detroit." *Jewish Telegraphic Agency* (4 September 2016); available online: <https://www.jta.org/2016/09/04/news-opinion/politics/pastor-gifts-trump-a-tallit-during-visit-to-detroit-black-church> (accessed 25 February 2018).

Duin, Julia (2008). "Obama, McCain Yarmulkes." *Washington Times* (26 July); available online: <https://www.washingtontimes.com/blog/belief-blog/2008/jul/26/obamamccain-yarmulkes/> (accessed 9 April 2018).

Eden, Ami (2016). "Why Bernie Sanders Isn't Beating Joe Lieberman on Jewish Pride." *Jewish Telegraphic Agency* (9 February); available online: <https://www.jta.org/2016/02/09/politics/did-bernie-sanders-just-steal-joe-liebermans-jewish-crown> (accessed 27 March 2016).

"Eisenhower I Like Ike Foreign Language Buttons, ca. 1952-1956" (2023). Susan H. Douglas Political Americana Collection, #2214. *Division of Rare and Manuscript Collections, Cornell University Library*; available online: <https://digital.library.cornell.edu/catalog/ss:10637465> (accessed 18 February 2023).

Eisner, Jane (2022). "Can AIPAC Still Claim the Middle Ground?" *Religion & Politics* (28 June); available online: <https://religionandpolitics.org/2022/06/28/can-aipac-still-claim-the-middle-ground/> (accessed 22 March 2023).

Enda, Jodi (2017). "Why Democrats Don't Like Joe Lieberman." *CNN Politics* (19 May); available online: <https://www.cnn.com/2017/05/19/politics/why-democrats-dont-like-joe-lieberman/index.html> (accessed 18 June 2023).

Engber, Corinne (2012). "Genderqueer Tallit Maker Weaves Nature and Prayer in Designs for LGBTQ+ Jews." *JewishBoston* (16 March); available online: <https://www.jewishboston.com/read/genderqueer-tallit-maker-weaves-nature-and-prayer-in-designs-for-lgbtq-jews/> (accessed 17 June 2023).

Estrin, Daniel (2020). "'Highly Motivated': In Israel, U.S. Voters Lean Toward Trump." *NPR* (3 November); available online: <https://www.npr.org/2020/11/03/930472425/highly-motivated-in-israel-u-s-voters-lean-toward-trump> (accessed 5 November 2020).

Feinberg, Ayal, Regina Branton, and Valerie Martinez-Ebers (2022). "The Trump Effect: How 2016 Campaign Rallies Explain Spikes in Hate." *PS, Political Science & Politics* 55, 2 (April): 257–265.

Freda, Ernie (1993). "It's a Hair-Raising Hanukkah Party in the Oval Office." *Atlanta Journal-Constitution* (9 December): A18.

Gerber, Drew (2016). "The 'Kippah Guy' Comes to Cleveland, Bearing Donald Trump (and Hillary) Yarmulkes." *Forward* (18 July); available online: <https://forward.com/news/345364/the-kippah-guy-comes-to-cleveland-bearing-donald-trump-and-hillary-yarmulke/> (accessed 22 April 2018).

Gersten, Lana (2008). "The Kippah Campaign." *Forward* (8 August): 2.

Gold, David L. (1987). "The Etymology of the English Noun yarmlke 'Jewish skullcap' and the Obsolescent Hebrew Noun yarmulka 'idem." *Jewish Language Review* 7: 180–199.

Goldberger, Frimet (2015). "Show Me Your Yarmulke: The Complete Guide to the Jewish Headgear." *Forward* (6 February); available online: <https://forward.com/articles/213738/show-me-your-yarmulke/> (accessed 9 December 2017).

Goldman, Ari L. (1989). "Reform Jews are Returning to Ritual." *New York Times* (26 June): A14.

Goodstein, Laurie (2000). "Lieberman Balances Private Faith with Life in the Public Eye." *New York Times* (18 August): A19.

"The GOP Dons a Kippah (and Even a Black Hat)" (2015). *Forward* (8 May): 8.

Gordan, Rachel (2013). "'What a Strange Power There Is in Clothing': Women's Tallitot." In *Fashioning Jews: Clothing, Culture, and Commerce*, ed Leonard J. Greenspoon, 167–176. West Lafayette, IN: Purdue University Press.

"Gov. Wilson's Head Cut in Auto Shake-Up" (1912). *New York Times* (4 November): 1.

Greenwald, Carol, Richard Allen, Eve Stieglitz, and Louis Sokol (2016). "Two Reasons Trump Deserves the Jewish Vote." *Forward* (12 August); available online: <https://forward.com/community/347562/two-reasons-trump-deserves-the-jewish-vote/> (accessed 20 March 2023).

Grossman, Lawrence (2010). "The Kippah Comes to America." In *Continuity and Change: A Festschrift in Honor of Irving (Yitz) Greenberg's 75th Birthday*, eds Steven T. Katz and Steven Bayme, 129–150. Lanham, MD: University Press of America.

Hajdenberg, Jackie (2023). "Embracing Their Place on 'the Fringes,' Queer Artists Reimagine Jewish Ritual Garments for All Bodies." *Jewish Telegraphic Agency* (3 January); available online: <https://www.jta.org/2023/01/03/religion/embracing-their-place-on-the-fringes-queer-artists-reimagine-jewish-ritual-garments-for-all-bodies> (accessed 17 June 2023).

Heil, Emily (2011). "Obalmulke or yarMITTkah?" *Washington Post* (15 December); available online: <https://www.washingtonpost.com/blogs/in-the-loop/post/obalmulke-or-yarmittkah/2011/12/15/gIQAh4eVwO_blog.html> (accessed 22 April 2013).

Heil, Emily, and Elizabeth Brotherton (2008). "Huck: Slim and CBS-Bound?" *Roll Call* (3 September): "Heard on the Hill."

Heilman, Samuel C. (2000). "The Lieberman Phenomenon." *Edah Journal* 1, 1: 1–4; available online: <http://www.edah.org/backend/JournalArticle/heilman.pdf> (accessed 25 February 2018).

Heilman, Samuel (2023). "The Modern Orthodox in America." In *Routledge Handbook of Jewish Ritual and Practice*, ed Oliver Leaman, 193–202. New York, NY: Routledge.

Herron, Michael, and Jeffrey Lewis (2007). "Did Ralph Nader Spoil a Gore Presidency? A Ballot-Level Study of Green and Reform Party Voters in the 2000 Presidential Election." *Quarterly Journal of Political Science* 2, 3: 205–226.

High, Brandon (2009). "The Recent Historiography of American Neoconservatism." *Historical Journal* 52, 2 (June): 475–491.

"Hillary Has Jewish Roots" (1999). *CBS News* (6 August); available online: <https://www.cbsnews.com/news/hillary-has-jewish-roots/> (accessed 4 March 2018).

Hoagland, Jim (1978). "The Stage Is Set for Decisive Action in Camp David Political Mystery-Thriller." *Washington Post* (11 September): A24.

"How the Candidates Go After the Jewish Vote" (1970). *New York Times* (13 September): E7.

Jewish Americans in 2020 (2021). *Pew Research Center* (11 May); available online: <https://www.pewresearch.org/religion/2021/05/11/jewish-americans-in-2020/> (accessed 7 June 2023).

"Jews Honor Eisenhower for Freeing Nazi Camps" (1965). *New York Times* (29 May): 12.

Joselit, Jenna Weissman (1990). *New York's Jewish Jews: The Orthodox Community in the Interwar Years*. Bloomington, IN: Indiana University Press.

Kaiser, Menachem (2014). "For Some Believers Trying To Connect With Jesus, the Answer Is To Live Like a Jew." *Tablet* (4 February); available online: <http://www.tabletmag.com/jewish-life-and-religion/161086/observing-torah-like-jesus> (accessed 25 February 2018).

Kamen, Al (2011). "Newt and Mitt for the Exacta?" *Washington Post* (16 December): A30.

Kampeas, Ron (2016). "Donald Trump, Bernie Sanders Leading the Candidate Kippah Race." *Jewish Telegraphic Agency* (19 April); available online: <https://www.jta.org/2016/04/19/news-opinion/politics/donald-trump-bernie-sanders-leading-the-all-important-kippah-race> (accessed 4 April 2018).

Kampeas, Ron (2017). "4 Times John McCain Went Maverick with Jewish Friends." *Times of Israel* (20 July); available online: <https://www.timesofisrael.com/4-times-john-mccain-went-maverick-with-jewish-friends/> (accessed 21 January 2022).

Kauffman, Matthew (2000). "Joe Goes to Their Heads." *Hartford Courant* (13 September); available online: <https://www.courant.com/news/connecticut/hc-xpm-2000-09-13-0009130293-story.html> (accessed 19 January 2022).

Kellman, Steven G. (2007). "Just A Jew Named Joe." *Shofar* 25, 2: 49–62.

Kennedy, Helen (2000). "The Buzz: As Skullcaps Go, It's a No-Brainer." *New York Daily News* (31 August); available online: <https://www.nydailynews.com/archives/news/buzz-article-1.879993> (accessed 24 February 2018).

Kershaw, Sarah (2000). "A Sign of Judaism Gets a Swoosh." *New York Times* (19 April): B1+.

Kestenbaum, Sam (2016). "Explained: Why Did Donald Trump Wear a Prayer Shawl—and Why Are Jews So Upset?" *Forward* (6 September); available online: <https://forward.com/news/349275/explained-why-did-donald-trump-wear-a-jewish-prayer-shawl-and-why-are-jews/> (accessed 24 February 2018).

"Kippa Election Tracker Predicts Big Trump Victory Among Orthodox Jews" (2016). [Teaneck, NJ] *Jewish Link* (3 November); available online: <https://jewishlink.news/features/15374-kippa-election-tracker-predicts-big-trump-victory-among-orthodox-jews> (accessed 19 January 2022).

Lieber, Valerie (2016). "We Need to Out Bernie Sanders as a Jew – For His Own Good." *Forward* (20 February); available online: <https://forward.com/opinion/333799/we-need-to-out-bernie-sanders-as-a-jew-for-his-own-good/> (accessed 8 June 2016).

"Mayor Urges U.S. Jews to Offset Nazi Ruin" (1946). *New York Times* (27 May): 2.

Miller, Jessica (2008). "Must Have: Obamica Yarmulkes from Vanity Kippah." *Jewcy.com* (15 August); available online: <http://jewcy.com/post/must_have_obamica_yarmulkes_vanity_kippah> (accessed 17 January 2018).

Milligan, Amy K. (2013). "Colours of the Jewish Rainbow: A Study of Homosexual Jewish Men and Yarmulkes." *Journal of Modern Jewish Studies* 12, 1 (March): 71–89.

Milligan, Amy K. (2014). "Expanding Sisterhood: Jewish Lesbians and Externalizations of Jewishness." *Journal of Lesbian Studies* 18, 4: 437–455.

Neal, Lynn (2014). "The Ideal Democratic Apparel: T-Shirts, Religious Intolerance, and the Clothing of Democracy." *Material Religion* 10, 2: 182–207.

Needleman, Sarah E. (2008). "Some Jewish Voters Wear Their Hearts on Their Heads." *Wall Street Journal* (29 September): A18.

"Obama's Yarmulke" (2007). *Forward* (5 September); available online: <https://forward.com/news/israel/11544/obama-s-yarmulke-00429/> (accessed 24 February 2018).

"On the Trail" (2000). *Economist* (30 September):30.

Oryszczuk, Stephen (2016). "Ex-IDF Men Selling Trump and Clinton Kippot to Gauge Support." [British] *Jewish News* (8 August); available online: <https://www.jewish-news.co.uk/ex-idf-men-selling-trump-and-clinton-kippot-to-gauge-support/> (accessed 19 January 2022).

Osnes, Larry G. (1967). "Charles W. Bryan: 'His Brother's Keeper." *Nebraska History* 48, 45–68.

"Palin Wigs Should Be Popular in Orthodox Jewish Neighborhoods" (2008). [Middletown, NY] *Times Herald-Record* (23 October); available online: <https://www.recordonline.com/story/news/2008/10/23/palin-wigs-should-be-popular/52222623007/ > (accessed 21 June 2023).

Phillip, Abby, and Jenna Johnson (2016). "Presidential Candidates Tell AIPAC They Will Stand Behind Israel." *Washington Post* (21 March); available online: <https://www.washingtonpost.com/politics/2016/03/21/854e1ede-ef7b-11e5-85a6-2132cf446d0a_story.html> (accessed 7 June 2023).

Philologos (2008). "Putting a Campaign Spotlight on the (Hebrew) Character Issue." *Forward* (23 October); available online: <http://www.forward.com/articles/14418/ (accessed 8 August 2011).

Philologos (2016). "Skullcap, Kippah, or Yarmulke?" *Mosaic* (27 January); available online: <https://mosaicmagazine.com/observation/2016/01/skullcap-kippah-or-yarmulke/> (accessed 17 December 2017).

"Photo Release: Governor Ron DeSantis Visits the Western Wall and the Church of the Holy Sepulchre" (2019). *Ron DeSantis: 46ᵗʰ Governor of Florida* (30 May); available online: <https://www.flgov.com/2019/05/30/photo-release-governor-ron-desantis-visits-the-western-wall-and-the-church-of-the-holy-sepulchre/> (accessed 12 May 2023).

Plaut, W. Gunther (1955). "The Origin of the Word 'Yarmulke." *Hebrew Union College Annual* 26: 567–570.

"Politics in Connecticut" (1884). *New York Times* (27 October): 1.

Posner, Nathan (2022). "RJC in Vegas Where Trump, Others Woo Jewish Voters." *Atlanta Jewish Times* (30 November); available online: <https://www.atlantajewishtimes.com/rjc-in-vegas-where-trump-others-woo-jewish-voters/> (accessed 20 March 2023).

Prager, Dennis (2016). "Bernie Sanders, the Non-Jewish Jew and Non-American American." *National Review* (7 June); available online: <https://www.nationalreview.com/2016/06/bernie-sanders-non-jewish-jew-non-american-american/> (accessed 8 June 2016).

Prothero, Stephen (2016). "WWJD? Maybe Vote for Bernie," *USA Today* (17 February); available online: <http://www.usatoday.com/story/opinion/2016/02/17/wwjd-vote-for-bernie-sanders-column/80426466/> (accessed 21 June 2016).

Reeves, Richard (1972). "Eleven Alligators in Florida's Political Swamp." *New York Times* (12 March): SM30.

Richman, Jackson (2019). "Top This? Presidential Candidates Get Covered in Yid-dishkeit." *Jewish News Syndicate* (12 September); available online: <https://www.jns.

org/top-this-presidential-candidates-get-covered-in-yiddishkeit/> (accessed 18 January 2022).

Richter, Greg (2016). "Trump Yarmulkes Sell Like Hotcakes at AIPAC." *NewsMax* (22 March); available online: <https://www.newsmax.com/Headline/aipac-trump-yarmulke-sold-out/2016/03/22/id/720384/> (accessed 27 March 2016).

Roberts, Sam (1989). "Giuliani Ads Remain Harsh in Last Days." *New York Times* (4 November): 27.

Rovell, Darren (2013). "Officially Licensed Yarmulke Catching On." *ESPN* (13 February); available online: <https://www.espn.com/blog/playbook/dollars/post/_/id/2816/officially-licensed-yarmulke-catching-on> (accessed 18 February 2023).

"The Royal Tennenhaus" (2009). *Seattle Met* (15 January); available online: <https://www.seattlemet.com/articles/2009/1/15/0209-mudroom-theroyaltennenhaus> (accessed 5 May 2018).

Saad, Lydia (2023). "Democrats' Sympathies in Middle East Shift to Palestinians." Gallup (16 March); available online: <https://news.gallup.com/poll/472070/democrats-sympathies-middle-east-shift-palestinians.aspx> (accessed 24 June 2023).

Sack, Kevin (1994). "2 Candidates Eagerly Pursue Pivotal Blocs Among Jews." *New York Times* (19 September): B1.

Safire, William (1984). "Hamlet of Nations." *New York Times* (29 October): A23.

Savage, Michael W. (2010). "Chelsea Clinton Marries Marc Mezvinsky in Rhinebeck, N.Y." *Washington Post* (1 August): A08.

Schoenburg, Bernard (2018). "Political Collectibles Convention Coming to Springfield." [Springfield, IL] *State Journal-Register* (5 July); available online: <https://www.sj-r.com/news/20180705/political-collectibles-convention-coming-to-springfield> (accessed 17 January 2019).

Schoenburg, Bernard (2019). "Springfield Man Travels Far to Encounter Candidates." [Springfield, IL] *State Journal-Register* (20 July); available online: <https://www.sj-r.com/story/news/politics/state/2019/07/20/springfield-man-travels-far-to/4647810007/> (accessed 13 November 2019).

Schumacher, Michael (2018). *The Contest: The 1968 Election and the War for America's Soul*. Minneapolis, MN: University of Minnesota Press.

Shameer, Sherry (2000). "Connecticut Woman Kicks Off a Joe Kippah Campaign." *Jewish News of Northern California* (15 September); available online: <https://jweekly.com/2000/09/15/connecticut-woman-kicks-off-a-joe-kippah-campaign/> (accessed 27 March 2018).

Siegel, Richard, Michael Strassfeld, and Sharon Strassfeld, eds. (1973). *The First Jewish Catalog*. Philadelphia, PA: Jewish Publication Society.

Silliman, Daniel (2020). "Trump Becomes the First President Since Eisenhower to Change Faiths in Office." *Christianity Today* (27 October); available online: <https://www.christianitytoday.com/news/2020/october/trump-nondenominational-presbyterian-religious-eisenhower.html> (accessed 26 January 2022).

Silverman, Eric K. (2013a). *A Cultural History of Jewish Dress*. New York, NY: Bloomsbury.

Silverman, Eric K. (2013b). "Aboriginal Yarmulkes, Ambivalent Attire, and Ironies of Contemporary Jewish Identity." In *Fashioning Jews: Clothing, Culture and Commerce*, ed Leonard J. Greenspoon, 177–205. West Lafayette, IN: Purdue University Press.

Spitzer, Eli (2022). "In Israel and American, Haredi Jews are Starting to Vote Like Everyone Else." *Mosaic* (21 November); available online: <https://mosaicmagazine.com/observation/jewish-world/2022/11/in-israel-and-america-haredi-jews-are-starting-to-vote-like-everyone-else/> (accessed 22 March 2023).

"'Stalling' on Jews Charged by Mayor" (1946). *New York Times* (16 September): 2.

Steinberg, Neil (2004). *Hatless Jack: The President, the Fedora, and the History of an American Style.* New York, NY: Penguin Publishing.

Sullivan, Amy (2017). "Clerical Speech Isn't Persecuted." *New York Times* (5 May): A31.

Talbot, Margaret (2015). "The Populist Prophet." *New Yorker* 91, 31 (12 October): 64–73.

Troy, Gil (2016). "Why Do Serious American Jews Wear Such Goofy Kippot?" *Jerusalem Post* (21 September): 14.

"U.S. Presidential Elections: Jewish Voting Record (1916–Present)" (2023). *Jewish Virtual Library*; available online: <https://www.jewishvirtuallibrary.org/jewish-voting-record-in-u-s-presidential-elections> (accessed 19 February 2023).

van Gelder, Lawrence (1968). "Kennedy Firm on the U.S. Commitment to Aid Israel." *New York Times* (6 June): 21.

Verdon, Joan (2000). "Campaign Yarmulke is a Head in the Polls." [Bergen County, NJ] *Record* (28 September): A8.

"Walker Defends City's 1927 Budget" (1927). *New York Times* (24 May): 5.

Walker, Hunter, and Julia Cannon (2014). "Inside the Launch of Hillary Clinton's Non-Campaign." *Business Insider* (10 June); available online: <http://www.businessinsider.com/inside-the-launch-of-hillary-clintons-non-campaign-2014-6?utm_source=hearst&utm_medium=referral&utm_content=allverticals> (accessed 8 May 2018).

Walters, Matt, Alex Sherman, and Josh Bloom (2007). "Letter from Walters, Sherman, and Bloom" (4 September); digital image provided to the author by Matt Walters.

Walters, Matt (2008). "Sold Out of Obama-kahs." *Jews for Obama* (22 October); available online: <http://www.jewsforobama.blogspot.com> (accessed 8 March 2011; link no longer active).

Weisman, Steven R. (1984). "Reagan Says Foes Fear to Attack Anti-Semitism." *New York Times* (27 October): 30.

Weiss, Michael (2003). "Joe in 2004." *Forward* (31 January): 19.

"The Yarmulke is Now a Fashion Item" (1990). *New York Times* (23 September): 5.

Yellin, Deena (2016). "Jews Using Their Yarmulkes for Political Statements." [Northern New Jersey] *Record* (5 November); available online: <https://www.northjersey.com/story/news/2016/11/05/jews-using-their-yarmulkes-for-political-statements/93448286/> (accessed 24 January 2018).

Yellin, Deena (2020). "For 2020 Presidential Race, Some Jews are Throwing Their Yarmulkes into the Ring." *NorthJersey.com* (21 February); available online: <https://www.northjersey.com/story/news/politics/2020/02/21/2020-presidential-race-some-jews-throw-yarmulkes-into-ring/4681197002/> (accessed 1 March 2023).

Zaltzman, Lior (2016a). "Kippah It Coming, Bernie!" *Forward* (21 January); available online: <https://forward.com/schmooze/331220/kippah-it-coming-bernie/> (accessed 7 May 2018).

Zaltzman, Lior (2016b). "Meet the Campaign Trail's Yarmulke Guy." *Forward* (8 February); available online: <https://forward.com/news/333104/meet-the-campaign-trails-yarmulke-guy/> (accessed 27 March 2016).

Zaltzman, Lior (2020). "Meet the Grandma Behind this Clever Jewish Biden-Harris Logo." *Kveller* (27 August); available online: <https://www.kveller.com/meet-the-grandma-behind-this-clever-jewish-biden-harris-logo/> (accessed 29 April 2023).

Zuckerman, Esther (2013). "Why Antonin Scalia Is Wearing that Hat to Inauguration." *Atlantic* (21 January); available online: <https://www.theatlantic.com/national/archive/2013/01/antonin-scalia-hat-inauguration/319242/> (accessed 22 November 2018).

7

FIRST THOUGHTS ON A SECOND QOMING

Reading QAnon's Occult Economy Through the Works of Jean and John Comaroff

Brian Hughes

Introduction: Occult Economy and the Comaroffs

For over a half-century, spouses and longtime collaborators Jean and John Comaroff have published influential and (as time has shown) perspicacious work on the role of witchcraft and the occult in postmodern and postcolonial contexts. Despite their disciplinary location within the field of anthropology, the Comaroffs' work offers a rich resource of insight into media. These insights offer particular insight into unconventional or "non-technological" mediations such as those belonging to the media of the occult. Media of this sort—sigils, rituals, hallucinatory visions, and demonic possessions—transmit information via an occultation by which the signified (concept) is metaphysically co-present and not merely conceptually indicated by a signifier (sound-image) (de Saussure, 1986). By the same token, media of this sort (sigils, rituals, etc.) are also congruent with occult content, that is, the proper means of transmitting messages which originate from outside the boundaries of reality itself. This transubstantial quality makes occult media and their corresponding messages one and the same.

This Janus-faced quality, by which form and content switch places and reverse order so easily, is common to magic and witchcraft and has been central to the Comaroffs' models of what they call *occult economies*, a "logic of concrete practices and rationales" (Comaroff & Comaroff, 2018, p. 291) that incorporates on one face "a material aspect founded on the effort to conjure wealth—or to account for its accumulation—by appeals to techniques that defy explanation in the conventional terms of practical reason" and on the other side "an ethical aspect grounded in the moral discourses and (re)actions sparked by the (real or imagined) production of value through such 'magical' means" (Comaroff & Comaroff, 2000, p. 310). That is, occult economy is the system of practices and beliefs which encompass

DOI: 10.4324/9781003342229-10

both occult explanations for abstract and dubious modes of capital accumulation (e.g., attributing others' wealth to magical origins) and the use of magic and the occult as a mode of capital accumulation in themselves (e.g., attempting to use magic to obtain wealth oneself).

The Comaroffs have traced occult economy in postcolonial South Africa and elsewhere through a library of manuscripts and books, perhaps most well-known among these *Millennial Capitalism: First Thoughts on a Second Coming* and *Occult Economies and the Violence of Abstraction: Notes from the South African Postcolony.* These essays provide an essential key to understanding the origins, nature, and perhaps even the future of QAnon and its subsidiary and progeny movements. This chapter will trace that key, reading the religious and marketing phenomena of the QAnon movement through the Comaroffs' model of occult economy and the social and economic relations which characterize the postcolony itself as they come home to roost in the United States.

Why QAnon and Why Now?

Before delving into the specifics of magic and marketing, it is necessary to argue that these phenomena "hang together," and that the model of occult economy does not "indiscriminately aggregate…disparate phenomena" (Comaroff & Comaroff, 2018; Murray, 2005). The perspicacity of *Millennial Capitalism, The Violence of Abstraction*, and corollary publications is demonstrated by the strong predictability which the authors impart to patterns of occult economy. It is as though they provide the magical formulae and incantations, the outcome of which can be brought about by the simple gathering of social, economic, political, and historical conditions. This model of occult economy (the deployment of magical means to achieve material ends) offers a clear framework to understand the emergence of QAnon as a religious and commercial phenomenon at the precise intersection of social, political, and economic conditions where it emerges: during a surge of far-right populism (arguably protofascist), among social classes (petit bourgeois and labor aristocracy) who have at last despaired of being made whole in the wake of economic catastrophe (the so-called Great Recession of the 2010s). The Comaroffs' model offers a clear and almost empirically predictable model by which magical-religious and commercial faces of occult economy will express themselves under these adverse socio-political-economic conditions.

First, the "violence of abstraction," in the form of "Liar's Loan" mortgage derivatives (Herndon, 2019) and the strip-mining of profitable business by venture capital (Covert, 2018; Morgan & Nasir, 2021), comes face-to-face with the fraud and hucksterism endemic to far-right populist movements (Sargent, 2022; Tager & Lopez, 2022). To the layperson's sensibilities, the vast wealth produced through opaque practices of destructive speculation might as well be a form of black magic. Occult economies emerge in "societies in which an optimistic faith in free enterprise encounters, for the first time, the realities of neoliberal economics:

of unpredictable shifts in sites of production and the demand for labor" (Comaroff & Comaroff, 1999, p. 294). They thrive in circumstances in which "the state can hardly be said to perdure at all, or to perdure purely as a private resource, a family business, a convenient fiction" (Comaroff & Comaroff, 2000, p. 325). Twenty years later, these words describe the very convergence of neoliberal austerity. It is a regime of social relations in which the state will rescue the financial architects of economic collapse while offering no relief to the economically dislocated save exhortations for people to undertake their own career retraining. This austerity, in turn, collides with the nepotism and cronyism that come to define elite power, such as that of the Trump White House, which all but rewrote the statutes against nepotism in the Executive Branch (Alexander, 2020), and a federal lobbying scene in which "building family empires" through lobbying and government relations "has become standard conceit" for the politicians across the political spectrum (Schweizer, 2018, p. 78). Contrary to complaints that the model of occult economy exoticizes the postcolony (Englund et al., 2000), the model's clear applicability to U.S. experience reveals the interplay of magic and markets as the outcome of objective material conditions.

Among these conditions lies the intersection of petit bourgeois and labor-aristocratic interests with conditions of economic precarity. Thus, QAnon, and occult economies in general, appears to emerge not out of poverty, but out of status threat, prototypicality threat, and symbolic threat—a cluster of dynamics which refers to socially dominant groups fearing for the loss of their privileged position (Bai & Federico, 2021). This interplay of economic and social threat occurs "[a]lmost everywhere that occult economies have arisen, the perceived need to resort to magical means of producing wealth is blamed, in one way or another, on the inability of the state to assure its national citizens a regular income: to protect them from destitution as productive employment migrates away across its borders; to stop the inflow of immigrants and others who divert the commonweal away from authochthons; to incarcerate criminals, witches, and other nefarious characters who spoil the world for upright, hardworking people" (Comaroff & Comaroff, 2000, p. 326). It has even been argued that far-right populism itself represents the application of colonial logics back onto the imperial core during moments of crisis. Far-right movements, fascism and its corollaries, merely return "colonialist procedures which until then had been reserved exclusively for the Arabs of Algeria, the coolies of India, and the [Blacks] of Africa" (Césaire, 2000, p. 36). Given the predictable applicability of occult economy to the United States in the 2010s and 2020s, this argument appears to have merit.

Contrary to popular fictions about the white working class's support for right-populism and participation in conspirituality movements like QAnon, "the roots of the rising occult economy are not to be found simply in poverty or deprivation…[but] rather in a doubling. On one hand was the perception that, behind the ordinary, visible workings of the market lie mysterious mechanisms that hold the real key to its bounty: to the rapid, often immaterial, invisible flow of value across time and space…On the other hand was a dawning sense—not only among the poor, also among those caught in the middle—of having been left out of the full promise of prosperity" (Comaroff & Comaroff, 2018, p. 300). This comports with the actual demographics of both QAnon and the Trump movement more generally. QAnon supporters generally fall at or around the median American income of $70,000, with 48% at or above $75,000/year annual household income and 35% between $30,000 and $74,999 (Kliger, 2021; Pew Research Center for the People and the Press, 2020). And while only 53.55% of QAnon adherents self-identify as Republican, this also comports with economic findings about Trump voters, who tended to cluster along two socio-economic axes: (1) non-college graduates making at or above the median U.S. household income (in fact, 20% non-graduates making $100,000/year) (Carnes & Lupu, 2016), and (2) people of relative affluent economic status in regions of relative precarity and/or poverty (Bump, 2021).

Here, at this juncture with far-right populism, marketing in its crassest form joins with occult economy—in the sense both of occulted finance and the commodification of magic. The far-right demagogue belongs to the genealogy of the humbug artist and snake oil salesman, fading seamlessly into the figure of the occultist and mystic. The novelist Nathanael West traces this continuity in his novel *A Cool Million*, in which "[a] hapless American Candide is destroyed by his gullible optimism, eventually murdered by a fascist demagogue (said to have been modeled on William Dudley Pelley) in order to transform him into a martyr" (Churchwell, 2020, p. 37). Pelley himself was a figure of occult economy during an earlier convergence of extreme right politics and socio-economic dislocation around the 1930s (Beekman, 2005). Pelley was a screenwriter, antisemitic conspiracist, dedicated occultist, and founder of the American fascist "silver shirts" organization, an "outspoken anti-Semite, an admirer of Adolf Hitler, and a true believer in esoteric religion and philosophy" (Toy Jr., 2006, p. 573) with "a penchant for exaggeration, if not for outright mendacity" (Harty, 2016, p. 64). More recently, Italian far-right president Silvio Berlusconi who, "with the air of a fairground huckster, and thanks to his TV monopoly…[set up] what Dario Fo describes as a 'new fascism'" (Ramonet, 2002). Berlusconi's legendary corruption is the very figure of occulted finance, spawning its own magical commodity market in the form of Berlusconi voodoo dolls, an example of "black magic which the damned communists used to beat Silvio Berlusconi's empire in 2021" (Reuters Staff, 2009). This is the Janus-face of occult economies, which the Comaroffs describe as their "essential paradox" (Comaroff & Comaroff, 1999, p. 284). On one hand, the occult represents a potential means to economic achievement, while on the other hand occult economy cries out "to eradicate people held to enrich themselves by those very means" (ibid). This resonates, too, with the observations of Michael T. Taussig that the rural people of Columbia and Bolivia treat the everyday social relations of contemporary economy as "vividly unnatural, even as evil" (Taussig, 2010, p. 3).

Occulted superhero of the Q movement, former President Trump, embodies the figure of what Krause-Jensen and Martin term the "business guru." The business guru is a populist figure, an expert in the creation of fortunes who "proclaims his disdain for the kind of numerical verifiable data produced by professional experts… instead emphasis[ing] the underlying and unquantifiable intuitive truths of 'culture' and individual energy" (Krause-Jensen & Martin, 2018, p. 92). He channels this power through the "impulses" of the "gut" to produce the "impeccable business instincts" of a Trump or TV producer Mark Burnett, who single-handedly revived the languishing businessman's career via the "alchemy of reality television" (Keefe, 2018). The business guru is "a mythical figure whose attraction and fascination lies in [his] ability to embody two structurally opposed principles…*suggests* new (im)possible logics" (2018, p. 102). The glitz of the political huckster presents an almost-literal magical glamor, "an illusory charm, a dangerous spell, a magical enchantment" (Bogusława Strawińska, 2014, p. 167), as well as the more prosaic "deliberate mystification, with the aim of creating interest in a particular movie or TV star…luxury goods or services" (2014, p. 170). This guru "resonate[s] with the idea of 'magic' and points to the central assumption…that enchantment, spectacle, and performance are simultaneously integral parts of the [capitalist] system's mode of operation" (Krause-Jensen & Martin, 2018, p. 97).

These material origins of occult economy drive the dynamics of the postcolony and the fevered supernatural populism of QAnon in a way that itself seems almost magical, appearing translocally and transtemporally with eerie similarity. So, too, this chapter will argue, do the expressions of QAnon mirror those of the Comaroffs' postcolony. The markets and the marketing of QAnon, the occulted finances and commodified magic which it sells, reflect the eerily identical desires, on one hand "to plumb the secret of those invisible means" and on the other "to stem the spread of a macabre, visceral economy founded on the violence of extraction and abstraction" (Comaroff & Comaroff, 1999, p. 293), all for the people whom Nathanael West described as those "poor devils who can only be stirred by the promise of miracles and then only to violence" (2009, p. 184).

Qase Studies in Occult Economy: Witches and White Hats in Esoteric and Exoteric Markets

The dual, inverted nature of occult economy reveals itself yet again in the QAnon movement's symptomology surrounding abstract finance. This chapter will now examine QAnon's supernatural interpretations of the wealthy and powerful, whose personal fortunes sometimes appear dubious at best. In the figure of former President Donald Trump, this mystery suggests a messianic character, evidence of talent and deservedness too great to be revealed except through omens and codes. On the other hand, the figure of Trump's presidential opponent Hillary Clinton comes to embody the very figure of the witch herself, whose power is derived not from a career of canny and perhaps cynical political dealings, but from practices of black magic, including human sacrifices.

By the same token, the production of magical commodities seeks to harness the apparent magic behind obscene, abstract wealth. QAnon cottage industries producing exegetical texts promise keys to the Q prophecies, in a marketing dynamic that combines the repetition compulsion of failed prophecy with the promise "to obtain true knowledge of hidden things" (Crowley, 1944, p. 250). Structurally, QAnon partakes in the same "each one teach one" recruitment pyramid of multi-level marketing (MLM) programs as the purveyors of modern-day snake oil become enmeshed in the world of conspirituality even while recruiting from its ranks. Conversely, QAnon conjures dark scenarios in which sinister forces produce poison apples in the form of saleable mass-market commodities, such as the case (described below) in which overstock furniture sales are imagined to conceal the trafficking of children. All come together in the Janus-face of the occult economy, which has, the Comaroffs write, a "bipolar character: At one level, they consist in the constant quest for new, magical means for otherwise unattainable ends; at another, they vocalize a desire to sanction even eradicate, people held to have accumulated assets by those very means" (Comaroff & Comaroff, 2000, p. 316).

Money from Nothing: Occulted Finance and Magical Commodities

Despite its protestations against the arcane, the central conceit of QAnon lies in a table of correspondences that would dazzle even the most demon-haunted Elizabethan warlock. The Q Clock, Great Awakening Map, and Deep State Mapping project, among others, "provide arcane, mysterious functions" (Hannah, 2021, p. 5), which promise to unlock the secret meaning of Q's cryptic "drops." The self-published e-book *An Invitation to the Great Awakening* promised to decode these decoding devices. QAnon expert Mike Rothschild describes *An Invitation* as "the gold standard" of Q exegesis, a "bestseller" unmatched at "red-pilling [recruiting] new converts" (Rothschild, 2021, p. 70). The book promised to "introduce new converts to the basics of how Q communicates, the messages that the Q poster is actually saying, how to interpret them, and why it all matters so much" (2021, p. 71). Through Amazon's self-publishing functions, the book climbed into the top 100 of sales (Collins, 2019), with its promise to give readers access into the mind of Q.

The systems of de-occultation which *An Invitation* sells are tools to interpret Q's posts by cross-referencing them with one another and with current events and prophesied future events (Hannah, 2021, p. 9). One may find correspondence here with the Enochian temple furniture of high Western Occultism (Dee et al., 1659), in which complex sigils and tables of angelic language promise to translate visions from beyond the veil (Crowley et al., 2008). Per the Comaroffs, these exegetical tools promise to repurpose "the translocal power of the black arts" (Comaroff & Comaroff, 1999, p. 286)—in this case, the secrecy of the Deep State—for the spiritual wealth of its readers and financial wealth of its authors.

These devices and the market which sprung up explaining their use to new recruits "[l]ink together a belief system that gestures toward religious belief…but exists apart from any actual transcendental referent" (Hannah, 2021, p. 6). And to be sure, "the minds behind creating and promoting QAnon didn't…sell currency or investments, but good feelings and community. It didn't promise vast riches, but the destruction of America's enemies" (Rothschild, 2021, p. 66). However, QAnon experts say, the movement has evolved beyond some of the conspirituality "affinity fraud" which mark its ancestry. Affinity fraud is a kind of marketing fraud dressed up in the guise of religion, which incorporates "some of Q's most important parts—secret intel from a guru, a massive event just around the corner, a secret battle between forces of light and darkness" (Rothschild, 2021, p. 55).

Some have traced precedents for QAnon to the NESARA affinity fraud (Crockford, 2022; Gulyas, 2021). The NESARA fraud is "a decades-old conspiracy theory whose followers believe that all their debts will be magically canceled" through a return to the gold standard, the abolition of the IRS, and federal fiat (BBC World Service, 2021). NESARA's popularity has ebbed and flowed in the 40 years since it emerged from the internet; however, recently, it "has increased since as it was taken up by the QAnon movement" (Crockford, 2022, p. 928). NESARA is the quintessential expression of occult economy in its desperate "desire to make money visible and tangible" (2022, p. 928) again out of the ether of fractional reserve banking and interest-bearing debt.

NESARA's resurgence coincides with several other currency speculation scams, most notably those focusing on the Iraqi Dinar and the Zimbabwean "Zim." In the former, which "Dinar promoters have claimed…will occur for nearly a decade," investors hope "that Trump and the Iraqi government will somehow 'revalue' the currency, boosting its current value of less than $0.001 to $3 or $4" (Sommer, 2018). The latter "Zim" speculation holds that the now-abandoned Zimbabwean dollar will be revalued as part of "a financial reset that will see billions of secret funds distributed to people across the globe and the erasure of all debts" (Mossou & Geiger, 2022). Similar QAnon currency speculation has focused on cryptocurrency as well (Piper et al., 2022).

These currency speculation schemes all share the central quality of messianic waiting[1] with the essential dream of occult economics, to spin straw into gold. "All of these things have a single common denominator: the allure of accruing wealth from nothing" (Comaroff & Comaroff, 2000, p. 313). They "promise to deliver almost preternatural profits, to yield wealth *sans* perceptible production, value *sans* visible effort" (Comaroff & Comaroff, 1999, p. 281). The dream of "financial relief through NESARA prompts another form of rematerialization of money: a desire to make money visible and tangible" (Crockford, 2022, p. 928), producing "vast, almost instantaneous riches to those who master its spectral technologies" (Comaroff & Comaroff, 2000, p. 298). True to the pattern of occult economy, they seek to mirror the practices of currency speculation with which QAnon boogeyman George Soros (Jewish-American billionaire stock trader/philanthropist) built much of his fortune (Morris, 2009). As "people ponder the interplay of mobility and compression in the production of new forms of wealth" (Comaroff & Comaroff, 1999, p. 291), all that is necessary is to buy the dip and keep the faith.

If Q Clocks and NESARA represent the receptive, even passive, side of QAnon's occult economy, then QAnon's tangled connections to the world of MLM schemes represent its active and outgoing path. Some of these MLMs, such as 7K Metals, center on precious metals speculation (Sommer, 2022). Others, like Young Living, Monat, and Arbonne, offer more practical consumer products, albeit charged with a spirit of patriotism and evangelical spiritual warfare (Adelakun, 2022; O'Donnell, 2021), that is, the practices through which humans "interced[e] in the supernatural war being waged on earth" between the people of God and "the Devil and his minions" (McCloud, 2015, p. 10). All offer a blend of "innovative occult practices and money magic, pyramid schemes and prosperity gospels" (Comaroff & Comaroff, 2000, p. 292) found throughout occult economies. Here, "[i]ndividual citizens, a lot of them marooned by a rudderless ship of state, try to clamber aboard the good ship Enterprise" (2000) "These are organizations built on foundational myths (that the establishment is keeping secrets from you, that you are on a hero's journey to enlightenment and wealth), charismatic leadership, and shameless, constant posting" (Tiffany, 2020). In so doing, MLM participants find themselves battling the eccentric currents of the "new world order" (Comaroff & Comaroff, 2000, p. 299). But "disillusioned MLM members have complained that they've been left badly in debt when their profits failed to materialize" (Sommer, 2022).

MLMs, while legal, "have been compared to illegal pyramid schemes, in which new members pay in money to join without any possibility of making their money back" (Sommer, 2022). This highly stratified structure of leadership and rank-and-file makes MLMs "uniquely fertile ground for conspiracism" (Tiffany, 2020), as "[t]he line between Ponzi schemes and evangelical prosperity gospels is very thin indeed" (Comaroff & Comaroff, 2000, p. 313). MLM "isn't just structurally conducive to spreading outlandish ideas: It also has some philosophical crossover with QAnon" (Tiffany, 2020). The products sold in Q-adjacent MLMs often amount to little more than potions and elixirs, speculative metals, and at-best pharmaceutically inert placebos buttressing a temporary dream of health, wealth, youth, or vitality (Imre-Millei, 2020; Jackson, 2022). Through the interweaving of MLM aspirations and QAnon mythology, products such as these come to represent a kind of sympathetic magic in the occult economy: everyday consumables imbued with the power and promise of the Q-eschaton. Kaitlyn Tiffany writes that "crucial to this process [of MLM recruitment] was the act of 'dream building'," and crucial to the longevity of their identification was that the dreams get bigger and bigger." Over time, "the dreams tended to move beyond money, or lifestyle aspirations, or even helping one's own family" (Tiffany, 2020). This is the very model of Q itself, as followers delve deeper down the rabbit hole of the conspiracy mythos, building and forking it, conjuring ever-more dimensions to the dream, even as they wander farther and farther from increasingly alienated friends and family (PERIL & NCRI, 2020).

Saints and Sickos: The Value of Revenge in the Occult Economy of QAnon

Obviously, the hoped-for economic blessings described above do not tend to arrive. And so, for every hope pinned to a magical commodity or debt-disappearing act via a half-understood complex financial instrument, there is a witch, someone who has mastered the black arts of wealth accrual through means that are so terrible they cry out for the ultimate revenge. "The antisocial greed of these predators was epitomized in the idea of unnatural production and reproduction, in images of toxic, degenerative sexuality, of adultery, rape, and abortion" (Comaroff & Comaroff, 2018, pp. 307–308). Within the system of the occult economy, people then become "convinced that their neighborhoods harbored trenchant human evil; that their familiar landscapes were alive with phantasmic forces of unprecedented power and danger" (Comaroff & Comaroff, 1999, p. 285). The quest for wealth becomes a witch hunt.

In their work on occult economies in South Africa, the Comaroffs return to stories of witch hunts and their victims, typically "men and women of conspicuous, unshared wealth…socially isolated and defenseless" (Comaroff & Comaroff, 1999, p. 287). While the QAnon subculture has indeed produced murders of the most lurid type, these do not seem to offer the correct parallel to tales of the "ha-Madura Witch Hunt," where a mob of young men murdered "an elderly woman by 'necklacing' and attacking two other elderly persons" (Comaroff & Comaroff, 2018, p. 305). One may, however, see parallels between the "repeated reference to [witches'] red vaginas, and to their lethal, rotten sperm" (Comaroff & Comaroff, 1999, p. 288) of South African witch scares and the figure of Hillary Clinton, who looms over the QAnon mythography in the form of a simultaneously desiccated and omnivorous sexual agent, a shriveled crone of prodigious sado-erotic appetites.

The figure of the witch is brought to apotheosis in the legend of the "Frazzle-drip" video, "a rumored dark web snuff film showing Hillary Clinton and longtime aide Huma Abedin sexually assaulting and murdering a young girl, drinking her blood and taking turns wearing the skin from her face as a mask" (Anti-Defamation League, 2023). The lurid details of this human sacrifice are essential, the conspiracy claims, in order to evoke sufficient terror in the victim that her blood will contain as much adrenochrome[2] as possible for the "drug-crazed satanic rites" carried on by a "global cabal of Democratic and Hollywood pedophiles" (Hitt, 2020). It is a pattern common to occult economies; this conspiracy theory proposes, "the malevolent ambitions of their elders, to whom the purloined parts were to be retailed…any disappearance of persons, especially children, was 'immediately linked to businessmen and politicians'" (Comaroff & Comaroff, 1999, p. 290). Themes of organ harvesting and human sacrifice are the common motif, "regularly used in potions for fertility, for success in business, and for luck in love. Those of white children fetched the best prices" (Comaroff & Comaroff, 1999, p. 280).

Clinton, like all witches, "distills complex, diffuse material and social processes into comprehensible human intentions and actions" (Comaroff &

Comaroff, 2018, p. 303). Along with husband Bill Clinton and others representing "third way" Democratic Party politics, Clinton is iconic of that "violence of abstraction" which characterizes governments' retreat from the provision of social good and toward the unleashing of abstract market forces throughout the 1990s, the very period of Millennial Capitalism which incubated the Comaroffs' model of occult economy. It is unlikely that many QAnon adherents would understand this process of personifying complex political-economic dynamics, but that is precisely why Hillary offers such a convenient screen on which to project their nightmares. As a woman, the intense misogyny of the populist far-right (Kalmoe & Mason, 2022) will naturally gravitate toward a female object of fear and loathing. And as guru-Trump's electoral antagonist, she perfectly suited the needs of the moment.

But cannibals cannot exist without victims, and here once more, the QAnon movement mixes the dynamics of late capitalist markets with fantasies of Satanic malevolence in a powerful attempt to reconcile the socio-political-economic contradictions for which they have no material frame of reference. In the summer of 2020, QAnon and the Q-adjacent internet buzzed with rumors that the discount home goods website Wayfair was in fact a front for human child trafficking. Wayfair, which uses algorithmic word combinations to name its products, had randomly assigned human names to storage cabinets, among many other smaller commodities (Dickson, 2020). The cabinets themselves were industrial grade and therefore significantly more expensive than those with which typical QAnoners were familiar. A new conspiracy and mode of "baking" clues were born. So it went, "Wayfair [was] using pricey storage cabinets to traffic children," and Q bakers set about "matching up the names of Wayfair products to those of missing children" (Seitz & Swenson, 2021).

This conspiracy, like the social/storytelling processes that built and elaborated upon it, is an attempt to magically explain complex economic processes which profoundly shape the lives of people like those in QAnon. These processes are inhuman, even antihuman, in their algorithmic efficiency. And yet the specific mechanisms of algorithmic naming and pricing remain hidden in the black box (or, if you prefer, the Saturnian Black Cube) of proprietary software and protected business secrets. This is an example of one way in which "[i]nterpersonal relations—above all, sexuality…come to stand, metonymically, for the inchoate forces that threaten the world as we know it" (Comaroff & Comaroff, 2000, p. 305). The destabilization of the American middle class, the replacement of physical retail by largely automated online processes, and contextless media grief-porn of child abduction merge "[d]iffuse concerns about cultural integrity and communal survival… in 'private' anxieties about sexuality, procreation, or family values" (Comaroff & Comaroff, 2000, p. 306). The future, represented by our children, is being consumed by the regime of global-digital economic efficiency. In this regime of exploitation, the United States becomes postcolonial without ever having been colonized, and the occult economy gives way to the common transcultural "mass panics about the clandestine theft and sale of the organs of young people" (Comaroff & Comaroff, 2000, p. 311). QAnon still cannot understand that "software is eating the world" (Andreessen, 2011), and so they must imagine that it is the people on TV.

One final rotation of the occult economy's Janus head returns us again to QAnon's messiah, the miracle worker foil to Hillary Clinton's diabolical cannibal. Once again, Donald Trump comes to embody the promise of magic in an unmanageable world. In the occult economy, the Comaroffs write, "there is a strong tendency for states to appeal to new or intensified magicalities and fetishes in order to heal fissures and breaches in the fabric of the polity" (Comaroff & Comaroff, 2000, p. 327). In the exercise of his celebrity, particularly in his rallies and revivals, Trump offers to remedy this through a kind of mass charismatic healing. But here, perhaps, is where the magical commodity is neither nightmare nor snake oil. In other words, maybe there is a dose of real magic in the man's ability to hold a crowd.

It has been remarked countless times by observers that Trump's campaign rallies (which persisted throughout his presidency) produced an air of eerie, electric, and threatening social energy, not unlike that which precedes a riot (and in at least two cases did precede riots) (Davey & Bosman, 2016; Savage, 2021). Trump's "rhetoric delivers catharsis to his audience by suspending any sense of accountability" (Samuels, 2020, p. 21). His physical and vocal presence acted as a dispensation to unleash "excitations that are characterized by a definite psychic and somatic state of excitation... the excitation experienced by submissive masses when they open themselves to a beloved leader's speech" (Reich, 1970, p. 156). In this role, Trump is the licensor and the dispenser of transgression. His audiences "identify with one another in terms of their ego, but they all put the leader in the place of their own ego-ideal" (Tarnopolsky, 2017, p. 7). The manic energy which spills out into violence in the streets of Chicago and the halls of the Capitol "should not be surprising since mania...is defined by the fact the individual's ego becomes conflated with his ego ideal" (Tarnopolsky, 2017, p. 7).

And here, perhaps, is where the books at last balance in the occult economy. "The specter of violence run wild is a caricature of postapartheid 'liberty': the liberty to transgress and consume in an unfettered world of desire, cut loose from former political, spatial, moral, sexual, and material constraints" (Comaroff & Comaroff, 1999, p. 293). In identification with the leader, the relation between adherents and the occult economy itself "becomes simultaneously truth and untruth: On the one hand, it holds out to the masses the promise of a collective release from the constraints of bourgeois civilization with its demand that all instinct (and perhaps especially violence) submit to a pathological repression" (Gordon, 2017, p. 48). In the figurehead of Trump, his most diehard adherents such as those of QAnon at last enjoy freedom from—if not control over—the social constraints of bourgeois civilization in the age of Millennial Capitalism. To the extent that is possible via the hyper-individualization that defines the occult economy, they are, at last, collectively made whole.

Conclusion

Perhaps the postcolony is everywhere, or perhaps the dynamics of occult economy which the Comaroffs have so extensively mapped over the course of their careers transcend the dynamics of colony/postcolony that were their focus. Whatever the case, the model of occult economy offers a chillingly predictive roadmap to the interplay of markets and magic which define QAnon, the American populist far-right movement, and increasingly, our society as a whole. Will there be yet another, third, coming? The dual-faced nature of the occult seems to promise there will. If the occult economy described in the preceding chapter comprises occulted finance, financialized occultism, witches and white hats, the magical and mundane, the aspirational and the violently resigned, it seems possible that some inversion of the whole might yet be slouching toward us. But rather than a return to normalcy, a Solomon-like containment of the spirits unleashed by Millennial Capitalism, might it not be something stranger still?

Notes

1 A complimentary phenomenon can be observed in a media cottage industry which emerged to serve liberal and progressive markets during the Trump administration (Marmura, 2020). A media ecosystem of columnists, podcasts, Twitter accounts, and mass-market books emerged that promised to reveal occulted legal and intelligence operations which would lead to the arrest of Trump and his associates on charges ranging from fraud to sex crimes to espionage. Sometimes termed "BlueAnon" (Bort, 2021), cheekily by critics on the left and earnestly by those on the right, this strange reflection of the Q phenomenon bespeaks the strange reflection which the Comaroffs identify between magic and the law. "Another crucial dimension is the fetishism of the law, of the capacity of constitutionalism and contract, rights, and legal remedies…Like all fetishes, the chimerical quality of this one lies in an enchanted displacement, in the notion that legal instruments have the capacity to orchestrate social harmony" (Comaroff & Comaroff, 2000, p. 328).

2 Adrenochrome is a naturally occurring chemical compound, produced by oxidized adrenaline. However, for reasons that remain unclear, it has become central both to Pizzagate and QAnon lore. So the legend goes: it confers powerful euphoric and psychedelic effects, as well as youth and longevity. However, the belief continues that it can only be extracted "from the pituitary gland of tortured children" (Hitt, 2020).

Works Cited

Adelakun, A. A. (2022). *Powerful Devices: Prayer and the Political Praxis of Spiritual Warfare*. New Brunswick: Rutgers University Press.

Alexander, D. (2020). *White House, Inc.: How Donald Trump Turned the Presidency into a business/Dan Alexander*. New York: Portfolio/Penguin.

Andreessen, M. (2011, August 20). *Why Software Is Eating the World*. Andreessen Horowitz. https://a16z.com/2011/08/20/why-software-is-eating-the-world/

Anti-Defamation League. (2023, May 30). *Frazzledrip*. ADL.Org. https://www.adl.org/glossary/frazzledrip

Bai, H., & Federico, C. M. (2021). White and Minority Demographic Shifts, Intergroup Threat, and Right-Wing Extremism. *Journal of Experimental Social Psychology, 94,* 104–114. https://doi.org/10.1016/j.jesp.2021.104114

BBC World Service. (2021, August 23). *Nesara: The Financial Fantasy Ruining Lives*. BBC. https://www.bbc.co.uk/programmes/w3ct1xzv

Beekman, S. (2005). *William Dudley Pelley: A Life in Right-Wing Extremism and the Occult/Scott Beekman* (1st ed.). Syracuse: Syracuse University Press.

Bogusława Strawińska, A. (2014). Glamour – Magic or Manipulation? A Short History and Definition. *Białostockie Archiwum Językowe, 14*, 165–176.

Bort, R. (2021, October 26). Marjorie Taylor Greene Uses Declaration of Independence to Defend Violent Capitol Riot. *Rolling Stone*. https://www.rollingstone.com/politics/politics-news/marjorie-taylor-greene-jan-6-declaration-of-independence-1248372/

Bump, P. (2021, October 23). Analysis | Places that backed Trump Skewed Poor; Voters Who Backed Trump Skewed Wealthier. *Washington Post*. https://www.washingtonpost.com/news/politics/wp/2017/12/29/places-that-backed-trump-skewed-poor-voters-who-backed-trump-skewed-wealthier/

Carnes, N., & Lupu, N. (2016, April 8). *Why Trump's Appeal Is Wider than You Might Think*. MSNBC.Com. https://www.msnbc.com/msnbc/why-trumps-appeal-wider-you-might-think-msna829531

Césaire, A. (2000). Discourse on colonialism/Aimé Césaire. In J. Pinkham (Trans.), *A Poetics of Anticolonialism/by Robin D.G. Kelley*. New York: Monthly Review Press.

Churchwell, S. (2020). All-American Fascism. *New Statesman (1996), 149*(5536), 31–37.

Collins, B. (2019, March 5). *On Amazon, a Qanon Conspiracy Book Climbs the Charts—With an Algorithmic Push*. NBC News. https://www.nbcnews.com/tech/tech-news/amazon-qanon-conspiracy-book-climbs-charts-algorithmic-push-n979181

Comaroff, J., & Comaroff, J. L. (1999). Occult Economies and the Violence of Abstraction: Notes from the South African Postcolony. *American Ethnologist, 26*(2), 279–303. https://doi.org/10.1525/ae.1999.26.2.279

Comaroff, J., & Comaroff, J. L. (2000). Millennial Capitalism: First Thoughts on a Second Coming. *Public Culture, 12*(2), 291–343.

Comaroff, J., & Comaroff, J. L. (2018). Occult Economies, Revisited. In B. Moeran & T. de Waal Malefyt (Eds.), *Magical Capitalism: Enchantment, Spells, and Occult Practices in Contemporary Economies* (pp. 289–320). Springer International Publishing. https://doi.org/10.1007/978-3-319-74397-4_12

Covert, B. (2018, June 13). The Demise of Toys "R" Us Is a Warning. *The Atlantic*. https://www.theatlantic.com/magazine/archive/2018/07/toys-r-us-bankruptcy-private-equity/561758/

Crockford, S. (2022). How to Manifest Abundance: Money and the Rematerialization of Exchange in Sedona, Arizona, USA. *The Journal of the Royal Anthropological Institute, 28*(3), 920–937. https://doi.org/10.1111/1467-9655.13772

Crowley, A. (1944). *Book of Thoth: (Egyptian Tarot)*. Newburyport: Red Wheel Weiser.

Crowley, A., Hyatt, C. S., & DuQuette, L. M. (2008). *Enochian World of Aleister Crowley: Enochian Sex Magick*. Tempe: Original Falcon Press, LLC.

Davey, M., & Bosman, J. (2016, March 12). Donald Trump's Rally in Chicago Canceled After Violent Scuffles. *The New York Times*. https://www.nytimes.com/2016/03/12/us/trump-rally-in-chicago-canceled-after-violent-scuffles.html

de Saussure, F. (1986). *Course in General Linguistics*. Open Court.

Dee, J., Kelly, E., & Casaubon, M. (1659). *A True & Faithful Relation of What Passed for Many Years Between Dr. John Dee and Some Spirits*. Moscow: Рипол Классик.

Dickson, E. (2020, July 14). A Wayfair Child-Trafficking Conspiracy Theory Is Flourishing on TikTok, Despite It Being Completely False. *Rolling Stone*. https://www.rollingstone.com/culture/culture-news/wayfair-child-trafficking-conspiracy-theory-tiktok-1028622/

Englund, H., Leach, J., Davies, C. A., Gupta, A., Meyer, B., Robbins, J., & Sangren, P. S. (2000). Ethnography and the Meta-Narratives of Modernity. *Current Anthropology, 41*(2), 225–248. https://doi.org/10.1086/300126

Gordon, P. E. (2017). The Authoritarian Personality Revisited: Reading Adorno in the Age of Trump. *Boundary 2, 44*(2), 31–56. https://doi.org/10.1215/01903659-3826618

Gulyas, A. J. (2021). *Conspiracy and Triumph: Theories of a Victorious Future for the Faithful.* Jefferson: McFarland.

Hannah, M. N. (2021). A Conspiracy of Data: QAnon, Social Media, and Information Visualization. *Social Media + Society, 7*(3), 205630512110360. https://doi.org/10.1177/20563051211036064

Harty, K. (2016). William Dudley Pelley, An American Nazi in King Arthur's Court. *Arthuriana (Dallas, Tex, 26*(2), 64–85. https://doi.org/10.1353/art.2016.0034

Herndon, T. (2019). Liar's Loans, Mortgage Fraud, and the Great Recession. *Review of Political Economy, 31*(4), 479–508. https://doi.org/10.1080/09538259.2020.1747746

Hitt, T. (2020, August 14). 'Adrenochrome': QAnon's Imaginary Drug Hollywood Is 'Harvesting' From Kids. *The Daily Beast.* https://www.thedailybeast.com/how-qanon-became-obsessed-with-adrenochrome-an-imaginary-drug-hollywood-is-harvesting-from-kids

Imre-Millei, B. (2020, November 30). Atop the Pyramid of the American Dream: The Politics Multi-Level Marketing. *The Observer.* https://theobserver-qiaa.org/atop-the-pyramid-of-the-american-dream-the-politics-multi-level-marketing

Jackson, E. (2022, May 17). How the Pandemic "Greased the Wheels" of Multi-Level Marketing Companies. *Canadian Business – How to Do Business Better.* https://canadianbusiness.com/ideas/multi-level-marketing-canada-pandemic/

Kalmoe, N. P., & Mason, L. (2022). *Radical American Partisanship: Mapping Violent Hostility, Its Causes, and the Consequences for Democracy.* Chicago: University of Chicago Press.

Keefe, P. R. (2018, December 27). How Mark Burnett Resurrected Donald Trump as an Icon of American Success. *The New Yorker.* https://www.newyorker.com/magazine/2019/01/07/how-mark-burnett-resurrected-donald-trump-as-an-icon-of-american-success

Kliger, Z. (2021, March 8). Who are QAnon Supporters? 5 Revealing Findings from Survey Data. *The Morningside Post.* https://morningsidepost.com/articles/2021/3/8/who-are-qanon-supporters-5-revealing-findings-from-survey-data

Krause-Jensen, J., & Martin, K. (2018). *Trickster's Triumph: Donald Trump and the New Spirit of Capitalism* (B. Moeran & T. de Waal Malefyt, Eds.; pp. 89–113). Springer International Publishing. https://doi.org/10.1007/978-3-319-74397-4_4

Marmura, S. M. E. (2020). Russiagate, WikiLeaks, and the Political Economy of Posttruth News. *International Journal of Communication, 14*(0), Article 0.

McCloud, S. (2015). *American Possessions: Fighting Demons in the Contemporary United States/Sean McCloud.* New York: Oxford University Press.

Morgan, J., & Nasir, M. A. (2021). Financialised Private Equity Finance and the Debt Gamble: The Case of Toys R Us. *New Political Economy, 26*(3), 455–471. https://doi.org/10.1080/13563467.2020.1782366

Morris, C. R. (2009). *The Sages: Warren Buffett, George Soros, Paul Volcker, and the Maelstrom of markets/Charles R. Morris* (1st ed.). New York: PublicAffairs.

Mossou, A., & Geiger, G. (2022, December 21). As QAnon Falters, European Followers Flock to a Financial Conspiracy. *Bellingcat.* https://www.bellingcat.com/news/2022/12/21/as-qanon-falters-european-followers-flock-to-a-financial-conspiracy/

Murray, C. (2005). *Medicine Murder in Colonial Lesotho: The Anatomy of a Moral crisis/ Colin Murray and Peter Sanders.* Edinburgh: Edinburgh University Press.

PERIL & NCRI (2020). *The QAnon Conspiracy: Destroying Families, Dividing Communities, Undermining Democracy*. Washington, DC: American University and Rutgers University.

O'Donnell, S. J. (2021). *Passing Orders: Demonology and Sovereignty in American Spiritual warfare/S. Johnathon O'Donnell* (1st ed). New York: Fordham University Press.

Pew Research Center for the People and the Press. (2020). *Study Info for Pew Research Center: American Trends Panel Wave 73 [Version 3]*. Roper Center for Public Opinion Research. https://ropercenter.cornell.edu/ipoll/study/31117706

Piper, E., Backovic, N., & Marland, T. (2022). *QAnon Crypto Trading Scheme Lost Investors Millions*. Logically.AI. https://www.logically.ai/articles/qanon-crypto-lose-followers-2-million

Ramonet, I. (2002, February 1). *Old Italy, New Facism*. Le Monde Diplomatique. https://mondediplo.com/2002/02/01berlusconi

Reich, W. (1970). *The Mass Psychology of Fascism*. London: Macmillan.

Reuters Staff. (2009, December 4). Italian Man Sells Voodoo Dolls of Berlusconi. *Reuters*. https://www.reuters.com/article/oukoe-uk-italy-berlusconi-voodoo-idUKTRE-5B33XG20091204

Rothschild, M. (2021). *The Storm Is Upon Us: How QAnon Became a Movement, Cult, and Conspiracy Theory of Everything*. New York: Melville House.

Samuels, R. (2020). Catharsis: The Politics of Enjoyment. In *Zizek and the Rhetorical Unconscious* (pp. 7–31). Springer International Publishing AG. https://doi.org/10.1007/978-3-030-50910-1_2

Savage, C. (2021, January 10). Incitement to Riot? What Trump Told Supporters Before Mob Stormed Capitol. *The New York Times*. https://www.nytimes.com/2021/01/10/us/trump-speech-riot.html

Schweizer, P. (2018). *Secret Empires: How the American Political Class Hides Corruption and Enriches Family and friends/Peter Schweizer* (1st ed). New York: Harper, an imprint of HarperCollins Publishers.

Seitz, A., & Swenson, A. (2021, April 20). *Baseless Wayfair Child-Trafficking Theory Spreads Online*. AP NEWS. https://apnews.com/article/social-media-us-news-ap-top-news-conspiracy-media-9d54570ebba5e406667c38cb29522ec6

Sommer, W. (2018, November 20). Trump Fans Sink Savings Into 'Iraqi Dinar' Scam. *The Daily Beast*. https://www.thedailybeast.com/trump-fans-sink-savings-into-iraqi-dinar-scam

Sommer, W. (2022, April 15). QAnon Leaders Push Followers Into Multi-Level Marketing. *The Daily Beast*. https://www.thedailybeast.com/qanon-leaders-push-followers-into-multi-level-marketing

Tarnopolsky, C. (2017). Melancholia and Mania on the Trump Campaign Trail. *Theory & Event*, *20*(1), 100–128.

Taussig, M. T. (2010). *The Devil and Commodity Fetishism in South America*. University of North Carolina Press. http://ebookcentral.proquest.com/lib/aul/detail.action?docID=565708

Tiffany, K. (2020, October 28). This Will Change Your Life. *The Atlantic*. https://www.theatlantic.com/technology/archive/2020/10/why-multilevel-marketing-and-qanon-go-hand-hand/616885/

Toy, E. V. Jr. (2006). William Dudley Pelley: A Life in Right-Wing Extremism and the Occult. *Journal of American History*, *93*(2), 572–573. https://doi.org/10.2307/4486338

West, N. (2009). *Miss Lonelyhearts & the Day of the Locust*. New York: New Directions Publishing.

PART III

Old Marketing in New Media

8

FAITH-CENTRIC TIKTOKS

Promoting Religion through Personalized Experience and Engagement

Mara Einstein

I have long argued that religion is a product (Einstein, 2008). The combination of faith, ritual, and community is promoted and packaged like other marketable goods and services. And like promotion for other goods, video content has become the predominant form of persuasive communication for faith-based groups. The Mormon Church had a successful, long-running campaign called "I am a Mormon." Scientology advised people to question their life and look for answers with a commercial called *Curious?* (Frazier, 2019), and evangelicals fund a $100 million-plus advertising campaign called, "He Gets Us," that has run in sports programming from March Madness to the Super Bowl.

While these broad-based appeals create awareness, their ultimate goal is to drive people online. HeGetsUs asks viewers to go to YouTube, Instagram, and their website. Mormons—or Latter-day Saints, as is now their preference—wanted to connect visitors with other believers online. Scientologists have a robust website with ways to connect with members, more commercials, and a trove of videos explaining the belief system. Traditional religion institutions, too, found that they had to pivot to providing online options during the COVID-19 pandemic. Religious services were streamed to congregants but also were widely available to seekers and the simply curious around the world (Campbell, 2021). Providing content this way had a two-fold benefit: digital services engaged current congregants while acting as marketing for prospective religious shoppers, reminiscent of religious radio and TV's past (Hangen, 2002).

Marketing on digital platforms prevails because broad-based, mass marketing tools are no longer as effective as they used to be for religion or any other product. This is especially true when communicating with younger generations like millennials and Gen Z who expect personalized, "authentic" content (Fils, 2020) presented in short-form, "snackable" videos (Jenkins, Ford, & Green, 2013). Customized

DOI: 10.4324/9781003342229-12

viewing experiences have driven viewers away from legacy media and toward social media outlets from Instagram to SnapChat to Twitch, and now TikTok.

Because social media (especially TikTok) and the influencers that populate them are a relatively new phenomenon, there is little theorizing in this area (Vrontis et al., 2021). Therefore, I will draw insights from marketing theory and industry "best practices" in conversation with Religious Studies. I will use content analysis to examine how influencers leverage resources (personal branding, content, engagement) to enhance religious promotion on this platform. Importantly, TikTok's algorithm is "hyperpersonalized," increasing opportunities for parasocial relationships, word-of-mouth marketing, and influence on a level not seen elsewhere. That trust and relatability is why one of the most popular hashtags on the platform is #TikTokMadeMeBuyIt.

TikTok can be used as a promotional tool that educates visitors or as a digital form of word of mouth, especially because of its ability to broadcast video in real time. For this chapter, I will analyze Orthodox Jewish women TikTokers who engage their audiences through personal, informative posts, and contrast those with posts about the Christian revival at Asbury University in early 2023, an almost continuous two-week Holy Spirit "outpouring" on a small Kentucky campus which was driven by TikTokers posting personal and event-based content in real time.

Gen Z: Religion, TikTok, and Religion and TikTok

National polling has pointed to the attrition of Americans who identify as religious, especially among younger generations (Burge, 2021; Lipka, 2015). The decline is part of a decades-long trend in the increasing number of the unaffiliated, or religious "nones." Thirty-four percent of Generation Z is unaffiliated versus 29 percent of millennials and 25 percent of Gen X. Not only is Gen Z unaffiliated, they also identify as atheist (9 percent) or agnostic (9 percent) at a higher rate than previous generations. And while religious disaffiliation (religious "dones") is increasing (Smith, 2021), Gen Z does not stand out because they are more likely not to have been associated with a faith to begin with (Cox, 2022).

At the same time, Gen Z is also "more socially conscious and politically active than previous generations," suggesting that they are finding community outside of religious institutions (United Way, 2022). Activism is fueled by the social upheaval they have experienced. This generational cohort has grown up not knowing a world without September 11th. They bore the fallout from the recession of 2008. Climate change is a steady drumbeat in their lives. Active shooter drills are a regular occurrence, as are active shooters. And, their formative school years were marked by the murder of George Floyd, the January 6th Insurrection on the Capital, and a global pandemic. Their lives have been a series of what research company Cassandra calls "permacrises" (2023).

Social media has been integral to their lives, and TikTok has become the social media platform for this generation. Almost three quarters of adult TikTok users are between the ages of 18 and 34, and slicing this still further, those between 18 and 24 are more heavily weighted than those between 25 and 34 (Oberlo, 2023: Vogels, E. A., Gelles-Watnick, R., & Massarat, N., 2022). Gen Z is defined as those born between 1997 and 2013, so the oldest part of the cohort is in the sweet spot of TikTok users.

For those unfamiliar with the platform, TikTok is a video-based social media platform. Creators produce videos up to 10 minutes long, though most are much shorter. These videos can be of events, or the person posting can perform (often dances) or speak directly into the camera like shooting a selfie. The app allows for a number of editing functions, such as filters (made popular on Snapchat), captions, music, and overlays (putting content on top of content). There is also an option to go live. Unique to the app is the ability to connect a video to a snippet of someone else's (called a "stitch") or put new content side-by-side with someone else's ("duet"). Like other social media, you can share content ("repost"), you can follow people whose content you like, and you can comment on individual posts. Another unique function of TikTok is the ability for the poster to respond to comments with another video. I like to think of TikTok as Twitter with video, though others' experiences may be different. For example, if all you watch are dance videos, there is unlikely to be a lot of intellectual interaction.

The algorithm is what makes TikTok unique and, frankly, a mystery. The platform has a "following" page which provides the visitor videos from people they follow and a "for you" page that presents content to visitors which is based on content they liked or viewed. Visitors are also given recommendations of content ("accounts you may like") or they can look for specific content using a search bar. Importantly, algorithmically recommended content fosters communities and subcultures. So if someone is looking to learn about what Orthodox Jews do, they may start by using the search bar and over time as they like, repost, and follow that content, more of that content will appear in their feed. Similarly, young Christians found their feeds overwhelmed with #Asbury2023 because the algorithm "knew" that was content they would spend time with.

Content runs the gamut, with the most popular categories being beauty, dance moves, fitness, and of course cats (or dogs). News and politics also has a strong presence on the site with groups like @GenZforChange and their affiliated influencers such as @OliviaJulianna presenting issues from gun control to the environment. As for news, many young people learned about the war in Ukraine from the app and according to Pew Research, 25 percent of U.S. adults under 30 get their news from TikTok (Matsa, 2022). Communities are formed through hashtags like #politicstiktok, #booktok, #foodtok, and #faithtok. There's even #potatotok, which has 200 million members sharing recipes and their love of the spud.

TikTok's growth is in no small part attributable to the pandemic when people spent time at home endlessly scrolling (as well as learning to produce) TikToks. Here are some statistics: TikTok is the second most widely used app around the world. Users spend 22.9 hours per month on the app, which is second only to

YouTube where visitors spend 23.4 hours per month (McLachlan, 2023). TikTok began to increase in popularity in 2019, but it was during the pandemic that TikTok reached critical mass. The app had 66.5 million U.S. users in 2020, which was up 800 percent from two years prior (Dean, 2022). Today, the app has 100 million monthly users.

Faith on TikTok covers a wide range of topics. Manifesting is popular (#manifestation has 32.8 billion views), as is #witchtok (40.4 billion views). Visitors can find more traditional religious content from practicing pastors (Pastor Noah,[1] @badpastor[2]) or they can engage with ex-vangelicals, like Melody Stanford Martin (@melodystanfordmartin). These posts entertain, engage, and inform. Importantly, they also act as marketing and evangelizing tools.

The Rise of Influencers and Their Advantages as a Marketing Tool

Social media spaces are more personal and more emotionally evocative (Berger, 2013) than traditional media. You are not watching TV from across the room. You are interacting with a person who is talking into a camera while you are, in essence, hold them in the palm of your hand. Our phones have become extensions of ourselves (Belk, 1988; Park & Kaye, 2019), and our social media interactions seem as if they are one-on-one, even when they are not. This gives rise to parasocial relationships, imbalanced interactions where the viewer feels an emotional connection to the content creator while the influencer or celebrity is unaware of who is on the other side. But that doesn't matter. For the follower, the connection is real, and it can lead to positive or negative outcomes (Hoffner & Bond, 2022).

Know, too, that self-representation and the need to belong (in community) are drivers for social media use (Goffman, 1956; Winter et al., 2014). It is a personally creative space and a place to commune. In doing so, creators and followers generate social capital. Likes and shares increase creators' credibility, while engagement builds social relationships between creators and followers as well as among followers.

Within the context of this intimacy, visitors do not want their experience interrupted by advertising. In response, marketers made commercial messages less obvious—first with native advertising (ads made to appear indigenous to the site where they appear) and then with branded content which are articles or video that look like editorial but are paid for by a sponsor (Einstein, 2016).

The natural evolution of covert marketing has been the widespread use of influencers. The Internet Advertising Bureau (IAB), the industry's leading digital advertising association, defines influencers as "those who are deemed to have the potential to create engagement, drive conversation and/or sell products/services with the intended target audience. These individuals can range from being celebrities to more micro-targeted professional or nonprofessional 'peers'" (IAB, 2018).

Influencers provide significant advantages for digital marketers. First, influencers have created relationships—seemingly authentic relationships—with their followers, which make them perfect brand ambassadors, whether selling roombas or religion. Second, influencers are content producers as well as message dissemina-tors. Customization enables higher engagement levels than found in other digital formats. Third, influencers offer a two-way conversation. Visitors/consumers might interact with a brand or their church, but they are far more likely to have a conver-sation with one of their favorite YouTubers or TikTokers. And, unlike most brands or religious institutions, influencers are entertaining and relatable; they evoke emo-tion and have a relationship with the visitor on a channel the audience opted into.

Content creators (influencers' preferred nomenclature) are no longer a monolith. The landscape segments by the number of followers. On TikTok, for instance, there is Mr. Beast—someone who has been posting stunts and challenges on YouTube for more than a decade—who has millions of followers across multiple platforms. He has the most subscriptions on YouTube (160 million) and his TikTok account has more than 83.9 million followers.

But not all influencers have millions of followers, nor do they have to (Collectively, 2018). Followers as a measure of marketing success have come into dispute with the rise of bots and the ability to buy followers (see Confessore, Dance, Harris, & Hansen, 2018), yet it continues to be used as a key performance indicator. The true value of influencers, however, is in their relationship with their audiences and their ability to get those audiences to buy into what they are sell-ing, whether it is a product or themselves. Broadly, then, there are thousands of influencers with follower numbers ranging from a few hundred to many millions. At the top of the list are the mega influencers, like Mr. Beast. At the next level are micro-influencers, with tens of thousands of followers, who can be important in persuading their fan base if their followers are loyal and passionate. Finally, there are nano influencers, with a few thousand followers, who present themselves as everyday people. These nano influencers have become increasingly popular as star influencers have become more expensive. Brands use nano influencers, but so do politicians because of their ability to create local impact.

Religious Content Creators

Religious content creators are unique. Unlike other product categories, faith is not homogeneous. There are different religions, different forms of practice, and a variety of ways to promote belief systems both within and outside of a traditional religious institution (Albanese, 1992; James, 2012). The product being endorsed is ill-defined in comparison to traditional packaged goods. Is the product being sold the Bible or a church leader or even clothes with a religious twist that is being hawked? In ad-dition, many influencers (particularly on Instagram) present themselves as religious to promote secular products rather than to promote religion per se.

Understanding all this, elsewhere I created a taxonomy of what was then called religious influencers (Einstein, 2020). These content creators exist on a spectrum from pure promotion of faith to using faith to promote secular products (Traditional Religious Leaders, Religious Innovators, Religious Social Celebrities, Faith-filled

Celebrities and Industrialists, Evangelicals/Televangelists, and False Profits). At one end of the spectrum are traditional religious leaders, such as the Pope or the Dalai Lama. These leaders are not so much selling faith as they are living their faith, and in presenting it affecting those who follow them. At the other are influencers who primarily sell products, like journals or candles, but use faith as a tool to persuade prospective customers. This presentation—using religious iconography, mentioning God or Jesus, etc.—becomes a form of promotion whether products or ideology is being sold. A great example here is Sazan Hendrix (@sazan), a fashion and beauty influencer and the creator of Bless Box, who now promotes candles and family and faith.

Creativity was surprisingly lacking when I analyzed religion on social media platforms like Twitter or Instagram. That has changed with the introduction of TikTok. Because of the sense of intimacy, the video content, and ease of production, TikTok has enabled dialogue in a way other platforms have not. I will examine this here first by looking at examples of Orthodox Jewish content.

The Orthodox Jewish (sort of) Ladies of TikTok

Three popular accounts that use TikTok to teach about Orthodox Judaism are @miriamezagui (1.6 million followers; 82.9 million likes), @therealmelindastrauss (811,000 followers; 81.2 million likes), and @nonjewishnanny (30k followers, 1.1 million likes).

Miriam Ezagui is a labor and delivery nurse by profession. She creates content for TikTok and Instagram, and some of it is repurposed across both platforms, though TikTok is her primary platform. She has 1.6 million followers on TikTok versus 74,000 on Instagram. Her content is a mix of family, cooking, celebrations, and lots and lots and lots of explanations of what it is like to be an Orthodox Jew. She wears a head scarf, so she is immediately identifiable as Orthodox. She labels each of her videos (another function of TikTok) so people will know what they are going to see before they click the post. Topics include "recap of Passover," "hard-boiled egg hack," and "shopping for a prayer shawl."

Most of Miriam's content is of her talking directly to the camera. She is teaching her followers, but she describes it as "sharing.": "I'm Miriam and I'm an Orthodox Jew and I share what my life is like." The style is very relatable and she exudes kindness and approachability, which you might expect from a labor and delivery nurse. Her posts get views in the hundreds of thousands and many have a million or more. Two stand out: one is about how on Shabbos Jews are not allowed to tear toilet paper. The frame people see if they go to her page is of Miriam sitting on the toilet—a visual that is arresting in and of itself. She then goes on to explain how Jews work around this requirement. This post has 466,000 likes, 11,800 people favorited it, and it has generated more than 7400 comments. Miriam responds to most of the comments—she actively engages with her audience—which is a key aspect of success on the platform. This post got 8.3 million views.

Another post was a response post. Someone had commented "go in the oven jew." The title of the post is "I'm a Jew & I'm Proud." Miriam looks directly into the camera, she takes off her glasses (which she rarely does) and she says, "Hi, I'm Miriam and I am a proud Orthodox Jew." Text is overlayed on the video. It says: "For thousands of years Jews has [sic] been persecuted. Great empires have tried to extinguish our flame, but we survive. We. Will. Always. Survive!" She subtly winks as the copy says, "Your hatred has no power over me." This has 2.4 million views, 297,000 likes, 4635 favorites, and 4737 shares. Comments are overwhelmingly supportive of Miriam.

Melinda Strauss (@therealmelindastrauss) presents as a typical influencer/content creator. Perhaps this is because she started as a kosher food blogger in 2011. Melinda wears a wig (usually in a bun) rather than a scarf, though I have to admit it is so naturally looking I wasn't even sure. She also wears distinctive glasses. She, too, talks directly to the camera. Her content is, not surprisingly, mostly about food. Examples of her posts include: Trader Joe's Kosher Food Haul, Making Challah is Spiritual for Jewish Women, and Packing Kosher Food for the Airplane. Periodically, she taps into other content, such as a discussion of the Holocaust and letting her followers know that it is okay to talk about the Holocaust—in fact it is encouraged—even if you are not Jewish. Like Miriam, she readily engages with her audience. Her "mantra": there are no stupid questions, thus encouraging followers to interact with her.

Like many influencers, she has a Linktree which includes links to "Shop my Merch" (sweatshirts and t-shirts, totes, etc. that include her signature glasses and bun), "Shop My Amazon" (product recommendations for which she is paid an affiliate fee), plus links to a website, another to recipes, and an option to request a video message, among a few others.

Adriana Rosie (@nonjewishnanny) is, as the handle suggests, a non-Jewish caregiver who works for Orthodox Jewish families. Similar to Miriam, she explains the intricacies of Orthodox Judaism, but she does it with an outsider's naivete. One video is about how she discovered there is makeup specifically for Shabbos (the Sabbath). In another, she talks about discovering how wild a holiday Purim is. Still others are videos with Miriam.

Adriana is younger than the other two women (she is 21 and Gen Z) and creates content that engages a younger audience. She takes advantage of TikTok's functionality, using a mix of trends and content rather than simply talking into the camera. For example, she is dancing in a video to music with the words, "I hate Kanye," a reference to Kanye West who has been spouting antisemitism. Part of the text on screen says: "2023 IN—Accepting others regardless of preconceived notions…2023 OUT—Kanye." She does not limit her content to Judaism or being a nanny but rather mixes it up to talk about her life as a young working person. She is frustrated by other drivers honking at her while she parks her car, she talks about how she was suckered into buying more makeup than she needed at Saks, and she laments that she is not making money from what she went to college for: she is a trained opera singer.

Adriana has a Linktree and sells merchandise on her blog, where she posts her mission: "my goal is to bridge the gap between the non-Jewish and Jewish morals that we can all use in our day-to-day lives and come together as one." She, too, has an Amazon affiliate page.

Individually and as a group, these content creators have opened a space for discussing Orthodox Judaism online. They are "authentic" or as much as one can be on one of these sites, but more importantly, they are engaging and engaged. They all receive numerous comments on their posts, and the creators take the time to respond to them. Like Melinda's philosophy, there are no dumb questions and explanations about the faith are presented as "let me share" rather than dogma or talking down. Maybe this is a function of the platform, or maybe it is effective salesmanship.

The possibility for video-based, personalized exchange among individuals at scale has not existed up until now. Twitter is language-based and so lacked nuance and intimacy. Instagram, while playing catch up to TikTok with Reels, still carries the imprimatur of being based on still photography and more importantly "perfect" still photography. TikTok, on the other hand, privileges messiness and appearing to be less practiced…except when it comes to dance moves.

What this means for the promotion of religion is the opportunity to have conversations about faith. The parasocial relationships created and the glimpse into lived religion are similar to those that emerged from reality TV, the rare programming where lived religion was presented on legacy media (Einstein, Madden, & Winston, 2018).

Asbury Revival 2023

For two weeks in February 2023 (8th–24th), tens of thousands of people made their way to Asbury University in rural Kentucky for what was called a modern-day revival. According to reported accounts, the event began spontaneously when a handful of students decided to remain in the chapel after a regular morning service to continue worshipping together. Others heard about the singing and praying, and by that evening, students were bringing mattresses to the building so they could spend the night. Slowly others joined until the venue reached capacity (1500-seats). Additional rooms had to be provided, and screens were erected outside to accommodate the overflow (Graham, 2023).[3]

The revival was shut down because 50,000 people who arrived from around the world overwhelmed the resources of the small community of 6000 residents. Some likened the event to Woodstock and it had a similar vibe—there was music, there were ecstatic experiences, and they had to bring in port-a-potties.

Initially, people were drawn to the event by one friend telling another (word-of-mouth marketing) and via Instagram. However, most were led to this small Christian college because of an unending stream of posts on TikTok.[4]

According to a hashtag search on TikTok, #asburyrevival2023 got 33.1 million views and #asburyrevival got 140.7 million views. Given this, it would be impossible in this limited space to discuss all the videos posted. Instead, I will provide examples of three types of posts that emerged and how they worked synergistically. These categories were: (1) videos from in and around the chapel, (2) testimonial videos of those who had been to Asbury, and (3) naysayers, who either had been to the event or who condemned it from afar.[5]

Videos from inside the chapel far outweighed any others. People were admonished not to record what was happening in the chapel, and yet hundreds if not thousands of these videos appeared so no one stopped people from pulling out their phones. Given the exigencies of the platform, it is easy to see why these videos were so popular. It is ready-made content. Posters only have to put titles on it and write a caption. One video posted by multiple accounts was of a young female college student with reddish hair standing and praying in front of the chapel. Her eyes are closed and she says, "…May they feel your presence in this very moment like they have never felt it before in their entire lives….God hears. God hears every prayer we have ever prayed…." An older woman is holding a microphone so all can hear, and this goes on for about 3 minutes.[6] Another popular version of "being there" content was to show how crowded the chapel was and then to pan outside to show the long line of people waiting in the cold to get it.

TikTok's algorithm favors short videos. So, snippets of people singing and swaying inside the chapel were popular. These were overlaid with information about where people could see the live stream or they were titled as "Update from Asbury" and noted with the day or hour of the revival (Day 8, 190+ Hours of Worship). One such video was a man who was supposedly healed by God.[7] The video was a response to a comment/question: "The man did he end up walking?"[sic] This got 28,000 likes. It also had over 500 comments, debating whether God could heal or making claims that He did such as "Another person who was partially deaf was healed as well. They didn't have to use their hearing aids anymore."

"I was there" videos began to take off after the first week. One person posted about how he and his wife drove more than 9 hours with his kids to get to Asbury. He was quick to say that not everyone would have the experience they did, but he said it was "wild" and that he felt the presence of God. Other videos show young people looking directly into the camera—either sitting in their car (a common TikTok venue because the lighting is perfect and it allows for optimum sound quality) or sitting behind a mic—talking about their experiences and how they felt that Jesus was in the room and this was a true revival. A typical one is by @kayyramos7, a young Hispanic college woman who sits in her car talking to the camera. She has a limited number of posts (15) and the only one that went viral is one she posted about Asbury. Her experiential video was done later and gets 1900 views, but it did not elicit much engagement. Her talk is rambling and stream of consciousness. She says in part:

> …you can sense like there was repentance in the air like you can just sense so much love, so much joy….before I went there, I prayed to God, and I asked like

what do you want me to see in this place? ... And to me, it just felt like, you know, in a way that was saying like "I'm coming back soon...go and tell others go...I need to go tell other people that God is real....if you're watching this video, and you don't know Jesus personally, I pray that Jesus will become so real to you that you encounter him that you will give up your life to him. So I just pray that you will know Jesus...He loves you. He died for you on the cross for you he died and if you believe in Him, your sins will be forgiven and Jesus is the only way, the way, the truth and the LIFE. Love you, guys

Naysayers, skeptics, and even the faithful who didn't believe that this was a true revival made for the most contentious content. They tagged their content with the appropriate Asbury hashtags so they knew they were opening themselves up to not only engagement from supporters but pushback from detractors.

One post was from an evangelical, 30-something pastor named A. G. Keeler. He is a regular TikToker and has more than 10,000 followers. He posted several times about Asbury, including one as he was on his way and one about LGBTQ and critical race theory (CRT) at Asbury. However, the one with the most views (419,000) was one labeled "I went to Asbury." He is sitting in a van talking to the camera and you can tell from his voice that he is hesitant about what he is about to say, which is where he begins:

It's actually a really difficult video for me to make. Now those of you who have called me a Pharisee over the last few days may not believe me, but I was really hopeful about what's happening at Asbury. Honestly, I felt like weeping because there's no gospel being proclaimed or offered. Instead, a distorted gospel is being presented and applauded.

...We were in the chapel for two and a half hours. Upon entering, the main leader was giving announcements and admitted that not much preaching has taken place. He said, "because we're not here to listen to a mesmerizing speaker." There was repetitive music which was rhythmic and emotional. There was great enthusiasm for meaningless phrases like "splashing in the love of Jesus" and "settling into grace," which was received with applause and amens....

Most concerning was the lack of the gospel. Two of the speakers said the word gospel as though they were communicating it, but it was absent. I wrote down some phrases that summarize the gospel I heard. "We know your life has been full of pain, but we're here to tell you Jesus loves you." "Your story is full of pain and Jesus receives you as you are," "Jesus is speaking, healing to broken, bleeding, wounded hearts, hear your testimonies," but not one of the testimonies we heard were about repentance and sadly, none really mentioned Jesus, if at all. That being said, I don't doubt anyone's sincerity. And I think people will get out of this what they want to. I in no way think that I have a definitive say or word on what is happening at Asbury. I'm simply sharing what I saw, what I experienced, and what I think about it.[8]

Another religious TikToker had a similar reaction, though with a less nuanced approach. @jeremystock5 (24,000 followers; 300,000+ likes) identifies himself as an Orthodox Christian, a former Calvinist and former evangelical, according to his bio. The Christian iconography visibly displayed behind him suggests his Christian identification, similar to when authors make sure you can see their book in the background.

His video starts with a stitch (a combining of videos) that asks the question: is this revival?[9] His answer is a definitive no. "I call it everything I see all in the time in evangelical Christianity in America." The post uses quick cuts of videos from a variety of Christian services, but all of them show young people jumping up and down with a gospel, rock soundtrack underneath. These are spliced with commentary from Jeremy, who is balding, wears a sweatshirt, and looks to be in his 40s.

He denounces the services saying that jumping and singing and emotion are all the current generation knows "as being filled in the Spirit." It is simply about emotional experiences and not the gospel. He admonishes viewers to go to the college's website where they claim to have had several revivals over the last century. Then he asks his viewers, "where to you go now? The next Hillsong concert?" The video goes on to be a rant against Protestants who he claims have stripped Christian of its true faith.

This TikTok has more than 200,000 views and very high engagement (7479 likes and more than 2500 comments). Most commenters attack Jeremy, claiming he doesn't know what it is like to feel the Holy Spirit. One positive commenter said, "Not to mention the fact that the majority of them were already Christian. It's not like there were mass conversions here or anything," which is the point of a revival. One commenter said that he hadn't been to church in years and went to Asbury and felt the Spirit, and Jeremy's response was, "ok, now what happens?"

A third type of detractor was ex-evangelicals or dones. Irene (@poullution) is one such poster. Her bio lists her as a historian and storyteller. She has 52,000 followers and more than a million likes. Many posts get tens of thousands of views, but the one that received the most (90,000+) was on Asbury, in which she said directly to the camera:

I will believe the Asbury College [sic] revival is the work of the Holy Spirit when someone stands on that stage and openly condemns Christian nationalism, and the conflation of Republicanism and Christianity. And if there's not someone moved by the Spirit of God in that fucking room to stand up there and claim that this is a fucking revival, and not speak that goddamn biblical truth, then I don't know what the fuck they're doing in there, but it's not the work of God. Because the God I grew up studying and worshiping and praying to would not allow a revival to happen in this cultural context that did not do such thing.[10]

The comment section for this was a mix of positive and negative responses. While some related to Irene and were skeptical about revivals because they had seen them in their youth or they were concerned about how manipulative gospel music is, many took offense at her swearing or claimed that religion was not tied to politics.

Irene looks to be in her late 20s, so she is on the young end of the millennial generation, and she responds with the wit and wisdom of her generation—she is smart, she is bold, and she has little problem slapping back if someone questions her thinking. She is an equal mix of angry ex-evangelical combined with the intellect of an academic. In one exchange, someone commented, "Your belief on if it is real has absolutely no bearing on its authenticity." To which Irene responded, "but it bothered you enough to comment 🐵 ♀."

At its essence, the promotion of Asbury was fueled by the variety of posts, the intense passion in terms of the engagement, and the emotion driven, especially by those who did not see the outpouring as a true revival. It is that emotion—especially anger—that works well on social media. These posts have virality, and the online virality spilled into real life.

Jumping on trends is encouraged on TikTok, and Asbury was nothing if not a trend. In marketing, this is known as "borrowed interest," using a celebrity or a trending popular culture event to grab people's attention so they will listen to your sales pitch. For example, CWC ministries (@cwc_youth) took advantage of the Asbury audience and created a TikTok just for the event. They even had t-shirts made that were sold through Amazon. The Daily Wire, the media company behind Ben Shapiro's conservative podcast, made sure to post about the event. Christian celebrities tried to claim the event, but most of those attempts were quickly quashed. While these posts were not central to the conversation, they opened up the information to a wider audience. Note, too, that it wasn't influencers who drove the revival but rather tonnage from a multiplicity of people posting. And those people could repurpose ready-made content that others had already posted.

At its base, then, TikTok worked as an effective promotional tool for the Asbury phenomenon because of the media-ready content of the event and because of its demographic target. First, charismatic Christian experiences lend themselves to social media.[11] This is especially true for a continuous event like Asbury. While there were a few videos of people "engaging with the Holy Spirit," most simply showed the filled chapel while music was playing and people were singing and swaying. This could be shown in short clips that do well on the platform.

Asbury was tailor-made for Gen Z. The revival occurred on a college campus, which automatically frames it as being for this generation. Further, the visuals were stage managed to appeal to young audiences. People aged 25 and under had a fast-track entrance into the chapel, and they were given seats in the front. While a handful of videos showed older folks (like the man being healed so he could walk), most were of college-age students praying at the front of the chapel or if a pastor was shown, they too were young, probably millennial.

Religion, Social Media, and the Market

Religion on TikTok provides an opportunity to conceive of social media marketing beyond a capital market context. After all, the examples studied here are not primarily platform capitalism, the use of a social media platform to grow one's business (Srnicek, 2016). Rather, these influencers define success through a broader range of metrics than simply product sales or revenues generated, but through replicating traditional promotion and education. Social media, when amplified by legacy media, can replicate broadcast's impact. Influencers have the ability to affect our thinking about politics, education, and, yes, religion.

Yet TikTok as a medium has proved itself to be more versatile and more engaging than other platforms. For the Orthodox Jewish community, it has provided a relatively safe space online for conversations to be had across belief systems—something people have been trying to do for decades. Is it selling the religion? No. I believe it is about selling acceptance and understanding. And unlike Holocaust education, it is explaining why Jews are different and that that is ok (Horn, 2023).

As for Asbury, whether this was a true revival (I'm not a religious scholar so I will not jump into that conversation) is beyond the point. It was good video. It was Gen Z focused, and it gave viewers an opportunity to put their pandemic trauma onto a platform and discuss it with a broad community. While older people might have had their physical ailments tended to, it was mental pain that this generation was looking to heal. As with any medium, viewers projected their beliefs onto the content (Hall, 1991). For some having gone through the trauma of the pandemic, this was the hope they were looking for. Others saw Christian Nationalism. But, being social media, posts functioned as social capital for those doing the TikToking.

Notes

1 https://www.tiktok.com/@pastor.noah/video/7051815160364813573
2 https://www.tiktok.com/@badpastor/video/7202282170642173230
3 CBN coverage of the event can see seen on YouTube: https://www.youtube.com/watch?v=VbEDKy1qRoA&t=122s
4 Other media outlets, like Fox News, reported in the event. Celebrities tried to attach themselves to the event for publicity purposes. These were quashed by the University which did not want to turn this into a political event.
5 There were posts of people who only watched Asbury via TikTok but not enough to warrant separate analysis. Most watching from afar engaged via interactions with other posters.
6 https://www.tiktok.com/@awakenedpoet/video/7200762463963319557?q=asbury%20revival&t=1682018686496
7 https://www.tiktok.com/@micah894/video/7201714631788842283?q=asbury%20revival&t=1682030265520
8 https://www.tiktok.com/@a.g.keeler/video/7200533075309202730
9 https://www.tiktok.com/@jeremystock5/video/7199511441685105963
10 https://www.tiktok.com/@poullution/video/7201236018094148907?q=asbury%20revival&t=1682018686496

11 Evangelicals have historically wasted no time adopting new media forms as "witnessing tools" and have strategically harnessed media delivery that engages younger generations. See "Jesus Music" documentary. https://www.amazon.com/Jesus-Music-Amy-Grant/dp/B09MYQD267/ref=sr_1_1?crid=1HZ0MKH4JD24&keywords=the+jesus+music&qid=1687059129&sprefix=the+jesus+music%2Caps%2C138&sr=8-1

References

Albanese, C. L. (1992). *America, religions and religion*. Belmont: Wadsworth Pub. Co.

Belk, R. W. (1988). Possessions and the extended self. *Journal of Consumer Research*, 15(2), 139–168.

Berger, J. (2013). *Contagious: Why things catch on* (1st Simon & Schuster hardcover ed.). New York: Simon & Schuster.

Burge, R. P. (2021). *The nones: Where they came from, who they are, and where they are going*. Minneapolis, MN: Fortress Press.

Campbell, H. A. (2021, November 15). Tech in churches during COVID-19 Research Project publishes first report. Exploring the Pandemic Impact on Congregations. Retrieved April 27, 2023, from https://www.covidreligionresearch.org/tech-in-churches-during-covid-19-research-project-publishes-first-report/

Cassandra (2023). Gen Z Values & Value: Consumer Confidence Report. Cassandra Report. https://cassandra.co/reports/2023/01/26/consumer-confidence

Collectively. (2018). The social influence business in 2018 & beyond. Retrieved from https://www.collectivelyinc.com/reports

Confessore, N., Dance, G., Harris, R., & Hansen, M. (2018, January 27). The Follower Factory. *New York Times*. Retrieved March 11, 2019 from https://www.nytimes.com/interactive/2018/01/27/technology/social-media-bots.html

Cox, D. (2022). *Generation Z future of faith*. American Survey Center. https://www.americansurveycenter.org/research/generation-z-future-of-faith/

Dean, B. (2022). *TikTok user statistics*. Backlinko. https://backlinko.com/tiktok-users

Einstein, M. (2008). *Brands of faith: Marketing religion in a commercial age*. London: Routledge.

Einstein, M. (2016). *Black ops advertising: Native ads, content marketing and the covert world of the digital sell*. New York: OR Books.

Einstein, M. (2020). "Religious Influencers: Faith in the World of Marketing." In R. A. Lind, eds. *Produsing theory in a digital world 3.0*. New York: Peter Lang Verlag, pp. 121–138.

Einstein, M., Madden, K., & Winston, D. (Eds.). (2018). *Religion and reality TV: Faith in late capitalism* (1st ed.). London: Routledge.

Fils, S. (2020). "The Rise of Cause Marketing." *Business2Community*, February 18. https://www.business2community.com/social-business/the-rise-of-cause-marketing-02286159

Frazier, K. (2019). Scientology's 2019 Super Bowl ad asks "Curious?" *World Religion News*. Feb 4, 2019. https://www.worldreligionnews.com/entertainment/scientologys-2019-super-bowl-ad-asks-curious

Goffman, E. (1956). *The Presentation of Self in Everyday Life*. Edinburgh: University of Edinburgh, Social Sciences Research Centre.

Graham, R. (2023, February 23). 'Woodstock' for Christians: Revival Draws Thousands to Kentucky Town. The New York Times. https://www.nytimes.com/2023/02/23/us/kentucky-revival-asbury-university.html

Hall, S. (1991 [1973]). "Encoding, Decoding." In S. During, ed. *The cultural studies reader*. London: Routledge, pp. 90–103.

Hangen, T. J. (2002). *Redeeming the dial: Radio, religion, and popular culture in America.* Chapel Hill: University of North Carolina Press.

Hoffner, C. A., & Bond, B. J. (2022). Parasocial relationships, social media, & well-being. *Current Opinion in Psychology, 45.* p. 101306

Horn, D. (2023). Is Holocaust Education Making Anti-Semitism Worse? *The Atlantic.* https://www.theatlantic.com/magazine/archive/2023/05/holocaust-student-education-jewish-anti-semitism/673488/#:~:text=IS%20HOLOCAUST%20EDUCATION,helping%20living%20ones.

IAB (2018). *IAB influencer marketing for publishers.* https://www.iab.com/wp-content/uploads/2018/01/IAB_Influencer_Marketing_for_Publishers_2018-01-25.pdf

James, W. (2012). *The varieties of religious experience* (M. Bradley, Ed.). Oxford: Oxford University Press.

Jenkins, H., Ford, S., & Green, J. (2013). *Spreadable media: Creating value and meaning in a networked culture.* New York: New York University Press.

Lipka, M. (2015). Millennials increasingly are driving growth of nones. Pew Research Center. https://www.pewresearch.org/fact-tank/2015/05/12/millennials-increasingly-are-driving-growth-of-nones/

Matsa, K. E. (2022, October 21). More Americans are getting news on TikTok, bucking the trend on other social media sites. Retrieved from https://www.pewresearch.org/short-reads/2022/10/21/more-americans-are-getting-news-on-tiktok-bucking-the-trend-on-other-social-media-sites/.

McLachlan, S. (2023, April 13). 50+ Important TikTok Stats Marketers Need to Know in 2023. Hootsuite. https://blog.hootsuite.com/tiktok-stats/

Oberlo (2023). TikTok Age Demographics. https://www.oberlo.com/statistics/tiktok-age-demographics#:~:text=According%20to%20recent%20research%20studying,750%20million%20TikTok%20users%20worldwide

Park, C. S., & Kaye, B. K. (2019). Smartphone and self-extension: Functionally, anthropomorphically, and ontologically extending self via the smartphone. *Mobile Media & Communication, 7(2),* 215–231. https://doi.org/10.1177/2050157918808327

Smith, G. A. (2021). About three in ten U.S. adults are now religiously unaffiliated. Pew Research Center. https://www.pewresearch.org/religion/2021/12/14/about-three-in-ten-u-s-adults-are-now-religiously-unaffiliated/

Srnicek, N. (2016). *Platform capitalism.* Hoboken, NJ: Wiley.

United Way (2022). Generation Z Social Issues & Their Impact on Society. https://unitedwaynca.org/blog/gen-z-social-issues/#:~:text=Gen%20Z's%20economic%20concerns%20stem,during%20the%20COVID%2D19%20pandemic

Vogels, E. A., Gelles-Watnick, R., & Massarat, N. (2022). *Teens, social media and technology 2022.* Pew Research Center. https://www.pewresearch.org/internet/2022/08/10/teens-social-media-and-technology-2022/

Vrontis, D., Makrides, A., Christofi, M., & Thrassou, A. (2021). Social media influencer marketing: A systematic review, integrative framework and future research agenda. *International Journal of Consumer Studies, 45(4).* DOI:10.1111/ijcs.12647

Winter, S., Neubaum, G., Eimler, S. C., Gordon, V., Theil, J., Herrmann, J., Meinert, J., & Krämer, N. C. (2014). Another brick in the Facebook wall—How personality traits relate to the content of status updates. *Computers in Human Behavior, 34,* 194–202.

9

SELLING TO "SMARTIES"

The Marketing Strategies of a Social Justice Influencer

Kristin M. Peterson

In recent years, Instagram has emerged as a social media platform primarily for commercial interests, where so-called lifestyle influencers peddle products for corporations seeking to tap into loyal followings of various sizes. As Leaver et al. (2020) argue, social media influencers have "commercialized Instagram into a marketplace" (p. 102). In turn, influencers have shifted Instagram from a space for casual images of daily life shared with a small network of friends to a capital-driven platform of professional quality images with branded messages distributed to a large number of unknown followers. As criticism mounts against the harm that is caused by social media influencers for promoting unachievable beauty and lifestyle standards, a smaller subset of influencers incorporate social justice themes into their content.

This chapter focuses on the work of Blair Imani Ali, who has developed a significant following as what I term a "social justice influencer." She centers her account on her intersectional identity as Black, bisexual, and Muslim. Imani Ali has developed a novel influencer approach of educating her followers, whom she terms "Smarties," about the historical background behind current social justice issues through videos, carousels of images, and captioned photos. Despite her distinct educational content, Imani Ali still incorporates typical influencer posts like fashion styles, reflections on her relationship with her romantic partner, skincare routines, and sponsored content. Although her sponsored content garners far lower engagement in terms of likes and comments, for this chapter, I focus on Imani Ali's sponsored posts in order to evaluate how an influencer who often posts about deconstructing capitalistic systems of power is framing content about consumption.

Through an analysis of several sponsored content posts from December 2020 to August 2022, it is evident that Imani Ali is aware of the critiques of influencer culture: a promotion of toxic beauty standards, a focus on entrepreneurship and

DOI: 10.4324/9781003342229-13

unachievable success, and an encouragement of endless consumption of products. Rather than opt out of consumer culture, I assert that Imani Ali promotes an intentional form of consumption that incorporates a concern for social causes and promotes self-care and individual expression. Related to what Taylor (2019) terms "consumopiety," this intentional consumption becomes a "pious practice," allowing individuals to feel better about how they spend their money (p. 39). Imani Ali models this intentionality in her own consumption of products and her explanation of how products and companies reflect her values. While Imani Ali identifies as Muslim, she promotes more generic, social justice-inflected religious ideals that involve consuming products that provide positive values for the self and the world. Her followers do not adhere to a particular religious tradition, but they are united by this deeper desire to connect their consumption to their overall spiritual well-being. Imani Ali appears to deliberately promote products that align with progressive values of social justice and environmental care, but she never addresses the negative practices of some of these companies. Instead, she promotes products with feel-good messaging, and it can be a religious practice to consume these products with the goal of improving the self and the wider world.

Lifestyle Influencers

While various communities have engaged with the visual elements of Instagram, lifestyle influencers[1] dominate the platform by combining an "authentic" glimpse into their lives with a focus on consuming products to achieve and maintain this lifestyle. Influencers often interweave visual styles and consumption, as Duffy and Hund (2019) note that Instagram promotes "a user experience focused on curated images and, increasingly, opportunities to shop" (p. 4984). Consequently, Instagram is primarily a platform for marketing and consumption. Leaver et al. (2020) elaborate on this shift, as influencers maintain a high follower-to-following ratio, create professionally produced content that is highly curated to show the perfect lifestyle, and schedule posts to get the most engagement (pp. 103–104).

Unlike regular social media users, influencers are distinct in maintaining large online followings and monetizing posts about their lives (Abidin, 2016, p. 3). Marketers find these content creators valuable because of their "influence" on followers and their promotion of a lifestyle that is relatable but aspirational (Hund, 2017, p. 2). Unlike the unachievable lives of Hollywood celebrities, the lives of influencers seem to be within reach, as long as followers consume the same products. An influencer lifestyle appears as aspirational, but studies that examine this industry address the difficulty of achieving success as an influencer (Duffy, 2017). In addition, influencers, especially women, often have to negotiate what Duffy and Hund (2019) term the "authenticity bind," in which followers want influencers to be relatable and spontaneous, but they still expect their lives to be aspirational and visually attractive (p. 4985).

Social Justice Influencer

This chapter focuses on a lifestyle influencer who incorporates social justice messaging into her aesthetically pleasing lifestyle content. Imani Ali occasionally posts content about fashion or make-up and sponsored content, but the majority of her page focuses on educational material on progressive causes, especially those that relate to her identity as a Black, bisexual, Muslim woman. The wider Instagram community of Muslim female influencers focuses primarily on faith and how it relates to lifestyle topics like fashion, makeup, relationships, child-rearing, and cooking (Beta, 2019; Baulch and Pramiyanti, 2018; Mahmudova and Evolvi, 2021; Peterson, 2016). Beta (2019) proposes the concept of a "social media religious influencer" to examine how Indonesian female influencers use their online platforms to promote a lifestyle that brings together consumption, creativity, and entrepreneurship with Islamic ethics (p. 2149). For Imani Ali, Islam is a significant and visible aspect of her identity, and this is reflected in the topics that she posts about. However, Islam is one aspect of her multifaceted identity, allowing her to focus on a variety of topics and reach an audience outside of the Muslim community.

Building on her undergraduate degree in history, Imani Ali takes on the role of a historian and educator, reflecting an emerging trend of influencers as experts on particular topics. In an analysis of health influencers, Hendry et al. (2022) propose the concept of "influencer pedagogy" to examine how influencers "cultivate authenticity and expertise" in order to educate their followers (p. 1). The authors discuss how one health influencer, Ashy Bines, relies on her authentic connection to her followers rather than professional training in fitness or nutrition to share her recommendations. In a similar manner, Imani Ali does not hold a graduate degree but claims the identity of a historian based on her fanbase and her popular press books. Likewise, Baker and Rojek (2020) discuss how health and wellness influencers eschew traditional expertise and instead share "carefully constructed personas and narratives of self-transformation, documenting their journey from illness to self-recovery" (p. 2). Wellness influencers reflect the larger trend of expertise being granted based on one's individual experience and research and not traditional and institutional authorities.

In recent years, some self-care and wellness influencers have expanded their focus to address progressive political causes. Stein (2021) discusses the collision of two movements: "an extremely online mode of social justice activism and the rebranding of diet and beauty culture as wellness and 'self care'." The popularity of influencers like Imani Ali reflects this recent trend of social media influencers posting about political activism. Digital media can be a space for political activism, such as hashtag activism (Jackson et al., 2020), the #MeToo (Clark-Parsons, 2021), and #BlackLivesMatter (Clark, 2016; Bonilla and Rosa, 2015; Bailey, 2021) movements online, and feminist activism (Banet-Weiser, 2018; Clark-Parsons, 2022), but lifestyle influencers face growing pressure to address political topics. For instance, when U.S. public discussion centered on anti-Black racism in the wake of the police killing of George Floyd in the summer of 2020, social media influencers were compelled to respond in order to sustain their loyal followings. As Wellman (2022) found in a study of the trend of posting black squares to support #BlackLivesMatter, this form of "performative allyship" was done "to build and maintain credibility with followers" by appearing to support the cause but contributing little to social change (p. 2).

In the summer of 2020, Instagram in the U.S. shifted from what Nguyen (2020) calls "an apolitical din" with beautiful pictures of mindless content to a space where people respond to political concerns. "It no longer felt appropriate—even for celebrities and influencers, who tend to exist unfazed by current events—to skip over politics and resume regular programming," Nguyen explains. Since Instagram privileges visual images over written captions, the dominant way that political information spreads on Instagram is through single images or slideshows that feature text in attractive font with beautiful colors. Imani Ali effectively blends together the visual styles and trends of Instagram with progressive messages. At the same time, she is still an influencer who needs to hawk products and services to stay financially stable. Her sponsored posts fit into the lucrative brand strategy of using "cause marketing" (Einstein, 2012) to connect a positive social cause to a product. In the case of Imani Ali, she promotes products that she argues align with the progressive causes of her page.

Curating a Community of Smarties

Before becoming an Instagram influencer and educator, Imani Ali was involved in Muslim American political activism, which led her to an appearance on Tucker Carlson's Fox News TV show in June 2017 to discuss safe spaces for Muslims. In the midst of Carlson's questioning, Imani Ali appears unintentionally to come out as queer. This moment solidified her identity as a bisexual, Black Muslim woman who deliberately challenges the assumption that Muslims cannot be queer (McNamara, 2017). In July 2019, she posted a TEDx Video on YouTube, "Queer & Muslim: Nothing to Reconcile," which had over 600,000 views in March 2023 (Imani, 2019).

Imani Ali has developed her own visual style and influencer tactics on Instagram by educating followers about the historical background behind current social justice issues. She builds on her undergraduate degree in history, along with several books that she has written about intersectionality and history (Imani, 2018, 2020, 2021). Her most popular posts are "Smarter in Seconds" videos, which she launched in August 2020, two months after she became an influencer (Toglia, 2020; Imani Ali, 2022d). As the name implies, the videos are only 15–30 seconds long and feature quick cuts of Imani Ali and guest experts with on-screen captions. The videos share soundbites of information in a way that is engaging and hopefully memorable. The overall style of Imani Ali's posts is bright, upbeat, and colorful, while also reflecting the energetic, pulsating pace of TikTok videos and Instagram Stories. Viewers' attentions must be captured in fractions of a second, and the content must be easy to digest. A *New York Times* profile describes her brand, as "combining progressive lessons with vibrant visuals and a perky, quirky delivery" (Jackson, 2020).

Imani Ali's approach has found a significant audience with over 530,000 followers on Instagram in March 2023, and a growing community of over 90,000 followers on TikTok. Alongside her promotional content, she receives financial support from followers through "tips" on various cash applications or by becoming an official "Smartie" on her Patreon page. She has also published several books, which she sells along with her own brand of lip liner and lipstick, stickers, T-shirts, and other products featuring Smartie sayings, such as "Getting smarter" and "Learning is a blessing."

Methods

This chapter seeks to understand how a social justice influencer negotiates the pressures to be a successful influencer by selling a particular lifestyle with the critiques that the influencer industry mainly promotes excessive consumption and an unachievable lifestyle. This pressure is especially heightened since Imani Ali's primary content focuses on power imbalances and inequalities within capitalistic societies. In order to analyze these negotiations, I collected all of the sponsored content posts starting on August 31, 2022, and working backward until I had gathered 60 posts. I determined that posts were sponsored content if they had labels like #ad or #[Insert name of company]Partner. I coded the posts based on the company that the ad was for and what type of product or service was promoted.

I analyzed the text of the posts to look at how Imani Ali talks about the products and her language around consumption. My analysis primarily focused on the language in the captions since that is the main avenue for elaboration on the products and her thoughts on consumption. In addition, the keywords in the captions help the content to spread through searches and algorithms. The visual contents, such as images and videos, that accompany the captions fit in with the overall style of the page. The still images incorporate bright and bold colors and feature Imani Ali using the products. For some posts, she shares a video about a topic that has some tie-in to the product or service being advertised.

On average, Imani Ali posts sponsored content to her page around three times a month. The posts address a variety of topics, including makeup (13), skincare (10), accessories (8), technologies (6), and web applications (5). She posts less frequently about shoes (4), food (2), books (2), and clothing (1). Some of the content is for well-known brands, such as Dove, Dell, Skittles, and Fossil watches, and other posts are for brands that are more popular among young people, like Sephora, Shutterfly, Slack, and Toms shoes. She also shares ads for smaller and niche companies like Visible Mobile, Birdies, Loti, and Muse Health.

Intentional Consumption

Overall, Imani Ali promotes companies that she finds have progressive values and support underrepresented groups. She models an intentional form of consumption by offering explanations of how these products and companies reflect her values.

In an ad for Dell laptops, she states, "It's important to me that the tools I use to educate people about equality are made by companies that are committed to equality" (2021a). Since Imani Ali takes on this role of being an educator, it is essential that the sponsored content does not contradict the progressive messaging of her account. She risks losing credibility with her followers if she were to mindlessly promote products that are harmful to the consumer or companies that cause social or environmental damage. However, in a lot of the sponsored posts, she often parrots the messaging from the companies, focusing on diversity, equality, environmentalism, and social responsibility. This form of "purpose-washing" (Einstein, 2023) may address significant social concerns but does not take action to create social change. Furthermore, she never discusses the harm causes by large corporations. For instance, Dell is one of several technology companies that is currently being sued in federal court for using child labor to mine cobalt for batteries (Toh, 2019).

Imani Ali is also deliberate in the language that she uses in advertisements so as not to support oppressive ideologies. For instance, an ad for Birdies shoes asks, "What are you running? And this isn't an invitation into hustle culture. Never that!" (2022c). Her statement contradicts the pressure in influencer culture to work nonstop. In the same post, she appears doing a yoga pose but explains in the caption that yoga should never be culturally appropriated. Another example of careful language use appears in a post for self-love decals that people can put on their mirrors as a daily form of affirmation. In the caption, Imani Ali writes, "for those who are sighted, we might spend a bit of time looking into the mirror," acknowledging in the caption those who cannot see (2021s). In all of these cases, the progressive messaging around proper language that appears in most of her educational posts is reflected in her sponsored posts, indicating continuity between progressive activism and intentional consumption.

Several of the sponsored content posts focus on the companies themselves and how they support marginalized groups. Two ads for Visible Wireless explain how this small company collaborates with LGBTQ creators on social media (2021k, 2022g), and a post for HBO Max discusses how the streaming platform promotes the work of Black creators (2021c). In an ad for Birdies shoes, Imani Ali appears wearing sneakers next to a pile of books, connecting her success as an educator and influencer with these shoes. She explains in the caption that this women-owned business is "thoroughly dedicated to empowering women" (2022a). One of several ads for Dell discusses how the company CEO spoke publicly about the need for more diversity in the company (2021a). She writes in the caption, "It's rare to see companies speak up and acknowledge how they must also play a role in addressing inequality." This quote indicates her support of companies that go beyond the marketing messages, but at the same time, she doesn't explain how Dell is actually doing the work to create more equality in the workplace and wider society.

Imani Ali also explains how companies support progressive causes, such as care for the environment, ethical business practices, accessible design, and positive messages on beauty. Several posts address how companies are helping the environment, such as a clothing line that uses upcycled materials (2021f), a jewelry company that is "ethically sourced" (2021r), a post about Dove Beauty Bars that mentions the benefits of using bar soap over "polluting makeup wipes" (2021q) and several ads for Dell computers that discuss their recycling initiatives and minimal package design (2021a, 2021b, 2021g). In an ad for a new type of Ray Ban sunglasses that takes photos and videos, Imani Ali mentions that these glasses offer "new levels of accessibility," presumably for those who have limited use of their hands (2021m). Finally, she supports a brand like Dove because of their Real Beauty campaign and how they took "a stand against digital distortion" by showing real women's bodies in their ads without touch-ups (2021h).

The visuals for these sponsored posts illustrate how Imani Ali incorporates these products into her influencer style and her work educating followers. For instance, the post about Dell computers features a photo of Imani Ali's lap as she is working on her Instagram page while a book about African American history lies next to her (2021b). The post for Dove bar soap reflects a pastel and natural look, as Imani Ali appears in a pastel pink blouse and headscarf, lying on a light blue blanket with the light-colored bars of soap arranged around her head (2021q). A post for jewelry engages with a bold style with Imani Ali wearing primary colors (green, yellow, blue, red) (2021r). In both cases, the advertisements easily fit in with the overall style of the page, as she uses either a bold and bright style or a pastel and natural approach. The sponsored posts, and the products in turn, are not anomalies in Imani Ali's content but are integrated into her style and her role as an influencer and educator.

Consumption as a Form of Activism

Several of the sponsored posts on Imani Ali's account are not necessarily about selling a particular product but instead highlight campaigns for various social causes. This relates to what Mukherjee and Banet-Weiser (2012) term "commodity activism," in which consumption of particular brands becomes a form of social activism. In these partner posts, the brands connect with some of the causes for which Imani Ali advocates. In turn, her Smarties can support these social causes and Imani Ali's educational work by purchasing products from these companies that maintain an affiliation with Imani Ali. Some of the partner posts are for companies that align a cause with their products, such as a Dove ad about frontline workers with a tie-in to antibacterial soap (2021i) and a post for a hand sanitizer company about their donation of sanitizer to organizations in need (2021d).

In other posts, the causes are unrelated to the products, such as a series of posts with Fossil watches about Pride month and the Trevor Project (2022e, 2022f), a Sephora campaign against online harassment (2021p), a post for Smarties candy for World Mental Health Day (2021o), and a Pride month posting for Skittles about the company's support for GLAAD (2021j). In the last post for Skittles, Imani Ali is cautious to avoid supporting any company that gives her money. She writes, "My Smarties know that I do my research before partnering with any brand" (2021j).

This illustrates how she wants to be intentional about the products that she collaborates with and doesn't want to promote a company that isn't sincere in their work. In all of these posts, the product is effortlessly incorporated into Imani Ali's usual educational content and vibrant posts. She wears a rainbow Fossil watch while discussing Pride history; an educational video about online harassment incorporates Sephora's social media campaign against hate; and Imani Ali holds a bag of Skittles in a typical rainbow-colored slideshow of self-portraits. Followers can feel good about consuming products that are tied to positive and progressive messaging, but these positive posts cover over the harmful business practices of these large corporations. For instance, Skittles has been found to contain an unsafe level of titanium dioxide (Myers, 2022), and Sephora claims to be "cruelty free" but continues to pay companies to test their products on animals (de Vlaming, 2023).

Comments on Imani Ali's posts sometimes discuss this commitment to promoting companies and products that align with progressive values. For instance, in response to the Fossil ad for Pride month, one person writes, "I love that you've vetted the company you're partnering with so thoroughly and it's amazing to know that it goes deeper for @fossil than just pride merch" (Ha, 2022). This comment illustrates that Imani Ali's fans put their trust in her to only promote products of the highest quality and ethics. When a few commenters criticize this post for promoting a product that is just trying to make money off Pride month, also known as rainbow washing, Imani Ali responds in the comment section, explaining how Fossil is donating 100% of their proceeds to the Trevor Project, but she does not clarify how much the proceeds are. One commenter expresses appreciation for Imani Ali's transparency, "I was skeptical at first (not critical), but I know your values too well to know that you wouldn't blindly partner up with a brand during Pride month" (Emalie, 2022). Her followers recognize that the ideals in Imani Ali's educational content are reflected in the products and the messages that she promotes in the sponsored content.

One relevant counterpoint is demonstrated in an ad for Johnson & Johnson about first-aid kits. While the vast majority of comments are positive and affirming Imani Ali's message about the need to be prepared in an emergency, a couple of people react with surprise that Imani Ali would partner with such an unethical company. One person wrote, "But J&J is an awful company that gave thousands of woman [*sic*] ovarian cancer and PCOS and more because their parents used their baby powder on them. Among other things... Really surprised by this partnership" (modernalchemytx, 2022). Another commenter discusses the company's history of abuse and contribution to the opioid epidemic, but this person also couches their comments by stating, "I hope this doesn't read as rude/judgemental [sic] towards Blair, I'm a huge fan and still loved this lesson!" (Jay, 2022). This poster is valid in her critiques of this company but feels the need to clarify that they still support Imani Ali's work and her overall goals. In this case, a few commenters point to a noticeable disconnect between Imani Ali's progressive values and a company with a history of unethical and unjust business practices. These comments likely fade into the background but still point to the possibility that influencers, no matter their progressive messaging, ultimately promote products to make money and not because they believe the company will improve the world. Furthermore, even a self-appointed expert like Imani Ali, who does thorough research, might be convinced by positive "purpose-washing" (Einstein, 2023) and neglect to dig deeper into the practices of these corporations.

Self-Care and Self-Expression

In addition to her work to model how to intentionally consume products with progressive values, Imani Ali also uses her sponsored posts to focus on consumption as a means of self-care and self-expression instead of endless consumption to achieve unhealthy beauty standards or unattainable levels of success. Rather than reject jewelry, fashionable clothes, and makeup as promoting toxic beauty standards, Imani Ali advises in a jewelry ad, "Adorn yourself in ways YOU choose" (2020). Expressing yourself with fashion, makeup, or jewelry is not inherently a bad thing, according to this post, but what matters is that you are not confined by narrow standards of beauty or fleeting trends. In another post, she explains that her style and elaborate makeup are her own form of expression but not an expectation for everyone (2021r). Since she has a bold fashion style and often wears elaborate makeup, these posts contradict the pressures for women to express their identities in similar ways.

In an ad for Birdies shoes, she discusses how a lot of fashion styles and trends for women often feature uncomfortable attire and restrict women's movements. As Imani Ali writes, "So much of feminine fashion involves us making ourselves uncomfortable in order to be viewed as professional or sexy" (2022b). The ad features fashion footage of Imani Ali, modeling her original style while wearing the comfortable Birdies sneakers. This ad reinforces that you can express your own original style without the restrictions of uncomfortable clothing or unachievable beauty standards. All of these posts focus on how the products help Imani Ali express her own individual identity and encourage followers to find their own style.

In other posts, she explains how various products promote self-love and self-care, such as motivational decals to stick on your mirror (2021s) and Dove body wash as part of a relaxing bath (2021n). While Imani Ali often posts about Dove and how they promote positive beauty messages and self-care, Dove has similar problems as Johnson & Johnson of putting harmful chemicals in their products (Edney, 2022). These examples illustrate how persuasive "purpose-washing" can be, as the brands appeal to positive emotions around self-love while covering up the dangerous chemicals in the product or the negative consequences of producing these products (Einstein, 2023). She often posts about skincare and shares honest reflections about her struggles with acne, but these posts center on loving oneself, including skin blemishes, and maintaining "healthy skin," not "perfect skin"

(2021l). Sometimes the post might be about an unrelated product but promote self-care, such as one that she did for Shutterfly photo prints in which she talks about the need to cherish memories with friends and family. She writes about a photo with her partner that she printed with Shutterfly, "That's one recent memory but it's reflective of the life Akeem and I are making together. One where we prioritize each other before our careers. One where we are working to live and not living to work" (2021e). In posts like this, Imani Ali models how to work as an influencer contrary to the pressures to endlessly labor and to always consume products to improve one's appearance.

Blending Progressive Activism with Entrepreneurship

With a loyal following already established, influencers like Imani Ali often launch their own companies to sell directly to their followers. Since March 2022, Imani Ali began focusing most of her sponsored content on promoting Fempower Beauty, a makeup company of which she is now a co-owner. Of the ten most recent sponsored posts, seven were for Fempower Beauty, potentially signaling a shift away from sharing ads for other companies. The posts about Fempower Beauty reflect Imani Ali's consistent message of bringing together progressive causes with entrepreneurship and consumption. She discusses how she wants to sell "makeup with a message," and each one of the lipstick sets correlates to messages in Imani Ali's book (2022j). This is a direct way to connect consumption of products with progressive ideals. In another caption, she discusses how the company is deliberatively working against unhealthy beauty standards, unethical business practices, unsustainable sourcing of products, and competitive and toxic work environments, especially among women (2022i).

In another post, Imani Ali discusses how a lot of women will tell her that they only wear neutral shades of lipstick and never wear bold red or purple shades. She elaborates on how this can be a form of self-censorship when the women do not feel comfortable breaking out of the beauty norms and embracing bold styles. She even compares this to women not being confident enough to ask for a raise at work. She writes, "If you decide not to do something I want it to be because YOU decided not to, not because you feel like it's off limits" (2022h). Again, the promotion of this new line of lipsticks is about empowering women to be bold in their makeup and in their lives.

Now with her own beauty products to promote, Imani Ali can potentially move away from her dependence on other companies for sponsorship. With her previous partner posts and advertisements, she had to fit the products into her overall educational content about progressive causes. The companies needed to use ethical practices that did not harm the environment, or at least use green messaging around recycled products and environmental concerns; to support women, people of color, queer individuals, and other marginalized people; and/or to create products that promote self-love and expression outside of dominant beauty standards. This often led her mainly to promote smaller companies with less name recognition and presumably less advertisement funds. On the other hand, when Imani Ali partnered with a larger brand, Johnson & Johnson, she was called out by some commenters for promoting a company that has committed several acts of exploitation, raising questions about Imani Ali's expertise as a smart consumer of brands that actually do the work. With her own company, Imani Ali is able to craft products and messaging that reflect her progressive values.

Self-Fulfillment and Spiritual Enlightenment through Consumption

Although Imani Ali occasionally posts about issues related to her Muslim identity, the primary content on her page relates to social justice topics, which sometimes intersect with her identity as a Muslim but also as a Black, queer woman. Unlike other Muslim influencers, she doesn't post hijab-wrapping tutorials, modest fashion images, or advice about fasting during Ramadan. Instead of centering on her Islamic faith, Imani Ali serves as a spiritual guide to living a meaningful life as a progressive activist. The primary content on her page educates followers on how to become more enlightened politically and how to live a life that contributes to the betterment of society. Her sponsored content, as this chapter has shown, is seamlessly integrated into her educational content by guiding followers in the entire lifestyle of a "Smartie."

An enlightened Smartie does not mindlessly consume products, but instead intentionally consumes items that reflect progressive values, contribute to justice and equality around the world, and improve the individual, inside and out. Imani Ali's work fits into the larger ecosystem of social media influencers from those on the progressive left to the far right and all the conspiracy theorists in between. In many of these examples, influencers may encourage followers to "do their own research" about politics, health, and consumer products, but at the same time, the influencers promote that their approach is the best. In the case of Imani Ali, she promotes a particular spiritual way of being—not necessarily tied to her Muslim background—that consumption can be a form of spiritual transcendence by making oneself a better person and helping improve the world. Imani Ali acknowledges critiques of capitalism in her captions and, in turn, frames her advertisements around her support only for companies that have ethical practices, aid marginalized communities, and work toward progressive goals. Her sponsored posts also promote that consumption can be a form of self-care and self-love by using products to celebrate one's individual identity outside of destructive norms and pressures. Her product promotions often reflect the goal of cause marketing—to get people to consume products that make them feel good rather than consider the harmful effects of capitalistic consumption or what might be effective practices to enact real social change.

Note

1 The use of the term "influencer" has become loaded in the last few years. Some people involved in this industry prefer the term "content creator," but academic research generally uses the term "influencer."

References

Abidin, C. (2016). "Aren't these just young, rich women doing vain things online?": Influencer selfies as subversive frivolity. *Social Media + Society*, *2*(2), 1–17. https://doi.org/10.1177/2056305116641342

Bailey, M. (2021). *Misogynoir transformed: Black women's digital resistance*. New York: New York University Press.

Baker, S. A., & Rojek, C. (2020). The Belle Gibson scandal: The rise of lifestyle gurus as micro-celebrities in low-trust societies. *Journal of Sociology*, *56*(3), 388–404. https://doi.org/10.1177/1440783319846188

Banet-Weiser, S. (2018). *Empowered: Popular feminism and popular misogyny*. Durham, NC: Duke University Press.

Baulch, E., & Pramiyanti, A. (2018). Hijabers on Instagram: Using visual social media to construct the ideal Muslim woman. *Social Media + Society*, *4*(4), 1–15. https://doi.org/10.1177/2056305118800308

Beta, A. R. (2019). Commerce, piety and politics: Indonesian young Muslim women's groups as religious influencers. *New Media & Society*, *21*(10), 2140–2159. https://doi.org/10.1177/1461444819838774

Bonilla, Y. & Rosa, J. (2015). #Ferguson: Digital protest, hashtag ethnography, and the racial politics of social media in the United States. *American Ethnologist*, *42*(1), 4–17. https://doi.org/10.1111/amet.12112

Clark, L. S. (2016). Participants on the margins: #BlackLivesMatter and the role that shared artifacts of engagement played among minoritized political newcomers on Snapchat, Facebook, and Twitter. *International Journal of Communication 10*(2016): 235–253.

Clark-Parsons, R. (2021). "I SEE YOU, I BELIEVE YOU, I STAND WITH YOU": #MeToo and the performance of networked feminist visibility. *Feminist Media Studies*, *21*(3), 362–380. DOI: 10.1080/14680777.2019.1628797

Clark-Parsons, R. (2022). *Networked feminism: How digital media makers transformed gender justice movements*. Berkeley, CA: University of California Press.

De Vlaming, S. (2023, March 8). Is Sephora cruelty-free? Here's the astounding truth. *Beautymone*. https://beautymone.com/is-sephora-cruelty-free/#:~:text=Report%20Ad-,FAQ,Sephora%20is%20not%20cruelty%2Dfree.

Duffy, B. E. (2017). *(Not) getting paid to do what you love: Gender and aspirational labor in the social media economy*. New Haven, CT: Yale University Press.

Duffy, B. E. & Hund, E. (2019). Gendered visibility on social media: Navigating Instagram's authenticity bind. *International Journal of Communication*, *13*, 4983–5002.

Edney, A. (2022, October 24). Dove, other Unilever dry shampoos recalled over cancer risk. *Bloomberg*. https://www.bloomberg.com/news/articles/2022-10-24/unilever-recalls-dry-shampoos-including-dove-bed-head-over-cancer-risk?leadSource=uverify%20wall#xj4y7vzkg

Einstein, M. (2012). *Compassion, Inc.: How corporate America blurs the line between what we buy, who we are, and those we help*. Berkeley, CA: University of California Press.

Einstein, M. (2023, June 14). Mental health ads are often harmful. They don't have to be. *Slate*.

Emalie. [@embolden.art.co]. (2022, June 1). *Thank you for your transparency! I was skeptical at first* [Instagram comment]. Instagram. https://www.instagram.com/p/CeROWhIJG-g/

Ha, V. [@bonesonstones13]. (2022, June 1). *I love that you've vetted the company you're partnering with* [Instagram comment]. Instagram. https://www.instagram.com/p/CeROWhIJG-g/

Hendry, N. A., Hartung, C. & Welch, R. (2022). Health education, social media, and tensions of authenticity in the 'influencer pedagogy' of health influencer Ashy Bines. *Learning, Media and Technology, 47*(4), 427–439, DOI: 10.1080/17439884.2021.2006691

Hund, E. (2017). Measured beauty: Exploring the aesthetics of Instagram's fashion influencers. *#SMSociety17: Proceedings of the 8th International Conference on Social Media & Society.* Association for Computing Machinery.

Imani, B. (2018). *Modern HERstory: Stories of women and nonbinary people rewriting history.* Berkeley, CA: Ten Speed Press.

Imani, B. [TedX Talks]. (2019, July 9). *Queer & Muslim: Nothing to reconcile* [Video]. YouTube. https://youtu.be/8IhaGUlmO_k

Imani, B. (2020). *Making our way home: The great migration and the Black American dream.* Berkeley, CA: Ten Speed Press.

Imani, B. (2021). *Read this to get smarter: About race, class, gender, disability, and more.* Berkeley, CA: Ten Speed Press.

Imani Ali, B. [@blairimani]. (2020, December 21). *Today I'm partnered again with @PiercingPagoda!* [Instagram photo]. Instagram. https://www.instagram.com/p/CJEYDUvnHLf/

Imani Ali, B. [@blairimani]. (2021a, January 26). *It's important to me that the tools I use* [Instagram photo]. Instagram. https://www.instagram.com/p/CKhCCdmJs7B/

Imani Ali, B. [@blairimani]. (2021b, February 10). *There's a lot of research that goes into* [Instagram photo]. Instagram. https://www.instagram.com/p/CLHk9S6J247/

Imani Ali, B. [@blairimani]. (2021c, February 25). *#ad Have you ever gotten THIS immersed in a show?* [Instagram photo]. Instagram. https://www.instagram.com/p/CLucxNupIev/

Imani Ali, B. [@blairimani]. (2021d, March 9). *Hello Smarties! Blair Imani and Papa Imani* [Instagram photo]. Instagram. https://www.instagram.com/p/CMOG7NdpS1u/

Imani Ali, B. [@blairimani]. (2021e, April 3). *While you enjoy this radiant #ShuttleflyWonderWalls* [Instagram photo]. Instagram https://www.instagram.com/p/CNNbpVnHqrJ/

Imani Ali, B. [@blairimani]. (2021f, April 14). *TWINNING WITH MY BESTIE!* [Instagram photo]. Instagram. https://www.instagram.com/p/CNp4zVMnXUW/

Imani Ali, B. [@blairimani]. (2021g, April 22). *How convenient! It just so happens to be Earth Day* [Instagram photo]. Instagram. https://www.instagram.com/p/CN-Rf2nH9BR/;

Imani Ali, B. [@blairimani]. (2021h, May 3). *#SmarterInSeconds: My Self Esteem Tips in partnership with @Dove!* [Instagram video]. Instagram. https://www.instagram.com/p/CObQNYvnu75/

Imani Ali, B. [@blairimani]. (2021i, June 7). *#DovePartner Take a moment to think of all of the unsung heroes* [Instagram photo]. Instagram. https://www.instagram.com/p/CP0n_Fmj2TZ/

Imani Ali, B. [@blairimani]. (2021j, June 9). *@Skittles gave up its rainbow this Pride* [Instagram photo]. Instagram. https://www.instagram.com/p/CP5590kDaNb/

Imani Ali, B. [@blairimani]. (2021k, June 16). *Meet a member of my chosen family* [Instagram photo]. Instagram. https://www.instagram.com/p/CQMF0dyjWKL

Imani Ali, B. [@blairimani]. (2021l, August 9). *I'd much rather have healthy skin* [Instagram photo]. Instagram. https://www.instagram.com/p/CSXAj9QnYzL/

Imani Ali, B. [@blairimani]. (2021m, September 14). *If you ask me, we're living in the future* [Instagram photo]. Instagram. https://www.instagram.com/p/CTzpqo_FuXR/

Imani Ali, B. [@blairimani]. (2021n, September 25). *#DovePartner One of the number one questions smarties love* [Instagram photo]. Instagram. https://www.instagram.com/p/CUQDTu_pfRG/

Imani Ali, B. [@blairimani]. (2021o, October 10). *How to fight mental health stigma* [Instagram video]. Instagram. https://www.instagram.com/p/CU2xHmkp8gm/

Imani Ali, B. [@blairimani]. (2021p, October 13). *#SmarterInSeconds: Online Harassment in partnership with @Sephora* [Instagram video]. Instagram. https://www.instagram.com/p/CU-TtYQpFe_/

Imani Ali, B. [@blairimani]. (2021q, October 24). *#DovePartner Imagine this: You tell me how you incorporate* [Instagram photo]. Instagram. https://www.instagram.com/p/CVavF-MJHUB/

Imani Ali, B. [@blairimani]. (2021r, November 3). *Taking a break from our regularly scheduled lessons to slay* [Instagram photo]. Instagram. https://www.instagram.com/p/CV0XFUoJ91Q/

Imani Ali, B. [@blairimani]. (2021s, November 15). *If you don't have time to read my wholesome story* [Instagram video]. Instagram. https://www.instagram.com/p/CWTqDTWqYLO/

Imani Ali, B. [@blairimani]. (2022a, March 15). *What are YOU running?* [Instagram photo]. Instagram. https://www.instagram.com/p/CbI_WPgOWwj/

Imani Ali, B. [@blairimani]. (2022b, March 23) It's been amazing to work with @birdies on everything [Instagram photo]. Instagram. https://www.instagram.com/p/Cbd1_ThpfUL/

Imani Ali, B. [@blairimani]. (2022c, April 1). *@Birdies and I want to know* [Instagram photo]. Instagram. https://www.instagram.com/p/Cb0D-JnrZ-4/

Imani Ali, B. [@blairimani]. (2022d, April 29). Behind the Scenes of #SmarterInSeconds [Instagram video]. Instagram. https://www.instagram.com/p/Cc8Z8TpOJ4E/

Imani Ali, B. [@blairimani]. (2022e, June 1). *#SmarterinSeconds: LGBTQ+ History in partnership with @Fossil* [Instagram video]. Instagram. https://www.instagram.com/p/CeROWhIJG-g/

Imani Ali, B. [@blairimani]. (2022f, June 2). *@Fossil has invited me to join them* [Instagram photo]. Instagram. https://www.instagram.com/p/CeU1MCap8F8/

Imani Ali, B. [@blairimani]. (2022g, June 30). #ad 🍫 *About 1/4th of @visiblemobile's partners are LGBTQIA+* [Instagram photo]. Instagram. https://www.instagram.com/p/CfcySgEpMyh/

Imani Ali, B. [@blairimani]. (2022h, August 2). *Art by @zeaink. You might know that I have a lipstick collection* [Instagram photo]. Instagram. https://www.instagram.com/p/CgxOZ33v1Kh/

Imani Ali, B. [@blairimani]. (2022i, August 19). *It's official! As of August 1, 2022* [Instagram photo]. Instagram. https://www.instagram.com/p/Chc_q4xuepT/

Imani Ali, B. [@blairimani]. (2022j, August 21). *Let's meet the shades one by one!* [Instagram photo]. Instagram. https://www.instagram.com/p/ChiS1IIvSgP/

Jackson, L. (2020, November 13). The work diary of Blair Imani, 'herstory' historian. *New York Times*. https://www.nytimes.com/2020/11/13/business/blair-imani.html

Jackson, S. J., Bailey, M. & Welles, B. F. (2020). *#HashtagActivism: Networks of race and gender justice*. Cambridge, MA: MIT Press.

Jay [@jay_alicex]. (2022, February 1). *Such an important lesson! personally however I won't be buying from Johnson & Johnson* [Instagram comment]. Instagram. https://www.instagram.com/p/CZcaSw0pT2P/

Leaver, T., Highfield, T. & Abidin, C. (2020). *Instagram: Visual social media cultures.* Cambridge, UK: Polity.

Mahmudova, L., & Evolvi, G. (2021). Likes, comments, and follow requests: The Instagram user experiences of young Muslim women in the Netherlands. *Journal of Religion, Media and Digital Culture, 10*(1), 50–70. https://doi.org/10.1163/21659214-bja10038

McNamara, B. (2017, September 12). Blair Imani opens up about being queer, Black and Muslim. *Teen Vogue.* https://www.teenvogue.com/story/blair-imani-queer-muslim-woman

modernalchemytx [@modernalchemytx]. (2022, February 1). *But J&J is an awful company that gave thousands of woman* [Instagram comment]. Instagram. https://www.instagram.com/p/CZcaSw0pT2P/

Mukherjee, R. & Banet-Weiser, S. (2012). *Commodity activism: Cultural resistance in neo-liberal times.* New York: New York University Press.

Myers, I. (2022, October 19). Thousands of children's sweets STILL contain additive unsafe for human consumption. *Environmental Working Group.* https://www.ewg.org/news-insights/news/2022/10/thousands-childrens-sweets-still-contain-additive-unsafe-human

Nguyen, T. (2020, August 12). How social justice slideshows took over Instagram. *Vox.* https://www.vox.com/the-goods/21359098/social-justice-slideshows-instagram-activism

Peterson, K.M. (2016). Islamic fashion images on Instagram and the visuality of Muslim women. In R. A. Lind (Ed.), *Race and gender in electronic media: Content, context, culture* (pp. 247–263). New York: Routledge.

Stein, L. (2021, March 5). The empty religions of Instagram. *New York Times.* https://www.nytimes.com/2021/03/05/opinion/influencers-glennon-doyle-instagram.html?smid=url-share

Taylor, S.M. (2019). *Ecopiety: Green media and the dilemma of environmental virtue.* New York: New York University Press.

Toglia, M. (2020, September 29). IG activist Blair Imani has a hack for beating imposter syndrome. *Bustle.* https://www.bustle.com/life/instagram-activist-blair-imani-social-media-educate

Toh, M. (2019, December 18). Apple, Google, Microsoft, Dell and Tesla are sued over alleged child labor in Congo. *CNN Business.* https://www.cnn.com/2019/12/17/tech/apple-microsoft-tesla-dell-congo-cobalt-mining/index.html

Wellman, M. L. (2022). Black squares for Black lives? Performative allyship as credibility maintenance for social media influencers on Instagram. *Social Media + Society, 8*(1), 1–10. https://doi.org/10.1177/20563051221080473

10

MARKETING MAINLINE CAMPUS MINISTRY

"God Loves Everyone, No Exceptions"

John Schmalzbauer

Declension narratives abound in public discourse about mainline Protestantism—the mainline is always headed for the grave—yet seldom has the mainline thrown itself an actual funeral (Bass, 1989; Hoge, Johnson & Luidens, 1994; Hudnut-Beumler & Silk, 2018; Hutchison, 1989; Sloan, 1994; Weeks, Coalter & Mulder, 1990). But that is exactly what happened in the fall of 1969 when a group of seminarians and undergraduates conducted a public memorial service for Luther Hall at the University of Minnesota. Proclaiming "dust to dust … earth to earth," a liturgist scattered dirt on the building. To clarify, the building was not closing, at least not yet. Rather, the funeral's organizers were protesting the closing of the ministry's cafeteria and food service. A handout distributed at the event declared, "Lutheran campus ministry is dead at the Minneapolis campus." However, the organizers did leave open the possibility for life after death, noting that "we do believe in the resurrection of the dead and look for the resurrection of Lutheran campus ministry." Lutheran campus minister Gordon Dahl was not amused, calling the funeral premature. Premature or not, the event was covered by the *Minneapolis Star*, ensuring a wide readership in one of the country's most Lutheran cities. While the 1969 funeral did not mark the death of Lutheran campus ministry at the University of Minnesota, it symbolized the start of a long decline in both student participation and financial resources. While campus Lutherans still had the use of an ecumenical center in St. Paul, a building near the main campus, and a coffeehouse across the river, the time would come when the ministry would be without a building of its own. In the early years of the twentieth century, the number of participants sank to new lows, this in a ministry that once drew hundreds of Lutherans to its events ("Lutheran hall mock funeral premature," 1969, p. 15).

Yet the decline did not last forever. As the seminarians noted back in 1969, Lutherans believe in the resurrection of the dead. Unlike the Easter accounts in the

DOI: 10.4324/9781003342229-14

gospels, the resurrection of Lutheran campus ministry took longer than three days. Far from an immediate turnaround, it required an intentional effort to position mainline Protestant campus ministry in the crowded marketplace of student religious life. Far from instant, it involved a new campus minister and a new mission statement that could bridge the religious and political divides in a polarized region and state (Denker, 2022; Orenstein, 2021; Wuthnow, 2012). In a state divided between a blue metro area and a red agricultural region, Lutheran Campus Ministry-Twin Cities publicly declares, "Whether conservative or liberal, introvert or extrovert, city kid or country kid, engineer or English major, queer or straight, questioning or certain, there's a PLACE FOR YOU here" (Lutheran Campus Ministry-Twin Cities, n.d.). In recent years, the ministry has welcomed LGBTQ students, Future Farmers of America, business majors, and environmentalists. Utilizing a rhetoric of hospitality and inclusion, it has recruited students dissatisfied with the evangelical parachurch groups that dominate campus religious life.

Despite this inclusive rhetoric, diversity remains a persistent challenge, as it does for many mainline Protestant campus ministries in the United States. Based in Minneapolis, Lutheran Campus Ministry-Twin Cities does not minister in just any city, but in the city of George Floyd's murder. While encompassing a mixture of geographies, identities, and majors, LCM-Twin Cities has reflected the racial homogeneity of the Evangelical Lutheran Church in America, a church that has been called the "the Whitest Denomination in the U.S." (Duncan, 2019). While articulating progressive positions on racial justice and systemic racism, LCM has remained largely white. Though there are new efforts to become more diverse, they are constrained by the denominational culture of the ELCA. The challenge of diversity is also part of the story of Lutheran campus ministry at the University of Minnesota.

Renewal and Revitalization in the Mainline

Analyzing the opportunities and the constraints shaping Lutheran campus religious life, this chapter looks at how mainline Protestants in the Evangelical Lutheran Church in America promote their organization in a crowded campus religious marketplace. Part of the Landscape Study of Chaplaincy and Campus Ministry in the United States, it is a case study of a mainline campus ministry. In the past decade, Lutheran Campus Ministries-Twin Cities has enjoyed an era of renewal and revitalization. In 2019, the ministry served 444 bowls of soup, reached 256 students at outreach events, engaged in 107 peer-to-peer conversations, provided 68 students with pastoral care, hosted 71 students at off-campus retreats, and involved 53 students in weekly worship, with an annual budget of nearly $300,000 (Lutheran Campus Ministry-Twin Cities, 2019, p. 6). In short, LCM-Twin Cities is anything but dead. While attendance has fallen since the pandemic, the ministry is still the largest mainline campus ministry at the University of Minnesota. What accounts for this revitalization? Though many factors are at work (including the dynamic leadership of Pastor Kate Reuer Welton), one of the key sources of LCM's recent turnaround has been an ability to position the ministry in the wider marketplace of campus religion. In short, Lutheran Campus Ministry has created a brand and found its niche, using stories, symbols, and material culture to appeal to moderate and progressive college students. Given the bland reputation of American Lutheranism, "Lutheran branding" may seem like an oxymoron (even in Minneapolis). Yet such marketing efforts are not unheard of in mainline denominations (Einstein, 2011), including the Evangelical Lutheran Church in America, where congregations like the House for All Sinners and Saints and its founding pastor Nadia Bolz-Weber have combined ancient liturgy with popular culture (Freudenberg, 2018). Through a series of engaging YouTube videos, Bolz-Weber (2018) has gained a following among Gen Z and Millennial viewers. In a similar way, LCM-Twin Cities has creatively marketed the mainline, carving out a space for both Lutheran identity and progressive Christianity at the University of Minnesota.

Studies of the marketing of contemporary religion have focused disproportionately on white evangelicals or on new forms of emerging spirituality (Einstein, 2008; Finke & Stark, 2005; Turner, 2008). Missing from the contemporary literature on religious marketing is a consideration of mainline denominational forms of Christianity. One of the few scholars to address this topic, Elesha Coffman (2017) writes about "marketing the mainline" in the *Christian Century* from its founding in 1884 into the post-war era. Focusing on an earlier era, R. Laurence Moore (1994) argues that the peak of mainline marketing was during Prohibition, adding that "when liberal Protestant moralists gave up battling, they ceased to be creative innovators in the marketplace of culture" (p. 236). The modern denomination was one of the first efforts to brand and market mainline Protestant Christianity. Despite the post-1960s "decline of denominationalism" charted by Robert Wuthnow (1989, p. 12) in *The Restructuring of American Religion*, denominational brand names still have meaning for many Americans, including millions of college students. As Nancy Ammerman (2005) documents in *Pillars of Faith*, denominational identity "largely results from relationships and narrative practices," including "[t]elling stories about denominational mission accomplishments, singing the songs of the faith and otherwise emphasizing its distinctive worship practices" (pp. 247, 251). Symbols and visual culture also play a role in the marketing of American denominations. As Mara Einstein (2008) writes in *Brands of Faith*, religious marketers make use of the shorthand of branding, noting that the "name or the logo appears and everything that is associated with that brand comes to mind" (p. 12). Focusing on a mainline denomination's use of marketing, Einstein (2011) explores similar themes in a case study of the United Methodist Church.

Part of the mainline Evangelical Lutheran Church in America (ELCA), Lutheran Campus Ministry-Twin Cities has leveraged the stories, symbols, and material culture of progressive Christianity to reach a new generation of students. With a rainbow flag and buttons that proclaim, "God loves everyone, No exceptions," they have marketed the mainline to the University of Minnesota. By gathering in the Gothic sanctuary of Grace University Lutheran Church and singing vespers music from a Lutheran conference center (Holden Village in the Pacific Northwest), they have connected students to the songs and stories of denominational identity, mixing contemporary music with the architecture of the past. In multiple ways, LCM-Twin Cities has remained connected to a Lutheran denominational ecology (Bass & Miller, n.d.; Coalter, Mulder & Weeks, 1992) of families, congregations, conference centers, and camps, ensuring a steady pipeline of new participants.

Despite decades of decline, moderate and progressive forms of Christianity are embraced by millions of Americans. Cultivating distinctive spiritual practices, the mainline has carved out pockets of vitality within the contemporary religious landscape base (Bass, 2009; Wellman, 2002). While denominational membership rolls continue their downward slide, more Americans are attracted to progressive Christianity in the abstract. According to data from PRRI, the percentage of Americans identifying with white mainline Protestant Christianity rose from 13 percent in 2016 to 16.4 percent in 2020 (McKibben, 2021). Conservative churches have stopped growing, and the mainline is a better fit for some young people (Jenkins, 2021). Surveys of Gen Z show overwhelming support for gay marriage and LGBTQ rights (PRRI, 2022). In this new environment, there are modest opportunities for mainline campus ministries that are ready to expand beyond their traditional constituencies. While denomination continues to matter at LCM, it is not the whole story of Lutheran marketing at the University of Minnesota. Reaching beyond its denominational niche, the ministry is also attracting a wider constituency of moderate and progressive Christian students, including those disillusioned with white evangelicalism, Catholicism, and more conservative forms of Christianity. As LCM's website announces (right after the sentence about city kids and country kids), "Though it says 'Lutheran' in our name, you don't have to be Lutheran (or even know anything about church) to get involved" (Lutheran Campus Ministry-Twin Cities, n.d.).

There are other reasons why college students might seek out a campus religious group, including Lutheran Campus Ministry. Research on Gen Z and American college students has uncovered a campus mental health crisis that has only been aggravated by the COVID-19 pandemic. Before the pandemic, the Healthy Minds Survey found that one-third of students experience psychological difficulties and ten percent have suicidal thoughts. Citing these figures, USC's Dean of Religious Life noted, "There's a Loneliness Epidemic on College Campuses" (Soni, 2019). During the pandemic, Lutheran Campus Ministry-Twin Cities found ways to connect and support its students, counteracting the effects of loneliness, anxiety, and stress. This focus on connection continues to be a part of its rhetoric and marketing.

Studying Mainline Marketing at the University of Minnesota

This chapter explores how Lutheran Campus Ministry-Twin Cities uses marketing and branding in a competitive religious marketplace. It is part of the Landscape Study of Chaplaincy and Campus Ministry in the United States, a five-year project funded by Lilly Endowment Inc. that includes a national survey, along with virtual and in-person field observations, and over 250 interviews in multiple regions of the country. A subset of the project, this chapter draws on interviews with ten students and two staff members, observation of online and in-person events, press coverage of the ministry, and an analysis of the ministry's web presence. Focusing on one field site in a much larger study, it looks at how Lutheran Campus Ministry-Twin Cities utilizes social media, material culture (sidewalk chalk, a Gothic church, and a rainbow flag, for example), and campus outreach to market itself. It explores the larger project of developing a brand that distinguishes LCM from other ministries. Finally, this chapter examines how the ministry builds upon the denominational ecology of Minnesota Lutheranism (camps, colleges, congregations, and family networks) in attracting students, as well as the limits of this strategy in a diversifying America.

Diversity remains a challenge for both LCM and its parent denomination. While articulating an inclusive vision of campus religion, the ministry has attracted a largely white constituency. Ministering in the city of George Floyd, LCM has sponsored discussions on racial justice and made pilgrimages to a church near George Floyd Square. In spite of these initiatives, the ministry has reflected the racial homogeneity of its parent denomination, the Evangelical Lutheran Church in America. Though new outreach strategies are in the works (including the hiring of a new staff person), it remains to be seen whether they can overcome the demographic weight of "the Whitest Denomination in the U.S." (Duncan, 2019).

Before exploring the contemporary marketing of LCM, this chapter will provide a brief historical background on Lutheran campus religious life at the University of Minnesota over the past century. It will place LCM-Twin Cities within the larger context of a heavily Lutheran state that has become less Lutheran over time, as the mainline has declined in numbers and as Minnesota has become more culturally and religiously diverse.

Lutheran Campus Ministry at the University of Minnesota: A Brief History

The ministry now known as Lutheran Campus Ministry-Twin Cities has a long and storied history at the University of Minnesota, beginning with the founding of a Lutheran student organization in 1914 (Ylvisaker, 2007). Emerging from a Scandinavian and German immigrant milieu, it was part of a larger ethno-religious subculture of Lutheran colleges, seminaries, and congregations. Indeed, one of the earliest accounts of the ministry appeared in the Norwegian language *Minneapolis Tidende* ("Lutheran Students' Association," 1921, p. 9). Many Lutheran students were the first in their families to go to college. When sociologist Luther Bernard came to Minnesota in 1917, he found a faculty "surrounded by German and Scandinavian peasants who still lived but little removed from the Middle Ages in their religious thinking" (Keillor, 2008, p. 112).

Maps of the Upper Midwest show a wide swath of counties where Lutherans are the largest or the second largest religious group. By the early twentieth century, they were the largest Protestant denomination in the state, outnumbering Episcopalians, Methodists, and Presbyterians (Noll, 2003). Reflecting Lutheranism's outsized role in Minnesota's religious landscape, the campus ministry maintained a high profile at the university. From the 1920s to the 1950s, the Lutheran Students' Association hosted leaders from denominational seminaries and colleges, drawing large crowds for special events ("500 will attend students banquet," 1941). Catering to its ethnic base, the Lutheran Student Association baked "lefse by the yard" (1949, p. 6) while sponsoring a holiday smorgasbord with Scandinavian delicacies ("Lutheran student group to have smorgasbord," 1957, p. 51).

By the late 1960s, the ministry was changing. Running a "hippie hangout" in the Bohemian Cedar-Riverside neighborhood, campus minister Gordon Dahl "had more contact with radicals and dropouts than typical Lutheran students." A 1969 profile from the *Minneapolis Star* described Dahl's approach: "Attired in psychedelic raiment, he conducts weekly experimental religious services at a West Bank church. He was tear-gassed six times last summer while serving as a volunteer medic during the riots at the Democratic National Convention in Chicago" ("Campus ministries run a hippie hangout," 1969, p. 22). By that time, many boomers had quit going to church. Reporting on a Lutheran Campus Ministry booth at the Minnesota State Fairgrounds, the *Minneapolis Tribune* declared, "It helps to have help when selling religion" (1974, p. 15).

In the midst of declining funds and decreasing student participation, Lutheran Campus Ministry-Twin Cities faced daunting challenges. Yet this was also a time of religious change and creativity. Between 1970 and the year 2000, the ministry staked out positions that have defined LCM to this day, positions that have helped the ministry appeal to a new generation of students. Employing one of the first Lutheran women ever ordained prior to her ordination (Zack, 1971) and a lesbian campus minister in the early 1980s (Miller, 1983), LCM was more progressive than its denomination. Co-sponsoring a worship service for Gay Pride Month, the Lutheran campus ministry became a reconciling in Christ congregation earlier than most congregations in the ELCA ("Gay pride month activities include religious services," 1997). Today, the ministry's website proclaims, "We are a queer inclusive community" (Lutheran Campus Ministry-Twin Cities, n.d.).

At the beginning of the twenty-first century, there are still a lot of Lutherans in the state of Minnesota, so many that Garrison Keillor can joke "that everyone in Minnesota is Lutheran, even if they're not" (Lagerquist, 2005, p. 98). Yet things are not the same. A few years ago, a front-page story in the Minneapolis newspaper announced, "As Churches Close, A Way of Life Fades," reporting a 30.5 percent national decline in the Evangelical Church in America since the year 2000 and a 22.1 percent decline among Minnesota Lutherans (Hopfensperger, 2018, p. A1). Along with the decline has come a shift in the ecology of Lutheran institutions. As historian Maria Erling notes, "The automatic 'marketing' that used to be directed toward the rising generation at camps and conferences and through their youth organizations, and pitched to parents and pastors in the denominational newspapers and magazines, has disappeared" (Erling, 2018, p. 97). Though such assessments may be overly pessimistic, the footprint of Midwestern Lutheran institutions is shrinking.

At a time when Minnesota has become more diverse, the state's Lutherans have remained overwhelmingly white. To quote a 50-year-old study that could have been written today, Lutherans "are racially homogeneous (98% white)," "native born (96%)," and "claim Scandinavian and German backgrounds" (Strommen, Brekke, Underwager, & Johnson, 1972, p. 29). According to the Pew Research Center (2014, p. 123), not much has changed demographically in 50 years. When the Evangelical Lutheran Church in America formed in the 1980s in a merger of three smaller denominations, it established a goal of ten percent racial and ethnic minorities for its national leadership, along with a more diverse membership (Goldman, 1987), affirming this commitment in 1991 and again in 1997 (Goldwyn, 1997, p. 10; Granquist, 2015). These goals remain largely unfulfilled. In 2019, the ELCA adopted yet another churchwide document on diversity, calling for "confession, reflection, and healing action." While acknowledging that "outreach efforts have increased the proportion of nonwhite members," it concluded that the ELCA remains a "predominantly white, middle-class church, most of whose members are of European descent" (Evangelical Lutheran Church in America, 2019, p. 2). The same year, African American minister Lenny Duncan (then a pastor in the ELCA) published *Dear Church: A Love Letter from a Black Preacher to the Whitest Denomination in the U.S.* (Duncan, 2019). Duncan's missive was published one year before the murder of George Floyd in one of America's most Lutheran cities, the hometown of Lutheran Campus Ministry-Twin Cities.

Beyond the implications for racial justice, Lutheran whiteness has also limited the potential constituency for Lutheran campus ministry. As Robert Jones (2016) notes in *The End of White Christian America*, white mainline Protestantism is a shrinking part of the American religious landscape. Amidst these many challenges, Lutheran campus ministers must also respond to a growing polarization between the state's red and blue counties. In a denomination made up of both red small-town congregations and blue metropolitan ones, campus Lutherans must figure out how to bridge the divide, a divide that includes conflicting responses to racism and white Christian nationalism (Denker, 2022). While most LCM students are progressive, they come from a divided state.

Marketing the Mainline in the Twenty-First Century

The marketing of Lutheran Campus Ministry-Twin Cities starts even before students step onto the University of Minnesota campus. In the summer of 2020, a notice went out to area congregations asking them for the names of young people headed for the state's largest campus. Written in the middle of the first year of the global pandemic, when the ministry was gathering mostly online, the announcement on the St. Paul Area Synod's website noted that the "always considerable challenge in connecting with students new to campus ... will only be amplified this semester—just as students' need for connection could be greater" (Welton, 2020, July 12). It included a video from LCM Pastor Kate Reuer Welton and footage of students singing and playing guitars in the Gothic revival chancel of Grace University Lutheran Church. As she noted in the interview for this study, "We do a lot of work trying to reach out to Lutheran pastors to get referrals."

Many students come to LCM because of the wider network of Lutheran institutions in the Midwest. Far from isolated, the campus ministry is connected to an extensive denominational ecology of congregations, camps, and church-related colleges. Though their influence has faded, some continue to serve as gateways to Lutheran Campus Ministry. While one student checked out the ministry because his mother knew Pastor Kate, another "wanted to be a part of a community" like she had known at Luther Crest Bible Camp. The same student "had heard that LCM was a place that at least some of my peers actually from camp had been in, had gone to." A third student followed the advice of her youth pastor, remembering, "I definitely was most influenced by the recommendation from my youth director at my home church." She later "realized that there was like a bunch of connections. Like I showed up and one of my mom's college friend's sons was there."

In the 2020 note to area clergy, the ministry promised incoming Minnesota Gophers "some special swag in a 'Welcome to the U' box that we'll send out in early August." Along with Starbursts and Skittles, the box included a rainbow sticker with the word "Beloved," another with the phrase "YOU ARE ENOUGH," and a card with the message, "THERE'S A PLACE FOR YOU HERE." These objects are a conscious effort to engage students who feel overwhelmed by the pressure of campus life. In an interview completed shortly after these care packages went out, LCM's Program and Outreach Coordinator Dana Rademacher Hansen talked about the stresses and strains of college life:

> I think college is a very stressful time and there's lots of things that can take priority, or sometimes like lies that get into students' heads about their worth ... I think it's really important to be maybe a countervoice to that and be the consistent voice that says, "No, you are beloved by God."

By telling students they are "beloved by God," LCM has presented itself as an antidote to the campus pressure cooker.

The iconography of LCM's packet has included more than just words. The rainbow colors, which also appeared on the ministry's t-shirt, hint that LCM is a more inclusive group than many of its competitors. Encouraging supporters to "GIVE ONE TO A STUDENT AND GET ONE FOR YOURSELF," the ministry created a rainbow-colored "God Loves Everyone No Exceptions T-Shirt." One of LCM's host congregations flies the rainbow flag. Located next to four large dormitories (nicknamed "Superblock"), Grace University Lutheran Church helps to promote the campus ministry. Grace is also where the ministry tables during Welcome Week, and for good reason. Thousands of students walk by the church every day, including some that end up joining LCM.

Commenting on the rainbow flag outside the Gothic church, Pastor Kate Reuer Welton noted the combination of tradition and inclusiveness: "We're like a visible church.... And we also have a rainbow flag. So I think they're just like, how can you be both?" Her colleague Dana Rademacher Hansen noticed the same thing during her undergraduate years. She remembered "seeing a rainbow flag outside of the church, and then I saw the word Lutheran and I remembered that my grandpa was Lutheran.... So I had this connection to my ancestry and also just like, wow, there's a rainbow flag at this church." Raised in the conservative Churches of Christ, Rademacher Hansen did not associate organized religion with inclusion until LCM. According to the ministry website, she is now "passionate about Queer Theology and Queer readings of scripture." The rainbow colors have attracted more than one student. Noticing the "God Loves Everyone" t-shirt, one woman said, "Something that stood out with me was just how accepting it was," adding that, "There's other Christian groups on campus that aren't, LGBTQIA affirming."

Besides its physical presence on the University of Minnesota campus, LCM maintains an active website, Facebook page, and Instagram account. While Facebook is used to cultivate its many donors, Instagram is much better suited for college students. With over 500 followers, the ministry's Instagram account extends LCM's reach beyond its regular participants. It includes much of the same iconography LCM uses outside Grace University Lutheran Church, including rainbow colors for National Coming Out Day. The account also includes stories from students that double as fundraising appeals. Reaching out to students experiencing anxiety and stress, many of the stories portray LCM as a home away from home, whether virtual or in person. As a junior woman wrote in the Fall of 2020, "LCM has been so important during these stressful times because it is a community that is doing things in such a different way right now."

"Whether Conservative or Liberal ... City Kid or Country Kid"

A well-crafted vision statement is a key element in LCM's effort to tell its story. In recent years, the ministry has had several statements and phrases that have served as official and unofficial mission statements. LCM's website lists "Three Expressions of Who We Are," in three two-word sentences: "Be Real. Be Curious. Be Community." While two students referred to one of the three "Bes" (Be Curious), others mentioned a longer sentence that also appears on LCM's website: "Whether conservative or liberal, introvert or extrovert, city kid or country kid, engineer or English major, queer or straight, questioning or certain, there's a place for you here." A key component in LCM's branding, it has also served as a gathering litany for the ministry's weekly services. Independently of each other, students said that this litany was important for understanding LCM. After noting its role as a gathering prayer, one made a point of telling the interviewer, "I feel like you should get a copy of this because I think it kind of, it embodies the whole, like, we really want to welcome people, aspect of LCM." After reciting it from memory, she concluded, "It doesn't matter where you align here. Like, we want you to feel welcome here."

Why did students mention the gathering litany? One reason may have to do with the current political climate. At a time of heightened polarization in Minnesota and the United States, it names something students are dealing with in their hometowns and on campus. In both high school and college, they have crossed paths with peers who do not share LCM's commitment to inclusion. One student recalled a "super, super, super religious" FFA (formerly known as Future Farmers of America) teammate in high school, who refused to speak to a transgender peer. She remembered thinking, "If that's what religion means to you, like I don't want it." When she first heard the gathering litany at LCM, it "was a big like Eureka moment … [I]t really told me that the church genuinely appreciated people no matter where they were at. And that was one of the things that encouraged me to stay." Celebrating the ministry's commitment to diversity, the gathering litany has helped LCM carve out a niche for progressive Christianity at the University of Minnesota.

The Limits of Diversity in the "Whitest Denomination in the United States"

Where does race fit into LCM's marketing? Where does race fit into this community of city kids and country kids, liberals and conservatives? Most of the interviews with Lutheran Campus Ministry-Twin Cities were conducted in 2020–21 academic year, in the months following the murder of George Floyd. Students talked about Floyd's murder and the protests that followed, as well as the ministry's response. Three days after his death, Pastor Kate Reuer Welton invited students to "an open space tonight on Zoom at 8 pm, to pray together, to listen to scripture, and for you to come with your questions, and your anger, and your despair, and whatever else it is you might be feeling." In the weeks and months that followed, LCM organized small group discussions of Layla Saad's *Me and White Supremacy* and a retreat on race. As one participant noted in a public post on the ministry's Facebook page, "[R]eading that book gave me something actionable to do in response to the murder of George Floyd and the ensuing protests. It opened my eyes to the fact that educating ourselves and those around us about white supremacy, and how it has become ingrained in our society, is really the first step we should take to help."

Reflecting the ministry's overwhelmingly white demographics, these conversations were framed as discussions of white supremacy by white students. As Pastor Kate (2020, October 30) wrote on the ministry's blog, "[T]he folks who identify as white in our community decided to read Layla Saad's *Me and White Supremacy*," adding that "If you are a person that identifies as white, feel overwhelmed by the work ahead of us as a country, and/or confused or a little annoyed with all of the competing narratives about what the next most faithful step is, please join in another round of our LCM Read Along." Rejecting the role of a white savior who tries to "fix" the problem, she noted her own "complicity in the systems that perpetuate the problems."

Dismantling those systems has been a much heavier lift. As a campus ministry serving the "whitest denomination in the United States," Lutheran Campus Ministry-Twin Cities faces special challenges, the most basic of which is its own whiteness. For the most part, students are aware of this reality, even if they are unsure what to do about it. Recognizing the obvious, a white male student said, "It's like, like most Lutheran churches, it's primarily white."

Reflecting the demographics of its parent denomination, Lutheran Campus Ministry-Twin Cities relies on a set of feeder institutions that reinforce its homogeneity. Part of the ecology of white ethnic Lutheranism in the Upper Midwest, Lutheran congregations, summer camps, and family networks serve as gateways to LCM. Students come from both the suburbs and from small towns outside of the Twin Cities. At the time of the interviews, several students were also involved in FFA and agricultural fraternities, reflecting targeted outreach on the University of Minnesota's St. Paul campus, home to the College of Food, Agricultural and Natural Resource Sciences. During the 2020–21 school year, a student said at least ten LCM students were members of agricultural fraternities and sororities, adding that they appreciate "being a part of both communities." While participation by St. Paul campus students has waned since then, the potential remains for future recruitment. For a season, Nordic skiing also served as a feeder for Lutheran Campus Ministry. Noting there were at least a half-dozen Nordic skiers in LCM in 2020–21, a student speculated about the connection: "This might just be the whole, like, Nordic skiing, Minnesota, Lutheran, Minnesota. So the overlap might be that more than anything else."

Unlike Lutheran summer camps, Nordic skiing, and agricultural fraternities, there is no great overlap between Minnesota's African American communities and the networks that feed into Lutheran Campus Ministry-Twin Cities. While such connections help LCM's white students feel at home (just like they did at camp), they do not serve that purpose for students of color and may have the opposite effect. Recognizing this fact, a student observed that "just in the fact that we are so white, that it's hard for a person of color, black person, to come in and feel like they're home and feel like they're comfortable enough to talk about their experiences."

To be sure, LCM is taking concrete steps to raise awareness of racial injustice and white supremacy, just as it did before the murder of George Floyd. In the year following Floyd's death, a book discussion, a retreat, and visits to a church near George Floyd Square sparked reflection and engagement in public issues. They have led white Lutheran students to see themselves as allies in the fight against racism in Minnesota. What they have not been able to do is change the larger religious and cultural ecology of Minnesota Lutheranism, which remains nearly as white as the days when the first German and Scandinavian students enrolled at the University of Minnesota.

Conclusion

Lutheran Campus Ministry did not die in the fall of 1969, when a group of seminarians held a memorial service for Lutheran House. Campus minister Gordon Dahl was correct in calling the funeral premature. Though LCM suffered a precipitous decline at the turn of the twenty-first century, it has enjoyed a period of modest revitalization over the past ten years. To be sure, this revitalization has been uneven. While attracting moderate-to-progressive students disenchanted with more conservative campus groups, it has also relied on the surviving denominational ecology of Minnesotan Lutheranism. Though more non-Lutheran students have joined the ministry since the pandemic, the ELCA remains a key part of LCM's constituency. While this has allowed LCM to survive, and even thrive, it has not helped the ministry to diversify. Having survived a near-death experience, diversifying the ministry may be the next challenge for one of the University of Minnesota's oldest campus ministries.

Nearly dying and rising again, LCM provides some larger lessons for the marketing of mainline Christianity in higher education. First, it is clear there remains a niche for progressive campus ministries on college campuses. Students with more inclusive views on LGBTQ rights do not feel comfortable in the evangelical parachurch groups that dominate the campus religious marketplace at many American universities. While many have joined the ranks of the "nones," those in search of religious community are a good fit for groups like LCM. A second and related lesson concerns the importance of using stories and symbols of inclusiveness to create a sense of belonging. LCM's message that "There's a place for you here," as well as its more poetic appeal to city kids and country kids, conservatives and liberals, resonates with students who are fed up with the polarization of the culture wars. Driven by LCM's inclusive theology and progressive commitments, such appeals have been about mission even before they have been about marketing.

As in the past, mainline campus ministries are dependent on the religious ecology of their denominations, including congregations, camps, church-related colleges, and informal friendship networks. While this network is shrinking, the denominational ecology of Minnesota Lutheranism remains an asset for LCM. Paradoxically, this asset, along with ties to Minnesota's suburbs, farm country, and small towns, is also a constraint on future growth and diversification. While providing a measure of comfort to students who miss these places, such connections do nothing to help students of color feel at home. While allowing LCM to attract its historic constituency of white European Lutherans, the denominational ecology of the ELCA does not help the ministry adapt to a diversifying state and metro area.

Ministering in Minneapolis, LCM has earnestly engaged with the topic of racial justice. While such conversations intensified following the murder of George

Floyd, they are not new to Lutheran Campus Ministry-Twin Cities. While raising the awareness of students, who increasingly see themselves as allies, they have not changed the racial and ethnic composition of the ministry. The challenge for LCM going forward will be to build on its current strengths, while diversifying its niche in the campus religious marketplace. This will mean attracting more students of color, especially those with more inclusive views on LGBTQ issues. Toward that end, LCM recently advertised a new opening for a Fellow for Outreach + Radical Welcome. The goal of the new position is to "gather students who are Black, Indigenous, and People of Color who are interested in a Queer affirming, curiosity driven Christian community" (Lutheran Campus Ministry-Twin Cities, 2023). Combining LCM's focus on LGBTQ inclusion with racial justice, it is an effort to diversify the ministry. Time will tell if such efforts help diversify LCM's demographics.

Another challenge may be staking a larger claim on the contemporary campus. While acknowledging the vitality of Lutheran Campus Ministry-Twin Cities, Pastor Kate Reuer Welton pointed to the far bigger footprint of an evangelical group that just concluded a multi-million dollar campaign. Noting the far more modest expectations of mainline Protestants, she said, "I wish the mainline could dream a bigger dream for itself." In her judgment, "[I]t's incumbent upon our ministry to take up space on campus in the progressive realm, which is why we invest heavily in our merch." For both Pastor Kate and her students, the t-shirts and buttons are "ways to show people that God loves everybody, no exceptions," whether or not they end up joining the ministry. In the end, that is why this mainline campus ministry has inserted itself so visibly in the public square.

References

"500 Will Attend Students Banquet". (1941, April 19). *Minneapolis Morning Tribune*, p. 10.
Ammerman, N. T. (2005). *Pillars of faith: American congregations and their partners*. Berkeley, CA: University of California Press.
Bass, D. B. (2009). *Christianity for the rest of us: How the neighborhood church is transforming the faith*. San Francisco, CA: HarperOne.
Bass, D. C. (1989). Ministry on the Margins: Protestants and education. In W. R. Hutchison (Ed.), *Between the times: The travail of the Protestant establishment in America, 1900–1960* (pp. 48–71). New York, NY: Cambridge University Press.
Bass, D. C., & Miller, G. (n.d.). Robert Wood Lynn, *Database: Christian Educators of the 20th Century*. https://www.biola.edu/talbot/ce20/database/robert-wood-lynn
Bolz-Weber, N. (2018). Separating self from selfie [video]. *Makers*. YouTube. https://www.youtube.com/watch?v=YgTTMt8ByRs
"Campus ministries run a hippie hangout". (1969, May 18). *Minneapolis Tribune*, p. 22.
Coalter, M. J., Mulder, J. M., & Weeks, L. (Eds.). (1992). *The pluralistic vision: Presbyterians and mainstream Protestant education and leadership*. Louisville, KY: Westminster John Knox.
Coffman, E. (2017). Marketing the mainline: *The Christian Century* and the business of ecumenism. In O. Scheiding & A. Bassimir (Eds.), *Religious periodicals and publishing*

in transnational contexts: The press and the pulpit (pp. 107–124). Newcastle upon Tyne, UK: Cambridge Scholars Publishing.

Denker, A. (2022). *Red state Christians: A journey into white Christian nationalism and the wreckage it leaves behind.* Minneapolis, MN: Broadleaf Books.

Duncan, L. (2019). *Dear church: A love letter from a black preacher to the whitest denomination in the U.S.* Broadleaf Books.

Einstein, M. (2008). *Brands of faith: Marketing religion in a commercial age.* New York, NY: Routledge.

Einstein, M. (2011). The evolution of religious branding. *Social Compass* 58(3), 331–338.

Erling, M. (2018). Futures for mainline Protestant Institutions. In J. Hudnut-Beumler & M. Silk (Eds.), *The future of mainline Protestantism in America* (pp. 83–105). New York, NY: Columbia University Press.

Evangelical Lutheran Church in America. (2019). *How strategic and authentic is our diversity; A call for confession, reflection and healing action.* https://download.elca.org/ELCA%20Resource%20Repository/Strategy_Toward_Authentic_Diversity.pdf

Finke, R., & Stark, R. (2005). *The churching of America, 1776–2005: Winners and losers in our religious economy.* New Brunswick, NJ: Rutgers University Press.

Freudenberg, M. (2018). Half-ass faith? Popular culture in Denver's house for all sinners and saints. *Journal of Religion and Popular Culture* 30(1), 62–73.

Gay pride month activities include religious services. (1997, June 21). *Minneapolis StarTribune*, p. 31.

Goldman, A. (1987, May 1). New Lutheran church formed from 3 roots. *New York Times*, p. 12.

Goldwyn, R. (1997, August 19), Veep has faith in cities: Top Lutheran want to 'sing a new song.' *Philadelphia Daily News*, p. 10.

Granquist, M. (2015). *Lutherans in America: A new history.* Minneapolis, MN: Fortress Press.

Hoge, D., Johnson, B., & Luidens, D. A. (1994). *Vanishing boundaries: The religion of mainline Protestant baby boomers.* Louisville, KY: Westminster John Knox Press.

Hopfensperger, J. (2018, July 8). As churches close, a way of life fades. *Minneapolis StarTribune*, A1.

Hudnut-Beumler, J., & Silk, M. (Eds.). (2018). *The future of mainline Protestantism in America.* New York, NY: Columbia University Press.

Hutchison, W. R. (Ed.). (1989). *Between the times: The travail of the Protestant establishment in America, 1900-1960.* New York, NY: Cambridge University Press.

It helps to have help when selling religion. (1974, August 28), *Minneapolis Tribune*, p. 15.

Jenkins, J. (2021, July 8). *Survey: White mainline Protestants outnumber white evangelicals, while 'nones' shrink.* Religion News Service. https://religionnews.com/2021/07/08/survey-white-mainline-protestants-outnumber-white-evangelicals/

Jones, R. P. (2016). *The end of white Christian America.* New York, NY: Simon & Schuster.

Keillor, S. J. (2008). *The basis of belief: A century of drama and debate at the University of Minnesota.* St. Paul, MN: Pogo Press.

Lagerquist, D. (2005). Being Lutheran in public: Contributions to social capital in the Midwest. *Anglican and Episcopal History* 74(1), 94–116.

Lefse by the yard. (1949, December 15). *Minneapolis Star*, p. 6.

Lutheran Campus Ministry-Twin Cities. (n.d.). Website. https://lcmtc.org/

Lutheran Campus Ministry-Twin Cities. (2019). *Lutheran campus ministry-Twin Cities 2019 annual report.* https://lcmtc.org/ar2019_digital/

Lutheran Campus Ministry-Twin Cities (2023). Job opportunities. https://lcmtc.org/job-opportunities/

Lutheran hall mock funeral premature, campus pastor says. (1969, October 11). *Minneapolis Star*.

Lutheran Students' Association (1921, June 9). *Minneapolis Tidende*, p. 9.

Lutheran student group to have smorgasbord. (1957, December 4). *Minneapolis Star*, p. 51.

McKibben, B. (2021, July 16). The unlikely rebound of mainline Protestantism. *New Yorker*.

Miller, K. (1983, February 7). Lesbian suffers emotional, spiritual pain after church ruling. *Minneapolis StarTribune*, p. 1.

Moore, R. L. (1994). *Selling God: American religion in the marketplace of culture*. New York, NY: Oxford University Press.

Noll, M. (2003). American Lutherans: Yesterday and today. In R. Cimino (Ed.), *Lutherans today: American Lutheran identity in the twenty-first century* (pp. 3–25). Grand Rapids, MI: Eerdmans.

Orenstein, W. (2021, September 9). When it comes to politics, Minnesota's urban-rural divide is alive and well. *Minnesota Post*.

Pew Research Center (2014). *America's changing religious landscape*. Washington, DC: Pew Research Center.

PRRI. (2022, March 17), Americans' support for key LGBTQ rights continues to tick upward. https://www.prri.org/research/americans-support-for-key-lgbtq-rights-continues-to-tick-upward/.

Sloan, D. (1994). *Faith and knowledge: Mainline Protestantism and American higher education*. Louisville, KY: Westminster John Knox Press.

Soni, V. (2019, July 14). There's a loneliness epidemic on college campuses. *Los Angeles Times*.

Strommen, M., Brekke, M. L., Underwager, R. C., & Johnson, A. L. (1972). *A study of generations: Report of a two-year study of 5,000 Lutherans between the ages of 15–65*. Minneapolis, MN: Augsburg Publishing House.

Turner, J. G. (2008). *Bill Bright and campus crusade for Christ: The renewal of evangelicalism in postwar America*. Chapel Hill, NC: University of North Carolina Press.

Weeks, L., Coalter, M., & Mulder, J. (Eds.). (1990). *The mainstream Protestant "decline": The presbyterian pattern*. Louisville, KY: Westminster John Knox Press.

Wellman, J. (2002). Religion without a net: Strictness in the religious practices of West Coast urban Liberal Christian congregations. *Review of Religious Research* 44(2), 184–199.

Welton, K. R. (2020, July 12). *Campus ministry: Made for a moment like this*. St. Paul Area Synod Blog. https://spas-elca.org/campus-ministry-made-for-a-moment-like-this/

Welton, K. R. (2020, October 30). *Read 'Me and White Supremacy' in community*. Lutheran Campus Ministry-Twin Cities Blog. https://lcmtc.org/read-me-and-white-supremacy-in-community/

Wuthnow, R. (1989). *The restructuring of American religion: Society and faith since World War II*. Princeton, NJ: Princeton University Press.

Wuthnow, R. (2012). *Red state religion: Faith and politics in America*. Princeton, NJ: Princeton University Press.

Ylvisaker, R. (2007, February 28). 100 years of campus ministry. *MetroLutheran*. https://metrolutheran.org/2007/02/100-years-of-campus-ministry/

Zack, M. (1971, May 30). Woman pastor doesn't fit old stereotypes. *Minneapolis Tribune*, p. 63.

11

INVENTING A DIGITAL EVANGELICAL AUDIENCE

Corrina Laughlin

On March 15, 2022, the satirical Christian website, *The Babylon Bee*, had their Twitter account suspended after they tweeted out a picture of Rachel Levine, the Biden administration's Assistant Secretary for Health, facetiously naming her their "Man of the Year." Twitter saw this as an act of hate speech that went against their terms of service because it misgendered Levine, a transgender woman. *The Bee*'s CEO Seth Dillon, however, refused to delete the tweet. *The Babylon Bee* was launched in 2016 as a conservative Christian version of the satirical news site *The Onion* and up to this point was a niche site, but when Dillion decided to take a stand against what he saw as "woke" censorship from Twitter, *The Bee* was catapulted into the national conversation. While *The Bee* was banned on Twitter, Seth Dillion was invited to the popular podcast "The Joe Rogan Experience" where, in a wide-ranging, nearly 3-hour-long conversation, Rogan asked Dillion why he chose not to take the post down. Dillion answered: "I feel like it's a protest. Look, I think you should be able to say that two and two make four and you shouldn't bake into your terms that two and two make five and you have to say that or else you can't tweet on this platform. I don't want to be on a platform like that. I'd rather stand up and say look we aren't going along with that" (Rogan, 2022). Here Dillion expresses his vision of Christian media's role as a bulwark against what he sees as liberal censorship of technology companies, and he couches his protests within the rhetoric of "free speech" that has become popular among right-wing politicians and celebrities. As their argument goes, the right to free speech guaranteed in the United States Constitution means that any attempt at content moderation by technology companies or other organizations is unconstitutional. Of course, Twitter and other privately owned technology companies are not infringing on the right to free speech by imposing and enforcing community standards on their platform, but the argument nevertheless remains popular and effective among conservatives.[1]

DOI: 10.4324/9781003342229-15

For his stand against Twitter, Dillon was widely praised, indeed lionized by many on the right. The hashtag #FreeTheBee trended on Twitter when Elon Musk acquired the platform and with Musk at the helm, *The Babylon Bee's* Twitter account was restored in November 2022.

The Babylon Bee is a digital-first company that has a website, a YouTube channel with 1.4 million subscribers, a podcast, and popular accounts across social media, including on Twitter where they boast 2.4 million followers. In all of these ways, and through the growing celebrity of Seth Dillon, who has become a Christian influencer,[2] *The Babylon Bee* has established itself as a successful digital media enterprise that caters to an evangelical audience. In this chapter, I take evidence gathered from a discourse analysis of advertisements featured on *The Babylon Bee's* newsletter in order to understand this audience. Predictably, many of *The Bee's* advertisers have a conservative bent, including those from fervent Trump supporter Mike Lindell of MyPillow and the Alliance Defending Freedom, an anti-LGBT lobbying organization, which a *Media Matters* report called, "one of the largest and most powerful anti-LGBTQ groups in the nation" (Damante & Suen, 2018), while other products advertised through the newsletter, such as dog food, wireless networks, and financial instruments are not explicitly political.

In what I chart below, "culture war" signifiers and discourses are meant to hail an adversarial digital evangelical audience across the variety of products marketed through the newsletter. In order to contextualize this trend, I begin with a consideration of the so-called culture wars and the place that evangelicals have occupied within them. I use this to understand how evangelical audiences and beliefs about popular culture evolved and, in turn, how marketers have attempted to engage and attract this audience. I then take the case of *The Babylon Bee's* advertisers to show how evangelical digital culture reflects the adversarial stance that evangelicals have developed with popular culture online. Ultimately, I claim that the digital evangelical audience—created and enforced by marketers—is potentially dangerous because of the capacity for radicalization in the digital ecosystem.

Evangelicals and the Culture Wars

The evangelical historian Randall Balmer has defined American evangelicalism with regard to its historicity, specifically the influence of Puritanism, Presbyterianism, and Pietism, as well as to three central beliefs held by most evangelicals: Biblical literalism, the centrality of conversion, and the importance of outreach (see Balmer, 2016, preface). Although there are thriving, growing evangelical churches in Black, Asian, and Latinx culture, the central understanding of American evangelicals in politics, news media, and popular culture is that of white evangelicalism as Anthea Butler's (2021) book *White Evangelical Racism* reveals. Butler writes, "The presupposition of the whiteness of evangelicalism has come to define evangelicalism" (2021, p. 11),[3] and she charts the formal policies and informal practices that have maintained and enforced the racial boundaries of white evangelical culture.

While white evangelicals have been studied as a political bloc and as powerful political activists (see Nelson, 2019; Stewart, 2019), in this chapter, I conceptualize them as a demographic target in order to understand how a digital evangelical audience is being created and reached by marketers using culture war signifiers. The precise beginning of the so-called culture wars in the United States has been debated by scholars,[4] but the consensus is that the culture wars are a series of battles between secular and religious visions of the United States. As James Davison Hunter (1991) explains, the central motivating idea for the religious faction became the protection of a normative American family structure against the supposed changes wrought around mid-century in America. Hunter explains that the idea of the family shared by religious conservatives was always a projection based on, "a certain *idealized* form of the nineteenth-century middle-class family: a male-dominated nuclear family that both sentimentalized childhood and motherhood and, at the same time, celebrated domestic life as a utopian retreat from the harsh realities of industrial society" (Hunter, 1991, p. 180). Though Andrew Hartman traces the culture wars to a different source than Hunter (namely the rise of the New Left), he agrees that the idea of a patriarchally structured family is central to the culture wars (2019, p. 86) and fear of the family in crisis has animated fights over abortion, public school curriculum, gay rights, and a panoply of other issues. That this fuzzy referent of a normative American family is central to the culture wars points to the affective structuring of the debates that define them. Hunter writes that "though competing moral visions are at the heart of today's culture war, these do not always take form in coherent, clearly articulated, sharply differentiated world views. Rather, these moral visions take expression as *polarizing impulses* or *tendencies* in American culture" (Hunter, 1991, p. 43). In other words, the culture wars are not necessarily about coherent understandings of the world as it is or as it should be, but rather, shared *feelings* about the country's ascension or decline.

For Jason Bivins (2022), the affect of the culture wars is central. More specifically, it is the affect of embattlement that is shared by both "the martyrs"—those Christians who believe they are being persecuted by secular elites—and "the whistleblowers"—those secularists who believe there is a sinister plot by Christian conservatives to convert the United States into a theocratic state. Embattlement, for Bivins, defines the stances of both of these groups, increases political and social polarization, and ultimately makes healthy democratic consensus impossible. This sense of embattlement helps to contextualize how American evangelicals understand themselves vis-a-vis popular culture and how marketers and advertisers understand the evangelical audience.

The Development of the Evangelical Audience

There are two stances that have defined and continue to influence American evangelicalism's understanding and consumption of popular culture and both of these stances contribute to the way digital marketers engage with evangelicals online.

First, there is the drive to create enclaved spaces that cater only to evangelical audiences. This is what I call the parallel popular culture of evangelicalism: as cultural forms become dominant in American media, evangelicals find ways to emulate them, or, to make versions of them tailored to evangelical tastes. Randall Balmer (2010) notes that this has been a prominent theme in evangelical culture since the Scopes Trial of 1925 when evangelicals and fundamentalists were ridiculed in the popular media of the time as backward and began to build alternate institutions. Balmer explains that at the apex of this period of building, around 1950, "evangelicals had burrowed into their own subculture. They socialized almost entirely within that world" (2010, p. 50). However, this impulse to separate completely from popular culture was tempered in the 1960s largely due to the influence of Billy Graham. Graham is sometimes referred to as "The Pope of Evangelicalism," because of his profound and enduring influence among American Protestants. Part of the lasting legacy he left on evangelical culture was his emphasis on the importance of media. He established the film studio Worldwide Pictures in 1951, the influential magazine *Christianity Today* in 1956, and a popular radio show, "The Hour of Decision," which ran until 2016. Graham believed that evangelicals had to engage with the secular tools that were popular with American audiences, and he showed, through his example, that there was nothing necessarily wrong with being a broadcaster or a magazine publisher as long as the values expressed by the cultural products one was producing were consistent with evangelicalism (see Wacker, 2014). The same understanding of popular culture as both a morally suspect sphere and, paradoxically, an important one for Christians to be producers and consumers of led to the birth of televangelism in the 1980s (see Bekkering, 2018; Hoover, 1988; Wigger, 2017) and the Contemporary Christian Rock scene in the 1990s (see Stephens, 2018). With these evangelical-targeted forms, Christians could produce media that they believed appealed to the popular zeitgeist while also maintaining and promoting Christian values. As they walked this line, evangelicals became innovators, developing distinct cultural forms[5] and creating lucrative media industries.[6] In the process, the media forms these industries have produced—for example the *Left Behind* book series (Shuck, 2005), televangelical fandoms (Bikkering, 2018), or the uber-popular music produced by Hillsong Church (Wagner, 2020)—have become touchstones for evangelicals to understand their own identity.

A second, related stance common to the evangelical engagement with popular culture, is adversarial. Perhaps no figure is as crucial for understanding the development of the adversarial evangelical audience as James Dobson. Through his influential organization, Focus on the Family, Dobson created and distributed books, pamphlets, magazines, devotionals and produced an influential radio show targeted toward evangelicals. In the 1960s and 1970s, as white evangelicals perceived the social world to be rapidly changing, they looked to Dobson for advice. In her book, *Practicing What the Doctor Preached*, on Dobson's influence, Susan Ridgely writes, "In the 1980s and '90s, as the 'culture wars' were heating up in the United States, Dobson stood almost alone as the easily accessible, biblically centered authority on children and family. That helped him attract a broad range of Christians to his growing media empire" (2017, p. 37).

What Focus' approach reveals is a wary understanding of popular culture sowed within evangelicalism. While evangelicals want to participate in what Stewart Hoover (2006) has called the "common culture" of media, they also see Hollywood and media elites as adversaries and they tend to believe that these elites look down on them. Not only that, they believe they have to be vigilant to avoid the ungodly influences in popular culture. This adversarial stance toward popular culture has been clearly illustrated by many Christian-led protests against popular media. Examples include the television show with a single mother protagonist, "Murphy Brown," or the fears of witchcraft within the *Harry Potter* book and film franchise (see Gilgoff, 2007, p. 62). Given this, marketers understand that evangelicals often remain mistrustful of secular forms of entertainment, even as they engage with them. However, the adversarial stance that evangelicals are known to have with popular culture has also been used by marketers as a way to activate evangelical audiences as I chart below with the case of Sony.

A Roadmap for Marketing to Evangelicals: The Case of Sony

A watershed moment in the history of marketing to evangelicals came with the 2004 film *The Passion of the Christ*. Directed by Mel Gibson, this film follows Jesus of Nazareth in his last days and depicts the violence of the crucifixion. The film garnered more than 600 million dollars at the box office largely due to the buzz the film generated among religious, particularly American evangelical audiences, which, as Mara Einstein (2008) explains, was part of a calculated marketing strategy targeted toward evangelical filmgoers. Hollywood took notice of this and at least one major studio, Sony, began to make a concerted effort to attract evangelical filmgoers.

Sony, whose music division had already made inroads in the CCM scene, created Affirm Films in 2007, as a production company devoted to making films for evangelical audiences. Affirm saw their first surprise hit with *Fireproof* which debuted in 2008. This film was ostensibly produced by Sherwood Baptist Church, a megachurch in Albany, Georgia, and its producers and director took care to make sure that the film was marketed as an evangelical, grassroots-funded production, which helped brand it as more authentic to Christian audiences. In fact, as James Russell (2010) writes, this strategy was meant to attract evangelicals who might not have trusted a major studio release. Sony's marketing used "culture war rhetoric as part of a larger promotional strategy, designed to maintain the Evangelical audiences' presumed sense of cultural distance from conventional entertainment cinema" (p. 407). Through Sherwood, the filmmakers strategically positioned themselves as Christian outsiders who were working to create media outside of the halls of power, and this was used to market the film to evangelicals trained to have an adversarial relationship with Hollywood. Watching *Fireproof* and other films, then, could almost be understood as an act of protest against the secular film industry, even as the film itself was distributed by one of the major global Hollywood studios, Sony.

Continuing their quest to corner the evangelical market, Sony purchased the Christian streaming service Pure Flix in 2020. As Sarah McFarland Taylor (2021) recounts, Pure Flix capitalized on culture war outrage from religious conservatives over the over-sexualization on young girls in the Netflix-produced film *Cuties*. McFarland Taylor notes that "Pure Flix self-positioned as the evangelical alternative to Netflix, has profited from the disaffection of some audiences with Netflix, capitalizing on a growing (no longer so 'niche') market for faith-based, family-friendly media in the U.S. and Canada." At the time of its acquisition, Pure Flix boasted 1 million subscribers. *The New York Times* has reported that Pure Flix attracts outspoken Christian celebrities like Tim Tebow and Jeff Foxworthy to their projects and explicitly market their films as "moral lessons" that both Christian and secular audiences can benefit from (see Rosman, 2017). With this strategic positioning (the idea, for example that secular culture *needs* to be redeemed by this religiously inflected moral content), they cast themselves as a "family friendly" alternative to Netflix and other streaming services.

The way that media companies like Sony have understood and marketed to the evangelical audience by highlighting self-fashioned Christian outsiders and explicitly positioning their content as a type of protest against the immoral entertainment industry is useful for understanding how digital marketers see the audience and how they use culture war signifiers and the evangelical affect of embattlement to attract and engage a digital evangelical audience.

Hailing Digital Evangelicals

The Alliance Defending Freedom

In my analysis of the marketing strategies employed by advertisers on *The Babylon Bee*'s newsletter, I found that marketers rely on culture war signifiers that activate the adversarial stance that evangelicals have developed in and through their cultural contestations with media industries and products. One of the most frequent advertisers on *The Babylon Bee* is The Alliance Defending Freedom, also known as the ADF. The ADF is a legal advocacy group whose central goal is drafting anti-LGBT legislation and using the courts to fight against gains made by gay rights groups. As *Media Matters* (2018) reports, The ADF has been involved in 54 US Supreme Court victories and takes in about 50 million dollars in annual revenue.

Although *Media Matters* pinpoints the clear agenda of the ADF, the rhetorical strategy they use in their marketing materials belies their intentions. Rather than concentrating on specific LGBTQ issues in politics, they instead evoke an American evangelical sense of embattlement by telling stories of individual Christians who have supposedly been targeted for their beliefs by various government agencies and corporations. For example, in one sponsored email message, The Alliance Defending Freedom tells the story of Paige, a Christian CVS employee who refused to prescribe "drugs that can end the life of the baby in the womb." The ADF goes on to explain, "Because she refused to act against her beliefs about good medical care and the right to life that every person has, Paige was fired a few months later. Adding salt to the wound, Paige had just two days prior received a merit-based raise, so her firing seemed especially unjust" (Alliance Defending Freedom, email communication, May 27, 2022). Another email tells the story of Maggie, who was pursuing a degree in counseling but was inexplicably barred from practicing because of her faith (Alliance Defending Freedom, email communication, October 17, 2022). Yet another email introduces Jack who is "standing up to Colorado's attempt to coerce speech and punish Christian business owners who choose to live out their faith in the marketplace" by refusing to bake a wedding cake for a same-sex couple (Alliance Defending Freedom, email communication, October 16, 2022). This list of righteous individuals who have supposedly been targeted by the government because of their evangelical faith invokes the idea of evangelicals as a persecuted social class, which reinforces what George Marsden (2006) has termed the "establishment-outsider paradox" characteristic of evangelical culture or, relatedly, what Jason Bivins (2022) explains as the American evangelical belief that Christians comprise an "Embattled Majority" (p. 6, capitalization in the original).

Taken alongside other advertisements in the evangelical digital ecosystem that call to mind the specter of persecuted Christians abroad, these personal stories of Christians in America who have supposedly been targeted because of their beliefs are effective as they elicit the common rallying tropes of persecution and martyrdom in evangelicalism. In her book on the history of American evangelical missionary work, Melani McAlister explains "American believers' identification with idealized and suffering Christians elsewhere also allows them to see themselves as persecuted by a secular American public, making them fellow victims in a global assault on Christianity" (2018, p. 12). Marketing tactics from the ADF trade in on the evangelical affect of embattlement and, in doing so, reinforce it as central to Christian identity in America.

Patriot Mobile—Ideological Infrastructure

While the ADF is an expressly political right-wing organization, a similar marketing strategy is used by more benign products. Patriot Mobile is an example of how culture war rhetoric has infiltrated the marketing of products as mundane as wireless. Patriot mobile advertises itself as "America's only Christian Conservative wireless provider" (Patriot Mobile, 2023). How can a wireless provider be political? As they note, "Patriot Mobile donates a portion of every dollar earned to support organizations that fight for First Amendment Religious Freedom and Freedom of Speech, Second Amendment Right to Bear Arms, Sanctity of Life and the needs of our Veterans and First Responders" ("Our Story", 2023). Their blog is made up of stories that enforce these same values. For example, you can find an account of how Patriot Mobile is empowering women to own guns, a story of the March for Life (anti-choice) rally, a story of how they have partnered with the right-wing organization, Turning Point USA. What is implicit in Patriot Mobile's marketing strategy is that theirs is the only wireless provider that is not progressive, they are enforcing the idea of Christian conservatives as an embattled social group that has to employ multiple strategies to fight against the so-called woke agenda. In offering an explicitly Christian conservative wireless provider, they create a moral choice for a digital audience as if to say: even in your choice of wireless, you are with us, or against us.

As companies market digital products to American evangelicals, they infuse digital consumerism with an adversarial stance that makes even seemingly ideologically neutral infrastructural choices like the choice of what wireless carrier to use, battles in the culture wars. And through this marketing, they are creating an adversarial digital realm for evangelicals to inhabit, and they are further polarizing and politicizing their digital lives.

Public Sq.

"Tired of supporting companies with a woke agenda? PublicSq. does the vetting for you so you can be more intentional with your spending without compromising on quality. Join the movement today!" (Public Sq., 2023). This is the text that greets visitors to Public Sq.'s webpage. Public Sq. is an app that users can download that directs them to anti-woke businesses in their area and online. Interestingly, the app directs users to companies that have no stated political agenda. Users are shown jeans, credit cards, snacks, all of which it is assumed have been vetted by the app and have been found to be suitably "anti-woke."

In an interview, Michael Seifert, the CEO of Public Sq., explained that the companies that add themselves to the app "are conservative, patriotic, freedom-loving businesses that have indicated that they agree with a set of values. And we basically expose them, whether that's coffee shops, restaurants, hotels, electricians, or plumbers, to this group of consumers that are ideologically aligned and ready to vote with their dollars" (Paul, 2022). While Seifert sees his app as a way to promote conservative consumerism, he also understands it as a challenge to businesses like Disney and Starbucks who have marketed themselves as more liberal leaning. As with *The Babylon Bee* and Patriot Mobile, Seifert sees his company as a dam against an elite establishment that he assumes is biased against conservatives and especially white evangelical conservatives.

The values that Seifert claims for his company are aligned with reads like a list of right-wing culture war grievances that include the recent anti-vaccination rhetoric that has infused evangelical discourses. In his interview with *The Texas Horn*, Seifert explains that his app does not endorse companies that ask their customers to provide proof of their COVID-19 vaccination statues. He explains that to do so would be discriminating against a group of people (the unvaccinated) and would go against the values of "freedom loving Americans." What's notable about the fact that Seifert chooses COVID-19 vaccination status as part of the set of values he wants to connect consumers to is that this is an issue, at the time that Seifert sat for this interview in 2022, that was being hotly debated in places like Truth Social and Gab, as well as the conservative corners or larger social media sites like Instagram and Facebook (see Pew Research Center, 2022). What this indicates is that the way that marketers advertise digital tools to their Christian audience is influenced by how those publics communicate about the issues du jour that they find important. There is a feedback loop, then, between conservative social media sites and the digital marketing that targets online evangelical audiences.

While Christian business people like Seifert claim that the values they promote are "biblical," as in eternal and unchanging, their marketing instead shows that they are influenced by trends in conservative social media. What is disturbing about this is the free flow of discourse that seems to take place as consequence. Misinformation about COVID vaccines, for example, can enter into the right-wing mediascape and become a cause that unites Christian conservatives, and these ideas are then used by companies to market to these same audiences. That misinformation and culture war politics in turn become baked into the identity of the digital evangelical.

Reckoning with a Digital Evangelical Audience

In their book chronicling the rise of the digital right, *Meme Wars*, Joan Donovan, Emily Dreyfuss, and Brian Friedberg (2022) theorize that there are "red pills" across the internet that can radicalize ordinary people into extreme positions. They use the emic term "red pill," which is often referenced in online discourses and which recalls a pivotal scene in the 1999 film *The Matrix*. In this scene, the hero, Neo, is offered a choice between a red pill that would show him the disturbing truth about the world and a blue pill that would let him continue to live his life in ignorance of this truth. Donovan, Dreyfuss, and Friedberg use the concept of the red pill to understand how, for example, young men are socialized into the online "incel" (short for involuntary celibate) community after ingesting, for example, misogynistic memes, jokes, or YouTube rants that they believe show them "the truth" about women. What is most concerning about the "red pilling" of digital denizens is the way that it leads to real-world violence, as in the case of Eliot Rodgers, who killed seven people in the college community of Isla Vista, California after being "red pilled" into an online "incel" community.[7] There is a long and tragic list of violent acts that have been perpetrated against marginalized groups by people who have been radicalized through online discourses.

There is evidence that evangelicals are more likely than others to accept QAnon conspiracy theories (General & Naik, 2021), meaning that evangelicals are being red pilled online already, and we might consider the concept of the red pill as we think about how evangelicals were led to the Capitol on January 6, 2021. Logistically, the insurrection was carried out by a large network of digital media users who used sites like Twitter and Facebook as well as alternative social media platforms like Parler and Gab to organize.[8] Emma Green (2021) called the events of January 6th "A Christian insurrection" and she has reported on the large evangelical presence at the Capitol. Concurring, Bradely Onishi (2023) argues that the way religious symbolism drawn from evangelical culture pervaded January 6th and "gave the rioters' actions a sense of divine permission" (174).

Can digital marketing be part of the mechanism of radicalization that is leading evangelicals to extreme ideas and even, in some cases, into engaging in violent behavior? The more that digital outlets, platforms, and products seek to attract an evangelical audience using the suite of so-called anti-woke discourses that have animated evangelical publics for the past several years, the more that these signifiers, ideas, and ideologies become central to evangelical self-understanding, and the more that evangelicals are siloed into online spaces and discourses based on their antagonism toward "woke" issues, the more they will identify with white Christian nationalists who seize on these grievances in order to organize. Bradley Onishi (2023) has asserted that white Christian nationalists are fighting an "American cold civil war," and the more that evangelicals are folded into this fight through their digital behavior, and through digital marketing, the more that they will feel the need to pick sides in this war.

This is why the use of culture war adversarial rhetoric in the marketing of digital tools, causes, and products for Christians should be cause for concern. Though this strategy has been used before to market films and other media to an assumed audience of adversarial evangelicals, what is more dangerous about the digital evangelical audience from those who have come before is the lack of gatekeepers, the flow of misinformation, and the tendency of digital platforms toward radicalization (Tufekci, 2018). When discourses from online conservative publics can be folded into marketing strategies for digital products, as seen in the case of Public Sq., there is a feedback loop that validates these discourses. And, ultimately, this feedback loop validates an American evangelical affect of embattlement.

The way that the adversarial evangelical audience has been activated in the digital realm is in no small part fueling the rise of Christian nationalism, a dangerous trend for American evangelicalism and for American democracy. Marketing strategies are effective tools for creating a digital evangelical audience, but they come with disastrous consequences.

Notes

1 The Pew Research Center (2022) found that right-wing social media sites promote themselves using the rhetoric of free speech and 22% of their survey's respondents flagged the importance of free speech as their reason for choosing an alternative social media platform.
2 See Rawnsley & Suebsaeng (2023) on Seth Dillon's influence.

3 Following Butler, when I refer to evangelicals in this article, I am referring to white evangelicals.
4 James Davidson Hunter's (1991) path-breaking work on the culture wars traces them to a shared sense of values and symbols in a religiously pluralistic society that "gave Protestants, Catholics, and Jews many of the common ideals of public life" (Hunter, 1991, p. 71) including collective symbolic understandings of the nation, common beliefs in the character of American progress. As immigration patterns changed after World War II, new faiths begin to gain prominence in American culture, and, during the same era, American culture was secularizing (Hunter, 1991, p. 75). In his book tracing the intertwining intellectual histories of culture war rhetoric and politics, Andrew Hartman (2019) instead sees the culture wars beginning with the social changes wrought by 1960s liberation movements. For Hartman, evangelicals and others on the right who joined their coalition occupied a reactionary stance against the New Left who advocated for Civil Rights for people of color, women, and homosexuals and in so doing, "lobbed the first shots in the culture wars that would come to define late-twentieth-century American political culture" (Hartman, 2019, p. 37).
5 See, for example, John Wigger (2017) on Jim Bakker's development of the evangelical talk show format. Tona Hangen (2002) has also written about the influence of Charles Fuller on the development of radio publics. And Stephens (2018) makes the case that rock music in America was influenced by Pentecostalism.
6 One of the most successful industries evangelicals have founded is that of book publishing. Daniel Vaca's (2019) book chronicles the evangelical publishing industry and Cohen & Boyer's edited volume *Religion and the Culture of Print in Modern America* (2008) outlines how evangelicals have become an enthusiastic reading public.
7 See *Meme Wars* Chapter 3 for the complete narrative of Eliot Rodgers' radicalization.
8 Parler was taken off of Apple's app store after the January 6th insurrection at the Capitol because of its refusal to moderate posts that explicitly promoted violence (Nicas & Alba, 2021).

References

Balmer, R. (2010). *The Making of Evangelicalism: From Revivalism to Politics and Beyond.* Waco, TX.: Baylor University Press.

Balmer, R. (2016). *Evangelicalism in America.* Waco, TX.: Baylor University Press.

Bekkering, D.J. (2018). *American Televangelism and Participatory Cultures: Fans, Brands, and Play With Religious "Fakes"* (pp. 1–228). New York: Springer International Publishing.

Bivins, J. C. (2022). *Embattled America: The Rise of Anti-Politics and America's Obsession with Religion.* New York: Oxford University Press.

Butler, A. (2021). *White Evangelical Racism: The Politics of Morality in America.* Chapel Hill, NC.: The University of North Carolina Press.

Cohen, C. L. & Boyer, P. S. (2008). *Religion and the Culture of Print in Modern America.* Madison, WI.: University of Wisconsin Press.

Damante, R. & Suen, B. (2018 July 26). The extremism of anti-LGBT powerhouse Alliance Defending Freedom. *Media Matters.* Retrieved from: https://www.mediamatters.org/alliance-defending-freedom/extremism-anti-lgbtq-powerhouse-alliance-defending-freedom

Donovan, J., Dreyfuss, E. & Friedberg, B. (2022). *Meme Wars: The untold story of the online battles upending democracy in America.* New York: Bloomsbury Publishing.

Einstein, M. (2008). *Brands of Faith: Marketing Religion in a Commercial Age.* New York: Routledge.

General, J. & Naik, R. (2021 May 23). QAnon is spreading amongst evangelicals. These pastors are trying to stop it. *CNN.com*. Retrieved from: https://www.cnn.com/2021/05/23/business/qanon-evangelical-pastors/index.html

Gilgoff, D. (2007). *The Jesus Machine: How James Dobson, Focus on the Family and Evangelical America Are Winning the Culture War*. New York: St. Martin's Press.

Green, E. (2021 January 8). A Christian insurrection. *The Atlantic*. Retrieved from: https://www.theatlantic.com/politics/archive/2021/01/evangelicals-catholics-jericho-march-capitol/617591/

Hangen, T. J. (2002). *Redeeming the Dial: Radio, Religion, and Popular Culture in America*. Chapel Hill, NC: The University of North Carolina Press.

Hartman, A. (2019). *A War for the Soul of America: A History of the Culture Wars*. Chicago: University of Chicago Press.

Hoover, S. (1988). *Mass Media Religion: The social sources of the electronic church*. Thousand Oaks, CA: Sage Publications.

Hoover, S. (2006). *Religion in the Media Age*. New York: Routledge.

Hunter, J. D. (1991). *Culture Wars: The Struggle to Define America*. New York: Basic Books.

Marsden, G. (2006). *Fundamentalism and American Culture*. New York: Oxford University Press.

McAlister, M. (2018). *The Kingdom of God Has No Borders: A Global History of American Evangelicals*. New York: Oxford University Press.

McFarland Taylor, S. (2021). Netflix' A Week Away is a world away. *Hypermediations*. Retrieved from: https://hypermediations.net/netflixs-a-week-away-is-a-world-away/

Nelson, A. (2019). *Shadow Network: Media, Money, and the Secret Hub of the Radical Right*. New York: Bloomsbury Publishing.

Nicas, J. & Alba, D. (2021 January 9). Amazon, Apple and Google Cut Off Parler, an App That Drew Trump Supporters. *The New York Times*. https://www.nytimes.com/2021/01/09/technology/apple-google-parler.html#:~:text=But%2C%20by%20Saturday%20night%2C%20Parler,that%20encouraged%20violence%20and%20crime.

Onishi, B. (2023). *Preparing for War: The Extremist History of White Christian Nationalism— And What Comes Next*. Minneapolis, MN: Broadleaf Books.

Patriot Mobile. (2023). *Our Story*. https://www.patriotmobile.com/

Paul, C. J. (2022). Interview with Michael Seifert. *The Texas Horn*. https://thetexashorn.com/2022/04/20/an-interview-with-michael-seifert/ https://doi.org/10.1080/15295030903583622

Pew Research Center. (2022). *The Role of Alternative Social Media in the News and Information Environment*. Retrieved from: https://www.pewresearch.org/journalism/2022/10/06/the-role-of-alternative-social-media-in-the-news-and-information-environment/

Public Sq. (2023). Home page. Retrieved from: https://publicsq.com/

Rawnsley, A. & Suebsaeng, A. (2023 May 31). DeSantis is scheming to steal the right-wing influencer vote from Trump. *Rolling Stone*. Retrieved from: https://www.rollingstone.com/politics/politics-features/donald-trump-ron-desantis-the-babylon-bee-conservative-influencers-feud-1234745140/

Ridgely, S. (2017). *Practicing What the Doctor Preached: At Home with Focus on the Family*. New York:Oxford University Press.

Rogan, J. (Host). (2022 August). Seth Dillon (No. 1857) [Audio podcast episode]. In *The Joe Rogan Experience*. Spotify: https://open.spotify.com/episode/2SOHGmqBL2Unhw CbYSF8uu

Rosman, K. (2017, April 23). Seeing, and streaming, is believing. *New York Times*, 166 (57576), 1–10.

Russell, J. (2010). Evangelical Audiences and "Hollywood" Film: Promoting Fireproof (2008). *Journal of American Studies*: JAS 44(2), 391–407. https://doi-org.electra.lmu.edu/10.1017/S002187580999140X

Shuck, G. (2005). *Marks of the Beast the Left Behind Novels and the Struggle for Evangelical Identity*. New York: New York University Press.

Stephens, R. J. (2018). *The Devil's Music: How Christians Inspired, Condemned, and Embraced Rock 'n' Roll*. Cambridge: Harvard University Press.

Stewart, K. (2019). *The Power Worshippers: Inside the Dangerous Rise of Religious Nationalism*. New York: Bloomsbury Publishing

Tufekci, Z. (2018 March 10). YouTube the great radicalizer. *The New York Times*. Retrieved from: https://www.nytimes.com/2018/03/10/opinion/sunday/youtube-politics-radical.html

Vaca, D. (2019). *Evangelicals Incorporated: Books and the Business of Religion in America*. Cambridge: Harvard University Press.

Wacker, G. (2014). *America's Pastor: Billy Graham and the Shaping of a Nation*. Cambridge: Harvard University Press.

Wagner, T. (2020). *Music, Branding, and Consumer Culture in Church: Hillsong in Focus*. New York: Routledge.

Wigger, J. (2017). *PTL: The Rise and Fall of Jim and Tammy Faye Bakker's Evangelical Empire*. New York: Oxford University Press.

PART IV

Spirituality and Multi-Level Marketing (MLM)

12

LIVE YOUR BEST LIFE NOW

Wellness, Spirituality, and Multi-Level Marketing in the Health Freedom Movement

Susannah Crockford

University of Exeter

Wellness Now

In 2019, Julie O'Shaughnessy filed a class action lawsuit against Young Living, an essential oils multi-level marketing (MLM) organization. The complaint's introduction described several elements of the overlaps between wellness, spirituality, and MLMs. Young Living sells essential oils under a "quasi-medicinal" guise promising "spiritual and material riches"; however, in practice, it was "an illegal pyramid scheme" and a "cult-like organization" that made false claims and used deceptive business practices (O'Shaughnessy v. Young Living Essential Oils, LC et al. 2019:2). Essential oils, as sold by Young Living – one of the two largest suppliers of essential oils in the US – are marketed as a universal panacea that can cure anything from cancer to COVID-19. Young Living also sells these distilled reductions of flowers, trees, and bark as spiritually elevating, offering a purportedly ancient connection to the sacred through scent (Ganga Kieffer 2021:299). MLM companies like Young Living offer buyers the opportunity to live their best life now, through purchasing the right products. While this may sound appealing, the combination of spirituality, wellness, and marketing in MLMs can be experienced problematically, or as the complaint states, "cult-like."

The structure of MLMs is problematic. Key to the business model is a reliance on the constant recruitment of people to sell products. These "sellers" do not receive a salary, are not directly employed by the MLM (they are independent contractors), and only get commission on products sold (Schiffauer 2019:3). However, to sell the products, they must pay a monthly membership fee or pay for the products before they can sell them, known as inventory loading. Sellers are told they can earn further commissions through recruitment, getting more people to sign up to sell the product (creating a downline). People at higher levels of MLMs earn

DOI: 10.4324/9781003342229-17

money almost entirely from recruitment, rather than sales. Lower levels struggle to sell products through face-to-face engagements within their social networks. This structure creates a pyramid shape, in which there are many more people at the bottom than at the top, but the money flows to the top – hence the common characterization of MLMs as pyramid schemes.[1] The O'Shaughnessy complaint sums up the problem: "Based on Young Living's own public disclosures, 94% of total Members earn an average of $1 per month in sales commissions, and more than half of those who joined in 2016 alone made no commissions at all" (O'Shaughnessy v. Young Living Essential Oils, LC et al. 2019:2). By contrast, Royal Crown Diamond members, the highest level of sellers, earned on average $1,684,354 annually, according to Young Living's public disclosure in 2022 (Young Living Corp 2022).

The pyramid structure of MLMs encodes hierarchy, which is given an extra dimension through the spiritual aspects of wellness. Wellness MLMs that sell essential oils, supplements, and related products are promoting more than just good health; they are also selling a route to spiritual development and betterment. They do so outside of, or skirting around, regulatory limits on advertising and medical claims. The wellness MLMs described in this chapter form part of a larger movement that rejects governmental regulation of personal health choice: the Health Freedom Movement (Crockford 2021). The first section of this chapter describes the religious, medical, and political worldview of the Health Freedom Movement. Like the pyramidal structure of MLMs, this worldview articulates hierarchically ascending levels of both spiritual development and personal perfection. This latter aspect is reflected in external markers of perfection; a peaceful and emotionally disengaged mind, a thin and tight able-body, and a lucrative career. Moreover, it is a career that offers women the elusive promise of "having it all" – a successful entrepreneur who can also be a stay-at-home mom with a flexible schedule that allows for childcare and domestic labor alongside a profitable business. Those who achieve this are not only the healthiest and wealthiest; they are also the spiritual elect.

Wellness MLMs are promoted as providing a route to that coveted ideal career, yet in reality, they only manifest it for the few who manage to ascend to the highest levels of the pyramid. Financial success and exterior beauty operate as marketing hooks for the lifestyle wellness MLMs promote and are often analogized to spiritual development. In this context, marketing the self is crucial; sellers must embody what they are selling. Since the COVID-19 pandemic, the Health Freedom Movement has also become more politically active, galvanized by mask and vaccine mandates interpreted as infringements on civil liberties to campaign for more personal choice over healthcare. The second section explores a case study of a group of American women who have shifted towards advocacy and political action over the course of the pandemic, called the Health Freedom Summit. The Health Freedom Movement overlaps political libertarianism, white evangelical Christianity, and new age spirituality, drawing interest across the political spectrum and from a diversity of religious traditions. In doing so, it creates a space for novel but unstable religious and political alliances among ostensible antagonists. They are drawn together through shared distrust of doctors and public health authorities. MLMs capitalize on this growing distrust to sell supplements and other unproven medical treatments.

The Health Freedom Movement

The Health Freedom Movement incorporates anti-vaccination advocates, naturopathic practitioners, and nutritional supplement salespeople, who use the term as a positive self-description. It is both branding (more optimistically valenced than "anti-anything") and also a point of conjunction between religion, health, and free market ideologies. In this section, I provide the history of the Health Freedom Movement in the US as a polyvalent symbol adapted to contestations of medical norms and practices as varied as medical marijuana, abortion access, and unapproved cancer treatments.

The long history of health freedom as a concept in the US links to ideas of personal choice over healthcare, coupled with the promotion of alternative practices. Historian Lewis Grossman (2021) traces the history of health freedom to the 1820s when the concept arose in opposition to new medical licensing regulations. The opposition to medical practitioners legally requiring accreditation to dispense medical treatment seemed largely motivated by an aversion to monopolies and to elite groups seen as undermining economic freedoms and freedom of inquiry (Grossman 2021:19–20). One perhaps surprising advocate of health freedom was the Founding Father and prominent physician of the early republic, Benjamin Rush (1746–1813). However, Rush's conversion to Jeffersonian Republicanism from Federalism and his alienation from local medical elites precipitated his advocacy for accepting a plurality of medical opinions and disagreeing with government regulation of medicine. Orthodox medicine at that time was characterized by aggressive application of physical interventions to heroically save the patient, including practices such as bloodletting, blistering, and emetic purging. Rush himself practiced this orthodox style of "heroic medicine" but his commitment to Republican values of freedom of inquiry and opinion meant that he believed there should be space for alternatives. And alternatives flourished in the nineteenth century, based on ideas about physiological matter as subject to universal laws, observance of which led to blessings of health and wealth, whereas violations led to disease and poverty (Albanese 2002:16–17). In this way of thinking, self-cure was more effective than orthodox medicine.

Alternative medical practices such as herbalism, osteopathy, and homeopathy were often offered by those outside of the regulatory licensing systems of the time. Samuel Thompson (1769–1843), an itinerant and unschooled herbalist, developed a system of six botanical treatments that could be administered without medical training, indeed he often ridiculed licensed medical doctors. His tinctures gained popularity in the 1830s–1850s to become a significant alternative medicine movement, called Thomsonianism. Advocates fought against medical licensing and got it effectively abandoned by the time of the onset of the Civil War (Grossman 2021:26). Thomsonianism laid the foundations for the subsequent development and widespread acceptance of complementary medicine in the US (Frey 2022). It was also the first popular movement advocating health freedom, promoting the principle that people have the right to choose their medical treatments, an emphasis that fed from the early Republican privileging of personal freedoms above all other concerns. Regulatory oversight of licensing was only reintroduced after the Civil War.

At the start of the twentieth century, increasing government regulation of pharmaceutical production and distribution as well as medical practitioners led to another wave of resistance in the name of health freedom. In 1909, magazine editor and journalist Benjamin Orange Flower (1858–1918) established the National League for Medical Freedom, which worked against government regulation of medical practice (Grossman 2021:94). Flower also engaged in the emerging metaphysical practices popular in Boston at that time such as psychic research, spiritualism, and New Thought, as well as libertarian political movements. Against a backdrop of medical professionalization, the NLMF opposed compulsory vaccination and supported homeopaths, osteopaths, chiropractors, faith healers, and their right to practice medicine. An emerging therapeutic ethos stressed salvation in this world, rather than the Protestant ethic of self-denial for salvific afterlife, which relied on physical and psychological health (Lears 2000). But how health was best maintained was still a matter of ongoing dispute. The NLMF campaigned against the American Medical Association and the Department of Health in their efforts to regulate and license medical practice, articulating health freedom through principles of economic freedom, freedom of inquiry, bodily freedom, and freedom of conscience and religion. In this articulation, choosing one's own therapies was the best way to maintain health, rather than following the advice of medical experts.

As medical authority was consolidated, physiological processes became medicalized so licensed practitioners using surgical interventions took precedence. This domination produced resistance that insisted on the naturalness of life processes, such as childbirth in the natural birth movement emerging in the 1940–1950s (Klassen 2002:27). The intervention of doctors in "natural" processes was met with suspicion, and nature was equated with spiritual value. In 1955, the National Health Federation was founded by businessman Fred Hart (1888–1976), after the Food and Drug Administration shut down his unproven cancer treatment using radionics, a form of electromagnetic therapy (American Cancer Society 1991:61). The organization published the periodical *Health Freedom News* and ran seminars and fairs, as well as lobbying activities aimed at promoting alternative treatments for cancer and other diseases.

In the late twentieth century, health freedom meant support for choosing non-regulated therapies and supplements and practitioners without medical licenses, as well as rejection of health practices and practitioners that were licensed and regulated by the state. It was part of a wider rejection of government authority common in libertarianism, operating on the principle that it is not the government's job to regulate healthcare and medical practitioners. However, health freedom is not always aligned with right-wing politics, as the concept has also been used to advocate for medical marijuana and abortion access (Grossman 2021:225–256). What connects these disparate political positions is often the spiritual valorization of nature, seen, for example, in the health and herbalism movement of the 1980s and 1990s that explicitly linked nature with women and femininity. Writers such as Susan Weed, founder and director of The Wise Woman Center in Woodstock, N.Y., and author of *Healing Wise* (1989), fought government regulation as a form of patriarchal oppression, in which male science dominated women's bodies. The Wise Woman Center still operates, training herbal healer apprentices or "Green Toed Witches" in practices such as herbal abortion, enabling women's bodily autonomy despite legislative restrictions.[2]

The term health freedom coalesced in the 1990s–2000s to refer to advocacy against regulation of nutritional supplements. It formed a mobilizing concept for political action in support of access to alternative medicines, able to draw in ideologically diverse constituencies from counterculture progressives to conservative Christians interested in questioning the efficacy and dominance of orthodox medicine (Grossman 2021:202). In 1998, the publication of Andrew Wakefield's article in *The Lancet* further undermined public trust in orthodox medicine through claiming a link between autism and MMR vaccines, even though the article was later retracted by the journal (Silverman 2012:203–205). Celebrities and other non-medical personnel, including actor Jenny McCarthy and environmental lawyer (and 2024 presidential candidate) Robert F. Kennedy Jr., promoted the idea that vaccines were unsafe. During the 2010s, anti-vaccination sentiments spread online, and blended with the notion of health freedom (Hotez 2021:2). As a preventive therapy given to healthy people, especially children, vaccines imbricate complex dynamics of personal choice and parental rights, as well as religious freedom.

The Health Freedom Movement accelerated from 2020 onwards, funded by private foundations and wellness companies, often selling supplements in tandem with disseminating material attacking medically authorized practices such as vaccination (Satija and Sun 2019). With the COVID-19 pandemic, it morphed into an anti-vaccination, anti-lockdown, anti-mask movement that shares affinities and adherents with the online prophetic movement QAnon (Baker 2022:4–5). Increased deaths from viral disease and increased online activity during lockdowns created conditions in which conspiracism flourished, using multivalent elaborations of the open symbol of apocalypse (Sturm and Albrecht 2021). Pandemic conspiracy theories may seem lurid, suggesting corrupt machinations of well-known scientists and politicians to cause immense harm, but underneath the details, such theories reveal spaces of contested values (Sobo and Drążkiewicz 2021:69). Public health measures proposed to mitigate COVID-19 became interpreted as affronts to not only civil liberties but also freedom of choice in medical treatment. Freedom as a value resonates deeply in the US on a cultural and historical level, and it also has religious elaborations. As indicated by the spiritual interests of early health freedom advocate Benjamin Orange Flower, there are deep spiritual currents in the Health Freedom Movement that rally feminist and new age spiritualities alongside evangelical Christians and free-market libertarians.

One of Flower's interests was New Thought, a spiritual movement that understood the sources of disease as spiritual and mental (Albanese 2006:395). Understanding the origins of ill health in this way renders the mechanistic worldview and primacy of physical interventions in biomedicine redundant, even harmful. In Flower's time such theories provided a counter to painful and unhelpful practices such as bloodletting; however, the Health Freedom Movement has maintained these theories into the twenty-first century offering a logic for undermining contemporary medicine. Another important spiritual strand that crosses over with health freedom is the Human Potential Movement, of which a significant center is the Esalen Institute in California. The fundamental principle is the human potential for supernormal dimensions of consciousness that lie dormant and require specific cultural practices and beliefs to be actualized and sustained, and that once stabilized have long-lasting, permanent effects on future experience (Kripal 2007:23–24). Health becomes optimizable through disciplined everyday practices, including dietary regulation, intense physical exercise, and meditation. The Human Potential Movement leads directly to the twenty-first-century cultural emphasis on wellness, which invokes the sense of not simply being free from disease and illness but of actively improving and enhancing health. This shifted the onus of health practices to producing certain types of bodies, and rebranded pervasive weight loss ideologies as wellness.

Wellness operates to support neoliberal capitalism because it renders health and illness an individual responsibility to be worked on for the sake of continued economic productivity (Cederström and Spicer 2015). Individualistic health ideologies provide another point of agreement between politically diverse positions, appealing across the spectrum from right-wing preppers and survivalists to feminist and new age spiritualities. Yet during COVID-19, some took the restrictions on going outside and emphasis on vaccines over natural immunity as an affront to the worldview wellness expresses (Baker 2022:4). At a confluence of wellness and new age spirituality, conspiracy theories provide a theodicy, an explanation for why bad things happen despite making the "right" decisions (Robertson 2016). Scholars have coined the term "conspirituality" to describe these overlaps (Ward and Voas 2011; Asprem and Dyrendal 2015). For those who elevate freedom as the pre-eminent value for determining their personal health, conspiracy theories filled a gap to explain why the "wrong" approach was being followed by orthodox medicine and politicians during the pandemic.

The Health Freedom Movement works not only through values and ideologies but also through businesses that directly benefit from the lack of regulations that the movement endorses. Corporations have cultures, and in some work is idealized as a form of spiritual quest (Lofton 2017:238; Chen 2022). While such cultures may be implicit, organizations in which the products sold are associated with spiritual elevation and personal betterment make these teleological claims explicit. The Health Freedom Movement campaigns for the use of supplements and other alternative therapies outside of orthodox medicine, and these products are sold through MLMs. Why should the corporate cultures and structures of MLMs appeal to health freedom advocates? Constant recruitment reflects a conversion model that could be called evangelical, and their pyramidal structure is ecclesiastical in its hierarchical structure. Moreover, the organizational structure means that members are not employees of the corporation, in fact, they pay the corporation for the products they sell, and therefore they, not the corporation, lose money if the product does not sell. This exploitative relationship is marketed, however, as an opportunity to be a small business owner or entrepreneur but with large corporate backing for product supply. This relationship resonates with the particular articulation of freedom found in the Health Freedom Movement. Direct sales primarily use the internet and social media to expand their customer base, and this information environment enables unsubstantiated claims of efficacy. In this way, the internet has taken over from the in-person parties that MLMs used to rely on (Chidester 2005:52–70). The MLMs limit their liability for the product because the sellers are not employed by the corporation; they are not legally responsible if their sellers, for example, claim that their essential oils can cure cancer. MLMs operate through a network in which the products are created and profit is collected by those at the top who are then legally disconnected from those working with them to distribute the product and generate the profits. Online disinformation also spreads through distributed networks of influencers, producing content for hire (Ong and Cabañes 2018). MLM-produced content about health freedom products can look indistinguishable from online disinformation. From a biomedical perspective, it is dangerous medical misinformation that undermines trust in science (Hotez 2021).

The use of online marketing in MLMs closely mirrors the role of online influencers in social media marketing more broadly. Social media marketing has shifted toward increased reliance on influencers in the past decade, who provide endorsement marketing for brands that pay them a fee (Kim and Kim 2021: 229–230). Followers trust influencers, who are supposed to embody what they are selling, know what they are talking about, and are similar to the audience themselves. The trust between influencers and followers is key to the success of this marketing strategy. For those influencers whose followers trust them to endorse alternative health products, such as supplements, they can also spread political ideologies of health freedom to a receptive audience through this relationship. Sociologist Stephanie Alice Baker (2022:4) calls alt-health influencers who spread conspiracy theories a "weaponization" of the democratizing ideals in wellness and web culture that are exploited for authoritarian purposes. In the Health Freedom Movement, the roles of online influencer, spiritual practitioner, political advocate, and supplement seller blur.

Warrior Moms for Wellness

The Health Freedom Summit constitutes the type of small advocacy organization that powers the Health Freedom Movement at a grassroots level, mixing speaking events with direct sales. The Health Freedom Summit began in 2020, prompted by opposition to the public health policies of the COVID-19 pandemic. The organization held online conferences in 2020 and 2021, featuring videos of famous Health Freedom Movement spokespeople such as Andrew Wakefield, Joseph Mercola, and Robert F. Kennedy, Jr (CCDH 2021; Frenkel 2021). The webinar format of the summit allowed registered attendees to watch at home for free, following pre-recorded videos on topics such as the health dangers of wearing a mask, vaccines, 5G and EMF (electromagnetic frequencies), lockdowns as a fascist takeover in Europe, and knowing your medical rights. While these topics follow from the history of the Health Freedom Movement, there are contemporary additions such as a transphobic attack on "the Gender Identity Industry" and a promotion of homeschooling. A closer examination of the Health Freedom Summit suggests what health and freedom mean in this context, as well as how it operates as a platform for MLMs selling wellness supplements.

Alongside the videos that are still available on the Health Freedom Summit's website is an advertisement for Touchstone Essentials' product Pure Body Extra. The price of $79.95 is slashed with a red line and replaced with the "summit special" price of $5. So not only does the Health Freedom Summit offer access to critiques of orthodox medicine and public health measures, it also offers a solution, for a lowered price. Pure Body Extra is a substance called zeolite, a dietary supplement, which Touchstone Essentials promises will help remove "toxins" from the body, such as mercury and lead.[3] Clicking on the ad for Pure Body Extra links to a site with testimonials from credentialed medical experts, with the domain name "healthfreedom.thegoodinside," a combination of the domain names for the Health Freedom Summit and Touchstone Essentials. The Health Freedom Summit is partnered with Touchstone Essentials, likely as a "Visionary Business Owner," meaning that they do direct sales for Touchstone Essentials, which is a transnational MLM corporation. Touchstone Essentials charges partners $19.95 annually to be a member plus a monthly $100 "auto-ship" for products, which means that partners are charged monthly for the products whether they sell them or not. There are more expensive "bundles" of products that allow partners to purchase access to higher rates of commissions.[4]

The Health Freedom Summit markets these products, for which its founders receive commission from sales, through Instagram (7,247 followers), Twitter (136 followers), Facebook (~3,200 followers) accounts, and a website. They run an online coaching platform, called Operation Flood, which costs $9.97 per month to join. Through this platform they seek to enlist advocates for the Health Freedom Movement through offering opportunities to work in the "parallel economy" – becoming members of MLMs for which they receive commissions for recruitment.

The Summit also has an email list, which sends out a monthly message of health advice or information, alongside affiliate links to MLM wellness products. The June email began with a message about the "spike glycoprotein bioweapon," or COVID-19 vaccine, that "was intentionally engineered to accelerate 'natural' diseases," so that when people increasingly die of cancer, heart disease, and strokes, it will never be linked back to "the jab." It also offers the chance to subscribe to a docuseries called "Disease in Reverse," which includes interviews with medical doctors and natural health experts sharing their "life-saving protocols." In the Health Freedom Movement, it is vaccinations that make people sick, on purpose, and their members are fighting to save people using alternative medicine and wellness supplements.

The Health Freedom Summit also offers live webinars in which the founders and their friends and associates offer direct advice on health problems and remedial products to buy. In November 2021, they hosted a Zoom meeting called "Disease Prevention Mastery Webinar," advertised through an email sent to their listserv. The "time sensitive" email advised readers to "avoid the hospitals," building up a sense of caution against orthodox medicine while simultaneously using the urgency incentive familiar in marketing. The email description alleged that "hospital treatment protocols are responsible for many deaths – not the C virus itself" so "it's time to figure out disease prevention so you never need to step foot in one of these houses of horrors ever again." Likely, they used the phrase "C virus" rather than the Coronavirus or COVID-19 to avoid being censored; whether they would be or not is perhaps not as relevant to the audience as the implication that the information that they are sharing would be censored by the powers that be because it is secret and dangerous. The meeting had 150 participants, and the founder of the Health Freedom Summit was the moderator, along with four co-hosts. The white women who organized the Summit identified themselves as mothers, fighting for their children's health; an important strand of their marketing was raising "21 children" between them. They depicted themselves not as distant health experts but as concerned moms motivated only by their desire to save children.

In the webinar, the critique of orthodox medicine had three main themes: environmental toxins in food, air, and soil; pharmaceuticals as ineffective or poisonous; and doctors having the wrong mindset. Speaking from their small boxes at the top of the Zoom meeting screen, they shared a PowerPoint that highlighted key phrases from the peer-reviewed literature they cited and diagrams to explain various biological mechanisms. About halfway through they stated: "We are being hijacked," accompanied with a slide with the same phrase as the title, with illustrations of air pollution, pharmaceuticals, EMFs, chemtrails, herbicides, pesticides, and processed foods. Here they identified the specific causes of illness in the modern world, the producers of the toxins that were damaging us at cellular level. They commented, "we've got the 5G now," to explain the health effects of phones. They talked about "things we don't see with our eyes," such as the herbicide glyphosate and unpronounceable ingredients in food. Darkly, they summarized: "This is the reality of where we live." The environment had been hijacked and that was why people were sick. Yet they did not advocate for strengthening environmental regulations or reigning in agribusiness to address these problems. Instead, they blamed toxins that produced free radicals that caused oxidative stress, and it was this oxidative stress that caused chronic and terminal illness.

However, they cautioned us that much of this information was still secret because our society did not promote health. But why not? They phrased the conundrum as, why are we so sick in our society when we have so much information and technology? Their answer was that we were being made sick on purpose by those in charge of our lives. But in the webinar, they did not dwell on that. Instead, they framed the problem among doctors as a problem of mindset. Medical interventions were modeled on war, as waging war on disease, and that destroys the body in the process. What was required was a "mindset shift" that could be achieved through "taking health advice from healthiest people I know," not people who stand to profit off illness. The implication here was that the well-presented, able-bodied white women who spoke to us were the healthiest people and therefore the best positioned to give health advice, and not doctors, who by implication stood to profit off keeping us sick.

Rather than linger on these implications, the presentation focused on solutions: Protandim, a supplement that activates the Nrf2 receptor. Backed up by selective quotations from supportive peer-reviewed studies, they told us we needed to activate the Nrf2 receptor, which they called a switch in our body, to eliminate a million free radicals every second of the day and activate our genes to stay healthy and "beat the system." They popped a link in the chat to buy the supplement, which was $50 a bottle per month. They described this as affordable. Clicking on the link led to a website where we could buy Protandim. In the corner of the webpage was the phrase, "referred by Santa Clara Services." The founder of the Health Freedom Summit confirmed in the chat that this was the name of her company. It also "curated" the Health Freedom Summit, something confirmed in the footer of every page of the Summit's handbook that carried the company's trademark.[5] Protandim is manufactured by LifeVantage products and sold by its "independent distributors." What this indicates is that this is an MLM scheme, and the Summit founder gets a percentage of the sales that she refers, the people who click on the link and buy. Like Young Living, LifeVantage has faced allegations that it is a pyramid scheme and a class action lawsuit (Smith et al. v. LifeVantage Corp. et al., Case No. 18-cv-135, D. Conn.).[6] Interestingly, in one of the clinical trials[7] referenced in the webinar, they describe Protandim as a nutritional supplement composed of "five botanicals," in an echo of Thomsonianism.

References to peer-reviewed studies and links to clinical trials formed one of the main marketing tactics in the webinar. With each claim about Protandim, we were told to check it out on PubMed, and see 32,000 results on it for ourselves. Or they assured us that this is not hype; this is real research; there are 28 peer-reviewed studies proving its effectiveness. This tactic is interesting because, on the one hand, we were being told not to trust doctors and pharmaceutical companies, and on the other, we were being told to trust peer-reviewed studies and clinical trials, produced by doctors and pharmaceutical companies. What was different was the conclusion. Peer-reviewed studies could be trusted when they supported the efficacy of the supplements they were selling. Other peer-reviewed studies, say on the efficacy of masking or the lethality of COVID-19, were not mentioned. Peer-reviewed studies were not left to stand alone, and it was acknowledged that some people did not want to engage with peer-reviewed research that would be a "rabbit hole." Testimonials were also used as another marketing tactic. One of the hosts told her story of her "awakening journey" over the past 11 years, after her son was injured by the MMR vaccination. That led to her becoming "awakened," and looking for solutions for her son, she dove into "true wellness." Years later her mother was diagnosed with triple negative breast cancer, as she was then "radically awake," she advocated for her and got her help outside of "the system." Part of that help was Protandim, which was "foundational in her healing," taking six doses per day. She told the story with a hint of predestination, framing her problems as "the things that we go through that take us where we need to be."

The idea of struggle as redemptive, and the repeated references to awakening provide coded references to religious themes that will be recognized by some, but not others. This tactic allows for religion to be present but is not so explicit that potential customers might be put off. But those familiar with the codes and themes of evangelical Christianity will hear references to "awakening" and link it to the conversion experience of being born again and the historical period of the Second Great Awakening (Elisha 2011:14). The term also resonates with the QAnon movement, a network of online conspiracy theories that use the term "awakening" to refer to the moment of realization that conspiracy theories are true, and the "mainstream media" narrative is a lie (Rothschild 2011:49). These references form part of an implicit opposition between religion and science that whispers the subtext that a fallen world has corrupted our perfect God-given bodies. In her testimonial, the host said she was able "by the grace of God" to help her mother outside of the system, even though the doctors recommended against that. They were "blessed" to walk down a different path outside of the system.

Coded references also lurk in a leaflet distributed by the Health Freedom Summit to advertise LifeVantage products, accompanied by images of the organizers. The last page of the leaflet has the header: "We know you have a servant's heart! You are a digital soldier working overtime for the future of our children, our families, and our country!" This sentence contains an evangelical motif, "a servant's heart," which is a code for a person motivated by kindness or God's grace rather than material reward (Elisha 2011:231). Whereas "digital soldier" is a QAnon reference, deriving from a speech given by Michael Flynn describing online supporters of Donald Trump (Rothschild 2021:9–10). The digital soldiers fight against the forces of the "deep state," often by posting memes on Facebook.

The Health Freedom Summit's social media pages make their engagement with conspiracy theories more explicit. For example, on their Facebook page a post from October 2021 details who "they" means, with a list of organizations and individuals, including the CIA, the Rothschilds, and the Trilateral Commission, all frequent figures in conspiracy theorizing (see Barkun 2003). The comment next to the image goes into more detail about "who are 'they'?" describing entire sectors of society, including Hollywood, the "deep state," NGOs, Big Pharma, and more. Another post from December 2020 depicts a Christmas tree with an ornament with Jeffrey Epstein's face in the center and a cursive caption, "This ornament didn't hang itself." This image refers to the online conspiracy theory that convicted sex trafficker and child abuser Jeffrey Epstein, who had many elite connections, did not hang himself in prison but was murdered, with the culprits often identified as Hillary and Bill Clinton. This event and the surrounding theorizing were drivers for posts related to QAnon, and the spread of the more complex network of conspiracy theories around it (Bleakley 2023). There are also photos from protests against pandemic restrictions in Louisiana taken in May 2020, showing individuals holding signs that say, "My Freedom Doesn't End Where Your Fear Begins," "Sunshine is Essential," and "No Virus Can Cancel the Constitution." These posts indicate an ongoing commitment and engagement with conspiracy theories related to QAnon and COVID-19, and participation in protests against public health measures to mitigate the pandemic. Alongside these posts are quotes from Summit speakers, and adverts for Touchstone Essentials and LifeVantage products, with links to purchase.

The Health Freedom Summit's engagement with MLMs contrasts with the older approach to direct sales as gender parties, typified by companies such as Tupperware and Mary Kay (Chidester 2005; Williams and Bemiller 2011:52–70). In the gender party approach, a (typically female) host invites her (again, primarily female) friends to a party, where an MLM distributor will sell them products, and try to recruit them into signing on to the MLM as members. The Health Freedom Summit is no longer a party, but rather an informational seminar combined with a political rally. They seek to recruit advocates for an overtly political movement, who will also be MLM members and distributors of wellness products. The Health Freedom Summit combined their political and medical priorities with making money, with videos on their website with explicit advice on how to "monetize your movement." The gender parties of Tupperware et al. were a way for women to work that was disguised as not-work, one that incorporated female-coded activities like hosting parties and could be accomplished alongside domestic labor (Williams and Bemiller 2011:2). In the case of the Health Freedom Summit, work is disguised as an advocacy meeting, but there remains the additional motivation of selling products, and they are still trying to recruit women to their cause. Their activism is embedded in the codes and logic of evangelical Christianity, albeit implicitly. Selling products for MLMs offers a way for women to work from home while looking after children, which appeals to homeschooling conservative mothers as well as spirituality-influenced yoga moms. As a form of activism that promotes conservative values of personal freedom and financial autonomy, it is also a way for evangelical Christian women to pursue success consonant with their political and moral values (Elisha 2011).

MLMs, Wellness, and Spirituality

As a concept, health freedom has blurry enough boundaries that it can be used to mobilize radically different religious and political commitments. Throughout the history of the term's use in the US, it has appeared as a banner under which vaccine refusal, medical marijuana, and abortion access can march together. In the case study of the Health Freedom Summit, it is used alongside codes and themes common in evangelical Christianity, but in a subtle enough way so as not to exclude non-Christians. For a concept that fuels an activist movement and marketing schemes, it is important to be as inclusive as possible. However, the connection between MLMs, wellness, and religion draws from deeper sources than the desire for a broad customer base. The conspiracy theories propagated by the Health Freedom Summit are also common among people engaged in new age spirituality, even if evangelical Christianity would seem to be their antipathy.

Conspiracy theories regarding health and medicine create common ground between religious and political antipodes. These theories provide an explanatory force for why doctors and public health authorities should not be trusted. MLMs can then step into the breach, advertising their products as trustworthy and valuable. Wellness is not anti-science as such but rather uses the methodologies and authority of science where and when it agrees with what they are selling. There is an instrumental and opportunistic logic that erodes the system being used as authoritative support.

Beneath the marketing veneer, the Health Freedom Movement has discernible ideologies that form the logic for its broad appeal. Perfection in this life is possible, if purchased through the right products, and supported with a positive attitude. While the larger movement is embattled by accusations of "cult-like" behavior,[8] financial exploitation of members, and digital censorship for dissemination of disinformation, they have rebranded themselves using a label that invokes the civil rights movement, thus posing themselves as an oppressed minority fighting against the "privileged" majority. But the words themselves are capacious enough semantically to allow for deceptive reinterpretation. Health is not the absence of disease, but the proactive creation of wellness through the purchase of supplements and the denigration of various aspects of modern society, such as phones, schools, and hospitals. Freedom in the context of the Health Freedom Movement is similarly partial. It is the freedom *to* choose medicines for yourself and your family, but not freedom *from* ineffective or potentially dangerous medicine marketed as cure-alls.

Notes

1 MLMs remain legal in the US despite this fundamental issue with their structure, due to the 1979 ruling in the landmark Amway case (*In re. Amway corp*). The difference between an MLM and a pyramid scheme is blurry but hinges on the product. MLMs claim that they sell a legitimate product, and so technically distributors have a way to make money beyond recruiting new members, even though this is extremely rare. Pyramid schemes do not have a real product and rely exclusively on recruitment, often using fees from new members to pay earlier members in a system akin to a Ponzi scheme (Schiffauer 2019:18).

2 Wise Woman Center, http://www.susunweed.com/Wise-Woman-Center.htm [accessed July 1, 2023].

3 The Memorial Sloan Kettering Cancer Center provides this information on zeolites: "Zeolites have not been shown to treat cancer or other conditions in humans. Zeolites are minerals that contain mainly aluminum and silicon compounds. They are used as drying agents, in detergents, and in water and air purifiers. Zeolites are also marketed as dietary supplements to treat cancer, diarrhea, autism, herpes, and hangover, and to balance pH and remove heavy metals in the body. However, there are no published human data to support these uses. Further, the FDA has issued several warning letters to distributors for misleading claims about zeolite products," https://www.mskcc.org/cancer-care/integrative-medicine/herbs/zeolite#:~:text=Zeolites%20are%20minerals%20that%20contain,heavy%20metals%20in%20the%20body [accessed June 14, 2023].

4 Touchstone Essentials is reviewed by the blog Smart Affiliate Success, which evaluates it as "not a scam" but also not a way to make significant profits due to the autoship requirements, https://smartaffiliatesuccess.com/is-touchstone-essentials-a-scam/ [accessed June 14, 2023].

5 Santa Clara Services also offered QuickBooks services, an accounting software: https://completebusinessgroup.com/santa-clara-services-llc/ [accessed June 14, 2023] although the website for the company itself is no longer working. It has been registered in Texas and in Louisiana as an LLC.

6 "LifeVantage Faces Pyramid Scheme Lawsuit," *Truth in Advertising*, Aug 9, 2018, https://truthinadvertising.org/articles/lifevantage-faces-pyramid-scheme-lawsuit/ [accessed June 14, 2023].

7 "The Effect of Protandim Supplementation on Oxidative Damage and Athletic Performance," *NIH US National Library of Medicine Clinical Trials*, Feb 12, 2019, https://clinicaltrials.gov/ct2/show/NCT02172625 [accessed June 14, 2023].

8 Accusations by former members, such as in the O'Shaugnessey complaint cited above, have led some in the anti-cult movement to include MLMs under their broad typological approach to defining "cults," for example Steve Hassan in his BITE model of authoritarian control: https://www.psychologytoday.com/gb/blog/freedom-mind/202201/multi-level-marketing-groups-operate-much-cults; and Rick Ross describes MLMs similarly as a form of "destructive cult," https://www.vice.com/en/article/epn3wa/is-lularoe-cult-mlm-lularich-documentary.

References

Albanese, Catherine L. (2002). *Reconsidering Nature Religion*. Harrisbury, PA: Trinity.

Albanese, Catherine L. (2006). *A Republic of Mind and Spirit: A Cultural History of American Metaphysical Religion*. New Haven, CT: Yale University Press.

American Cancer Society. (1991). "Unproven Methods of Cancer Management: National Health Federation." *CA-A Cancer Journal for Clinicians* 41, 1: 60–64.

Asprem, Egil, and Asbjørn Dyrendal. (2015). "Conspirituality Reconsidered: How Surprising and How New Is the Confluence of Spirituality and Conspiracy Theory?" *Journal of Contemporary Religion* 30, 3: 367–382.

Baker, Stephanie Alice. (2022). "Alt. Health Influencers: How Wellness Culture and Web Culture Have Been Weaponised to Promote Conspiracy Theories and Far-Right Extremism during the COVID-19 Pandemic." *European Journal of Cultural Studies* 25, 1: 3–24.

Barkun, Michael. (2003). *A Culture of Conspiracy: Apocalyptic Visions in Contemporary America*. Berkeley, CA: University of California Press.

Bleakley, Paul. (2023). "Panic, Pizza and Mainstreaming the Alt-Right: A Social Media Analysis of Pizzagate and the Rise of the QAnon Conspiracy." *Current Sociology* 71, 3, 509–525.

CCDH. (2021). "*The Disinformation Dozen.*" Center for Countering Digital Hate, 1–40.

Cederström, Carl, and André Spicer. (2015). *The Wellness Syndrome*. Cambridge: Polity.

Chen, Carolyn. (2022). *Work Pray Code: When Work Becomes Religion in Silicon Valley*. Princeton, NJ: Princeton University Press.

Chidester, David. (2005). *Authentic Fakes: Religion and American Popular Culture*. Berkeley, CA: University of California Press.

Crockford, Susannah. (2021). "The 'Health Freedom Movement' Enters the Covid Era by Disseminating Medical Disinformation." *Religion Dispatches*, May. https://religiondispatches.org/the-health-freedom-movement-enters-the-covid-era-by-disseminating-medical-disinformation/.

Elisha, Omri. (2011). *Moral Ambition: Mobilization and Social Outreach in Evangelical Megachurches*. Oakland, CA: University of California Press.

Frenkel, Sheera. (2021). "The Most Influential Spreader of Coronavirus Misinformation Online." *The New York Times*, November 25, https://www.nytimes.com/2021/07/24/technology/joseph-mercola-coronavirus-misinformation-online.html [accessed June 14, 2023]

Frey, Rebecca J. (2022). "History of Complementary Medicine." Salem Press Encyclopedia of Health. Online edition.

Ganga Kieffer, Kira. (2021). "Smelling Things: Essential Oils and Essentialism in Contemporary American Spirituality." *Religion and American Culture* 31, 3: 297–331.

Grossman, Lewis A. (2021). *Choose Your Medicine: Freedom of Therapeutic Choice in America*. Oxford: Oxford University Press.

Hotez, Peter J. (2021). "America's Deadly Flirtation with Antiscience and the Medical Freedom Movement." *Journal of Clinical Investigation* 131, 7: 1–4.

Kim, Do Yuon, and Hye Young Kim. (2021). "Trust Me, Trust Me Not: A Nuanced View of Influencer Marketing on Social Media." *Journal of Business Research* 134, May: 223–232.

Klassen, Pamela E. (2002). *Blessed Events: Religion and Home Birth in America*. Princeton, NJ: Princeton University Press.

Kripal, Jeffrey J. (2007). *Esalen: America and the Religion of No Religion*. Chicago, IL: University of Chicago Press.

Lears, T. J. Jackson. (2000). "From Salvation to Self-Realization: Advertising and the Therapeutic Roots of the Consumer Culture, 1880–1930." *Advertising & Society Review* 1, 1. 1–17.

Lofton, Kathryn. (2017). *Consuming Religion*. Chicago, IL: University of Chicago Press.

O'Shaughnessy v. Young Living Essential Oils, LC et al. (2019). Case no. 1:19-cv-00412-LY, D. W. Tex.

Ong, Jonathan Corpus, and Jason Vincent A. Cabañes. (2018). "Architects of Networked Disinformation: Behind the Scenes of Troll Accounts and Fake News Production in the Philippines." *ScholarWorks@UMass Amherst* 74, 1–67.

Robertson, David G. (2016). *UFOs, Conspiracy Theories and the New Age: Millennial Conspiracism*. London: Bloomsbury.

Rothschild, Mike. (2021). *The Storm Is upon Us: How QAnon Became a Movement, Cult, and Conspiracy Theory of Everything*. New York, NY: Melville House.

Satija, Neena, and Lena H. Sun. (2019). "A Major Funder of the Anti-Vaccine Movement Has Made Millions Selling Natural Health Products." *The Washington Post*, December 20, https://www.washingtonpost.com/investigations/2019/10/15/fdc01078-c29c-11e9-b5e4-54aa56d5b7ce_story.html [accessed June 16, 2023]

Schiffauer, Leonie. (2019). *Marketing Hope: Get Rich Quick Schemes in Siberia*. New York, NY: Berghahn Books.

Silverman, Chloe. (2012). *Understanding Autism: Parents, Doctors, and the History of a Disorder*. Princeton, NJ: Princeton University Press.

Smith et al v. LifeVantage Corp. et al. (2018). Case No. 18-cv-135, D. Conn.

Sobo, Elisa J., and Elżbieta Drążkiewicz. (2021). "Rights, Responsibilities and Revelations: COVID-19 Conspiracy Theories and the State." In *Viral Loads: Anthropologies of Urgency in the Time of COVID-19*, edited by Lenore Manderson, Nancy J. Burke, and Ayo Wahlberg, 68–90. London: UCL Press.

Sturm, Tristan, and Tom Albrecht. (2021). "Constituent Covid-19 Apocalypses: Contagious Conspiracism, 5G, and Viral Vaccinations." *Anthropology and Medicine* 28, 1: 122–139.

Ward, Charlotte, and David Voas. (2011). "The Emergence of Conspirituality." *Journal of Contemporary Religion* 26, 1: 103–121.

Weed, Susan S. (1989). *Healing Wise: Wise Woman Herbal*. Woodstock, NY: Ash Tree.

Williams, Susan L., and Michelle Bemiller. (2011). *Women at Work: Tupperware, Passion Parties, and Beyond*. Boulder, CO: Lynne Rienner.

Young Living Corp. (2022). U.S. Income Disclosure Statement. Available at: https://static.youngliving.com/en-AU/PDFS/IDSOnlineVersion_PDF_US_Page3.pdf [accessed June 14, 2023].

13

#BECAUSEOFLULAROE

MLMs and the Rhetoric of Freedom, Girlboss Feminism, and Retail Ministry

Deborah Whitehead

University of Colorado Boulder

As the 2019 Showtime series *On Becoming a God in Central Florida* opens, protagonist Travis Stubbs is listening intently to a motivational tape titled "Dream a Big Dream," recorded by Obie Garbeau, the enigmatic millionaire founder of the fictional Founders American Merchandise ("FAM") multi-level marketing (MLM) enterprise. "There is a place, a mighty and transcendent place, where progress is inevitable," he intones. "A place where the pursuit of happiness is a priority and the right to dream is a guarantee. That place is called America. God Almighty made this great nation so that you and your business could prosper. A future not just for you but for the people you love. For your family" (Higgins, 2019). Religion, nationalism, capitalism, and masculinity intersect in the FAM imagination, which promises unlimited wealth and happiness to all who follow the Garbeau "system," which adherents pledge is "above all others." Central to the system is the promise of "freedom": Garbeau preaches a version of the American dream that links capitalism with nationalism, religion, and white masculinity. By joining FAM, they become "Founders men," joining the ranks of Jesus and the Founding Fathers, though their path is one of entrepreneurship, not revolutionary struggle or sacrifice. Garbeau promises freedom *from* the 9 to 5 grind of soul-sucking and exhausting hourly wage work that we see the protagonists engaged in, and freedom *to* become great men: working for others requires that you give up your soul to survive, but being your own boss is the true path to wealth and salvation. "I sell people back their souls," he explains. On Travis's last day of work, in an elaborate ritual performance that he has planned with his upline for months, he dons a tuxedo and white gloves, announces to his boss that he is quitting, and walks out of the office onto a red carpet and through a cheering crowd of FAM members to a waiting limousine, believing he is destined for glory and greatness. "You're not a boy anymore, you're a Founders man!" Garbeau promises, one who will now command and

DOI: 10.4324/9781003342229-18

enjoy "respect … luxury … [and] security." In this ritual enactment of wealth and success, converts to the Garbeau system hope to follow the path of their founder, eventually becoming "gods" like him. Garbeau's tapes narrate his own journey from insignificant cog in the capitalist machine to master of his own destiny and creator of FAM, inviting others to follow him in a process of capitalist diviniza-tion or theosis.[1] While Garbeau's system is addressed to men, relegating women to supporting and decorative roles as wives in the organization, it is Stubbs' widow, Krystal, who inherits Travis's dream after his untimely death. Though she is not a true believer like Travis, she tries to use the Garbeau system to secure a better future for herself and her infant daughter.

This chapter will explore how these themes – religion, nationalism, capitalism, and gender – intersect in 21st-century U.S.-based MLM and direct sales companies, such as LuLaRoe, that primarily market to and recruit women. Using the example of LuLaRoe, I seek to unpack the connections between the rhetoric of "freedom," "girlboss feminism," and the use of religious language to sacralize MLMs as not just retail businesses but also "retail ministries" that provide divine promises and blessings to their followers.[2] Direct selling is "a business model that provides en-trepreneurial opportunities to individuals as independent contractors to market and/ or sell products and services … through one-to-one selling, in-home product dem-onstrations or online" and one in which "compensation … may be earned based on personal sales and/or the sales of others in their sales team" (Direct Selling Asso-ciation, 2023). The terms MLM, direct selling, social selling, and network market-ing are defined synonymously and succinctly by the Federal Trade Commission as "businesses that involve selling products to family and friends and recruiting other people to do the same" (Federal Trade Commission, 2022).[3] According to the most recent industry fact sheet, direct selling generated over $40 billion in sales in the U.S. in 2022, with 6.2 million direct sellers working either full or part time in the industry (Direct Selling Association, 2023).[4]

MLMs promise sellers the ability to work from home and set one's own hours; they hold particular appeal for women and especially mothers in conservative reli-gious communities, who are drawn to the compelling opportunity for work that, at least theoretically, can be easily arranged around a stay-at-home mom's schedule and responsibilities. If the FAM dream was about achieving a particular version of 1990s white masculinity and suburban family life, where success was measured in part by the idea that women would no longer need to work for wages and could devote themselves entirely to their roles as wives and mothers, 21st-century MLMs presume a different economic reality. Instead, they are based on the presumption that women must earn wages to support their families, either because their hus-band/partner is absent, because his income is insufficient, or because they desire a higher standard of living. MLMs today tout themselves as "recession-proof," even using the 2008 recession to drive recruitment through advertising; for example, a 2009 Avon ad featured a woman confidently claiming, "I can't get laid off. It's my business" (Jones, 2009). In the wake of the loss of millions of jobs during the 2008 recession, the ranks of direct sales swelled; 100,000 Americans joined an MLM in 2009 (Johnson, 2009).[5] The dream being sold reflects an aspirational vision of 21st-century white womanhood, combining the ideal of stay-at-home motherhood with that of the entrepreneurial "boss babe." MLMs promise these women that despite what they've been told about having to choose between being a stay-at-home mom and having a rewarding career, they *can* "have it all." They trade on a version of 21st-century white neoliberal feminism that defines feminism as "women working to optimize themselves to succeed within capitalist contexts" through "individual behavior modification and attitude adjustment," rather than critiquing existing structures (Mastrangelo, 2021). These promises help to explain why 75% of direct sellers are women, half of them are between the ages of 35 and 54, and 83% are white (Jones, 2009). As LuLaRoe retailer Jill Drehmer puts it, "this is a white girl business," with "not a lot of diversity" (Faust and Stern, 2021).

Many MLMs sell products primarily marketed to women, such as cosmetics, skin care, clothing, dietary supplements, and other products geared toward health or "wellness." Sales of many of these products remain high despite inflation (Peiser, 2023). Over 34% of the direct sales market is wellness products, including weight management products, herbal formulas, protein shakes, and essential oils; other categories include home and family care, personal care, clothing and accessories, and leisure/educational (Direct Selling Association, 2023). Women are often attracted to work as recruiters for these companies by the promise of receiving discounts on products they wish to buy for themselves. The practice of using women to sell products directly to other women dates back to the first "Avon Lady," Mrs. Persis Foster Eames Albee of Winchester, NH, a mother of two who was recruited in 1886 by David McConnell, founder of the California Perfume Company (renamed Avon in 1929), to sell his perfumes. He "saw business advantages in having women sell to other women for their ability to add a personal and understanding touch to the exchange" and thought that women were more likely to trust other women and therefore to buy from them; Albee was so successful that she began to recruit other women as sales agents as well (Klepacki, 2005). Avon provided a source of part-time employment for Albee and other U.S. women during a time when they faced very limited work options and decades before they received the right to vote.

Utah has been called the "unofficial world capital of multi-level marketing and direct sales companies" because over 100 are headquartered there, more per capita than any other U.S. state (Team Business for Home, 2017). In fact, Utah's reputation as a "mecca for multilevel marketing companies" is such that businesses in other sectors of the Utah economy have to work hard to overcome negative perceptions when recruiting investors and new hires from out of state (Bluestein, 2020). Because Utah also has a large population of members of the Church of Jesus Christ of Latter-day Saints, there are various theories regarding the linkages among Utah, Mormonism, and MLMs. An executive at doTERRA, an essential oils company that has 50,000 direct sales representatives in Utah alone, acknowledges that "It would be very difficult for doTERRA to experience the success it's had in any other state"; LDS direct sellers are skilled at "connecting with their friends, they know the languages, they're tech savvy" (Lindsey, 2016; Mencimer, 2012). Another theory is that experience serving missions gives LDS men and women the ability to withstand rejection: after all, sales is "missionary work turned into a business" (Johnson, 2009). As Guy Raz, host of NPR's *How I Built This*, puts it: "If you are an entrepreneur and you have got this idea, you might go to 1,000 people and 900 of them will say, 'This is a stupid idea,' or 900 of them will say 'I'm not interested in investing or giving you money.' You have to be willing to tell that story again, and again, and again and hear 'no' again and again. Believe it or not a lot of Mormons have developed this skill" (Williams, 2020).[6] These products may also hold particular appeal for LDS women because of cultural pressures to look young, thin, and beautiful. A 2017 study found that Utah had more plastic surgeons per capita than Los Angeles, leading some to dub Salt Lake City the "Vainest City in America"; the launch of Bravo's *Real Housewives of Salt Lake City* in 2020 added to the stereotype (Zaragoza, 2020).[7] But perhaps the most compelling factor in the success of MLMs in Utah has to do with cultural pressures on LDS women to be stay at home wives and mothers, even when economic necessity dictates otherwise; a 2015 *New York Times* study found that nonemployment rates for women of childbearing age in some parts of Utah are as high as they were for U.S. women in the 1950s (Aish et al., 2015).

The 2021 Amazon Prime documentary *LuLaRich* explored the history of LuLaRoe, a MLM company specializing in women's clothing that skyrocketed to over $2 billion in sales within five years of its founding (Faust and Stern, 2021). The company was founded in 2012 by DeAnne Stidham and her husband Mark, both lifelong entrepreneurs and members of the Church of Jesus Christ of Latter-day Saints. *LuLaRich* featured interviews with the Stidhams, their children (many of whom worked in the business), other employees, and independent distributors (called "fashion consultants" or "retailers"), tracing the spectacular success of the company as well as its highly publicized problems, including multiple complaints and lawsuits by former retailers. LuLaRoe's signature comfortable, stretchy fabric with its colorful, limited-edition prints made the clothing both instantly recognizable and the source of high, sometimes frenetic demand as distributors and customers competed to find and purchase particular patterns, called "unicorns" in company parlance. The company's success can be traced to several factors, including the growth of social media and the growth of the athleisure market in the 2010s. Among athleisure brands, LuLaRoe stood out for their size inclusivity, with sizes ranging from 2 to 18+, and their "buttery-soft" leggings in exuberant prints that the company calls "the perfect blend of comfort and imagination" (Print Leggings, 2023).[8]

In *LuLaRich*, DeAnne Stidham credits her parents with starting her on the path to entrepreneurship, saying that they "built dreams" and "taught us to believe that we could do anything." To underscore this point, she relates a story from her childhood when her mother, who started her own catering business, promised her 11 children that she would have a surprise for them when she got home from work one night. Gathering her children at the bottom of the stairs, she began throwing cash down to them. "All we saw was money just coming down," DeAnne remembers. "She goes, 'Pick it all up! It's all yours, whatever you can get, it's all yours! Mom did this for you! And we're gonna go shopping, we're gonna go get ice cream!'" In this story, money rains down like manna from heaven from a hardworking mother to her children; now the whole family can get what they want. She tells the story to underscore that LuLaRoe can do this for your family, too. DeAnne's version of the "boss babe" is explicitly tied not just to the dream of being able to provide for your family but also unlimited consumption: shopping, ice cream, whatever you want! "I wanted to be that kind of person that could say, 'I've earned it, I'm gonna buy that,'" she says while explaining her motivation for starting the company (Faust and Stern, 2021).[9]

LuLaRoe leans heavily into the #bossbabe rhetoric, encouraging retailers to tag their social media posts with hashtags like *#beinspired #passion #dreambig #mywhy #goalcrusher #goaldigger #momboss #mompreneur* and *#girlboss* and devoting an entire page on its website to "Mompreneur Inspiration" (Mompreneur Inspiration, 2022).[10] The company's website invites women to "Become a Fashion Entrepreneur," "Start Your Own Boutique," and run "your own clothing business with the flexibility to reach **your goals** on **your schedule** ("Join LuLaRoe," emphasis in original). The company also promises that selling LuLaRoe will make your kids proud of you: "Oh, to be an entrepreneur and a fantastic parent. There is no more incredible feeling than charting your course, making your own rules, and having control over your life, but most importantly, making your kids proud of what you can accomplish" (Mompreneur Inspiration, 2022). Another promise to would-be entrepreneurs is that they are "not alone – the LuLaRoe community has your back" and that they will be joining not just a company but also a community, a "support system," a "sisterhood," and a "movement" that is designed to "help others to succeed" (Join LuLaRoe, 2023). The company's annual incentive "D.R.E.A.M" trips, which only the top 4% of retailers qualify for, both celebrate and perform this success. Company videos and photos depict smiling women dancing and enjoying luxurious cruises, concerts, and meals. But this is a version of success that also celebrates traditional heterosexual marriage, albeit with a girlboss twist. In a video from the 2022 D.R.E.A.M. trip to Cancun, couples pose wearing matching pink t-shirts. The women's read "Resting Rich Face" and the men's read "She's My Sugar Mama" (D.R.E.A.M. Trip 2022 Recap, 2022).

According to the company's founders, fashion, entrepreneurship, and wealth are not ends in themselves, but rather means to the acquisition of goods of a higher order nature. The company's tagline is "creating freedom through fashion," and its mission statement tells would-be recruits that by signing up as direct sellers, they will gain access to the opportunity to "create freedom, serve others, and strengthen families" (About LuLaRoe, 2021). In her work on fashion and the women's movement, Einav Rabinovitch-Fox describes how fashion "enabled women to articulate claims of freedom and modernity, turning fashion into a political assertion of rights" (Rabinovitch-Fox, 2021). She shows how historical innovations in women's fashion, such as the knee-length hemlines of the flappers and the popularization of pants in the 1960s and 1970s, have opened up new possibilities for literal freedom of movement, while at the same time generating broader understandings of gender, activism, and individual freedom. The type of freedom promised by LuLaRoe also combines freedom of dress with individual freedom in its marketing. According to its website, LuLaRoe is "magic": "it both empowers women to dress to their fullest potential and provides retailers the opportunity to turn their passion into a career," and as a result, "thousands of women … have gained freedom in their lives" (About LuLaRoe, 2021). LuLaRoe's conception of freedom is also strongly linked to patriotism and a version of U.S. nationalism that promises women the ability to realize (and wear) the American dream. The company issues its popular "Americana" collections each year for the Fourth of July, featuring stars, stripes, exploding fireworks, and flags in patriotic colors; some patterns include U.S. landmarks and hundred dollar bills. A company promotional video, "We Are LuLaRoe," proclaims "We Embrace Freedom," showing the words superimposed on images of individual women dressed in Americana prints, riding bikes, holding their arms outstretched, and playing outdoors with their children (We Are LuLaRoe, 2022).

This layered rhetoric of freedom is powerful: the company promises women that they are joining a "movement," and that by joining they will gain total freedom: freedom to dress to their fullest potential, to earn to their fullest potential, and ultimately to live to their fullest potential. Here fashion, patriotism, economic success, and a particular notion of women's empowerment collide in a dizzying kaleidoscope of red, white, and blue prints. LuLaRoe employs a neoliberal and religious rhetoric of infinite abundance, or "blessings," that are freely available to, and enough for, everyone, if we just believe in them and work at them hard enough, promising women an unlimited opportunity whose outcome is dependent only upon their individual choices and actions. According to the Stidhams, "anyone who wants to join this business can be absorbed in the blessings that it can provide for all" (Faust and Stern, 2021). Viewed in this way, the leggings, skirts, tops, and dresses that comprise the LuLaRoe collection are not just ordinary articles of mass-produced clothing; rather, they are extraordinary, quasi-sacred instruments and vehicles of power. Likewise, LuLaRoe is not just a business opportunity but also a magical space of endless possibility, where dreams come true and blessings of freedom, strength, love, hope, happiness, and personal growth flow freely to women and their families. Employing the language of transcendence to market goods that are positioned as transcending the market, LuLaRoe promises an almost messianic vision of bringing "life more abundantly," to paraphrase John 10:10.[11]

By describing itself as "a place where lives are being improved," LuLaRoe uses the language of Christian ministry to frame itself as a site and source of infinite abundance that is freely available to, and enough for, everyone. Another dimension of the "magic of LulaRoe," says its website, "is the culture and people behind it. … Like a rising tide that lifts all ships – everyone contributes to the whole and together everyone achieves more" (About LuLaRoe, 2021). As Mark Stidham puts it, "we're not in the clothing business, we're in the people business. We know if you're happy and confident, you can sell anything" (Faust and Stern, 2021). Its high startup costs ($5000–$10,000 at its height, now lowered to $500) served to reinforce the perception of the value of the opportunity – one whose outcome was limitless, or rather, limited only by its distributors' individual choices and actions. The company hashtag *#becauseofLLR* expressed this idea by implying that everything good in a consultant's life was "because of LuLaRoe," thereby "enticing [prospective] consultants with social media posts boasting large bonus checks and other lavish material possessions," according to one lawsuit (Pierson, 2017).

The language of blessing can be used to cover many sins: fast fashion, overconsumption, greed, exploitation. Kate Bowler argues that the prosperity gospel in the U.S. is characterized by the themes of "faith, wealth, health, and victory," and the confidence that believers are promised these things. "Though believers argue that Christian prosperity differs from worldly acquisitiveness," she argues, theirs is a message that "inscribes materiality with spiritual meaning" (Bowler, 2018, 8). We see similar connections between material success and theological virtue in the linkages between the prosperity gospel and the LDS doctrine of self-reliance, despite LDS leaders' attempts to differentiate the two (Oaks, 2018; Whitehead, 2023). A similar connection can be made with the language of blessing in Christian ministry; "Bless" is even the name used to sanctify LuLaRoe's point of sales app.

But LuLaRoe is careful to promise "equal opportunity," not "equal outcome" to its consultants. As Marcel Mauss famously argued, gifts establish social and economic networks of relationship and create obligations of reciprocity (Mauss, 2002). In LuLaRoe, the gift of infinite abundance is contingent on individual action and must be reciprocated with hard work and loyalty. This notion is symbolized in LuLaRoe parlance by "the box," that is, the large cardboard boxes of LuLaRoe product that are purchased by individual distributors for resale to their customers but whose contents remain a mystery until they are opened. Each LuLaRoe print is produced in a limited run of 5000, and company policy is that patterns are never reused. Distributors place orders for particular quantities of items (dresses, tops, leggings, etc.), but they do not have control over the particular patterns they will receive. This means that each unboxing has an element of randomness and surprise. The popularity of Facebook Live "unboxing" videos at the height of LuLaRoe's fame, where retailers would film themselves excitedly opening up their boxes and holding up each item of clothing for their online audiences, demonstrates this well: some retailers would sell their entire boxes in one Facebook Live session, while others were not so fortunate. Sellers do their best to generate enthusiasm for each pattern, but they don't know if their boxes will contain highly coveted and therefore easily sellable prints or undesirable, old, unpopular, or even damaged ones that are practically impossible to sell.[12] In each box, there will likely be some duds; to address this problem, retailers are told to keep using social media to drum up excitement and to keep purchasing more boxes of new inventory. What will you do when you open your box? Will you be able to sell all of its contents, trade them with other consultants to get what you want, absorb your losses, and keep buying and selling, or will you give up and quit? According to the company, it's all up to you: what will you do with your gift? As Mark Stidham puts it, LuLaRoe "is the greatest psychological experiment in history! Because everybody gets a box of stuff, and what did you do with it?" (Faust and Stern, 2021). When disaffected former distributors complained that they lost money because they received unpopular prints or damaged merchandise that they could not sell, he uses the same logic: "some people took that box of clothing and turned it into one million dollars, others put it in the closet because it scared them. What did you want out of it?" Or as Deanne states at the end of the series, brushing off critiques from former retailers, "We are creating something that is creating that sense of courage, confidence, and security. You get to take charge, you get to be the boss. You know, it's easy. And if [women] could just understand, you gotta work at it, I'm gonna put my head down and put my heart and soul into it" (Faust and Stern, 2021). In other words, the problem is with the retailer, not the product. The "magic" and "blessings" of the box to transform lives are available to everyone, but not everyone will be able to receive them. In the language of ritual, you didn't perform the ritual correctly or with the correct intention; in the terms of the prosperity gospel, you didn't have enough faith; in the language of neo-liberal capitalism, you didn't work hard enough, have the right attitude, or want it badly enough.

From the start, LuLaRoe targeted stay-at-home moms with its recruiting. Mark Stidham explained the company's success in this way:

> if you want to create incredible wealth, identify an underutilized resource. And … there is an underutilized resource of stay-at-home moms [who] have chosen to be a mother. And if you make that choice, you pay a price career-wise in our country right now. We have a lot of people of faith that have been attracted to this business [and] we've got this army of women who are smart, passionate, beautiful, funny, educated, and want to do things, and we want to give them … all of that (Faust and Stern, 2021).

In corporate and social media messaging like this, LuLaRoe recognized and capitalized on a "hole in the American economy": "the near-universal desire of working parents to truly manage a work-life balance: to participate in the economy and realize achievements for themselves while also spending meaningful time with their children" (Gilbert, 2021; see also Petersen, 2021). Using the language of women's empowerment for traditionalist ends, the company simultaneously appeals to "people of faith," stay at home moms, and women who feel "underutilized" and undervalued in the American economy. Videos produced as part of their "We Are LuLaRoe" advertising campaign deliver messages such as: "You are beautiful, amazing. You are smart, compassionate, confident, free. We are mothers building a community, making a difference through social retail" (We Are LuLaRoe, 2022). As Sarah Banet-Weiser has argued, these messages of "empowerment, confidence, capacity, and competence" characterize "corporate feminism," a highly visible form of 21st-century "popular feminism" that is expressed in product merchandising and advertising campaigns and generates the desire for consumption by appealing to notions of personal freedom and ability (Banet-Weiser, 2018, 3–4).

Frankie Mastrangelo shows how such messages also constitute "girlboss feminism," which she defines as "emergent, mediated formations of neoliberal feminism that equate feminist empowerment with financial success, market competition, individualized work-life balance, and curated digital and physical presences driven by self-monetization" (Mastrangelo, 2021, 4). Girlboss feminism, according to Mastrangelo, mobilizes digitized spaces to sell products, promote aspirational lifestyles, and create communities for the purposes of individual advancement and economic stability; they also promote a version of feminism that is devoid of collective struggle. While it is not restricted to multi-level companies, also operating in the wellness industry and self-help coaching, it is a key feature of MLM marketing in social media.

The example of LuLaRoe demonstrates how girlboss feminism and corporate feminism are used to generate sales of the clothing as well as recruitment of direct sellers. In so doing, it promotes very specific religiously, corporately, and nationally conditioned versions of "freedom" and "having it all" through a combination of generically popular feminist language, references to the American dream, and the Christian language of ministry. LuLaRoe's messaging defines women's "freedom" in terms of individual *feeling* (happy, sexy, beautiful), *opportunity* (for work-life balance and economic success), and *consumption* (having it all), while also framing the actual labor involved in building the business as well as the labor of reproduction and childcare as a matter of individual women's responsibility, psychological fortitude, and "hustle," as opposed to being conditioned or constrained by broader structural, political, or economic issues. The strength of LuLaRoe's recruitment messaging has been in its ability to generate not just opportunity but also FOMO (fear of missing out on) the opportunity to have an ideal work/life balance. Testimonials from women who joined the business as retailers bear this out. In one woman's words, "I was a mom to two kids and I was on low income assistance. I wanted to be able to go to the store and swipe my card and not wonder if it was gonna be declined, and LuLaRoe said 'you can make full time income on part time work.' In that moment I fell in love with the opportunity." Or as another put it, "I love being a mom and I love being this independent person, how do I make those two mesh? That's it, you have a store in your house, it's perfect!" "It just is … the Dream," said another. "I can be at home with my kids, I can make money, I can own my own business" (Faust and Stern, 2021).

MLMs appeal to women with the language of empowerment, but as a former executive in the Utah, home office of Younique, a makeup company, notes, "You can't say that you're uplifting or empowering women when you're trying to convince them that you need these products and that they will ultimately improve their lives ... The makeup is not what Younique is marketing. They're marketing a lifestyle, they're marketing a dream, they're marketing a support group. So the majority of emotions we put on are focused on recruitment" (BBC Stories, 2019). Another former LuLaRoe consultant, Roberta Blevins, says that "MLMs target women mostly – stay at home moms, single moms, retired women at home, people on disability, people of color, low income, people who don't have the advantages that other people have." She also notes that the company preys on people who are lonely and seeking community: "that's the reason I got into LLR in the first place, was to create a community" (Faust and Stern, 2021)."I felt like I was missing out on [my children] growing up," said retailer Courtney Harwood. "Part of what attracted me to joining LuLaRoe was the hope that I could make what I was making [in corporate America] if not more, working less and being able to spend more time with them." Yet after quitting her marketing job to focus on LuLaRoe full time, Harwood felt "humiliated," not empowered, when the Stidhams invited her to company events with the requirement that she bring her husband (from whom she was separated and contemplating divorce) and counseled her not only to remain married but also to "focus on being subservient" to him. "LuLaRoe hid behind the guise of uplifting and empowering women," she said. "We were supposed to be empowered at first and then the husband was supposed to take over" (Faust and Stern, 2021; see also Suddath, 2018 and Gray, 2021).

Harwood says that the Stidhams encouraged her husband to quit his job to sell LuLaRoe with her full time; many consultants have similar stories of being pressured to earn enough money so they could "retire their husbands." But the goal of "retiring your husband" was not, as it might first appear, a feminist one designed to make women the sole breadwinners and men the stay-at-home parents. Instead, the goal was to retire husbands from their outside jobs so that they could take over their wives' LuLaRoe businesses, thereby making the entire family dependent on LuLaRoe. Many women, including Harwood, also found that rather than giving them the "freedom" to stay at home with their children while doing part-time work for full-time pay, working for LuLaRoe actually meant they were working constantly and having very little time to spend with their kids.

Many consultants also say that DeAnne continually offered unsolicited personal and marriage advice, including pressuring them to dress and look a certain way, lose weight, and get gastric sleeve surgery, as well as tips on how to please their husbands. "All the consultants dressed alike, most of them were blond, most of them were white, and all *obsessed* with the prints," said one; "I came to this realization ... oh my god, I'm in a cult," said another (Faust and Stern, 2021). DeAnne even recruited a select group of retailers to come with her to a clinic in Mexico for gastric sleeve surgery, calling them the "Tijuana Skinnies" and pressuring them until they agreed to the surgery.

She told retailers that "all you have to do is spend five minutes on your knees every day and your husband will let you buy anything you want" (Faust and Stern, 2021). DeAnne's advice appeared to follow similar principles as her parents, Maurine and Elbert Startup, who were active proponents of a particular form of women's identity. They co-authored a book called *The Secret Power of Femininity: The Art of Attracting, Winning, and Keeping the Right Man for You, for Unmarried, Ex-Married, and Married Women* in 1969, founded the American Family and Femininity Institute in Pasadena, and organized "Femininity Forums," charging women $300 to attend 12 3-hour sessions on how to properly cultivate their "femininity" (Warren, 1972). Among the elder Startups' advice to women in the book was that they "must drop every suggestion in speech, apparel and manner that you are able to … take care of your own affairs or to spurn the guidance and care of man" (Warren, 1972). Maurine Startup also served as chairwoman of the California STOP ERA movement, worried that the ERA would "limit women's options to be housewives and mothers," and encouraged women to observe Valentine's Day as "Femininity Day" and to spend it reflecting on "such topics as 'improving your home' and 'keeping your man'" (Feminist Majority Foundation; L.A. Times, 1975). While DeAnne's views may not be identical to her mother's, these examples locating the "power of femininity" in women's subservience indicate more than just coincidental connections between LuLaRoe's language of women's empowerment and what Jana Riess calls a "distinct brand of anti-feminism that was popular in Mormon circles in the 1960s and 1970s" (Riess, 2021).

So what exactly are LuLaRoe and other MLMs selling? A set of contradictions that confuse empowerment with subservience, scarcity with abundance, freedom with constraint, and gift with opportunity in order to promote a certain type of women's labor (working from home as a MLM consultant) as preferable to forms of labor that involve working outside the home, promising endless blessings for women and their families if they shape their entrepreneurial aims around traditional gender roles. Fusing the rhetoric of freedom and neoliberal feminism with the religious language of ministry, LuLaRoe uses digital spaces to market a particular version of the American dream to U.S. women.

Notes

1 The model of divinization in the Garbeau system is similar to the LDS doctrine of exaltation as reflected in President Lorenzo Snow's famous couplet, "As man now is, God once was: As God now is, man may be" (Church of Jesus Christ of Latter-day Saints).
2 Thanks to Sarah MacFarland Taylor for the term "retail ministry," see also Shellnutt (2015).
3 According to the FTC, "If the MLM is not a pyramid scheme, it will pay you based on your sales to retail customers, without having to recruit new distributors" (Federal Trade Commission, 2022).
4 In addition to the 6.2 million direct sellers, there are an additional 41 million "preferred customers and discount buyers" who purchase products/services at wholesale or discount prices from a direct sales company but do not sell them to others (Direct Selling Association).

5 Lauren Woolley discusses the negative LDS "summer sales bro" stereotype (Woolley, 2022).
6 Mencimer also notes that returned missionaries are "natural recruits for companies that need salespeople with a high tolerance for rejection" (Mencimer).
7 The study cited is Madsen, Dillion and Scribner (2017). However, Jana Riess points out that the number of plastic surgeons per capita may be a misleading measure, given that plastic surgery rates among Utah women are in line with the national average (Riess, 2017).
8 LuLaRoe featured inclusive sizing during a time when most athleisure brands, including Lululemon, Beyonce's Ivy Park line, and Serena Williams' S by Serena line, did not go beyond size 14, though 67% of U.S. women are plus size (Nittle, 2018). In 2012, the same year LuLaRoe was founded, Lululemon founder Chip Wilson stated in an interview that "quite frankly, some women's bodies just actually don't work" in Lululemon leggings (Memmott, 2013).
9 Wearing $1100 Valentino Rockstud pumps throughout the documentary, she certainly gives the impression of having fulfilled that goal.
10 The term "girlboss" was coined by Sophia Amuroso in her 2014 book of the same name (Amuroso, 2014). "Boss Babe" was coined by Natalie Ellis and Danielle Canty when they founded Boss Babe, an online community and female entrepreneur coaching program, in 2014 (Ellis and Canty).
11 Mara Einstein argues that religious language is often used to reframe the "material aims of capitalism … as somehow not only about capital accumulation" but about attaining higher order goals such as personal growth and transformation (Einstein, 2008, 13).
12 The rapid growth of the company between 2015 and 2017 led to major quality control issues, with many sellers complaining that the inventory they received contained damaged, defective, or smelly leggings that were either impossible to sell or returned by unhappy customers, leaving retailers to absorb the losses. Sellers said that when they posted on social media about these issues and were told to take their posts down, they were blocked and unfriended. This became one of the primary motivations for the creation of the private LuLaRoe "Defective" Facebook community in 2017, which grew to 27,000 members that same year (Mash, 2017). LuLaRoe Defective was an important precursor to the "anti-MLM movement" that has proliferated on social media, particularly YouTube, Reddit, and TikTok, since 2017 and has been accelerated by criticisms of MLM recruitment tactics during the COVID-19 pandemic (Tiffany, 2021).

References

Aish, G., Katz, J. & Leonhardt, D. (2015, January 6) "Where Working Women Are Most Common." New York Times. https://www.nytimes.com/interactive/2015/01/06/upshot/where-working-women-are-most-common.html?mtrref=www.google.com&gwh=5D85E39AC84DC7C00069ED83C9087D89&gwt=pay&assetType=PAYWALL.

Amuroso, S. (2014) #GirlBoss. Portfolio/Penguin.

Banet-Weiser, S. (2018) Empowered: Popular Feminism and Popular Misogyny. Duke University Press.

BBC Stories (2019, April 26) "MLM: Are Make-Up Empires Exploiting Mums?" YouTube. https://www.youtube.com/watch?v=o5xhNXVfPYQ

Bluestein, A. (2020, January 15) "How Mormons Built the Next Silicon Valley When No One Was Looking." Marker, Medium. https://marker.medium.com/how-mormons-built-the-next-silicon-valley-while-no-one-was-looking-c50add577478

Bowler, K. (2018) Blessed: A History of the American Prosperity Gospel. Oxford University Press.

Direct Selling Association. (2023) "Direct Selling in the United States: 2022 Industry Overview," https://www.dsa.org/docs/default-source/industry-fact-sheets/dsa-2022g-ofactsheetv4.pdf?sfvrsn=c51ed2a5_2, accessed June 16, 2023.

Einstein, M (2008) *Brands of Faith: Marketing Religion in a Commercial Age.* Routledge.

Ellis, N. & Canty, D. (2023) "About Boss Babe." Boss Babe.com. https://bossbabe.com/about.

Faust, B. P. & Stern, C.S. (Executive Producers). (2021). *LuLaRich,* directed by Jenner Furst and Julia Willoughby Nason. Amazon Prime Video.

Federal Trade Commission. "Multi-level Marketing Businesses and Pyramid Schemes," Federal Trade Commission Consumer Advice, July 2022, https://consumer.ftc.gov/articles/multi-level-marketing-businesses-pyramid-schemes, accessed June 16, 2023.

Feminist Majority Foundation, Part II: 1975, https://feminist.org/resources/feminist-chronicles/the-feminist-chronicles-2/part-ii-1975/.

Gilbert, S. (2021, September 25) "*LuLaRich* Reveals a Hole in the American Economy." Atlantic Monthly. https://www.theatlantic.com/culture/archive/2021/09/lularich-parents-parttime-work-american-economy/620211/

Gray, E. (2021, September 20) "Amazon's 'LuLaRich' Perfectly Explains the Demise of the Girl Boss." MSNBC. https://www.msnbc.com/opinion/amazon-s-lularich-perfectly-explains-demise-girl-boss-n1279597

Higgins, J. (Executive Producer). (2019). *On Becoming a God in Central Florida.* Showtime, 2019.

Jones, C. (2009, May 13) "Direct Sales (Like Avon, Mary Kay) Offer Recession-Proof Jobs." ABCNews.com. https://abcnews.go.com/Business/story?id=7582313&page=1

Johnson, K. (2009, June 11) "Door to Door as Missionaries, Then as Salesmen." New York Times. https://www.nytimes.com/2009/06/12/us/12coldcalls.html

Klepacki, L. (2005) *Avon: Building the World's Premier Company for Women.* John Wiley and Sons.

Lindsey, D. (2016, September 8) "Follow the Profit: How Mormon Culture Made Utah a Hotbed for Multi-Level Marketers." KUTV. https://kutv.com/news/local/follow-the-profit-how-mormon-culture-made-utah-a-hotbed-for-multi-level-marketers

LuLaRoe. (2022, January 6) "We Are LuLaRoe." YouTube. https://www.youtube.com/watch?v=y6SHebWhri0.

LuLaRoe. (2022, October 6) "D.R.E.A.M. Trip 2022 Recap!." Facebook. https://www.facebook.com/watch/?v=1133025887610018

LuLaRoe. (2022, October 19) "Mompreneur Inspiration." LuLaRoe.com. https://www.lularoe.com/blog/mompreneur-inspiration.

LuLaRoe. (2021) "About LuLaRoe." LuLaRoe.com. https://news.lularoe.com/about-lularoe.

LuLaRoe. (2023) "Join LuLaRoe." LuLaRoe.com. https://www.lularoe.com/join-lularoe.

LuLaRoe. (2023) "Print Leggings." LuLaRoe.com. https://www.lularoe.com/women/leggings.

Madsen, S. R., Dillion, J. & Scribner, R. (2017, April 10) "Cosmetic surgery and body image among Utah women." Utah Women Stats Research Snapshot (No. 8). Office of the Utah Women & Leadership Project. http://www.uvu.edu/uwlp/docs/uwscosmeticsurgery.pdf.

Mash, J.K. (2017, April 28) "LuLaRoe Leggings Responds to Customer Concerns Over Tears." Today. https://www.today.com/style/lularoe-leggings-under-fire-after-customers-say-it-easily-tears-t108835

Mastrangelo, F. (2021) *Theorizing #Girlboss Culture: Mediated Neoliberal Feminisms from Influencers to Multi-level Marketing Schemes.* Ph.D. dissertation, Virginia Commonwealth University. https://scholarscompass.vcu.edu/cgi/viewcontent.cgi?article=7768&context=etd.

Mauss, M. (2002) *The Gift: The Form and Reason for Exchange in Archaic Societies*. Translated by W.D. Halls. Routledge.

Memmott, M. (2013, November 7) "Lululemon Founder: Our Pants Won't Work for Some Women." National Public Radio. https://www.npr.org/sections/thetwo-way/2013/11/07/243706174/lululemon-founder-our-pants-wont-work-for-some-women

Mencimer, S. (2012) "Get-Rich-Quick-Profiteers Love Mitt Romney, and He Loves Them Back," Mother Jones. May/June. https://www.motherjones.com/politics/2012/05/mitt-romney-nu-skin-multilevel-marketing-schemes/

L.A. Times. *The Los Angeles Times*, December 1, 1974, page 75.

Nittle, N. (2018, July 10) "Activewear Brands Are Ignoring Plus-Size Women." Racked. https://www.racked.com/2018/7/10/17550018/activewear-brands-plus-size-women

Oaks, D.H. (2018, August 7) "President Oaks Tackles Why Mormons Fall for Get-Rich-Quick Schemes." LDS Living. https://www.ldsliving.com/president-oaks-tackles-why-mormons-fall-for-get-rich-quick-schemes/s/82898

Petersen, A. H. (2021, September 15) "What Got Left Out of *LuLaRich*." Culture Study. https://annehelen.substack.com/p/what-got-left-out-of-lularich?s=r

Peiser, J. (2023, April 16) "Inflation Can't Smudge the Glowing Beauty Industry," Washington Post. https://www.washingtonpost.com/business/2023/04/17/beauty-industry-inflation/

Pierson, D. (2017, December 12) "LuLaRoe Has Turned Your Facebook Friends into a Leggings Sales Force. But Is It a Pyramid Scheme?" Los Angeles Times. https://www.latimes.com/business/la-fi-tn-tech-multilevel-marketing-20171211-story.html

Rabinovitch-Fox, E. (2021) *Dressed for Freedom: The Fashionable Politics of American Feminism*. University of Illinois Press.

Riess, J. (2017, March 17) "Mormon Women Have More Cosmetic Surgery – Or Not," Religion News. https://religionnews.com/2017/03/17/mormon-women-have-more-cosmetic-surgery-or-not/

Riess, J. (2021, September 16) "LuLaRoe and the Shadow Side of Mormon Gender Roles." Religion News. https://religionnews.com/2021/09/16/lularoe-and-the-shadow-side-of-mormon-gender-roles/

Shellnutt, K. (2015, November 23) "The Divine Rise of Multilevel Marketing." Christianity Today. https://www.christianitytoday.com/ct/2015/december/divine-rise-of-multilevel-marketing-christians-mlm.html

Suddath, C. (2018, April 17) "Thousands of Women Say LuLaRoe's Legging Empire Is a Scam," Bloomberg BusinessWeek. https://www.bloomberg.com/news/features/2018-04-27/thousands-of-women-say-lularoe-s-legging-empire-is-a-scam

Team Business for Home. (2017, June 12) "Network Marketing the Second-Biggest Industry in Utah with $8.5+ Billion in Revenue," Business for Home. https://www.businessforhome.org/2017/06/network-marketing-the-second-biggest-industry-in-utah-with-8-5-billion-in-revenue/

The Church of Jesus Christ of Latter-day Saints. "Chapter 5: The Grand Destiny of the Faithful." *Teachings of Presidents of the Church: Lorenzo Snow*. https://site.churchofjesuschrist.org/study/manual/teachings-of-presidents-of-the-church-lorenzo-snow/chapter-5-the-grand-destiny-of-the-faithful?lang=eng&adobe_mc_ref=https://www.churchofjesuschrist.org/study/manual/teachings-of-presidents-of-the-church-lorenzo-snow/chapter-5-the-grand-destiny-of-the-faithful?lang=eng&adobe_mc_sdid=SDID=43240E3F7641DE10-27710D7393238EF8|MCORGID=66C5485451E56AAE0A490D45%40AdobeOrg|TS=1687456685&v=V01

Tiffany, K. (2021, January 27) "How the Pandemic Stoked a Backlash to Multilevel Marketing." Atlantic Monthly. https://www.theatlantic.com/technology/archive/2021/01/anti-mlm-reddit-youtube/617816/

Warren, V. (1972, August 6) "New Lift for Old-Fashioned Femininity." New York Times. https://www.nytimes.com/1972/08/06/archives/new-lift-for-oldfashioned-femininity.html

Whitehead, D. (2023) "Startup Culture: MLMs, Mormons, and Entrepreneurship." *Mormon Studies Review*, 10, 31–41.

Williams, L. (2020, January 28) "What NPR's Guy Raz Told Jimmy Fallon about Why Latter-day Saints Are Successful in Business," LDSLiving. https://www.ldsliving.com/what-nprs-guy-raz-told-jimmy-fallon-about-why-latter-day-saints-are-successful-in-business/s/92292

Woolley, L. (2022, October 12) "The Returned Missionary to Summer Sales Pipeline," The Daily Universe. Brigham Young University. https://universe.byu.edu/2022/10/12/the-returned-missionary-to-summer-sales-pipeline/

Zaragoza, A. (2020, December 11) "Is Mormon Culture Really Plastic Surgery-Obsessed?" Vice. https://www.vice.com/en/article/pkd3b7/housewives-of-salt-lake-city-plastic-surgery-mormon-church

PART V

Cult Branding, Purpose Marketing, and the Body Politic

14

DRINKING THE CROSSFIT KOOL-AID

Cult Marketing Meets Functional Fitness

Cody Musselman

"Excuse me, CrossFitters coming through!" yells a sweaty woman in workout attire as she brushes past two coworkers casually chatting in the break room. Her workout partner follows her and, unprompted, begins to explain their daily workout. "I did 6,000 burpees and I feel great!", he shares before vomiting. The coworkers recoil in disgust. "CrossFit's not just an exercise, it's a cult," the sweaty woman proclaims before catching her slip. "I mean it's a way of life." The two CrossFitters continue to exercise and vomit in the breakroom until one of their coworkers can no longer stand idly by. "Stop! This is disturbing," he yells. "I respect that you have this new hobby that you're really excited about, but you don't have to let it change your personalities." His appeals are immediately undercut by one of the CrossFitters. "WRONG! CrossFit is not a hobby. It's a cult."

This absurd scene appears in a 2014 parody video posted by CollegeHumor, an internet-based comedy company, which pokes fun at the intensity and high degree of devotion members of the CrossFit community show to their exercise regimen. Founded in 2000, CrossFit combines high-intensity cardio, Olympic weightlifting, gymnastics, and odd object movements with diet recommendations in an approach to exercise called functional fitness. Functional fitness trains exercisers in the strength and agility needed for everyday tasks, like carrying in heavy grocery bags from the car or lifting luggage into the overhead compartment on an airplane. Yet CrossFit is perhaps better known for its tight-knit communities that span the globe. With over 13,000 affiliated gyms worldwide, CrossFit is one of the fastest growing fitness communities of the twenty-first century, and it has become a way of life for millions of people who eat, train, and commune within the world of CrossFit.

The CollegeHumor video relies upon the well-known passion CrossFitters express for "forging elite fitness" for its critique to land. In the comments section of the video, both diehard CrossFitters and detractors affirm the kernel of truth at the

DOI: 10.4324/9781003342229-20

heart of the CollegeHumor parody: that the fanaticism of CrossFitters boarders on that of cult members. "I'm a CrossFit addict, and I LOVE THIS! Ironically [this video is] pretty accurate," one viewer posted. "Friends don't let friends do Cross-Fit," reacted another viewer. "CrossFit in a nutshell," one comment reads. "I do CrossFit and I agree with this." "Long live the CrossFit cult!" proclaimed another. "Best hobby in the world…and the best cult to join" (CollegeHumor, 2014). While the viewers reveled in the apparent hyperbole of the CollegeHumor video, else-where, more serious accusations against CrossFit suggested that, like a cult, Cross-Fit could have a detrimental impact on the lives of its followers (Havrilesky, 2014; Weathers, 2014; Michaels, 2019; Glassman, 2020). From fears of injury to lament-ing the cost (roughly $120–200/month at most gyms), critics used their comparison of CrossFit to a cult to warn prospective members of the toll it could take on their body, on their finances, and on their relationships. To say CrossFit is a cult was, to many, a joke, but for others it was no laughing matter. Yet, in the face of such criticisms, CrossFitters wore the cult accusations as a badge of honor, claiming, in reference to Jim Jones and the People's Temple movement, to have drunk "the CrossFit Kool-Aid" (Herz, 2014, p. 232).

Claims that CrossFit is a cult or a lifestyle distract, however, from the real seri-ousness of CrossFit as a business. Around the time CollegeHumor published their parody, CrossFit Inc. made roughly $100 million annually and with the success of its thousands of affiliate gyms, the brand generated approximately $4 billion in annual revenue (Ozanian, 2015). In the fall of 2015 CrossFit's founder, Greg Glassman, visited Harvard Business School and shared with students how CrossFit had forgone exclusive brand deals in favor of supporting a broader economy of CrossFit-related businesses started by CrossFit enthusiasts. In short, the cult of CrossFit is big business.

In this essay, I want to pause on the use of the word "cult" to describe CrossFit, its business, its brand, and its consumer culture. Scholars of religion have argued that the cult designation operates by labeling some religions as dangerous, abnor-mal, or bad in opposition to the broadly acceptable, normal, and good religions (Melton & Bromley, 2002; Lewis, 2004; Oliver, 2012; Thomas & Graham-Hyde, 2021). Cult is therefore a subjective term that serves to place some religions, sects, and religious movements under greater public scrutiny and government surveil-lance than others. To avoid imposing judgment, scholars suggest using the term New Religious Movement (NRM) when referencing groups that fall outside the religious mainstream. This is a useful and sensitive suggestion that has contributed to the growth of the NRM subfield over the last 20 years.[1] Yet this emphasis on NRMs risks missing how cult accusations circulate in popular culture and through the market. This essay examines the cult of CrossFit and situates the emergence of CrossFit as a cult brand within the early twenty-first-century trend of cult mar-keting. Separated into two sections, the first section of this essay traces popular attitudes toward cults in the latter half of the twentieth century and shows how re-ligious fanaticism inspired a new approach to brand marketing. The second section introduces CrossFit as a cult brand. CrossFit bursts onto the global fitness scene, while brand strategists and marketing specialists were codifying what it meant to be a cult brand. With CrossFit serving as a paradigmatic cult brand, this essay shows how religion and economy mixed and mingled in the early twenty-first century to produce cultlike market offerings and to remake the cult designation into an economic category.

Cults Meet Cult Marketing

The word cult comes from the Latin word *cultus*, meaning to cultivate, grow, or worship. From the seventeenth century onward, it has been used to describe religious sects and or groups that direct their veneration to a particular figure, deity, or object. By the mid-nineteenth century its meaning had expanded to include the adoration of non-religious things, like the "cult of success." Its meaning further evolved during the mid-to-late twentieth century during a boom in alternative religions and new religious and spiritual organizations, and "cult" became a pejorative label used to describe and denigrate fringe religious groups. At first, in the 1950s and 1960s, cults were thought of as anomalous and largely harmless oddities. From the 1970s onward, however, the notion that cults were dangerous and housed social deviants increased. During the heyday of the cult controversies in the 1970s and 1980s, being accused of membership in a cult was decidedly bad, and anti-cult groups like Ted Patrick's FREECOG and "cult deprogrammers" emerged to manage the public concern around cults. The fear of cults intensified with media coverage of sensational and sometimes violent events such as the Manson Family murders in 1969, the mass suicides of the People's Temple at Jonestown in 1978, Heaven's Gate in 1997, and the stand-off between federal agents and the Branch Davidians in Waco, TX, in 1993.

Cult allegations likewise mapped onto "true religion/false religion" and "good religion/bad religion" binaries, in which the cult always stood for the "false" or "bad" religion in opposition to the "true" and "good" religion, which in the United States usually meant mainline Protestant Christianity. The legitimacy of the cult designation was rarely questioned in American popular discourse in the late twentieth century, as Sean McCloud writes. Even when fringe groups like Hare Krishnas, Scientologists, and Mormons made appeals to *not* be considered cults, their arguments nevertheless reinforced the power of the word cult to sanction or ostracize minority religious groups (McCloud, 2004; Goodwin, 2020). "To label a movement a cult can be to suggest that it is a dangerous pseudo-religion with satanic overtones which is likely to be involved in financial rackets and political intrigue, to indulge in unnatural sexual practices, to abuse its women and children, and to use irresistible and irreversible brainwashing techniques in order to exploit its recruits," Eileen Barker explains (Barker, 2014, p. 236). To label a movement a cult is to suggest that it is not the kind of religion that benefits society or produces good citizens. The "cult" label even goes so far as to suggest that the movement is not a religion at all. Writing an editorial in 1993 for the *Christian Century*, Michael

Barkun summarized the opinion many Americans held in the late twentieth century. "To be called a cult is to be linked not to religion, but to psychopathology," he wrote (McCloud, 2004, p. 185).

The popular impression of cults began to change slightly, however, by the late 1990s and the early 2000s. Even with the tragedies of Heaven's Gate and the Branch Davidians in the 1990s, journalists began to disassociate the cult label from specific groups and theologies and used it to instead describe specific actions and activities. It became a shorthand and "conjured images of brainwashing, financial exploitation, child abuse, and sexual impropriety that might be attributed to any group" (McCloud, 2004, p. 173). Popular media also began to change the way it represented cults, often presenting cults as a comedic punchline rather than as a real and horrifying threat. This transition to the comedic genre is indicative of changing attitudes toward New Religious Movements, Joseph Laycock argues (2013, p. 92). The use of the word "cult" likewise changed in news media during the 1990s, as Philip Deslippe explains in his study of cult references in American newspapers. "In simple terms, if the word 'cult' was used in a newspaper during the Nineties, chances are it was not in reference to a religious group," Deslippe writes. In fact, "the most common application of these 'non-religious' uses of the word 'cult' was for cult media and cult followings" (2021, p. 206). Popular opinion around cults had shifted and returned to a pre-"cult menace" attitude toward cults as oddities and anomalies. Cults could still be dangerous, but they were now also sources of creative inspiration and references for parsing out the depths of human emotionalism, commitment, and zeal.

Deslippe's observation that most cult references in news media sources during the 1990s were for fandoms directs us to another trajectory the word cult took during the late twentieth century. As mentioned above, the notion that the word cult could be applied to non-religious objects, people, activities, and groups pre-dated the surge of cult controversies from the 1960s onward. Yet, the idea that a piece of media might gather a cult following and become a "cult classic" arose in tandem with the "cult menace" in the latter-half of the twentieth century. At the same time, the proliferation of niche markets in post-war America encouraged new forms of media that appealed to small yet passionate audiences. Likewise, new forms of media distribution emerged that made repeat viewings or readings possible. "Cult classic" movies, for example, took off when movie theaters began to license cheap and offbeat movies to show during their late nighttime slots as "midnight movies." These movies could play at the theaters for months or years at a time and would gain a devoted fanbase, with crowds developing viewing rituals such as wearing costumes, reciting dialogue, and throwing objects or speaking back to the screen at particular moments in "call backs." Cable television and other home media innovations like VHS, DVD, and DVR likewise made repeat viewings possible for dedicated fans (Jancovich et al, 2003).

Cult fandoms were related to yet distinct from the "cult menace" but nevertheless added to the idea circulating in the 1990s and early 2000s that cults could be harmless and fun. This idea was at the heart of a new trend within the world of marketing and brand management called cult marketing or cult branding. At the core of cult marketing is the idea that brands can engender fierce loyalty in their customers in the way that cult groups in the late twentieth century compelled members to become evangelists and devotees at all costs, while channeling the fun and harmlessness of media cult followings. "A cult brand is a product that has found a market niche and dominates it," writes Jon Berry in a 1992 issue of *AdWeek.* "Its consumers have intense brand loyalty." Berry cites the motorcycle manufacturer Harley-Davidson Inc. and the computer company Apple Inc. as examples of successful cult brands that have been able to develop a seemingly close relationship between brand and consumer. "To get ahead in the 1990s, a growing number of converts believe, more companies will have to learn how to think like cult marketers," Berry explains (1992). The goal of cult branding and cult marketing, as an article in *BusinessWeek* clarifies, is "to foster a sense of shared experience and belonging" among consumers and to tie the brand to the consumer's identity such that they become brand evangelists and a volunteer salesforce. "The fastest-growing [cult brands] often project an aura, an attractive group identity," the *BusinessWeek* article adds (Brady et al, 2004, p. 65). Customers want to feel like insiders, like they have ownership over the product and their community of consumer fandom. Cult brands benefit from consumer enthusiasm and exchange, and the most successful cult brands "give empowered consumers a great product and the tools to use it however they want" (Brady et al, 2004, p. 66). Marketing professionals watched in amazement as Harley-Davidson fanatics organized motorcycle rallies and Mac groupies traveled around the country volunteering as staff for the opening of new Apple stores (Kahney, 2004, p. 18). And they began to ponder how other companies might recreate the seemingly unflappable brand loyalty that companies like Apple and Harley-Davidson enjoyed.

While journalists and social commentators were remarking upon the emergence of cult brands in the early 1990s, it was not until the early 2000s that marketing experts published a spate of books on how to actively cultivate and market a cult brand. Dave Arnott published *Corporate Cults* in 2000, Matthew Ragas and Bolivar Bueno published *The Power of Cult Branding* in 2002, followed by Douglas Atkin's *The Culting of Brands* in 2004 and Shep Hyken's *The Cult of the Customer* in 2009. This first wave of cult marketing inspired later books in the same vein, like Jody Raynsford's *How to Start a Cult* (2021), and Michael Schein's *The Hype Handbook* (2021). In these books, authors try to dispel any fear readers may have about cults before offering practical tips for brand building. "First things first," writes Shep Hyken, "there's nothing scary about the word *cult*" (2009, p. 1). Even if the word cult had spent decades accruing negative connotations, there was still some desirability and utility in being associated with cults, these authors argue. Cults are not all bad. Bueno and Ragas, for example, consulted cult experts to distinguish between two types of cults: destructive cults and benign cults. Destructive cults, they write, "hurt, harm, manipulate, and often brainwash their members."

Benign cults, on the other hand, "help fill the emotional wants and needs of their followers in a positive way." "Whenever we discuss cult brands," they write, "we will always be talking about benign cults" (Ragas & Bueno, 2002, p. xxii). Atkin (2004) makes a similar argument, writing, "the position of this book is that *cults are a good thing*, that *cults are normal*, and that people join them for *very good reasons*" (emphasis in original, p. xiv).

What is notable about this move to renovate the image of the "cult" for the purposes of brand building is that these authors are using real-life examples of famous cult groups as inspiration for their marketing techniques. Rather than borrow the word cult from "cult classic" fandoms or merely apply the word cult to explain the fanaticism of certain consumers, these authors turn to examples from the heyday of the "cult menace." "One thing led to another, and soon the two of us were reading about the history of cults and infamous cultic groups and leaders," Bueno and Ragas explain. "Jonestown and Jim Jones. David Koresh and the Branch Davidians. Marshall Applewhite and Heaven's Gate. Which followers of an organization have ever shown more loyalty, devotion, and attraction to some person or some thing than members of a cult?" (2002, xxi). Raynsford is even more explicit, encouraging his readers to "extract what your brand can learn from cults and cult leaders" (2021, p. 12). Atkin takes a similar approach, writing that "the insights we derive from cult members, and the techniques used to generate devotion amongst them *are* transferable to a more general context" (2004, p. xv). The logic in turning to cults for inspiration, as Atkin explains, is because "*the same dynamics are at play behind the attraction to brands and cults*. They may vary in degree of strength (although not always), but not in type. … the sacred and profane are being bound by the essential desires of human nature, which seeks satisfaction wherever it can" [emphasis in original] (2004, p. xiii). The market, these authors argue, provides the same kind of outlet for finding community, identity, meaning, and expressing devotion as religious sects or cults.

In their marketing tomes, these authors are picking up on the long history of exchange between religion and business in American marketing that scholars like Mara Einstein (2008) and R. Laurence Moore (1995) have detailed at length. With the disestablishment of religion and free market capitalism, the United States has been fertile ground for developing creative techniques for winning people over—and that win may be equally sought after in saving souls as it is in making sales. To pinpoint moments of tactical exchange between religion and marketing, we might variously turn to thespian-turned itinerant preacher George Whitefield, the salesman-turned-revivalist Dwight Moody, the Christian service ethos of Wal-Mart, and the charismatic spirituality of Oprah (Stout, 1991; Moreton, 2010; Lofton, 2011; Gloege, 2015). We might also, as Atkin, Ragas, Bueno, and Raynsford show us, turn to the spectacle and fascination behind the late twentieth-century American "cult menace."

While these cult-branding authors all agree that cults possess some characteristics worth copying in marketing, their suggestions for how brands emulate cults vary. First marketers must contend with the paradox at the heart of a cult's appeal, Atkin explains (2004). Cults (and consequently cult brands) make people feel like they're more fully embracing and expressing their individuality while also feeling like they belong to a community. What sets cults apart, then, is that they are often in opposition to the status quo and are decidedly exclusionary. The proposition that marketing and sales teams ought to mimic this dynamic is likely to make any marketer nervous about losing potential customers. Brand marketers need to rid themselves of this aversion, Atkin (2004) advises:

> To generate cultlike devotion to your brand, the kind of attachment that leads to large profits and word of mouth, you cannot expect to secure every man, woman, and child on the planet. Instead of trying not to alienate anyone, you must target the alienated and simultaneously separate your organization from the mainstream.

pp. 17–18

Cult brands do not need to be small, Atkin clarifies, but they should fill a specific niche. Michael Schein (2021) suggests leaning even further away from the mainstream through a pugnacious strategy he calls "picking fights and making enemies." Cult marketers and cult brands that follow this strategy "identify a person or a status quo idea and position themselves and their ideas in opposition to it," he explains (p. xiii). Jody Raynsford shares Schein's approach, as is evident in the second commandment of his seven cult-brand commandments. "Thou shalt pick an enemy," Raynsford instructs. According to Raynsford, this step is essential since every cult needs "an external enemy against which the cult leader and their followers can rally" (2021, p. 94). What Atkin, Schein, and Raynsford underscore in their recommendations is the power of setting one's brand apart not only through the quality of product or service that is sold but also through a reputation based on an oppositional attitude. Raynsford's other six commandments (2021, pp. 94–95) drive this point home:

1　Thou shalt develop a polarizing cult message.
2　Thou shalt pick an enemy.
3　Thou shalt be different. And celebrate it.
4　Thou shalt bang thy drum over and over and over. [i.e. proselytize]
5　Thou shalt target outliers and misfits. [for recruits]
6　Thou shalt build belonging.
7　Thou shalt give thy followers plentiful opportunities to demonstrate belonging.

The strong emphasis these cult-marketing authors place on antagonism and identity formation is perhaps what makes CrossFit most appear like a cult to outside observers and insiders alike.

Cult Marketing Meets the Cult of CrossFit

Greg Glassman founded CrossFit in 2000 with his then-wife Lauren. Glassman, a former gymnast and fitness trainer, was an iconoclast and clashed with the management of several fitness studios he worked for before starting his own gym. The first CrossFit gym, or "box" as CrossFitters call them, opened in Santa Cruz, CA, where Glassman had already been training the Santa Cruz police department in methods of functional fitness that would help officers stay fit on the job. Shortly after the Santa Cruz box proved to be successful, Glassman began to publish his daily workouts (or WODs, "workout of the day," in CrossFit argot) online for free. An online community of people who resonated with Glassman's high-intensity approach to fitness soon sprang up and they followed his unique fitness program that combined gymnastic movement, cardio, and Olympic weightlifting. In discussion threads people posted their scores for timed workouts, recorded their personal best performances, celebrated each other's successes, and swapped workout tips. Glassman also began publishing notes on his theories and approach to fitness in the *Cross-Fit Journal*. Within a few years of CrossFit Inc.'s founding, a CrossFit enthusiast in Seattle approached Glassman about starting an affiliated gym and the affiliate model was born. In the affiliate model, gyms that want to use CrossFit's brand name and unique athletic programming license the name for an annual fee of $3,000. The only other requirement is that gym instructors, or "coaches," must be trained according to the CrossFit methodology through courses offered by CrossFit Inc. (courses cost approximately $1,000 each). CrossFit then began offering instructor training courses, alongside higher level and specialty certification courses, like CrossFit Adaptive for differently abled athletes, and CrossFit gymnastics for people who wanted extra coaching tips on gymnastic movements. With a relatively low threshold for entry, CrossFit gyms began to pop up across the United States before spreading across the world (Herz, 2014; Hart, 2021; *The Morning Chalk-Up*, 2023).

The growth of CrossFit was supported by early adopters in the military, police force, and firefighters who embraced CrossFit's ethos of "preparing for the unknown and unknowable" (Musselman, 2019). Plus CrossFit's emphasis on functional fitness helped them to train for the physical rigors of their professions. The popularity of CrossFit likewise expanded with the creation of the CrossFit Games, an annual competition among CrossFitters who compete for the title of "Fittest Man and Fittest Woman in the World." What started as a backyard barbeque "festival of fitness" in Aromas, CA, in 2007 has grown into a multimillion-dollar sport with title sponsorships from Reebok and No Bull and five days of televised competition among an international cadre of professional CrossFit athletes (CrossFit Games, 2012).

Despite this explosion in growth and popularity, CrossFit gained and retained a reputation for being insular and cult-like. The affiliate model afforded independent box owners a lot of freedom and flexibility in how they wanted to run their gyms. Without much oversight from CrossFit Inc., each gym developed its own personality, attracting some types of people and driving away others. Some CrossFit gyms, for example, fashioned themselves as women-only gyms, while others advertised themselves as LGBTQ-friendly gyms, and some were known for being conservative Christian gyms. Some CrossFit gyms gained reputations for training elite athletes to be contenders at the CrossFit Games, while other CrossFit gyms were geared toward senior citizens. As a result of this variation, CrossFitters became incredibly attached to their box communities, which also became an outward manifestation of their personal identity. CrossFit boxes exemplified the cult paradox outlined by Atkin (2004): CrossFit gyms became a place where it was "more possible to *be* yourself with people you consider to be more *like* yourself" (p. 5). Plus the variability worked to the advantage of CrossFit evangelists who folded the sectarian nature of CrossFit into their pitch: if you don't like the CrossFit gym you sampled, try another.

As CrossFit's influence over the fitness industry increased over the first two decades of the twenty-first century, the zeal CrossFitters expressed for their CrossFit communities did not go unnoticed by the outside world. Jokes began to circulate like: "A vegan, atheist, and a CrossFitter walk into a bar. You know because they tell you." In an interview, CrossFit's CMO remarked that "CrossFit is tighter than a religion" (Pathak, 2015). The comparison to religion even garnered CrossFit Inc.'s executives an invitation to speak at Harvard Divinity School in 2015. Despite its increased association with religion, CrossFit was still mostly compared to cults, even among its members. In a CrossFit-produced documentary, John Welbourn, a former NFL lineman and a competitor in one of the first CrossFit Games, reflects upon the tight-knit community he found through CrossFit. "In college, in one of my classes we defined what a cult was. The number one [trait] was a special diet. CrossFit promotes a diet: the Zone. They have a certain terminology that only people within the cult understand. If you were to say to somebody 'what's your Fran time?' on the street, he doesn't understand. But if you tell it to a CrossFitter, he knows exactly what you're talking about." ["Fran" is a CrossFit workout of barbell thrusters and pull-ups.] He continues to detail the ways that CrossFit resembles a cult. "Special clothing: I see these CrossFitters, their biggest thing is to go get t-shirts from other CrossFit gyms and wear them proudly. Meeting places: your CrossFit gym, that's your community. A lot of CrossFitters tend to only associate with other CrossFitters." Having made this comparison and seeing the criteria stack up, Welbourn ponders, "Now is it a good cult? Yeah. It's a fitness cult—it's making you better. It is a cult? Yeah, it is" (CrossFit Pictures, 2009).

Welbourn was not the only insider taking stock of CrossFit's distinctive social practices and wondering if they had inadvertently joined a cult. As early as 2006, members logged onto CrossFit's online discussion forum to weigh in on CrossFit's cult status and how to handle cult accusations. Given the broader cultural turn in the 1990s and early 2000s toward treating cults as anomalies, comedic fodder, punchlines, and fandoms, the allegations that CrossFit was a cult were mostly lighthearted. Still, one discussant took the charge head-on and used a cult questionnaire to evaluate CrossFit. Like Welbourn, this member wanted to see how

CrossFit would measure up and posted the results to the forum: "Is Crossfit a cult? Let's put it to the test" (Walsh, 2006).

Q: Does the group display excessively zealous and unquestioning commitment to its leader and (whether he is alive or dead) regards his belief system, ideology, and practices as the Truth, as law?

A: Yes

Q: Are questioning, doubt, and dissent discouraged or even punished.

A: Yes.

Q: Are mind-altering practices (such as meditation, chanting, speaking in tongues, denunciation sessions, and debilitating work routines) used in excess and serve to suppress doubts about the group and its leader?

A: No.

Q: Does the leadership dictate, sometimes in great detail, how members should think, act, and feel (for example, members must get permission to date, change jobs, marry—or leaders prescribe what types of clothes to wear, where to live, whether or not to have children, how to discipline children, and so forth)?

A: No.

Q: Is the group elitist, claiming a special, exalted status for itself, its leader(s), and members (for example, the leader is considered the Messiah, a special being, an avatar—or the group and/or the leader is on a special mission to save humanity)?

A: Yes, most definitely.

Q: Does the group have a polarized us-versus-them mentality, which may cause conflict with the wider society?

A: Yes.

Q: Does the leadership induce feelings of shame and/or guilt in order to influence and/or control members. Often, this is done through peer pressure and subtle forms of persuasion.

A: Yes.

Q: Does subservience to the leader or group require members to cut ties with family and friends and radically alter the personal goals and activities they had before joining the group?

A: No.

Q: Is the group preoccupied with bringing in new members?

A: Yes.

Q: Is the group preoccupied with making money?

A: Somewhat.

Q: Are members expected to devote inordinate amounts of time to the group and group-related activities?

A: No.

Q: Are members encouraged or required to live and/or socialize only with other group members?

A: No.

Q: Do the most loyal members (the "true believers") feel there can be no life outside the context of the group? Do they believe there is no other way to be and often fear reprisals to themselves or others if they leave (or even consider leaving) the group?

A: Yes.

It is unclear where the member found this questionnaire, although it resembles cult definitions and anti-cult resources published by the International Cultic Studies Association. Nevertheless, with half of the questions answered "yes" and the other half answered "no," the questionnaire did little to settle the lively debate happening among CrossFitters on the forum about whether CrossFit was a cult. Amused by the comparison, another poster suggested, "I guess it should be called CultFit" (Shereyk, 2006).

Elsewhere, Greg Glassman had responded to accusations that CrossFit was a cult, telling a journalist, "We keep being asked: are you a cult? And after a while I realized, maybe we are? This is an active, sweating, loving, breathing community. It's not an insult to a CrossFitter to be called part of a cult. Discipline, honesty, courage, accountability—what you learn in the gym—is also training for life. CrossFit makes better people" (ReasonTV, 2014). Like the cult marketers who were publishing their books around the same time that CrossFitters were preoccupied with cult comparisons on the CrossFit discussion forums, Glassman reframed cults as a good thing. CrossFit, if anything, was a benign cult, perhaps even a good cult because it was in the business of health, wellness, and community building.

While Glassman believed CrossFit was in the business of making better people, he had not always represented CrossFit as something benign. In the first-ever feature published about the upstart fitness brand in the *New York Times*, Glassman underscored CrossFit's hardcore and exclusive nature. "It can kill you," Glassman said. "I've always been completely honest about that" (Cooperman, 2005). The article introduced CrossFit broadly as a fitness trend gaining popularity and momentum, but it mostly focused on risk, injury, and a condition from over-exertion called Rhabdomyolysis that occurs when muscles break down quickly and proteins enter the bloodstream and cause kidney damage. One of the main interview subjects for the article had returned to CrossFit after recovering from Rhabdomyolysis and his testimony highlighted the degree of devotion CrossFitters held in the face of naysayers and other fitness experts who warned CrossFit neophytes of injury. In this 2005 interview, Glassman was not only responding to criticisms that CrossFit was dangerous, but he was also upping the ante and making a claim about the culture of CrossFit. "If you find the notion of falling off the rings and breaking your neck so foreign to you, then we don't want you in our ranks," Glassman proclaimed (Cooperman, 2005). In this interview, Glassman communicated that as a fitness methodology and as a brand, CrossFit was doing things differently, and it didn't care if it was exclusionary or ostracizing potential customers. It had found its niche among hardcore fitness enthusiasts. It was a cult brand.

While the reputation of CrossFit as something dangerous has lessened over the years (thanks in part to the litigiousness of CrossFit Inc.), an adversarial attitude remains at the heart of the CrossFit culture (Helm, 2013). Like other cult brands, CrossFit has an enemy or two. One of CrossFit's first and most enduring "enemies" is the standard fitness gym, or what CrossFitters call "Globo-gyms." "*Globo-gym* was, and remains, CrossFit's code-word shorthand for The Way Things Are Is Wrong," J.C. Herz explains in her history of CrossFit, *Learning to Breathe Fire*. "It's a loaded phrase, like 'factory food' or 'the 1%' or 'the mainstream media,' that defines a culturally dominant Them, and by opposition, a scrappy, righteous Us" (2014, p. 170). In more precise terms, Globo-gyms are high-volume fitness club franchises like Planet Fitness, LA Fitness, Anytime Fitness, the more upscale Equinox, or the now defunct former fitness industry giant Bally Total Fitness. "High-volume health clubs—facilities that sell year-long memberships to use cardio machines and weight circuits—have a financial model that succeeds when members pay but don't actually exercise," writes Herz. "The gym's billing system is going to extract money from members' bank accounts every month, regardless of whether they work out" (Herz, p. 177). From CrossFit's inception, with its open-source workouts, affiliate model, Libertarian ethos, and dispersed online community, it has positioned itself in opposition to the high-volume health club model. Rather than sell you a membership and hope you do not show up, the highly engaged CrossFit community generates a profit from a small yet devoted group of fitness enthusiasts who pay a premium (roughly $120–200/month) for small-group coaching and who come to the gym four or more times a week. In turn, these customers expect their physical results and social benefits to justify the cost. "What keeps them going, and makes it almost impossible to go back to a Globo-gym, is a change in their identity: they become athletes," Herz writes (2014, p.191). They also become evangelists.

As evangelists, CrossFitters proselytize the CrossFit methodology neatly summarized in "Fitness in 100 Words" (Glassman, 2021):

Eat meat and vegetables, nuts and seeds, some fruit, little starch and no sugar. Keep intake to levels that will support exercise but not body fat.

Practice and train major lifts: Deadlift, clean, squat, presses, C&J, and snatch. Similarly, master the basics of gymnastics: pull-ups, dips, rope climb, push-ups, sit-ups, presses to handstand, pirouettes, flips, splits, and holds. Bike, run, swim, row, etc., hard and fast.

Five or six days per week mix these elements in as many combinations and patterns as creativity will allow. Routine is the enemy. Keep workouts short and intense.

Regularly learn and play new sports.

At first glance, this physical prescription does not seem to adhere to Raynsford's suggestion to "develop a polarizing cult message," but at the time of CrossFit's founding many high-volume health clubs were populated with specialized cardio and weight machines. Group fitness classes were dedicated to honing particular muscles and movements (Pilates for the core, for example, or cardio for heart health). Elite athletes also trained with specialization in mind, hoping to run further faster, or to bulk up to tackle or lift heavy weights. Glassman's provocative "cult message" therefore was to eschew specialization. "Our specialty is not specializing," Glassman wrote in one of his foundational articles "What is Fitness?" (2002) for the *CrossFit Journal*. With CrossFit, Glassman wanted to train a generalist— someone who would not run as fast as the trained sprinter or lift as much as the accomplished Olympic weightlifter, but who could run *nearly* as fast as the sprinter while lifting *nearly* as much as the weightlifter. Elsewhere, Glassman explained his approach, stating "I believe there is a physical capacity that would lend itself generally well to any endeavor. Optimally? No. Generally well" (CrossFit Journal, 2009). This approach to fitness was attractive to people who shared Glassman's idea that the purpose of fitness exceeds proficiency in sports. Rather, when in the gym, one is training for life.

For those who resonated with CrossFit's simple yet rigorous fitness method, its sports-team-like community, its emphasis on a hardcore attitude, and its outsider status within the broader exercise culture, it was easy to "bang thy drum over and over and over"—in the words of Raynsford—and provide testimony affirming their devotion to the cult brand of CrossFit. For those subjected to CrossFitters' evangelizing efforts, the CrossFit nomenclature was most notable. WOD, box, AMRAP, Fran, EMOM, Globo-gyms, L1, and The Hopper are just a few of the specialized words and acronyms CrossFitters use. In 2019, CrossFitters once again debated the cultlike status of their community online in a Reddit thread and one commenter made note of CrossFit's distinctive vocabulary. "To the average punter you're speaking in your own lingo that makes no sense to anyone that doesn't do it, but [makes] total sense to anyone who does." The commenter gave an example:

A: Yeah, I just PR'd on the WOD earlier.
B: Yeah, Grace?
A: Nah, it was Isabell, I RX'd it.
B: Good job man, the oly lifting is hard.

("Why Do Some Consider CrossFit a Cult" Reddit, 2019)

"Screams of cult," the commenter concluded. Amanda Montell affirms this conclusion in her book *Cultish: The Language of Fanaticism*, in which she argues that language is at the center of cult formation. From technical terms to thought-terminating cliches, language shapes worldviews, she suggests, and specialized language signals insider status while laying the groundwork for fanaticism (Montell, 2021, p. 14). The cultish capacity of specialized language was not lost on cult marketers either. In a 2004 edition of *Adweek*, Rob Schwartz details the cult characteristics brands might appropriate to become cult brands and suggests that brands develop an insider language to communicate in ways that add mystique and reward loyal members (Schwartz, 2004). For CrossFitters, expressing their unorthodox approach to fitness through their own vocabulary helped accomplish the feeling of community and solidarity and cemented their status as a cult brand.

Conclusion

This essay has examined the rise of cult marketing within the broader history of cults in the United States to show how marketing and brand strategists turned to cults for inspiration. The logic of cult marketing suggests that the fidelity and fanaticism people express while in cults can be redirected to sales. In the early 2000s, cult marketers hypothesized that brands could generate consumer loyalty through cult tactics, and real-life religious groups that made headlines for their radical, deviant, or even dangerous behavior became models for marketing professionals. CrossFit emerges within this context as a paradigmatic cult brand. To be clear, there is no evidence that Greg Glassman or executives at CrossFit Inc. were consciously adopting cult-marketing techniques as they shaped and developed the CrossFit brand. Rather, the founding story of CrossFit and the subsequent devotion CrossFitters began to display for the brand is often narrated as arising organically. Members and executives explain CrossFit's cultlike status through the appeal of its product. "The magic is in the movement, the art is in the programming, the science is in the explanation, and the fun is in the community," according to Glassman (CrossFit, 2005). Nevertheless, this essay argues that the proliferation of cult-marketing books and advice columns in the early 2000s laid the conceptual groundwork for CrossFit insiders and outside observers to interpret a for-profit fitness business in terms of a cult. Comparisons of CrossFit (or other businesses) to cults are not mere hyperboles or analogies. Rather, these comparisons stem from a moment in marketing history in which marketing experts were actively mining New Religious Movements for tactics and techniques to bring into the marketplace. While scholars of religion debate the utility of the word cult and often suggest using a less politically charged description like "New Religious Movement" to discuss minority religions, this essay demonstrates how the word cult circulates outside of academic discourse and takes on new meanings as a category of economic consequence.

Note

1 Eileen Barker has discussed how the designation "New Religious Movements" is likewise imperfect because the newness and religiousness of NRMs may often be contested. Eileen Barker, "The Not-So-New Religious Movements: Changes in 'the Cult Scene' over the Past Forty Years," *Temenos* 50, no. 2 (2014): 238. Janja Lalich and Karla McLaren likewise argue that the term "New Religious Movements" is inadequate because some cults include religious ideas, while others, like multi-level marketing and high-control political groups, do not. Janja Lalich and Karla McLaren, *Escaping Utopia: Growing Up in a Cult, Getting Out, and Starting Over* (New York: Routledge, 2018).

Bibliography

Atkin, Douglas. *The Culting of Brands: When Customers Become True Believers*. New York: Portfolio, 2004.

Barker, Eileen. "The Not-So-New Religious Movements: Changes in 'the Cult Scene' over the Past Forty Years." *Temenos* 50, no. 2 (2014): 235–56.

Berry, Jon. "The Power of Cult Brands." *AdWeek's Marketing Week*, February 24, 1992.

Brady, Diane, Robert Hof, Moon Ihlwan, and Kerry Capell. "Cult Brands." *BusinessWeek*, August 2, 2004.

Cooperman, Stephanie. "Getting Fit, Even If It Kills You." *The New York Times*, December 22, 2005. https://www.nytimes.com/2005/12/22/fashion/thursdaystyles/getting-fit-even-if-it-kills-you.html.

CollegeHumor. Your CrossFit Friends (Hardly Working), 2014. https://www.youtube.com/watch?v=pqb9pBJweVU.

CrossFit. "Sunday 051113." *Workout of the Day*, November 13, 2005. https://www.crossfit.com/workout/2005/11/13#/comments.

CrossFit Games History: 2007–2013, 2012. https://www.youtube.com/watch?v=5y92hjZNEjI.

Deslippe, Philip. "Past the Pejorative: Understanding the Word 'Cult' Through Its Use in American Newspapers During the Nineties." *Implicit Religion* 24, no. 2 (2021): 195–217.

Einstein, Mara. *Brands of Faith: Marketing Religion in a Commercial Age*. London; New York: Routledge, 2008.

Every Second Counts. CrossFit Pictures, 2009.

Glassman, Greg. "What Is Fitness?" *The CrossFit Journal*, 2002.

———. "World-Class Fitness in 100 Words." *Morning Chalk Up*, August 11, 2021. https://morningchalkup.com/2021/08/11/world-class-fitness-in-100-words/.

Glassman, Suzie. "I Left a Cult and Survived–Okay CrossFit but Same Thing." *Medium* (blog), October 24, 2020. https://medium.com/the-haven/i-left-a-cult-and-survived-okay-crossfit-but-same-thing-1e0f7ff8cbf6.

Gloege, Timothy E. W. *Guaranteed Pure: The Moody Bible Institute, Business, and the Making of Modern Evangelicalism.* Chapel Hill: University of North Carolina Press, 2015.

Goodwin, Megan. *Abusing Religion: Literary Persecution, Sex Scandals, and American Minority Religions.* New Brunswick: Rutgers University Press, 2020.

Harvard Divinity School, *CrossFit As Church!?*, 2015, https://www.youtube.com/watch?v=9oc8ZRKDCyU.

Hart, Matt. "Does CrossFit Have a Future?" *The New Yorker*, July 20, 2021. https://www.newyorker.com/sports/sporting-scene/does-crossfit-have-a-future.

Havrilesky, Heather. "Why Are Americans So Fascinated with Extreme Fitness?" *The New York Times Magazine*, October 14, 2014. https://www.nytimes.com/2014/10/19/magazine/why-are-americans-so-fascinated-with-extreme-fitness.html?_r=0.

Helm, Burt. "Do Not Cross CrossFit." *Inc.com*, July 2, 2013. https://www.inc.com/magazine/201307/burt-helm/crossfit-empire.html.

Herz, J.C. *Learning to Breathe Fire: The Rise of CrossFit and the Primal Future of Fitness.* New York: Three Rivers Press, 2014.

Hyken, Shep. *The Cult of the Customer: Create an Amazing Customer Experience That Turns Satisfied Customers Into Customer Evangelists.* Hoboken: Wiley, 2009.

Jancovich, Mark, Antonio Roboll Lazaro, Julian Stringer, and Andy Willis, eds. *Defining Cult Movies: The Cultural Politics of Oppositional Taste.* New York: Manchester University Press, 2003.

Kahney, Leander. *The Cult of Mac.* San Francisco: No Starch Press, 2004.

Laycock, Joseph. "Where Do They Get These Ideas? Changing Ideas of Cults in the Mirror of Popular Culture." *Journal of the American Academy of Religion* 81, no. 1 (March 2013): 80–106.

Lalich, Janja, and Karla McLaren. *Escaping Utopia: Growing Up in a Cult, Getting Out, and Starting Over.* New York: Routledge, 2018.

Lewis, James R. "Overview." In *The Oxford Handbook of New Religious Movements*, 3–15. New York: Oxford University Press, 2004.

Lofton, Kathryn. *Oprah: The Gospel of an Icon.* Berkeley: University of California Press, 2011.

McCloud, Sean. *Making the American Religious Fringe: Exotics, Subversives, & Journalists, 1955–1993.* Chapel Hill: University of North Carolina Press, 2004.

Melton, J. Gordon, and David Bromley. "Challenging Misconceptions About the New Religions–Violence Connection." In *Cults, Religion, and Violence*, 42–56. Cambridge: Cambridge University Press, 2002.

Michaels, Jillian. "The Good & Bad of CrossFit." *The Good & Bad of CrossFit | Jillian Michaels*, February 27, 2019. http://www.jillianmichaels.com/blog/health-and-fitness/good-bad-crossfit.

Montell, Amanda. *Cultish: The Language of Fanaticism.* New York: Harper Wave, 2021.

Moore, R. Laurence. *Selling God: American Religion in the Marketplace of Culture.* New York: Oxford University Press, 1995.

Moreton, Bethany. *To Serve God and Wal-Mart: The Making of Christian Free Enterprise.* Cambridge, MA; London: Harvard University Press, 2010.

Musselman, Cody. "Training for the 'Unknown and Unknowable': CrossFit and Evangelical Temporality." *Religions* 10, no. 11 (November 2019): 624. https://doi.org/10.3390/rel10110624.

National War College Speech: Part 1. CrossFit Journal, 2009. http://journal.crossfit.com/2009/01/national-war-college-speech-part-1.tpl.

Oliver, Paul. "Conceptual Analysis and New Religious Movements." In *New Religious Movements: A Guide for the Perplexed*, 3–19. New York: Continuum, 2012.

Ozanian, Mike. "How CrossFit Became A \$4 Billion Brand." *Forbes*, February 25, 2015. https://www.forbes.com/sites/mikeozanian/2015/02/25/how-crossfit-became-a-4-billion-brand/?sh=1e2c6fb41f96.

Pathak, Shareen. "CrossFit CMO Jimi Letchford: 'CrossFit Is Tighter than a Religion.'" *Digiday* (blog), March 27, 2015. https://digiday.com/marketing/crossfit-cmo-jimi-letchford-crossfit-tighter-religion/.

Ragas, Matthew W., and Bolivar J. Bueno. *The Power of Cult Branding: How 9 Magnetic Brands Turned Customers into Loyal Followers (and Yours Can, Too!)*. New York: Crown Business, 2002.

Raynsford, Jody. *How to Start a Cult: Be Bold, Build Belonging, and Attract a Band of Devoted Followers to Your Brand*. Monee: Known Publishing, 2021.

ReasonTV, "CrossFit Founder Greg Glassman: "I'm a Rabid Libertarian." 2014, https://www.youtube.com/watch?v=-EB0XyBUl0U

Schein, Michael. *The Hype Handbook: 12 Indispensable Success Secrets from the World's Greatest Propagandists, Self-Promoters, Cult Leaders, Mischief Makers, and Boundary Breakers*. New York: McGraw-Hill Education, 2021.

Schwartz, Rob. "Cult-Ural Marketing." *Adweek*, November 29, 2004. https://www.adweek.com/brand-marketing/cult-tural-marketing-76372/.

Shereyk, Adam. "Could It Be Cult Fitness?" *CrossFit Discussion Board*, December 17, 2006. https://board.crossfit.com/showthread.php?t=18903.

Stout, Harry S. *The Divine Dramatist: George Whitefield and the Rise of Modern Evangelicalism. Library of Religious Biography*. Grand Rapids: W.B. Eerdmans, 1991.

The Morning Chalk-Up. "The Original CrossFit Box: Then and Now." *Newsletter*. Accessed March 10, 2023. https://morningchalkup.com/newsletters/original-crossfit-box-now/.

Thomas, Aled, and Edward Graham-Hyde. "The Return of the 'Cult.'" *Implicit Religion, Special Issue: The Return of the Cult: Bad Religion in the Age of Trump and COVID* 24, no. 2 (2021): 129–34.

Walsh, John. "Could It Be Cult Fitness?" *CrossFit Discussion Board*, December 20, 2006. https://board.crossfit.com/showthread.php?t=18903&page=2.

Weathers, Cliff. "CrossFit Is a Cult: Why so Many of Its Defenders Are so Defensive." *Salon*, October 22, 2014. https://www.salon.com/2014/10/22/crossfit_is_a_cult_why_so_many_of_its_defenders_are_so_defensive_partner/.

"Why Do Some Consider CrossFit a Cult?" *Reddit*, June 4, 2019. https://www.reddit.com/r/crossfit/comments/bw0lkp/comment/eq0rina/?utm_source=reddit&utm_medium=web2x&context=3.

15

PURPOSE-DRIVEN FOOD

Evangelical Diet Marketing and Conscious Capitalism

Chad E. Seales

University of Texas at Austin

In 2011, Rick Warren, the California-based Baptist minister who authored the New York Times #1 best-selling book *The Purpose Driven Life* (2002), launched a diet plan to help his church congregants lose weight. He called it *The Daniel Plan*, named after Daniel in the Bible, and co-authored a book by that title with the help of two celebrity doctors: Daniel Amen and Mark Hyman (Warren and Hyman 2013). The goal of *The Daniel Plan* was to motivate church members to eat more vegetables and fruits. In the biblical story, Daniel was an Israelite held captive in Babylon who refused to eat King Nebuchadnezzar's meat or drink his wine, saying to the chief official, "Give us nothing but vegetables to eat and water to drink. Then compare our appearance with that of the young men who eat the royal food and treat your servants in accordance with what you see" (Daniel 1: 1–18 NIV). Daniel likely refused to eat the King's food because he did not want to break Jewish prohibitions against eating meat sacrificed to other gods (White 2000: 269). But for Warren, who updated the story to make it relevant to the modern moment, Daniel was not just a Jew worried about his religion's dietary restrictions, but he was also a faith-filled guy who "refused to eat junk food and challenged a king to a health contest" (15).

Never mind that there were no empty calories in biblical times—no candy bars or bags of chips—what Warren wanted his audience to know was that the rulers of this world tempted you with bad food that made you sick, while God expected you to eat good foods that kept you fit and trim. Even though the authors said *The Daniel Plan* wasn't a weight loss plan, their loudest message was that bodily appearance was the visible measure of healthy eating. In the opening chapter, Warren wrote that a sudden awareness of obesity led him to find an alternative diet for himself and his congregants. It was on the day he baptized over 800 adults at his church, lowering each new believer underwater and lifting them back up, that

DOI: 10.4324/9781003342229-21

he said he knew something was wrong. After all that heavy lifting, he declared, "Wow! Everybody's FAT!" (13).

A decade later, in 2022, the food technology company Pairwise launched a "new purpose-driven brand called Conscious Foods" (Petrak 2022). Based on the company's self-description, "Pairwise is a health-focused food and agriculture company that is transforming what we eat" (Pairwise 2023a). Like *The Daniel Plan*, Pairwise stated, "our mission is to build a healthier world through better fruits and vegetables," which it says is motivated by the problem of "low-quality diets" in the United States. Citing a CDC report from 2019, Pairwise noted that only one in ten adults eats the daily recommended amounts of fruits and vegetables. In response to this problem, again like *The Daniel Plan*, Pairwise states, "we believe that if we can get more people to sub in fruits and vegetables for their regular meals and snacks, we can move the needle upward on fruit and vegetable consumption with the aim of yielding the related health benefits" (Pairwise 2023b). Rick Warren and Pairwise were not the first to tell people to eat more vegetables and fruits. But they were among those who consolidated this advice into a marketing strategy rebranding mundane diet plans and health products to sell as a moral lifestyle with a higher purpose. In *The Daniel Plan*, that higher purpose was rooted in biblical faith in God's natural order. For Pairwise, the higher purpose developed out of the scientific promise of industrial agriculture to develop new technologies to feed the world. Within the marketing world of purpose-driven companies and products, these causes were interchangeable, as both shared the same economic view of entrepreneurship and free markets.

This chapter examines the marketing trend of plant-focused "purpose driven food" that developed around Rick Warren's management model of the "purpose driven life," popularized in his first best-selling book and later infused into *The Daniel Plan*, and compares it to the purpose-driven marketing of plant-based health foods by biotech companies like Pairwise. Over the decade plus following the publication of *The Purpose Driven Life*, the phrase "purpose driven" circulated widely within corporate branding and product marketing to signal that profit could be used to promote positive social change. Within purpose-driven marketing, a product is tied to a cause. Most often these causes relate to global issues like climate change, poverty, or health and assume that corporations are well suited to address those issues by offering solutions that are financially and socially profitable.[1] *The Daniel Plan* and biotech marketing of "conscious foods" shared the social cause of improving personal health as measured by lower rates of obesity and Type II diabetes. The two marketing strategies differed, however, in that *The Daniel Plan* carried a religious critique of industrial food production as against God's plan for a healthy lifestyle, whereas biotech corporations rebranded industrial agriculture as able to produce health products that were better suited to consumer demand. Ultimately, the chapter argues that religious resistance to industrial agriculture highlighted in *The Daniel Plan* was compromised by a cultural evangelicalism that focused spiritual attention on personal management and body image, which made its health message interchangeable with biotech marketing of conscious foods as improving personal health. As such, purpose-driven food marketing undermined producer sovereignty by offering the feeling of personal agency as a consumer's right to choose healthy food without changing the modes of food production owned and controlled by the biotech industry that contributed to environmental factors that negatively impacted public health.

Cultural evangelicalism is defined here as a political theology of moral management that did not require confessional consent but nonetheless defined public values (Kyle 2018: 7). In the case of purpose-driven food, public values related to food consumption moved across traditionally understood religious and secular spaces, including churches and businesses, with corporate marketing providing the medium for shared consumer practices. Cultural evangelicalism was embedded within purpose-driven marketing, which collapsed the distinction between marketing religion as a product and marketing products as a religion by merging both into a spiritual lifestyle of healthy choices. Purpose-driven marketing expressed cultural evangelicalism in ways that could appear religious or secular to consumers. *The Daniel Plan* buffered between confessional Christian diet plans and healthy food choices as a secular spiritual lifestyle. What distinguished *The Daniel Plan* from other Christian diet plans was the way it marketed biblical diet advice as a management strategy that encompassed social life, from church to home to work and beyond, including sports and entertainment. Warren named this strategy "the purpose driven life" and combined the business ideas of management by objectives and self-control taken from Peter Drucker, a key figure in the post-WWII development of corporate management, with evangelical understandings of soul salvation as an individual decision and a personal relationship (Starbuck 2017: 99).[2]

The implication that strong and thin believers were ideal Christians contributed to the popularity of *The Daniel Plan*, as it fit within the marketable categories of Christian diet plans and health products. The book version of *The Daniel Plan* was another best seller for Warren, debuting as number one on *The New York Times* best seller list. It sold over 2 million copies, not as popular as *The Purpose Driven Life*, which sold over 30 million copies by 2012, but still among the more popular Christian diet plans of the twenty-first century.[3] *The Daniel Plan* garnered support from a range of evangelicals, including at least one member of the People for the Ethical Treatment of Animals (PETA), often perceived as having an antagonistic relationship with religion. Michelle Reynolds, who posted her testimony to the PETA website in 2017, described herself as a person who grew up in a "traditional, Southern, Christian family" and was surrounded by people who had health problems like "heart attacks, strokes, cancer, obesity, and diabetes." After taking an agriculture class in college, Michelle learned of the "horror of factory farming for the first time" and decided to stop eating animals. For years, Michelle tried to reconcile her new veganism with her Christian faith, until she found in *The Daniel Plan* a way to do that. In the post, Reynolds highlighted the health benefits of the plan, emphasizing weight loss and noting how the plan claimed "improvement or resolution of chronic diseases, including type 2 diabetes" among the 15,000 people in Warren's congregation. To bolster her point, she referenced a Facebook post from Franklin Graham, a conservative evangelical, who had recently in January of 2017 made a New Year's resolution to become a vegan to lose weight, joking that he wanted to return to the same size he was as a high school freshman (Reynolds 2017). "Vegetables and fruit anyway you can fix them," Graham declared to the thousands of people attending an outdoor meeting in Madison, Wisconsin as part of the "Decision America Tour," an evangelical political campaign that supported the 2016 presidential candidacy of Donald Trump. Then he stopped and asked the crowd, "Do you think I'll survive?" (Smith 2016).

Michelle Reynolds' PETA post on the health benefits of veganism and Franklin Graham's resolution to become vegan to lose weight demonstrated the tension between collective critique and body weight that persisted in popular media coverage of *The Daniel Plan* that focused on weight loss success. *Publishers Weekly*, for example, noted the frequently cited stat, which Reynolds also referenced, that members of Warren's Saddleback Church had "collectively lost 250,000 pounds during the first year of the program." This emphasis on body type and weight loss in Christian diet plans resonated within American culture. Before *The Daniel Plan,* Don Colbert's *What Would Jesus Eat?* (2002) promoted a biblical-based Mediterranean diet as an alternative to fast food and processed foods that contributed to 15 "adverse health conditions" with obesity at the top of the list. And George Malkmus's *The Hallelujah Diet* (2006) offered a biblical model for eating raw and organic foods as a way to reclaim the "vital nutrients God meant for us to eat." Christian diet plans offered consumers a range of theological opinions on how to survive nutrition-scarce food markets produced by industrial agriculture (Patel 2012). The emphasis on obesity and body image as a measure of poor health that resulted from bad personal choices, however, limited the potential for a radical critique of food production in the United States that was latent in Christian diet plans, especially *The Daniel Plan*, to develop into a social movement that could challenge public policies that supported an industrial agricultural system that produced environmental factors that contributed to a range of public health outcomes beyond the control of the individual (Griffith 2004; Kwan and Sheikh 2011).

In the early 2000s, critiques of industrial agriculture brought increased public attention to the environmental problem of industrial food production and its health impacts on consumers. Food corporations and governmental authorities responded by branding this environmental crisis as a personal problem of poor choice and lack of education that resulted in higher rates of obesity and Type II diabetes in the U.S. population (Guthman 2011). In this highly marketed moment of medical diagnoses, Christian diet plans like *The Daniel Plan* offered moral solutions to public health crises in America. These moral solutions were religious calls for help from individuals suffering from health ailments better understood as problems of inflammation than as weight gain (Marya and Patel 2021). When gathered in churches and congregations, personal pleas for better health, even when misdirected toward body size, had the potential to coalesce into social movements for political action. Because of *The Daniel Plan,* an increasing number of consumers were motivated as religious collectives, as churches and congregations, to find nutrient-dense foods. This religious shift in consumer behavior supported alternative food markets that benefited small-scale farmers, local producers, co-ops, and natural food stores by directing spending away from big-box grocers and fast-food chains.

Because the primary religion of this consumer movement, cultural evangelicalism, however, shared overlapping economic assumptions with industrial agriculture, particularly assumptions concerning consumer freedom and corporate sovereignty, it was unable to challenge the problem of environmental health in the United States as a problem of food sovereignty in which biotech industrial corporations controlled the agricultural system. This brand of cultural evangelicalism in its most basic economic form was individual, personal, privatized, and libertarian—no government policies or regulations needed—emphasizing neoliberal "private choices" solutions offered to a collective, broadscale, systemic food industry problem.[4] *The Daniel Plan* held in tension mainstream diet marketing emphasis on weight loss and personal health with collective religious critique of industrial agriculture. Beyond the personal moral attention to individual weight loss, *The Daniel Plan* was filled with shared moral reasons to resist industrial agriculture. "Real, whole food that comes from the earth—food that was created by God—heals," Warren wrote, "while industrial-processed food created in factories by man harms" (37).[5] The book stated plainly that "the best thing you can do for your health is to avoid factory-made science projects with weird and strange molecules that haven't been made by God in nature" (114). In favor of returning to God's natural order for humans, animals, and the environment, the authors promoted grass-fed beef as superior to factory-farmed beef (91), asserted that "factory foods are loaded with toxic fats, sugars, and salt" (107) and singled out sugar—we see you high fructose corn syrup—as "the main cause of disease" (109). The plan further brought attention to the economic and environmental impact of genetically engineered (GE) crops, recounting a story told by a church member about Nigerian farmers "Who were given seed by a large agricultural company at a cheaper price than their regular seed, but then the seeds from that crop couldn't be replanted (They are designed that way.) The farmers then were forced to buy the seed from the same company at a higher price the next year and eventually couldn't afford to farm" (114). Citing personal testimony, the authors of *The Daniel Plan* claimed that resisting industrial agriculture was not just good for your health in the way God intended; it was a social mission to heal the planet and help small farmers around the world, including those in Africa.

The Daniel Plan distilled social critiques of industrial agriculture into consumer takeaways that resembled anti-industrial diet messages in health food stores, books, and documentaries that circulated throughout American culture and coalesced into an alternative food-choice lifestyle. In the late 1990s, Whole Foods consolidated small chains of natural food stores across the country into a nationally recognized brand, later bought by Amazon in 2017. Journalist Eric Schlosser's *Fast Food Nation: The Dark Side of the All-American Meal* (2001) called on consumers to resist the corporate power of large-scale restaurant chains that limited the availability of healthy food and suppressed the wages of workers who served Americans their daily meals. Michael Pollan's *Omnivore's Dilemma* (2007) moved countervailing foodie cultures closer to the mainstream. Schlosser and Pollan were later featured in the documentary film *Food, Inc.*(2009), which increased public awareness of the dangerous working conditions of employees at slaughterhouses, the horrific cruelty inflicted upon animals in factory farming, the environmental impact of industrial agriculture, and the role of government subsidies for GE crops of corn and soybean used primarily as animal feed and sweeteners for soft drinks. *The Daniel Plan* incorporated these critiques of industrial agriculture into its practical diet advice: eat more vegetables, forsake fast food, avoid added sugar, cut back on processed snacks, watch out for herbicide and pesticide residue from conventional and GM crops, and if you can, don't eat animals from factory farms. In this way, *The Daniel Plan* was not that different from other plant-based anti-industrial agriculture diet plans. But unlike the others, Warren offered a religious reason to make better diet choices that, unlike most Christian diet plans, did not require the consumer to declare themselves religious. He did so by using a secularizing religion that appealed to the broadest segment of the consumer market: cultural evangelicalism.

Warren's bible-based diet plan was part of his larger evangelical marketing strategy to promote religion as a lifestyle choice. Despite being influenced by previous marketing styles, Warren refused to label his purpose-driven approach as a marketing strategy (Vaca 2019: 5). Part of Warren's obfuscation was a pastoral attempt to give God the credit for the popularity of *The Purpose Driven Life*. If the best seller was just the result of savvy marketing, then that would undermine the mystique and power of the product being sold, which was a self-help guide to finding God's purpose for your life. Take out God and you were left with friendly guidance from a guy known for wearing Hawaiian shirts. Take out Daniel from the Daniel Plan and all you had is more diet advice. Warren's main contribution to religious marketing in America was to resist the notion that what he was doing had anything to do with marketing at all and instead consolidate various denominations of conservative Protestantism in the United States into a purpose-driven brand of what American religious historian Daniel Vaca labeled as "ambient evangelicalism" that established "a presence in people's worlds without seeking deliberate or conscious commitment" (157). The Daniel Plan wasn't just diet advice. It had a biblical mandate. But to follow the biblical diet, you didn't have to commit to any church doctrine. You didn't even have to commit to reading the bible. You just had to commit to the higher purpose of the plan.

While biblical commitment was optional for cultural evangelicalism at the level of consumption, making it interchangeable with the liberal multiculturalism of purpose-driven marketing, it was much more strident at the level of production. The liberal messaging of healthy food was detached from the more conservative practices and beliefs of the farmers and ranchers who produced that food. As an organic food inspector in Iowa told author Laura Sayre, "Organic farming is conservative small-time rural farmers making food for white liberal yuppie and hippie types" (Sayre 2011: 39). In the marketing of purpose-driven food, Warren's expression of cultural evangelicalism for the spiritual consumer contrasted more conservative religious beliefs that prevailed among fundamentalist evangelical food producers. These farmers and ranchers were motivated by biblical principle to raise animals in accordance with what they considered a divinely sanctioned natural order in which cows were made by God to eat grass instead of grain as men were made to be the head of the household. Each animal and each person had a place in this natural order (Walker 2009).

The religious motivations of fundamentalist evangelical food producers were noticeably absent from liberal critiques of industrial agriculture as well as later marketing of purpose-driven food. *Food Inc.*, for example, not only featured progressive figures like Schlosser and Pollan, but it also brought attention to fundamentalist evangelical farmer Joel Salatin of Polyface Farms. The film, though, never addressed Salatin's religious motivation for farming. Rather, it emphasized the rotational grazing technique for his cows and chickens as an alternative agricultural model to factory farming. Salatin soon became the face of local food producers with grit and entrepreneurial spirit, while Schlosser and Pollan were marked as enemies of the industrial food state (Enzinna 2010).

There was a reason why Joel Salatin's conservative Christianity wasn't featured in *Food Inc.* His biblical justifications of gender norms with the man as spiritual head of household, his claim that Jesus was the only way to be saved and enter heaven, and his pro-life political stance would have offended at least half the audience. It was hard enough to get self-identified liberals to stop eating animals from factory farms. If you told them that to do that, they would have to buy from farmers and ranchers like Salatin who discounted structural constraints against black farmers and said "we do not believe America is systemically racist," then suddenly big corporations like Mars, Incorporated, which stopped using a headshot of an African American man on the packaging of "Uncle Ben's" rice and PepsiCo distributor Quaker Foods, which stopped promoting the name and image "Aunt Jemima" on its line syrups and baking products, appeared socially progressive by comparison (Booker 2020; Philpott 2020; Selyukh 2020; Alcorn 2021). When it came to talking about biblical doctrine and racial history, there was always the risk of revisiting the culture wars, which is perhaps why Warren did not directly reference any of his own conservative theological positions, some of which overlapped with Salatin, particularly his pro-life stance, in *The Purpose Driven Life* or *The Daniel Plan*.

The spiritual version of cultural evangelicalism expressed in *The Daniel Plan* was better suited to corporate multiculturalism and the myth of consumer agency than the more fundamentalist evangelicalism practiced by anti-industrial food producers, including but not limited to organic, biodynamic, regenerative, and sustainable farmers and ranchers. Not all these farmers were evangelical, but many of them were. Within the evangelical marketing model of *The Daniel Plan* was a latent political tension between conservative religion that promoted anti-industrial food production as a return to divinely sanctioned natural order and consumer liberalism that promoted individual freedom to buy healthy food products within a deregulated marketplace. The same might be said for a more conservative evangelical consumer, who purchased vegetables at the market from a hippie farmer with a different perspective. Akin to the political space of a farmer's market in a progressive city, purpose-driven marketing reconciled political incongruity through a corporate multiculturalism that set apart the consumption of the product as the expression of a universal spiritual act from the production of the product as motivated by a particularly religious belief.

American evangelicals have been savvy with marketing because they were able to thrive within the corporate spaces of the secular marketplace (Moreton 2009; Grem 2016; Lofton 2017; Porterfield et al. 2017). When it came to business, evangelicals knew what they were doing. And what modern evangelicals like Warren did was develop a marketing strategy that was neither public nor private, and in this way neither liberal nor conservative, as illustrated in Warren's ability to stand between presidential candidates John McCain and Barack Obama and bring them together on stage at his church in 2008 and later offer the invocation prayer at President Obama's inauguration in 2009. As an extension of this marketing strategy, *The Daniel Plan* combined the ambient faith of evangelicalism presented in *The Purpose Driven Life* and the consumer lifestyle of healthy living offered as an alternative to industrial agriculture. This combination was what defined Warren's marketing strategy as a form of cultural evangelicalism that could be practiced with or without a faith commitment. By 2005, a quarter of Americans, or roughly 75 million people, claimed to have read *The Purpose Driven Life* without claiming to be an evangelical (Vaca 2). What brought them together was a commitment to corporate management as the ideal business model.

Warren wasn't offering a doctrinal product message, like a theological plan of salvation, but a life method for finding personal meaning in the greater purpose behind the product message. For Vaca, this was what made Warren's evangelicalism a kind of background music in the consumer marketplace. It didn't require anyone to believe in it. It was just there, and it got in people's heads, and they started to like it. But it wasn't *just* there. For the actual book sales of *The Purpose Driven Life,* the marketing style was strategically reformatted over time within the specific institutional context of book publishing until it became less doctrinally specific and more generically pop. Ambient evangelicalism, argued Vaca, became the elevator music of a specific kind of religious marketing strategy. And *The Purpose Driven Life* was the textual equivalent of that kind of background evangelicalism.

In *The Daniel Plan*, Warren translated in layperson's terms a theological defense of the priesthood of the believer to work out their personal salvation as a faith choice to the individual consumer right to pursue individual health by choosing not to eat GE and processed foods. As in moments past, such radical individualism challenged institutional authority. *The Daniel Plan* presented a consumer threat to industrial agriculture and corporate control of the food system. For the biotech industry, around which industrial agriculture was consolidated since the 1990s, the most significant aspect of this evangelical threat was the spiritual invitation for consumers to eat more vegetables. Of all potential changes to consumer behavior, choosing to eat more vegetables would have the greatest impact on corporate control of GE plants because animals, especially chickens and pigs, but also cows and fish, were the biggest consumers of GE crops, consuming more than "70% of harvested GE biomass," according to the *Journal of Animal Science and Biotechnology* (Van Eenennaam 2013). And it's not like chickens, pigs, cows, or fish had options. According to the FDA, as of 2022, "95% of animals used for meat and dairy in the United States eat GMO crops" (FDA 2023). If humans stopped eating animals that ate GE crops, that would cut out a huge market share for the biotech industry.

Previously, the meat industry responded to potential market threats by trying to silence public criticism. In the early 1990s, 13 states, most of them in the Sunbelt, enacted "food libel laws," also known as "veggie libel laws," or "food disparagement laws," that made it possible for food companies to sue any person who disparaged the industry. The laws were enacted in response to a *60 Minutes* episode that informed the public that most apples sold in the United States contained a chemical residue that could cause cancer. After the episode aired, the sale of apples plummeted (Roberts 2016: 313–315). At the time, the industry strategy was to threaten legal action or sue a complainant to avoid potential loss to corporate profits. Such lawsuits were rare, but even the threat of legal action significantly impacted free speech. The highest profile case of a veggie libel suit happened in 1996, when Oprah dedicated an episode of her show to the dangers of eating beef produced through factory farming, bringing national attention to the deadly Mad Cow Disease, and the Texas Beef Group sued her for over $10 million in damages. She eventually won that legal battle—this was Oprah after all—but she never again made the kind of bold declaration she made before the trial, when she said, "It [the fear of dying from mad cow disease] has just stopped me cold from eating another burger" (Batheja 2018).

Warren, who was closely aligned with Oprah, having appeared in her Life Class in 2013 to discuss the purpose-driven life, was able to do something not even she could do. He was able to convince people to eat vegetables without facing backlash from industrial meat producers. While diets and dieting carried on within Oprah's media networks, including a 21-day vegan cleanse in 2008 that briefly addressed concerns of animal cruelty in factory farming, none offered the kind of religious invitation to collectively resist the health impacts of industrial agriculture in the way *The Daniel Plan* did. But even as Warren preached to his congregation and told the millions of readers of *The Daniel Plan* to avoid processed foods, including factory-produced meat, he never found himself in the kind of lawsuit that was waged against Oprah. When it came to talking bad about the meat we eat, it seemed that religious criticism, at least a particular kind of religious criticism, an evangelical bible-based kind of cultural criticism, was exempt from corporate liability.

To understand this shift from the 1990s, when Oprah was sued by the meat industry for saying she was scared to eat a hamburger, to the 2010s, when Warren spoke freely on avoiding toxic industrial foods as a spiritual practice, it's important to consider how the broad appeal of Warren's evangelical marketing strategy overlapped with emerging new health markets that made such criticism profitable, including the rise of veganism among consumers with climate concerns. The plant-based meat company Impossible Foods was founded in 2011, the year Warren announced *The Daniel Plan* to his congregation, and a similar company, Beyond Meat, launched its first plant-based chicken product in 2012 (Quart 2013: 139; García-Martínez and Li 2022: 2). Longstanding investors in biotechnology and industrial agriculture, like Bill Gates, invested in plant-based meat alternatives, while celebrities, including actors, musicians, chefs, and athletes promoted plant-based lifestyles (Garcés 2019; Frazier and Cheeke 2021). Within the emerging market of plant-based food products, the economic realities of profit and the evangelical imagination of moral goodness were interchangeable in the same way a Forbes contributor substituted the word "business" for "church" when he read *The Purpose Driven Life* (Karlgaard 2004). Such interchangeability eventually would even allow meat-based meat to return alongside plant-based meat, so long as it served a higher purpose. The Atlanta-based eco-friendly, health-conscious burger franchise YEAH! BURGER, for example, which opened around 2012, offered consumers hamburgers that according to Natasha Smith of *Data, Strategy, and Technology (DMN)*, "fit [consumers'] health-conscious lifestyles; gluten-free, vegan, organic—you name it." If consumers wanted grass-fed beef that they thought was better for themselves and the environment, then that was just as good as consumers who didn't want to eat beef because they thought it was bad for themselves and the environment. A self-described "purpose driven company," YEAH! BURGER offered the menu of consumer lifestyle choice. Or as marketing and business director Kelly Wallace told *DMN*, YEAH! BURGER has "been trying to connect with customers on a deeper level. We're not just selling a product; we're selling a lifestyle" (Smith 2015).

What YEAH! BURGER sold the consumers was the idea that they were in control. The consumer set the agenda for the company that served them. The YEAH! BURGER purpose-driven marketing model for sustainable food options though did not carry over after the COVID pandemic, which forced the restaurant to close in 2020. When it reopened in 2021, the company decided to only offer plant-based burger options, stating that was the prevailing trend. But then a year later, it decided to return to its original menu of beef, bison, chicken, and plant-based meals in response to consumers who walked out of the restaurant once they learned there were no meat options. Company founder Erik Maier told *Atlanta Magazine* that they "underestimated the popularity of—and loyalty to—the old menu." But when YEAH! BURGER returned to the previous offerings, it offended vegan loyalists who decided the company had just chosen making "money and profit over making the ethical choice," as one customer posted on Instagram (Cooper 2022). By June 2023, YEAH! BURGER had closed and was taking suggestions for where to reopen in a new location (YEAH! BURGER 2023).

The story of YEAH! BURGER was one of consumer choices tied to corporate supply. The purpose-driven marketing model intended to bring choice and supply together into a profitable relationship. Sometimes it worked. Sometimes it didn't. The challenge with food marketing was that it literally was a matter of consumer taste. And when it came to changing patterns of food consumption, it seemed that consumers liked things the way things used to be and preferred foods that tasted like that to which they were accustomed. *The Daniel Plan* tried to change consumer behavior over time through disciplined eating habits, offering journaling guides and support groups in local churches. Warren asked his congregants to learn how to enjoy leafy vegetables and raw fruits, to give them a try and eventually they would realize they tasted better than fast food, even if at first, they might not like it. The biotech industry, though, which had engineered food taste for decades, didn't want to change consumer behavior. They just wanted to make healthy foods more palatable to consumers or make the foods they already eat more nutritious. In this way, they could profit from the problem they created—a scarcity of nutrient-dense foods—by creating new healthier foods that they owned.

Enter "purpose driven food" as a profitable product for the concerned consumer. Pairwise uses gene editing, including what is known as CRISPR, which stands for "clustered regularly interspaced short palindromic repeats," to turn genes on and off within a plant. This approach differs from previous forms of genetic engineering because it doesn't extract genes from one plant or animal and insert them into another. Rather, it edits the genes of a particular plant to produce a more profitable product, altering a vegetable to make it taste better to consumers or removing a thorn gene from a plant to make it possible for laborers to harvest it more efficiently (Conscious Foods 2023). The first product Pairwise planned to bring to market in 2023 was a leafy green that was nutrient dense but in its original form had a horseradish kind of taste that the company believed most consumers wouldn't eat. By genetically editing out the bitter taste, Pairwise hoped the trademarked Conscious Greens, marketed under the brand of Conscious Foods, would be more palatable to consumers. Unlike *The Daniel Plan*, which encouraged consumers to change their food taste over time through healthy habits, learning to prefer say spinach and strawberries to chips and candy, Pairwise didn't want to challenge consumer taste. From a sales perspective, it didn't think that was feasible. Dr. Tom Adams, co-founder and chief executive officer of Pairwise said that consumers generally choose taste over nutrition, in addition to wanting to save money, noting that most consumers will say they want to eat more leafy greens, but they typically choose the kinds of lettuce like iceberg that are tastier to them but less nutrient dense than other options like kale. To deal with this problem, Pairwise identified green-leafed plants in the Brassica genus, which included cabbages and mustard greens that had a comparable nutritional profile to kale, and edited out the genes from the plant that caused bitterness, in order to make it more appealing to a broader range of consumers (Pairwise 2023c).

After Conscious Greens, Pairwise planned to add seedless blackberries, black raspberries, and pitless cherries to the purpose-driven Conscious Foods (Pairwise 2023c). Megan Thomas, head of marketing and communications at Pairwise, described the launch of the new food line by saying, "As a purpose-driven brand, we are supporting access to healthy food in the communities where we operate. We know that consumers, especially younger adults, are increasingly interested in mission-focused brands, and we are excited to bring purpose into the produce aisle with Conscious Foods" (Businesswire 2023). To emphasize the purpose of accessible nutrition, Pairwise highlights its relationship with the Partnership for a Healthier America, a non-profit that supports healthy eating by providing produce and education to low-income communities. Pairwise promotes this partnership as evidence of its purpose-driven company culture that recognizes how families on "tight incomes" often need "help from nutritionists and monetary support to encourage a lifelong habit of choosing fruits and veggies" (Pairwise 2023b).

To understand how this purpose-driven missionary enterprise is potentially profitable, it's important to consider how industrial agriculture overwhelmed the food system in the United States with poor nutrition at the same moment that neoliberal economic policies defunded public health services, including FDA and food safety inspectors (Cordelli 2020). The net effect was that U.S. residents were left to figure out how to survive in a world of nutrition scarcity with limited access to healthcare or medical advice for those who couldn't afford it. Returning to *The Daniel Plan*, what Warren offered unhealthy Americans was akin to what Oprah offered overwhelmed shoppers on her show and in her magazine, a blueprint to navigate what appeared to be the endless options of consumer choice. That so many Americans listened to an evangelical celebrity and not a governmental authority about their health and diet signaled the presence of an empty space in public life that religion and corporations filled. After industrial agriculture took nutrition out of the food system and conservative evangelicalism supported the privatization of public services, they both stood to gain, financially and spiritually, by selling back what they took away from Americans.

Absent from the Pairwise marketing of its purpose-driven brand are the proprietary implications of gene-editing technology. While patent laws are evolving to keep up with the biotechnology innovations, all signs indicate that genetically or genome-edited plants will follow the same proprietary rules of previous GMO crops, in which the company that altered the DNA of an organism in a lab owns the property rights to that altered organism as a patented product. Many critics have focused on the ethics of genetic editing and the health safety of the biotechnology. While these are important conversations, they are difficult to argue because corporate interests are so entangled with scientific studies. As such, the ethical concerns of biotechnology are secondary to the economic implications of gene-editing as a proprietary technology that will extend corporate control of the food system by pharmaceutical and biotech companies. In the previous model of GMO technology, companies, like Bayer, which acquired Monsanto in 2018, owned all engineered seeds that a farmer was required to purchase annually from the company, along with its accessory chemicals. If a farmer attempted to save seed to replant the following year, they would be sued by the corporate owner. In this way, GMO farming was another expression of labor dependency that eroded food sovereignty, or the ability of a community to feed itself by its own democratic means. While the relations of production may vary in the development and farming of genetically edited plants, the technology remains privately controlled by multinational corporations. To this point, Pairwise partners with Bayer to edit corn in order to make it produce more yield on less land. And the biotech industry invests in the genetic editing of plants to match them with patented herbicides and pesticides.

The major differences between GMO and genetic editing are in the way they are marketed to different sets of consumers. As GMO was to animal feed, genetic editing is to the emerging market of human health. There is a concept called "poverty capital" that Ananya Roy used to explain how the kind of global poverty produced through colonization, resource extraction, and neoliberal economic policies, can be made profitable in the economic marketplace of corporate philanthropy and international development (Roy 2010). What genetic editing offers biotech companies is a way to profit, for a lack of a better term, from "undernutrition capital." There is money to be made in finding government subsidized corporate controlled solutions to a global nutrition crisis that ultimately is a sign of the ecological catastrophe of climate change to which industrial agriculture is a major contributor. Capitalism produces poverty (Desmond 2023). This is a social fact. The reason for this is scarcity. In the United States alone, there are not enough jobs that pay a living wage, not enough housing that everyone can afford, not enough healthcare available to all, not enough public transportation, not enough of a lot of things. It's not like capitalism doesn't work. It just doesn't work for everybody. Likewise, industrial agriculture produces some healthy food, but just not enough for everybody. Its major products, GMO corn and soybeans for animal feed and soft-drink sweetener, contribute to nutrition scarcity in the food market. As proponents of deregulated capitalism look to solve the problem of poverty with solutions offered by private corporations, industrial agriculture intends to fix undernutrition by designing new products, healthy fruit, and vegetables, which can survive climate change and feed the world.

Using the technology of genetic editing, biotech companies scour the planet for the healthiest plants to tweak just enough to patent them. Once they do this, once they own the earth's pantry, they can, if they so choose, destroy the original plant varieties on which human civilization has depended upon for thousands of years. If they do this, then they own the entire food chain. While Pairwise intends to offer new and improved plant products that look like the originals, whether it is a leafy green or red raspberry, other companies like Calyxt want to inject genetically edited nutrition into previously nutrient-poor foods, so that consumers can continue to eat Wonder Bread, if they so choose, and still get their daily requirements of fiber, vitamins, and minerals (Molteni 2019). For Calyxt, the purpose is to take existing products and make them healthier. Rather than find a plant in nature, Calyxt identifies food products already in the industrial agriculture system, like soybean oil, which the biotech industry introduced into the market in 2015 as derived from GM soybean crops, then edits its genes to get rid of trans fats and reduce saturated fats.

These kinds of genetically edited food products are integrated into purpose-driven food marketing as interchangeable with smaller scale produce grown using non-biotech methods, whether that be organic, regenerative, biodynamic, or otherwise. Purpose-driven, like other labels such as natural, green, sustainable, or environmentally friendly, is relativized in these marketing approaches as a health concept that obfuscates the social and economic relationships between consumers and producers. As one example, consider how the event and meetings management group, Thrive!, touted in 2022 that "purpose driven food and beverage" was "on-trend for events," offering advice on how to organize an event that addressed labor concerns, offered attendees refrigerator space to store their own food, promoted sustainable practices, like "eliminating plastic and designing menus based on water usage," labeled "buffets with allergens and other dietary needs," and provided "attendees with complete, nourishing and balance meals" (Stuckrath 2022). Nowhere in that advice is biotech or corporate ownership mentioned. As such, Thrive! offers another example of a purpose-driven marketing model for consumer choice dependent upon the availability of food products within an agricultural system controlled by large-scale industrial producers.

London-based consumer goods corporation Unilever, which includes among its products Dove soap, Axe body spray, and Ben and Jerry's ice cream, launched a "Future Foods" campaign in 2020 that committed to introducing more plant-based meat and dairy alternatives into the market with stated goals to "double the number of products delivering positive nutrition globally by 2025—defined as products containing impactful amounts of vegetables, fruits, proteins, or micronutrients like vitamins, zinc, iron and iodine" and to "continue lowering calorie, salt and sugar levels across products."[6] Unilever acknowledged its presence in the market "as one of the world's largest food companies" and summarized the global food system as "inequitable and inefficient," saying that "one billion people around the world are hungry while two billion are obese or overweight" (Unilever 2020). In the stated mission of Future Foods to transform the global food supply, Unilever recognized consumer concern for biotechnology and vowed to "respond to [consumer] demands in our different local markets to provide products that meet their needs." But it also declared that the company will "retain capability to include GM ingredients in our food products in the future when these are shown to be safe, are approved by the relevant authorities and are wanted by consumers" (Unilever 2004). Although elsewhere in the statement Unilever appears more open to regulation and labeling of GM food ingredients, its ambivalence regarding the role of biotechnology in the future of foods, which will include the developing technology of genetic editing that differs from GM foods but will remain under the control of biotech corporations, is a long way from *The Daniel Plan* pronouncement cited earlier that "the best thing you can do for your health is to avoid factory-made science projects with weird and strange molecules that haven't been made by God in nature."

Warren's evangelical diet plan challenged the health impacts of a corporately controlled industrial food system; however, its sharp edge of social critique was dulled by a moral emphasis on good choices through diet and exercise. The religious morality of the diet plan shielded Warren from industry retaliation, as he was able to issue bold criticism as biblically based. However, because *The Daniel Plan* was just a diet plan and not a policy prescription, because it translated criticism of industrial food into the good news of consumer choice, and because its primary goal was weight loss, any criticism of industrial agriculture, factory farming, and junk food, or Foods of Minimal Nutritional Value (FMNVs) as the USDA defined them, was redirected by industrial biotechnology companies into an emerging marketing campaign for their own proprietary brand of nutrient-dense "purpose driven" foods. The ability of industrial agriculture to absorb religious critique was possible at the consumer level, as purpose-driven marketing rendered religion and secularity interchangeable as a spiritual lifestyle of personal product choice. Corporate marketing of purpose-driven foods focused on nutrition and health without offering a direct critique or rejection of biotech control of the food system that contributed to a lack of nutrition and health as an environmental problem. Thus, purpose-driven marketing demonstrated the religious and secular limits of consumer movements to transform modes of food production in the United States.

Notes

1 According to the United Nations Global Compact, "consumer demand for purpose-driven brands means that companies who amplify their positive social and environmental impacts will also maximize their revenues" (n.d.). For a description of how cause marketing morphed into purpose-driven marketing as well as how purpose marketing made it increasingly difficult for a consumer to discern between the marketed idea of the product and its actual impact, see Einstein (2012). See also Richey and Ponte (2013) and Aziz and Jones (2016).

2 Warren was trained as a Southern Baptist minister, though he resisted many of the strictures of the Southern Baptist Convention (SBC), particularly the denomination's refusal to ordain women, and promoted a more non-denominational brand of church polity. Still, he emphasized a radical Protestant doctrine of the priesthood of the believer, which meant that every individual was responsible for working out their own salvation, a doctrine shared among Baptist traditions, while also wanting to maintain a congregational connection to the SBC without having to explain denominational identity in his church marketing (Warren 2007: 199).

3 Megachurch pastors have used church marketing networks to purchase mass numbers of books, often at a discount, which gets the authors on the best seller lists. Evangelical pastors have relied on marketing strategies promoted by George Barna and at times, as was the case with Mark Driscoll of Mars Hill Church, have used their own funds to purchase thousands of books through a third party. Such tactics are controversial among

4 On the role of religious individualism in neoliberal economic solutions, see discussion of ecopiety/consumopiety as it relates to global climate change in Taylor (2019).

5 *The Daniel Plan* emphasis on eating whole foods made by God is wide ranging in American Christianity and popular culture. For additional examples, see Leto (2016, 2023).

6 The Pepsi Corporation also tried to introduce alternative food products as healthier. They recently, however, admitted defeat and went back to selling the same soda and chips as before, only marketing them now as "healthier" (Maloney 2023).

Works Cited

Alcorn, Chauncey. (February 9, 2021). "Aunt Jemima Finally Has a New Name." *CNN Business*. *https://www.cnn.com/2021/02/09/business/aunt-jemima-new-name/index.html*. Accessed December 6, 2021.

Aziz, Afdhel, and Jones, Bobby. (2016). *Good Is the New Cool: Market Like You Give a Damn*. New York: Simon and Schuster.

Batheja, Aman. (January 10, 2018). "The Time Oprah Winfrey Beefed with the Texas Cattle Industry." *The Texas Tribune*. https://www.texastribune.org/2018/01/10/time-oprah-winfrey-beefed-texas-cattle-industry/. Accessed June 25, 2023.

Booker, Brakkton. (September 23, 2020). "Uncle Ben's Changing Name to Ben's Original After Criticism of Racial Stereotyping." *National Public Radio*. https://www.npr.org/sections/live-updates-protests-for-racial-justice/2020/09/23/916012582/uncle-bens-changing-name-to-ben-s-original-after-criticism-of-racial-stereotypin. Accessed December 6, 2021.

Businesswire. (May 16, 2023). "Pairwise Introduces Conscious™ Greens, Into U.S. Restaurants." https://www.businesswire.com/news/home/20230516005522/en/Pairwise-Introduces-Conscious%E2%84%A2-Greens-Into-U.S.-Restaurants. Accessed June 28, 2023.

Christensen, David A. (2020). *The Persuasive Preacher: Pastoral Influence in a Marketing World*. Eugene, OR: Wipf and Stock Publishers.

Colbert, Don. (2002). *What Would Jesus Eat? The Ultimate Program for Eating Well, Feeling Great, and Living Longer*. Nashville, TN: Thomas Nelson.

Conscious Foods. (2023). "Our Process." https://consciousfoods.net/process. Accessed June 28, 2023.

Cooper, Carly. (March 3, 2022). "Meat Is Back on the Menu at Yeah! Burger – Atlanta Magazine." https://www.atlantamagazine.com/dining-news/meat-is-back-on-the-menu-at-yeah-burger/. Accessed June 27, 2023.

Cordelli, Chiara. (2020). *The Privatized State*. Princeton, NJ: Princeton University Press.

Desmond, Matthew. (2023). *Poverty, by America*. New York: Crown.

Einstein, Mara. (2012). *Compassion, Inc.: How Corporate America Blurs the Line between What We Buy, Who We Are, and Those We Help*. Berkeley, CA: University of California Press.

Enzinna, Wes. (2010). "Big Meat vs. Michael Pollan." *Mother Jones*. December. https://www.motherjones.com/environment/2010/12/michael-pollan-backlash-beef-advocacy/. Accessed May 25, 2023.

FDA. Center for Food Safety and Applied Nutrition. (2023). "GMO Crops, Animal Food, and Beyond." January. https://www.fda.gov/food/agricultural-biotechnology/gmo-crops-animal-food-and-beyond. Accessed June 26, 2023.

Frazier, Matt, and Cheeke, Robert. (2021). *The Plant-Based Athlete: A Game-Changing Approach to Peak Performance*. New York: HarperCollins.

García-Martínez, Javier, and Li, Kunhao. (2022). *Chemistry Entrepreneurship*. Weinheim, Germany: John Wiley & Sons.

Garcés, Leah. (2019). *Grilled: Turning Adversaries into Allies to Change the Chicken Industry*. London: Bloomsbury Publishing.

Gibbs, Eddie. (2009). *ChurchMorph: How Megatrends Are Reshaping Christian Communities*. Grand Rapids, MI: Baker Academic.

Grem, Darren E. (2016). *The Blessings of Business: Christian Entrepreneurs and the Politics and Culture of Sunbelt America*. Oxford and New York: Oxford University Press.

Griffith, R. Marie. (2004). *Born Again Bodies: Flesh and Spirit in American Christianity*. Berkeley and Los Angeles: University of California Press.

Guthman, Julie. (2011). *Weighing In: Obesity, Food Justice, and the Limits of Capitalism*. Berkeley and Los Angeles: University of California Press.

Karlgaard, Rich. (2004). "Purpose Driven." Forbes. https://www.forbes.com/forbes/2004/0216/039.html. Accessed June 27, 2023.

Kenner, Robert, director. (2009). *Food, Inc*. Magnolia Pictures.

Kwan, Samantha, and Sheikh, Christine. (2011). "Divine Dieting: A Cultural Analysis of Christian Weight Loss Programs." In Albala, Ken, and Trudy, Eden, eds. *Food and Faith in Christian Culture*. New York: Columbia University Press, pp. 205–220.

Kyle, Richard. (2018). *Popular Evangelicalism in American Culture*. New York: Routledge.

Leto, Kim Dolan. 2023. *Fit God's Way: Your Bible-Based Guide to Food, Fitness, and Wholeness*. Paperback Original edition. Washington, D.C: Salem Books.

Leto, Kim Dolan. (2016). *F.I.T. 10 Steps to Your Faith Inspired Transformation: Healthy, Happy, & Fit God's Way*. Newtype. https://www.newtypepublishing.com/

Lofton, Kathryn. (2017). *Consuming Religion*. Chicago, IL: University of Chicago Press.

Maloney, Jennifer. (April 22, 2023). "Pepsi's New Healthy Diet: More Potato Chips and Soda." *Wall Street Journal*. https://www.wsj.com/articles/pepsi-lays-doritos-soda-sugar-fat-salt-health-62047e07. Accessed July 12, 2023.

Malkmus, George H., Shockey, Peter, and Shockey, Stowe D. (2006). *The Hallelujah Diet*. Shippensburg, PA: Destiny Image Publishers.

Marya, Rupa, and Patel, Raj. (2021). *Inflamed: Deep Medicine and the Anatomy of Injustice*. Farrar, Straus and Giroux.

Molteni, Megan. (March 28, 2019). "The First Gene-Edited Food Is Now Being Served." *Wired*. https://www.wired.com/story/the-first-gene-edited-food-is-now-being-served/. Accessed June 28, 2023.

Moreton, Bethany. (2009). *To Serve God and Wal-Mart: The Making of Christian Free Enterprise*. Cambridge, MA and London, England: Harvard University Press.

Pairwise. (2023a). https://www.pairwise.com/home. Accessed June 28, 2023.

Pairwise. (2023b). "Nutrition & Sustainability." https://www.pairwise.com/nutrition-sustainability. Accessed June 28, 2023.

Pairwise. (2023c). "Introducing Conscious™ Foods." https://www.pairwise.com/news/introducing-conscious-foods. Accessed June 28, 2023.

Patel, Raj. (2012). *Stuffed and Starved: The Hidden Battle for the World Food System – Revised and Updated*. New York, NY: Melville House.

Petrak, Lynn. (March 23, 2022). "New 'Purpose-Driven' Produce Brand Debuts." *Progressive Grocer*. https://progressivegrocer.com/new-purpose-driven-produce-brand-debuts. Accessed June 27, 2023.

Philpott, Tom. (November 2020). "The Racist Roots of Joel Salatin's Agrarian Dream." *Mother Jones*. https://www.motherjones.com/food/2020/11/joel-salatin-chris-newman-farming-rotational-grazing-agriculture/. Accessed May 26, 2023.

Pollan, Michael. (2007). *The Omnivore's Dilemma: A Natural History of Four Meals*. New York, NY: Penguin Books.

Porterfield, Amanda, Grem, Darren, and Corrigan, John. (2017). *The Business Turn in American Religious History*. Oxford and New York: Oxford University Press.

Quart, Alissa. (2013). *Republic of Outsiders: The Power of Amateurs, Dreamers and Rebels*. New York and London: The New Press.

Reynolds, Michelle. (April 28, 2017). "Thinking of Trying 'The Daniel Plan'? Start Here." PETA. https://www.peta.org/living/food/the-daniel-plan/. Accessed June 20, 2023.

Richey, Lisa Ann, and Ponte, Stefano. (2013). *Brand Aid: Shopping Well to Save the World*. Minneapolis, MN: University of Minnesota Press.

Roberts, Michael T. (2016). *Food Law in the United States*. New York: Cambridge University Press.

Roy, Ananya. (2010). *Poverty Capital: Microfinance and the Making of Development*. New York: Routledge.

Sayre, Laura. (2011). "The Politics of Organic Farming: Populists, Evangelicals, and the Agriculture of the Middle." *Gastronomica* 11 (2): 38–47.

Schlosser, Eric. (2001). *Fast Food Nation: The Dark Side of the All-American Meal*. Boston, MA and New York: Houghton Mifflin Harcourt.

Selyukh, Alina. (June 17, 2020). "Aunt Jemima Will Change Name, Image As Brands Confront Racial Stereotypes." *National Public Radio*. https://www.npr.org/sections/live-updates-protests-for-racial-justice/2020/06/17/879104818/acknowledging-racial-stereotype-aunt-jemima-will-change-brand-name-and-image. Accessed December 6, 2021.

Smith, Natasha. (January 9, 2015). "YEAH! BURGER Bites Into Purpose Branding." *DMNews*. https://www.dmnews.com/yeah-burger-bites-into-purpose-branding1/. Accessed June 28, 2023.

Smith, Samuel. (December 28, 2016). "Franklin Graham Reveals His 'Drastic' New Year's Resolution." *The Christian Post*. https://www.christianpost.com/news/franklin-graham-reveals-his-drastic-new-years-resolution.html. Accessed June 20, 2023.

Starbuck, Peter. (2017). "Peter F. Drucker's Management by Objectives and Self-Control." In Wilkinson, Adrian, Armstrong, Steven J., and Lounsbury, Michael, eds. *The Oxford Handbook of Management*. Oxford and New York: Oxford University Press.

Stuckrath, Tracy. (June 6, 2022). "Purpose-Driven Food & Beverage Is On-Trend for Events." *Thrive Meetings and Events*. https://thrivemeetings.com/2022/06/purpose-driven-food-beverage-is-on-trend-for-event-attendees/. Accessed June 23, 2023.

Taylor, Sarah McFarland. (2019). *Ecopiety: Green Media and the Dilemma of Environmental Virtue*. New York: NYU Press.

Unilever. (November 18, 2020). "Unilever Sets Bold New 'Future Foods' Ambition." https://www.unilever.com/news/press-and-media/press-releases/2020/unilever-sets-bold-new-future-foods-ambition/. Accessed June 28, 2023.

Unilever. (March 2004). "Growing for the Future." Accessed June 28, 2023. https://www.unilever.com/files/origin/51022cd86978d58e18523a410507d8008d70e030.pdf/es_growing_for_the_future_3rd_ed.pdf

United Nations Global Compact. (n.d.). "Purpose-Driven Marketing: How Brands Are Attracting Socially Conscious Consumers and Creating Change in the World." https://unglobalcompact.org/take-action/purpose-driven-marketing. Accessed May 31, 2023.

Vaca, Daniel. (2019). *Evangelicals Incorporated: Books and the Business of Religion in America*. Cambridge, MA: Harvard University Press.

Van Eenennaam, Alison L. (2013). "GMOs in Animal Agriculture: Time to Consider Both Costs and Benefits in Regulatory Evaluations." *Journal of Animal Science and Biotechnology* 4 (1): 37.

Walker, Pamela. (2009). "Rehoboth Ranch and Windy Meadows Farm: For the Love of God and Family." In *Growing Good Things to Eat in Texas*. College Station, TX: Texas A&M Press, pp. 92–119.

Warren, Rick. (2002). *The Purpose Driven Life: What on Earth Am I Here For?* Grand Rapids, MI: Zondervan.

Warren, Rick. (2007). *The Purpose Driven Church: Growth Without Compromising Your Message and Mission*. Grand Rapids, MI: Zondervan.

Warren, Rick, and Hyman, Mark (2013). *The Daniel Plan: 40 Days to a Healthier Life*. Grand Rapids, MI: Zondervan.

White, Edward Joseph. (2000). *The Law in the Scriptures: With Explanations of the Law Terms and Legal References in Both the Old and the New Testaments*. Union, NJ: The Lawbook Exchange.

YEAH! BURGER. https://www.yeahburger.com/. Accessed June 27, 2023.

PART VI

Religion, Marketing, and the Spirit of Capitalism

16

HINDUISM AND THE NEW SPIRIT OF CAPITALISM

Vocational Theology in 21st-Century Spiritualist Self-Improvement Literature

Justin W. Henry

In December 2022 while visiting a colleague in Kolkata, I joined in on a hunt for pornographic magazines among the book stalls lining a busy section of Park Street. My colleague, who was conducting research on youth sexuality in India, recalled from her school days that male classmates would clandestinely purchase Playboys and similar titles concealed in polythene and discretely arrayed amid more mundane merchandise from the vendors of this district. After 20 minutes of searching and some bashful inquiries, we were disappointed to learn what should perhaps have been intuitively obvious at the outset: that in the age of readily available online pornography of every imaginable type, demand for the antique magazine variety of this particular photo-literary genre had plummeted to effectively zero. No one had anything of the kind on offer. There, among the eclectic titles ranging from teach-yourself C++ programming, to textbooks on advanced accounting, to paperback reimaginings of Hindu epics sporting tawdry fantasy art covers, a preponderance of books of a certain type did make an impression on me in the course of our brief, abortive research venture. On the basis of volume, the best-sellers of the Park Street scene appeared to be works by Indian authors promising "lifehacks" involving a slight adjustment of one's outlook or a simple modification to one's daily routine guaranteeing to revolutionize one's life in every imaginable way: titles such as *Magic Mindset*, *The Art of Attracting Abundance*, and *Think Like a Monk: Train Your Mind for Peace and Purpose Every Day*—books written by self-proclaimed successful people promising to reveal their secret—the secret to not only becoming rich yourself but also doing so in a way that promises to be personally, even spiritually, fulfilling.

Such a school of thought and such a genre of literature have of course been known to us for over a century at this point, with origins traceable to the "New Thought" and Metaphysical movements of the late 19th century—ideas adopted

DOI: 10.4324/9781003342229-23

by the "Human Potential Movement" of the mid-20th century and augmented and rebranded many times since (Albanese 2008). There are however several novel themes among the voluminous paperbacks and YouTube lectures of the newest generation of "lifestyle gurus." One discovers, for example, a seeming consensus among works of this type over the applicability of "Eastern wisdom" to techniques for career advancement and financial success. The conceit that Hindu Dharma and Indian culture historically emphasized minimum state intervention in economic affairs has in recent years made strange bedfellows between some on the progressive end of the political spectrum and media commentators with allegiance to Narendra Modi and his BJP government. In this domain, liberal best-selling mythologist, self-help author, and "leadership consultant" Devdutt Pattanaik finds himself in agreement with "Hindu first" provocateur Rajiv Malhotra (along with others in orbit around Malhotra's "Infinity Foundation") in their shared insistence that Kautilya's *Arthashastra* (a classic Sanskrit work on Indian statecraft) outlined the basic principles of *The Wealth of Nations* two millennia prior to Adam Smith.[1]

Beyond such innovative projections of 21st-century social life into the distant past (an example of what Banu Subramaniam has referred to as interpreting history through the lens of "archaic modernities"[2]), another, more esoteric, trend stands out amid the most recent generation of self-improvement literature. Some of the most popular of these authors, although writing independently of one another, advance similar worldviews proposing a certain harmony between the psychology of the individual reader and the organization and *telos* of the cosmos itself. One repeatedly encounters amid the pages of books promising "abundance," "fulfillment," and professional and personal success proclamations that the minds of individual people are fragmentary instantiations of cosmic consciousness, participating in the teleological cosmic project—an insistence that we are each *active* contributors to the evolution and advancement of the human civilizational project (enabled by the spark of *creativity* that each of us possesses, sharing in the essence of the Divine, the fundamental nature of which is creativity).

Leaving a broader scholarly survey of self-improvement literature of this type as a desideratum, I restrict my discussion in this chapter to the work of Deepak Chopra (b.1946) and Vishen Lakhiani (b.1976). What I will refer to as the "vocational theologies" of these two figures overlaps in many respects, with the elder Chopra having established his reputation as an internationally best-selling, preeminent spiritually oriented self-improvement author and public speaker over the past three decades, and Lakhiani representing an emerging voice in this market. Giving an overview of their respective counseling projects, I go on to highlight continuities between the worldviews of these two figures and those of Friedrich Taylor and Mary Parker Follett, formative early 20th-century thinkers in the field of scientific management, specifically their shared insistence that free-market, corporate modernity offers a portal to the most equitable, most peaceful, and most humane future world.

While Taylor and Follett advance such a notion on the basis of their understanding of a teleology of corporate efficiency given the implementation of a perfectly attuned, empirically grounded "managerial science," Chopra and Lakhiani stray into the realm of the mystical and the metaphysical in their accounts of the moral necessity of big business. While they are by no means systematic theologians, at their loftiest, the cosmological worldviews which Chopra and Lakhiani articulate are in essential respects approximate to other well-known theological concepts from both the Hindu and contemporary Christian traditions. Their insistence on *creativity* as archetypal principle of cosmic design and evolution is reminiscent of Alfred North Whitehead's innovative "process philosophy," which has furnished inspiration for serious-minded professional theologians for nearly a century at this point.[3] The notion that the individual psyche reflects or contains a spark of "divine consciousness" is of course also congruent with the essential Upanishadic equivalence between the *Atman* (individual soul) and the *Brahman* ("the Godhead"). On the other hand, alongside such esoteric ruminations we discover amid the writings of 21st-century lifestyle gurus the frequent deployment of corporate jargon in an effort to equate entrepreneurial innovation with personal creativity and fulfillment. The frames in which Chopra and Lakhiani situate their transformational programs may be ambitiously cosmic in scope, but, as I argue below, the actual prescriptions they offer with respect to how one is to conduct oneself in the course of one's daily routine are steeped in the ethos of 21st-century corporate productivity: Chopra and Lakhiani's admonitions for us are essentially the same as those of corporate managers who today speak not of "work-life balance" but of "work-life integration."

I suggest furthermore that the "holistic lifestyle" advocated by Chopra and Lakhiani—in which the boundary between "work" and personal time dissolves—represents a "spiritualization" of the demand for near constant creative productivity germane to the modern workplace and to the "new spirit of capitalism," that is, the new philosophy of managerial best practices articulated in Business and Management university curriculum which has taken shape since the 1980s. The term derives from the work of Luc Boltanski and Eve Chiapello, who note a transition from the spirit of mid-20th-century textbooks in Management Studies, involving a movement away from concerns over ensuring maximal industrial productivity and toward an emphasis on "innovation and creativity" as desiderata of the present-day, "network firm" oriented workplace. Boltanski and Chiapello are of course building from Max Weber's well-known argument in *The Protestant Ethic and the Spirit of Capitalism* (1991 [1930, 1905]), in which Weber maintains that early modern Protestant theology effected a cultural norm of consistent devotion to one's "vocation" (*Beruf*), both as a means of alleviating psychological anxiety with respect to the status of one's salvation and as a result of the notion—originating with Luther—that God had assigned a "calling" to each person. Boltanski and Chiapello trace the organizational structure of Western capitalism from the "domestic" or "family firm" based model of the 19th and early 20th centuries, to the "industrial model" of the mid-20th century, in which "activity means 'work' and being active means 'holding a steady and wage-earning position,'" concluding that the late 20th- to early 21st-century "project-oriented model" of capitalist model represents a qualitatively different mode of production. According to them, the "new spirit of capitalism" embodied in this model:

> overcomes the oppositions between work and no-work, steady and unsteady, paid and unpaid, profit-sharing and volunteer work, and between that which can be measured in terms of productivity and that which cannot be assessed in terms of accountable performances.[4]

Amid the "new spirit of capitalism," where there is an expectation that leaders and other visionaries will be "capable of managing people who are autonomous and creative," according to Boltanski and Chiapello, "activity" has become the rubric against which all workplace performance is measured, generating an ethos in which:

> Life is conceived as a series of projects, all the more valuable when different from one another. What is relevant is to be always pursuing some sort of activity, never to be without a project, without ideas, to be always looking forward to, and preparing for, something along with other persons whose encounter is the result of being always driven by the impulse of *activity*.[5]

While Chopra and Lakhiani speak to a general audience desiring to enhance their personal and spiritual lives in addition to their workplace performance and financial portfolios, their presuppositions regarding the necessity of inner transformation for maximal job performance are, as evidence would suggest, symptomatic of a broader trend within the way that vocational readiness is conceptualized. Indeed, essays and editorials in major Indian newspapers and American business trade magazines have noted the ascendency of quasi-spiritualist discourse in Business and Management pedagogy for two decades at this point, including the introduction of courses in "self-mastery" at major business schools.[6]

Deepak Chopra

The confluence of the new spirit of capitalism and Hindu-adjacent spiritualism is nowhere better exemplified than in the writing and social media evangelism of Deepak Chopra, former practitioner and professor of internal medicine turned self-help guru and purveyor of alternative medical remedies. Chopra's turn away from mainstream, empirically grounded medical science was no doubt influenced by the years he spent as an understudy to Maharishi Mahesh Yogi, the founder of Transcendental Meditation which became a pioneering brand in the realm of commodified "eastern wisdom" (Lucia 2014). Chopra's most recent book, *Abundance: The Inner Path to Wealth*, represents a return to form with respect to his writing career, reprising major themes of one of his first works, *Creating Affluence: Wealth Consciousness in the Field of All Possibilities* (1993). *Abundance's* subtitle, "the inner path to wealth," must be interpreted in the context of Chopra's vocabulary, where nearly all words are capacious and irreducibly polysemic: "wealth," he explains, refers to more than simply monetary wealth, encompassing instead the totality of things an individual might possess ensuring the highest level of life satisfaction (including physical health and positive social relationships).

Chopra by no means eschews *monetary wealth* as anathema to a spiritual lifestyle, though, and indeed casts the pursuit of financial success as one, apparently central, aspect of a maximally rewarding life.[7] (*Abundance* repeatedly avers that the "path to abundance" includes "wealth" qua financial prosperity.) Chopra has marketed his recent work enthusiastically on social media, where recent interviews with him have also been shared on the accounts of various American free-market advocacy groups. In his messaging and in these interviews, Chopra presents a close association between entrepreneurialism and personal creativity, maintaining that the two should necessarily go hand-in-hand and insisting that for the entrepreneurially inclined, a remunerative outlet for creative products ensures a path to joy (to "follow one's purpose" is to "follow one's joy," he says). Comfortably espousing industry buzz words, Chopra speaks of "disruptive creativity" as a means to personal fulfillment.

In interviews promoting *Abundance*, Chopra illustrates his strategy of "incubating" a germinal idea to a state of entrepreneurial utility—this through a process of market research and analysis following which one awaits further "insight" to arise out of passive exercises such as meditation or listening to music or dreaming during sleep. In connection with this method, Chopra invokes a lofty metaphysics in which he insists that the ground of being of the universe itself is one of *creative dynamism*, invoking the phenomenon of quantum entanglement in support of his view of the universe itself as a conscious agent. Chopra's idealist metaphysics—referring to the fabric of the universe as "thinking nonstuff"—parallels the "holographic theory of the universe" articulated by David Bohm, Karl Pribram, and others, which posits that the (to us) unpredictable outcomes of quantum wave collapses are informed by subtle forces determining these events by taking into account the distribution of outcomes of a certain kind simultaneously and instantaneously, thus presenting the fabric of space-time itself as a sort of intelligent, decision-making organism.[8] Chopra understands this modern concept in theoretical physics to have been anticipated by the Hindu concept of *maya* (the notion that the material world as we experience it is in some sense an illusion) as well as by the Buddhist concept of *shunyata*, or the ultimately insubstantial nature of all physical things. Invoking Hindu theological vocabulary, he summarizes his view to explain:

> The universe is a big dream machine, churning out dreams and transforming them into reality, and our own dreams are inextricably woven into the overall scheme of things. The mechanics for the fulfillment of these dreams are contained firstly in the power of knowledge, known in ancient India as *gyan shakti*, and secondly, in the power of intention or desire, known in ancient India as

iccha shakti. But the power of knowledge and the power of intention or desire find their immeasurable strength and potentiality in the power of transcending, known as *atma shakti. Atma shakti,* the power of the self, is the power of Brahman, where the infinite organizing power of the universe resides.

(1993, pp. 93–94)

Chopra concludes furthermore that the subtle forces governing the "thinking nonstuff" pervading experiential reality suffuses each individual person's mind and physical body. He explains that the "creative intelligence" of the universe operates at the cellular level, connecting this thought with a reassurance that, by way of some sort of osmotic principle, every person has the capacity to draw from the creative force which governs the self-regulation of the body:

without creative intelligence, you cannot explain how every cell does trillions of things every microsecond and communicates with every other cell [...] this is the expression of "creative intelligence," and it is infinitely abundant. Look at nature—in every seed there is the promise of 1000s of forests! For every creative idea, you have infinitely more creative ideas available to you.

(Nasdaq Entrepreneurial Center)

We are each then according to Chopra, both *guided by*, as well as *co-participants in*, an intelligent cosmos which is directing the development of the world we all experience toward ever greater levels of organizational complexity (1993, pp. 21–23).

Receptivity to the fact that the intelligent cosmos directs the operation of our own bodies as well as the world with which we interact promotes a kind of Daoist imperative to yield to the "natural path" of action rendered for every person at a given point in time. Chopra invokes the Hindu concept of Dharma in service of this sentiment, though it must be clarified that his application of the term has the very specific sense of *sva-dharma* or "personal duty," rather than the more general (and commonly understood) senses of Dharma as either prescribed social duty or ethical commandments: "Each of us has a dharma, a purpose in life. When we are in dharma, we enjoy and love our work" (1993, p. 30). From Chopra's point of view, a spiritually fulfilling existence—one lived in accordance with the direction that the cosmos continually supplies for us—may be lived out through vocational means. There is no imperative that one renounce family life or material possessions in order to achieve self-actualization and to harmoniously participate in the cosmic order. Chopra takes an opportunity to contrast Western monotheist traditions in which, according to him, "you have to be poor in order to be spiritual," with the *purusha-arthas* (life objectives) of traditional Hinduism, which allow for *artha* (material wealth) and *kama* (physical pleasure) as dimensions of the good life. Chopra claims that in the Hindu tradition, "if you are poor, then you are not spiritual! You have missed out on the opportunity that is called 'generosity of spirit'—'spirit' being awareness which is infinitely creative" (Nasdaq Entrepreneurial Center).

Vishen Lakhiani

Vishen Lakhiani, author of the NY Times best-seller *The Code of the Extraordinary Mind* (2016) and follow-up companion work *The Buddha and the Badass: The Secret Spiritual Art of Succeeding at Work* (2020), echoes much of Chopra's lifestyle guru messaging, all the while branding himself, his company, and his products with a younger, hipper aesthetic. A computer programmer by training, Lakhiani has gained fame through his recent books, his many high-profile speaking engagements, and through Mindvalley, a company he founded in 2002 offering digital products to facilitate healthy living, financial planning, personal and spiritual growth (including numerous online tutorials as well as the meditation app "Omvana"). Mindvalley also organizes "A-Fest," an annual retreat for aspiring innovators and business elite hosted in a different exotic international getaway location each year, featuring a lineup of inspirational speakers, immersive workshops, meditation and yoga instruction, and live entertainment.

Lakhiani was raised in a Hindu family in Malaysia but explains that he discarded religion at the age of 19, remaining "spiritual" but not wanting a single nominal religious identity to separate him "from the billions of spiritual people who weren't Hindu" (Lakhiani 2016, p. 25). Lakhiani relates that he went on to find solace in "models such as humanism and pantheism," and that he sustains his "belief in a higher power" (p.88).

At the core of Lakhiani's brand is his self-enhancement program distilling of the choicest nuggets of wisdom he has collected from his personal encounters with titans of industry, lifestyle gurus, and celebrity consultants. His monographs and lecturers are peppered with anecdotes of time spent with the likes of the Dalai Lama, Richard Branson, Elon Musk, Tony Robbins, Srikumar Rao, Cameron Herold ("the CEO whisperer"), Jim Kwik, Michael Beckwith, and a host of others. Lakhiani also partners with female motivational speakers such as Mel Robbins and Elon Musk's mother, Maye Musk (the title of his recent book gestures to Jen Sincero's *You Are a Badass* (2013), a thematically similar work). Lakhiani's program which promises to unlock "the extraordinary mind within" is modeled on his own transformational experiences originating with a single meditation class he took in Los Angeles in the early 2000s. Lakhiani relates that through this one-day course he learned to immerse himself in a relaxed state, allowing him to return to his job cold calling law offices selling case management software with greater "empathy" for those he was speaking to over the phone. With his newly cultivated "alpha state of mind," Lakhiani explains that he was better able to anticipate in the course of a short conversation with a stranger whether or not his sales product was truly suited for the potential customer's needs, to navigate the sale effectively, or to abort the attempt if it became clear that product was not a good fit. Straying into the realm of the telepathic, Lakhiani furthermore claims that with the aid of his newfound meditative absorption, he was able to run his fingers down the law office listings in the phone book until he "felt an *impulse*," or an intuition that the number he had landed on would yield a receptive client—an intuition which he concedes "makes no logical sense" but which, he asserts, allowed him to double his sales in a single week by employing this divinatory method (Lakhiani 2016, pp. 48–51). The foundational practice for the "lifehack" method Lakhiani goes on to outline begins, therefore, with a 20-minute daily regimen of meditation, during which practitioners are to take up six subjects of meditation in turn.[9]

Lakhiani emphasizes the necessity of cultivating entrepreneurial *vision* to building a successful company, which demands first that one understand the values and motivations unique to oneself—one's "soulprint," as Lakhiani puts it, the essence of one's aspirations and moral orientation to the world, determined by significant life experiences, each of which leaves a "trace" on one's personal psychology. Knowing one's soulprint offers one clarity of vision in entrepreneurial endeavors, Lakhiani explains, since "you need to mark up your creations with the unique stamp of your soul," ensuring that one's work is meaningfully aligned with one's values (Lakhiani 2020, pp. 17–29). This imperative braids intimately with the message abiding at the heart of Lakhiani's instruction—that self-fulfillment depends on one's work corresponding to one's "calling." A fully self-actualized entrepreneur (Lakhiani defines "entrepreneur" in the most capacious sense possible) is one for whom "the old model of work disappears," wherein a "job" or "career" is not merely a means of financial subsistence but instead a vehicle transporting you to your "vision board" image of yourself, generating meaningful and fulfilling experiences and relationships along the way (Lakhiani 2016, p. 194).

Lakhiani reassures readers that the universe itself offers direction with respect to opportunities that may shepherd one toward work of the most fulfilling variety, introducing his theory of each individual as a "Godicle" or fragmentary aspect of the Divine. Lakhiani's understanding of the direction of this hypothetical collective divine consciousness is apparently teleological in nature, ensuring readers that receptivity to the vocational direction that the universe offers each of us will compel innovation in "humanity plus" (i.e., "pro-humanity") entrepreneurial initiatives, resulting in the future in a maximally humane, maximally technologically efficient world. The valence of this hypothetical collective divine is one of pure *creative force*, with Lakhiani introducing the oceanic proposition that each of us as a "Godicle" or "particle of God" experiences and simultaneously participates in this creation in every moment of our lives (Lakhiani 2016, p. 202).

Vocational Theology and the New Spirit of Capitalism

Chopra and Lakhiani are by no means the first to synthesize spiritual "technologies of the self" with the normative demands of modern capitalism.[10] Addressing an audience of upwardly mobile Baby Boomers in the 1980s, popular mythologist par excellence Joseph Campbell issued his iconic commandment to "follow your bliss," suggesting that a vocational commitment of any kind might furnish a spiritually fulfilling life trajectory (a personal "hero's journey"), so long as it remains something personally rewarding.[11] Echoing Campbell, Chopra admonishes his students to "follow your joy"—advocating not "inner worldly asceticism" but "inner worldly *spiritualism*." Similarly, Lakhiani employs a portmanteau of his own construction—"Blissipline"—which he identifies as a cornerstone of his transformational project, indicating the necessity of discipline in one's daily routine which does not come at the expense of personal "bliss." Scholars such as Kimberly Lau (2000), Jeremy Carrette and Richard King (2005), Meera Nanda (2009), and Jeff Wilson (2014) have from more than 20 years ago noted a trend in New Age spiritualism in the West accompanying the commodification of "eastern wisdom" involving an insistence that transformational practices can find primary application in professional success. Carrette and King were early observers of the eager integration of meditational and Asian-inspired wellness techniques into the workplace by some among the American corporate top-brass, with the expectation that such technologies of the self would result in more efficient workers.[12]

What I wish to illustrate here are the significant intersections between the promises of 21st-century lifestyle gurus and the exuberant utopianism of several foundational figures in the discipline of "scientific management," which has today evolved as the field of Management Information Systems. Pioneers of "the science of work," such as Fredrick Taylor, Jules Amar, and Mary Parker Follett, a century ago expressed utopian visions involving the potential for maximal efficiency in the workplace to bring about not only positive transformations of individual psychological but even, in time, a more just, fair, and abundant society for all. While absent the meditation spaces, hammocks, foosball tables, and Kegger Fridays found in hip office spaces of today, Frederick Taylor's seminal *Principles of Scientific Management* (1911) foresaw the science of precision workflow as a means of achieving "close, intimate, personal cooperation between the management and the men" (1967 [1911], p. 21), predicting that his method would soon effect a "mental revolution" which would go so far as to result in "the substitution of peace for war; the substitution of hearty brotherly cooperation for contention and strife [...] replacing suspicious watchfulness with mutual confidence; of becoming friends instead of enemies."[13]

Mary Parker Follett, a contemporary of Taylor who spent a significant portion of her career working to articulate the most efficient forms of business management, social work, and local government, attributes an almost demiurgic character to her theoretical, maximally systematic managerial system—one which she thought would serve, as did Taylor, to one day create the best possible world. Follett's guarantee of this outcome is not based on any esoteric metaphysics or theological speculation regarding the intelligent unity of atomic matter, but rather on expansive research in the then-incipient fields of empirical psychology and scientific management. In her most abstract ruminations, however, Follett approaches Chopra and Lakhiani not only in referring to the efficiency of management science as deriving its truth from "the powers of the universe," but also in her reassurance to readers that in submitting to the recommendations of this science (as applied in the real-life

conditions of the workplace), employees participate in atomistic fashion in the teleological construction of a perfect world, even if ignorant of the dynamics by which
it continues to develop:

> Circular response is the psychological term for the deepest truth of life. We
> move always within a larger life than we are directly cognizant of. But many
> men have deliberately shut their eyes to that larger life because they felt that
> any view must be false which made the individual seem to "transcend" what
> we know he can never transcend. But the theory of creative experience given to
> us by the most profound philosophy throughout the ages, and now so happily
> strengthened by recent research in several fields, shows that the individual can
> create without "transcending." He expresses, brings into manifestation, pow-
> ers which are the powers of the universe, and thereby those forces which he is
> himself helping to create, those which exist in and by and through him, are ever
> more ready to respond, and so Life expands and deepens; fulfils and at the same
> moment makes possible larger fulfilment.
>
> *(Follett 1924, p. 116)*

We see therefore within the thought of Chopra, Lakhiani, Taylor, and Follett a
shared insistence that—far from being mundane, dehumanizing, or alienating—
vocational work involves participation in a transcendent, intersubjective dimension
of reality, the operation of which *is vital to the realization of humanity's ultimate
potential.* A key point of contrast deserves notice in the audiences germane to the
early scientific management paradigm of Taylor and Follett and the vocational theologies of Chopra and Lakhiani, respectively. While Taylor and Follett were preoccupied with managerial best practices attuned to 20th-century industrial production,
Chopra and Lakhiani are addressing a 21st-century workforce populating job sectors oriented toward the "new spirit of capitalism." Management science in Taylor
and Follett's "Fordist" paradigm primarily calculates an efficient distribution of
tasks within a corporate setting and, as such, depends upon hierarchical employee
obedience and conformity. By contrast, Chopra and Lakhiani tailor their message
to a present-day workforce concentrated on finance, information-technology, and
social media freelance. Accordingly, both stress the necessity of *individual creativity* for a fulfilling career work-life—personal creativity being especially relevant
for those ensconced in a more structured "project-oriented" corporate environment,
branding and marketing, social media, and startups (Chopra speaks often of the
necessity of being a "creative disruptor").

Chopra and Lakhiani practice what they preach—in addition to their books and
frequent speaking appearances, both make felicitous use of social media in promoting their products and brands. Their insistence on living one's life as a kind of
creative meditation is an understandable desideratum for many today immersed
in the project-oriented workplace, especially in light of the demand for perpetual
content creation in the realm of social media. Furthermore, whereas Taylor and

Follett restrict their concerns to the management of the workplace proper, Chopra and Lakhiani's insist that readers orient *their entire lives and daily routine* toward maximum productivity, perhaps reflecting the erosion of the home-workplace barrier consequent to the rise of remote work in recent years (also related to the irregular hours sometimes demanded by the project-oriented work paradigm articulated by Boltanski and Chiapello). While Chopra and Lakhiani underwrite their vocational theologies through appeals to the cosmic and the transcendent, and Taylor and Follett to the mundane and the empirical, all are united in their vision of the corporate mission to create a more harmonious social world, and in their understanding that disciplinary technologies of the self in service of this mission will be positively transformational at the level of the individual.

The movement to integrate work and personal life in certain elite sectors of the business world has of course been ongoing for some time. Readers will recall to mind the novel work environments of "Ben & Jerry" in the 1970s, Yvon Chouinard's Patagonia, and the early days of Bill Gates' Microsoft—prototypes of later Silicon Valley corporations offering employees a self-contained social environment, all the while blending conventional business practices with in-house therapeutic and spiritual resources, alongside progressive, socially conscious rhetoric and branding.[14] Accepting that Boltanksi and Chiappello are correct in their recognition of a new spirit in management culture demanding *constant activity* from employees, in closing I would like to update the range of vocations which might be included within the purview of the "new spirit of capitalism." Beyond the "network firms" which form the basis of Boltanksi and Chiappello's analysis, and beyond the integrative campuses of Google and Facebook, the "new spirit of capitalism" remains intensely relevant to the remote work and gig economies which have come to encompass an increasingly substantial segment of the labor force in recent years. Without the physical confines of a traditional office place and the regularity of defined work hours, these new cultures of labor permit workers to devote an unlimited proportion of time to "activity" of all manner of vocational applications. In connection with this, I would like to take the opportunity to flag a significant departure in the prescriptions of Chopra and Lakhiani from the Protestant "spirit of capitalism" as defined in its classical sense: for Weber, an essential consequence of Lutheran theology was the supposition that each (redeemed) person had a specific vocation (*Beruf*) envisioned and assigned by God. Strict application to one's vocation was, in Weber's understanding, an outward demonstration of one's place among the "elect," as well as a means of alleviating psychological anxiety regarding the status of one's salvation. Chopra and Lakhiani—who have themselves enjoyed careers spanning an extremely varied set of job descriptions—both eschew the notion that any individual should limit themselves to a single occupation for a lifetime. The "creativity" that they both insist is accessible to every person (with the proper training to access it) is rather meant to empower readers to embrace *vocational flexibility*, which is obviously essential to the atomized (and precarious) labor force of the 21st-century gig economy.

Notes

1 Pattanaik expresses this view in his social media posts and YouTube videos. An extensive rendering of his understanding that the foundations of free-market capitalism are intimately a part of Vedic theology and ritual is contained in his *The Business Sutra: A Very Indian Approach to Management* (2013), as well as his follow-up abridged version, *The Success Sutra: An Indian Approach to Wealth* (2015).

2 I borrow this term from Subramaniam (2019, p. 7).

3 See Whitehead (1929, pp. 21–22). For a commentary on Whitehead's philosophical theology, see Lowe (1962, pp. 95–113).

4 Boltanski and Chiapello (2005, p. 169 (emphasis added)). For a full-length study, see Boltanski and Chiapello (2018 [2005]).

5 Boltanski and Chiapello (2005, p. 169). Isabelle Darmon (2011) has critiqued Boltanski and Chiapello's thesis on the grounds that Weber anticipated the necessary "adaptation" of employees who would allow vocational commitments to displace personal ones, owing this to the dynamic potential of modern capitalism to mobilize novel worker subjectivities. Darmon notes that Weber recognized "a decisive impulse for all economic action under conditions of a market economy" to assume "an inner adjustment (*Eingestelltheit*) to economically productive work as form of life (*Lebensform*)" (Darmon [2011, p. 205]; quotation and translation from Weber [1922, p. 60]). Acknowledging Darmon's intricate and insightful analysis of Weber's view of the processes by which capitalist logic interrupts care for "extra-occupational" social obligations, I defend the proposition that the "new spirit of capitalism" represents a rupture from prior capitalist epistemologies by way of the prevalence of rhetoric concerning personal ethical prerogatives into discourse associated with capitalist maintenance. Such rhetoric contrasts with Weber's insistence on the attenuation of any emphasis on "personal moral qualities" and "ethical maxims" germane to capitalist epistemologies preceding the modern industrial era. See discussion of Weber's view in Darmon (2011, p. 205).

6 Weiss (2018) tallies electives on topics, including "mindfulness," "compassionate leadership," "purpose," and "self-mastery," currently on offer at major business schools, including Harvard's Kennedy School, The University of Pennsylvania's Wharton School, The University of Michigan's Ross School, and (her own) Stanford Graduate School of Business. For a survey of recent scholarship on the role of "humanistic management" in business ethics, see Acevedo (2012).

7 Chopra hedges somewhat in advising readers to cultivate detachment toward money: "To have true wealth of affluence is to be totally carefree about everything in life, including money. True wealth consciousness is, therefore, consciousness of the source of all material reality. This source of all material reality is pure consciousness. It is pure awareness. It is the unified field. It is the field of all possibilities" (1993, p. 66).

8 For an explanation of the holographic theory of the universe in theoretical physics, see Pitts (1990, pp. 80–89).

9 Lakhiani's six subjects of meditation are Connection, Gratitude, Freedom from negative charges, Creative visualization, Intentions for the day, and Blessing.

10 Michel Foucault introduced the phrase "technologies of the self" in his later life lectures in the context of his continued exploration of discourse concerning the constitution and transformation of "the self" across the premodern-modern periods in western Europe. Foucault's specific concern was the "practices whereby individuals, by their own means or with the help of others, acted on their own bodies, souls, thoughts, conduct, and way of being in order to transform themselves and attain a certain state of perfection or happiness, or to become a sage or immortal, and so on" (Martin 1988, p. 4). See Foucault (1988) for his posthumously published lecture on the subject.

11 For an evaluation of Brendan Gill's contention that Campbell's "follow your bliss" mantra represented the philosophy of Reagan era "Wall Street yuppies and junk-bond dealers," or that of the "Ann Ryan type of elitist individualist with no discernable social conscience," see Ellwood (1999, pp. 127–169, quotation on p. 132).

12 See discussion in Urban (2015, p. 182), citing Lau (2000) and Carrette and King (2005). See also Meera Nanda's (2009) analysis of "karma capitalist" figures, including Swami Dayananda, Mata Amritanandamayi, and Deepak Chopra (pp. 96–105).
13 From Taylor's address to the United States House Labor Committee, January 25, 1912; cited in Kanigel (1997, p. 473).
14 I thank Mara Einstein for pointing out to me these pioneers of "work life integration" and their relevance to this discussion.

References

Acevedo, Alma (2012). "Personalist Business Ethics and Humanistic Management: Insights from Jacques Maritain." *Journal of Business Ethics*, *105*(2), 197–219.
Albanese, Catherine (2008). *A Republic of Mind and Spirit: A Cultural History of American Metaphysical Religion*. New Haven: Yale University Press.
Boltanski, Luc and Eve Chiapello (2005). "The New Spirit of Capitalism." *International Journal of Politics, Culture, and Society*, *18*(3/4), 161–188.
——— (2018 [2005]). Trans. Gregory Elliott. *The New Spirit of Capitalism*. Verso.
Carrette, Jeremy and Richard King (2005). *Selling Spirituality: The Silent Takeover of Religion*. London: Routledge.
Chopra, Deepak (1993). *Creating Affluence: Wealth Consciousness in the Field of All Possibilities*. San Rafel, CA: New World Library/Amber-Allen Publishing.
——— (2022). *Abundance: The Inner Path to Wealth*. Harmony Books.
Darmon, Isabelle (2011). "No 'new spirit'? Max Weber's Account of the Dynamic of Contemporary Capitalism Through 'pure adaptation' and the Shaping of Adequate Subjects." *Max Weber Studies*, *11*(2), 193–216.
Ellwood, Robert (1999). *The Politics of Myth: A Study of C.G. Jung, Mircea Eliade, and Joseph Campbell*. Albany, NY: SUNY Press.
Follett, Mary Parker (1924). *Creative Experience*. London: Longmans, Green and Co.
Foucault, Michel (1988). "Technologies of the Self." In Luther Martin, Huck Gutman and Max Hutton (Eds.), *Technologies of the Self: A Seminar with Michel Foucault* (pp. 16–49). Amherst, MA: The University of Massachusetts Press/Tavistock Publications.
Kanigel, Robert (1997). *The One Best Way: Frederick Winslow Taylor and the Enigma of Efficiency*. New York: Viking Press.
Lakhiani, Vishen (2016). *The Code of the Extraordinary Mind: 10 Unconventional Laws to Redefine Your Life and Succeed on Your Own Terms*. New York: Rodale Books.
——— (2020). *The Buddha and the Badass: The Secret Spiritual Art of Succeeding at Work*. New York: Rodale Books.
Lau, Kimberly (2000). *New Age Capitalism: Making Money East of Eden*. Philadelphia, PA: University of Pennsylvania Press.
Lowe, Victor (1962). *Understanding Whitehead*. Baltimore, MD: The Johns Hopkins Press.
Lucia, Amanda (2014). "Innovative Gurus: Tradition and Change in Contemporary Hinduism." *International Journal of Hindu Studies*, *18*(2), 221–263.
Martin, Luther H. (1988). "Introduction to *Technologies of the Self*." In Luther Martin, Huck Gutman and Max Hutton (Eds.), *Technologies of the Self: A Seminar with Michel Foucault* (pp. 3–8). Amherst, MA: The University of Massachusetts Press/Tavistock Publications.
Nanda, Meera (2009). *The God Market: How Globalization Is Making India More Hindu*. Gurugram, Haryana: Penguin Random House India.
Nasdaq Entrepreneurial Center (2022, March 7). *Abundance: The Inner Path to Wealth with Deepak Chopra, M.D.* [Video]. YouTube. https://www.youtube.com/watch?v=YMrlRc0S-Jg

Pattanaik, Devdutt (2013). *The Business Sutra: A Very Indian Approach to Management*. New Delhi: Rupa Publications.

——— (2015). *The Success Sutra: An Indian Approach to Wealth*. New Delhi: Aleph Book Company.

Pitts, Mary Ellen (1990). "The Holographic Paradigm: A New Model for the Study of Literature and Science." *Modern Language Studies*, 20(4), 80–89.

Subramaniam, Banu (2019). *Holy Science: The Biopolitics of Hindu Nationalism*. Seattle, WA: University of Washington Press.

Taylor, Frederick Winslow (1967 [1911]). *The Principles of Scientific Management*. New York: Norton Press.

Urban, Hugh B. (2015). *Zorba the Buddha: Sex, Spirituality, and Capitalism in the Global Osho Movement*. Berkeley, CA: University of California Press.

Weber, Max. (1922). *Grundriß der Sozialökonomik, III. Abteilung. Wirtschaft und Gesellschaft [Economy and Society]*. Ed. Marianne Weber. J.C.B Mohr [Paul Siebeck].

——— (1991 [1930, original German edition 1905]). *The Protestant Ethic and the Spirit of Capitalism*. Trans. Talcott Parsons. London: Routledge.

Weiss, Leah (2018). *How We Work: Live Your Purpose, Reclaim Your Sanity, and Embrace the Daily Grind*. New York: Harper Wave.

Whitehead, Alfred North (1929). *Process and Reality: An Essay in Cosmology*. London: Macmillan/Cambridge University Press.

Wilson, Jeff (2014). *Mindful America: The Mutual Transformation of Buddhism Meditation and American Culture*. New York: Oxford University Press.

17

VINTAGE NOT RETRO

The Secondhand Social Life of Christian Material Culture

James S. Bielo

There is a thriving secondhand market in the United States for Christian material culture. Bibles, Bible study guides, prayer books, hymnals, rosaries, icons, relics, statues, holy cards, pilgrimage souvenirs, liturgical objects, devotional plaques and prints, denominational periodicals, and evangelical pamphlets are just a few of the diverse genres from diverse theological traditions. Items are sourced from shuttered churches, estate sales, auctions, flea markets, thrift stores, antique malls, and garage sales and resold in brick-and-mortar shops and online venues such as eBay, Instagram, and Etsy. What organizes the circulation of the secondhand sacred?

Instagram is a lively space for this market; every day, dozens if not hundreds of items are posted for sale. Some sellers host "live sales" that exclusively feature Christian materials. In May 2022, I attended one of these sales and learned an important lesson about how valuation works in this marketplace. Four sellers joined the live stream from their respective locations (southern Michigan, central Florida, and two in separate Chicagoland suburbs). For 3 hours (5–8 pm), they took turns presenting their inventory. Each auction lasted 5–10 minutes, allowing each seller about 15 turns. The sequence for each turn was consistent. An initial presentation focused on the item's material qualities (e.g., size, weight, substance), as well as any information the seller could share about its use, production history, or previous owner. Following this description, attendees use the chat window to comment on the item and enter bids. While bidding is open, sellers talk with each other, usually making complimentary observations about the item's aesthetic details, proposing potential uses, or exchanging stories about their own related "finds." The seller eyeballs the chat, and when bidding stalls, they ask for a "bid end."

The conversation among sellers is especially important; it is a time when the valuation of an item is actively constructed, a time when bids can stagnate or escalate. It was during this talk about the seventh item up for sale that a particular

DOI: 10.4324/9781003342229-24

comment caught my attention. The Florida reseller was offering a pair of two decorative plates featuring renderings of Mary, Our Lady of Lourdes, and Our Lady of Medjugorje, stamped with the date 1994. As attendees contemplated a bid, she paused over how best to characterize the plates: "I wouldn't say vintage, maybe retro." One of the Chicagoland sellers responded immediately, raising her finger to disagree: "If it's 2002 or older it's vintage." She did not name a particular source for this designation; rather, she seemed to be referencing an accepted definition that "vintage" means at least 20 years old. While I suspect she was remembering a particular source and I also suspect that there are competing definitions, the referential meaning of "vintage" is not most crucial here. It is the indexicality of the term, and the value attached to its indirect indexical meanings, that really matters. In the secondhand market of Christian material culture, "vintage" means desirability: worth buying, worth keeping, worth collecting, of a time separated from our present and unspoiled by any accusation of newness.

Classification

This Instagram moment caught my attention because it highlights a vital process: the categories used to classify materials and the dynamics of valuation that develop in relation to those categories. One reason to dwell on classification as a generative process is because it advances a rich vein of interest in the study of material religion. In an important methodological essay, David Morgan (2017) names classification as a pivotal process scholars use to understand objects and their attendant uses, meanings, and sensations (i.e., the social life of the object). When classifying religious objects, Morgan argues that scholars should attend to material affordances, functionality, how an object compares to related objects and fits within a broader class of things, and how objects can be remediated over time (that is, "reissuing of a product in a new medium or format" [p. 25]). In short, scholarly classification entails a range of practices that demand close attention to detail and an understanding of religious culture and history. By making classification a central process in the work of doing material religion scholarship, Morgan rightly observes that naming, categorizing, and conceptualizing are crucial for apprehending the social work performed by and through materiality.

This chapter builds on this attention to classification, but with a riff. I shift the focus from the classificatory work of the analyst to the classificatory work of sellers who are engaged with the secondhand circulation of Christian material culture. In doing so, this chapter resonates with scholarship in material religion and material culture studies more broadly that seeks to understand how practices of classification play an instrumental role in broader assemblages of circulation.[1] "Kitsch" is a prime example (Primiano 2015). This category is typically invoked in the register of "evaluation and criticism" (p. 286). Kitsch is used to index objects that are mass-produced, non-durable, and unworthy of serious consideration. The social life of this classification is thoroughly normative. To name an object as kitsch is to place it lowly on a hierarchy of consumer taste. By extension, the "classifier" (Bourdieu 1984: 6) places themselves on that hierarchy by asserting a capacity to distinguish non-kitsch from kitsch, valuable from unworthy. Classifications of kitsch can accomplish other social work as well. For example, McDannell (1995) argued that judgments of taste in popular Catholic art ultimately reproduced a gendered hierarchy, in which images associated with masculinity were legitimized and those associated with feminine devotion were deemed "kitsch."

Classifications are discursive acts with material effects, and this generative quality is true across scales. It is famously true as a fundamental act in the making and imposition of the category "religion." The term was mobilized by theologians in the 16th century to draw boundaries between acceptable and unacceptable ways of being Christian and was continually used by colonizers and new nations seeking to join global modernity to categorize diverse indigenous traditions and to fashion essentialized models of tradition for what we now call Hinduism and Buddhism (Smith 1978; Chidester 2014; Van der Veer 2014). Classifications of "religion" also circulate in contemporary law. In the U.S. context, organized groups must file to be recognized as such if they wish to access the benefits that accompany the status, from property tax exemptions to resources from the Office of Faith-Based Initiatives (Sullivan 2020).

This process of dividing "religious" from not also finds expression in the everyday exchange of secondhand resale. In December 2022, I experienced a curious example of this in a northwest Chicago thrift store. The store is a for-profit ministry created by a local progressive evangelical church. On this particular visit, I sourced two objects: a Catholic Bible (1968 Jerusalem edition) and an Italian pewter statue of Mary holding baby Jesus. When the clerk told me the total price, it was less than I expected. I asked if she included both items, and she said that all Bibles are always free. I asked if it mattered what kind of Bible. "No, that's just our policy. We don't want to profit off of people's faith." She said this while still holding the statue. How is it that one of these is classed as a "faith" object and the other not? At least for this Protestant ministry, Bibles of any sort occupy a special place, categorically set apart and distinct from other forms of Christian material culture. *Sola scriptura*, secondhand style.

In the remainder of this chapter, I take up two examples of classification that circulate among resellers and, in turn, help structure the ongoing circulation of Christian material culture. The secondhand market is decentralized, composed of a diverse network of online and brick-and-mortar venues of consumption. In turn, the value attached to different classifications is not authoritatively set but is contingent on particular performances and social arrangements. Given this centripetal environment, this chapter illustrates how classifications impact the multiple valuations of Christian material culture. In this way, classification contributes to the never-finished process of constructing value as "not an inherent characteristic of commodities, but something that is open to constant relational and active negotiation" (Gregson and Crewe 2003: 112).

Excess

The four women who opened this chapter are resellers; they scavenge secondhand venues in search of donated, discarded, and passed over items.[2] Some resellers source and sell as a "side hustle" to supplement other income streams, while others resell full-time, circulating a greater mass of materials to sustain a livelihood. Some source only to sell, while others curate personal collections that exist alongside and in tandem with inventories for sale. For those who deal heavily in Christian material culture, some are devout adherents of a particular tradition, others self-identify as "spiritual but not religious," and still others are non-theist or atheist.

Irrespective of these differences, a particular sentiment is widely shared among resellers. There is a decided sense that an abundance of materials exists, a condition of unending excess. This sentiment resonates with a broader fact about late modern consumer culture: that our earth is "filled with more things than at any time in history" and that a majority of those things eventually circulate in the secondhand world (Minter 2019: xvii; cf. Strasser 1999; Jhally 2006). For workers in the circular economy, this abundance can be experienced as burdensome (Berry 2022), but for resellers, it is an evergreen well of excitement and enticement. Excess fuels the enthusiastic expectation that any given sourcing outing could produce unexpected and valuable discoveries.

For Christian material culture, the material excess emerges from several interlaced sources. First, religion and consumer capitalism are deeply enmeshed in the United States (Taylor and Einstein 2022). For example, the mass production of goods designed to aid personal and familial devotion and religious education increased dramatically during the 20th century (Primiano 2015). Christian producers also have a longstanding habit of adapting to new media. As technologies are developed and commodity forms are generated, Christians are quick to adopt them (Moore 1994; McDannell 1995; Hendershot 2004; Campbell 2010; Wagner 2012). The result is a material culture environment dense with objects born of a particular ritual purpose and Christian-themed versions and alternatives of popular commodities. The social life of this abundant Christian materiality fosters collection, accumulation, donation, resale, and the circulation of the sacred through market exchange (cf. Belk, Wallendorf, and Sherry 1989).

Second, the 20th century experienced significant growths in both the general population and in Christian affiliations. Here in the third decade of the 21st century, we are experiencing increasing death rates of individuals and institutions. The estate sale industry is booming with the passing of Baby Boomers, and for millions who have accumulated Christian materials, their personal collections are being sold. In many cases, there is a question of why the families who manage estates do not retain the Christian material culture of their dead relatives. A few scenarios are potentially at work: living relatives may have examined the available materials and extracted certain items to keep; they may have divergent aesthetic preferences from the deceased and are uninterested in the materials despite being devout themselves;

they may have a divergent religious identity from the deceased and deem the materials uninteresting devotionally, sentimentally, aesthetically, and historically; or, despite a desire to keep or gift away, they make the difficult decision that selling is necessary for financial reasons.

Third, churches are also closing at an advancing rate across denominational lines, as are Christian-related organizations, such as local Masonic chapters.[3] In some cases, such as liturgical items that have received a clerical blessing, materials are transferred to other congregations in a local or regional network. In southwest Ohio, I encountered another way by which materials remain in circulation but out of the secondhand market. The Episcopal Diocese of Southern Ohio created a Freecycle Marketplace. When congregations in the diocese close, all remaining materials from church buildings are transported to the Cincinnati headquarters, sorted, and listed as available for free for any Episcopal church in need (Stateside or abroad). While institutional mechanisms can account for a certain range of materials, large quantities still enter the secondhand market through estate sales, auctions, and donations.

Fourth, there is a widespread resistance to trashing materials that are socially classified as "sacred" (Stengs 2014). Devout and non-devout people alike are reticent to throw a Bible in the garbage, opting instead to donate it to a thrift store, leave it in a neighborhood Little Free Library, or follow ritual procedures for authorized disposal (Parmenter 2010). Every reseller I have interviewed has a story along these lines: receiving Christian materials at no cost because someone would rather gift a "religious" item than imagine it in a landfill heap, bound for incineration.

Resellers operate amid this condition of excess. The question I turn to now is this: how do resellers interact with two particular classifications that are operative in the secondhand circulation of Christian material culture? For each, I draw from ethnographic data collected with resellers, online examples, and my own experience apprenticing as a reseller. Throughout, I consider the performative work of classification, in particular the ways in which classification helps to structure valuation.

Oddities

What do you imagine when you hear the word "oddities"? Perhaps the indexical range triggers terms like weird, strange, bizarre, unusual, obscure, creepy, ghoulish, mysterious, and/or macabre. "Oddities" was popularized by a reality television program of the same name that aired on the Discovery Channel from 2010 to 2014. The show profiled a New York City store that specialized in the secondhand trade of rare material culture designed to fascinate and disturb, to make you laugh and cringe. While "oddities" might most immediately conjure images of mummified human and animal remains or artwork made from bone or hair or nail clippings, it has also come to include a range of Christian materiality. In early February 2023, I searched "#oddities" on Instagram and the top featured post was not an articulated

bat skeleton; it was a "rare and precious 1700's reliquary presenting a rock crystal cross containing a first-class relic of the true cross." The post was from a resale company based in France specializing in "relics and reliquaries, religious objects, engravings, instruments of penance, [and] devils."[4] What do we make of "oddities" encompassing Christian material culture, and what classificatory work is being done with this category?

I took this question to Adam Rust, the owner of an "antiques and oddities" store in Chicago's Andersonville neighborhood.[5] The store is a destination in the city and the region, often included in celebratory "best of" lists of places for residents and tourists to visit. Walking into the store, you can immediately appreciate why. The small shop (~500 square feet) is densely packed with large, small, and miniature items: situated on tables and shelves, hung on walls, propped along the floor. is full, but not disorganized. With every scan around the room, your eye lands on something different: taxidermy animals, outmoded medical devices, a preserved animal fetus in a jar, Victorian hair wreaths, the artwork of an infamous serial killer, a crucified Jesus.

Adam and his wife created the store in 2010, just after completing their MFAs together. Based on their experience as consumers in local secondhand stores, they decided that reselling "vintage" could be a successful business model. It was on their honeymoon in Romania, tracing the route of Vlad III (a.k.a. Vlad the Impaler [to Bram Stoker fans, "Dracula"]), when they decided to take a chance and pursue the venture. Their vision for the store is to be a kind of "dark comedy" or "physical satire" that ruminates on the lifecycle of physically entering and exiting the world, the membrane between life and death, and the mysteries that ensue from a terminal existence. It is death, as a specter and as an unavoidable though deferrable fact, that Adam finds most compelling in relationship to Christianity.

Raised in a nominally Presbyterian home, Adam disconnected from churchgoing as a teenager and has identified as an atheist throughout this adult life. He described his interest in Christian material culture as detached from theological meaning, grounded more in an attachment to "darkness." Namely, he is fascinated by the idea that the cross, arguably the primary symbol for Christians across traditions, is "a torture device." His art school education included significant attention to Christian themes and figures, and he felt especially drawn to examples like the bodily stigmata of St. Francis of Assisi. On local and international sourcing trips, Adam seeks items that fit this motif of "dark" existential expressions. Just before the COVID-19 pandemic, he returned to Paris, France, a favored city of his to source in. He recalled one item in particular: a monastic self-flagellation kit being sold for $4000. He decided against it due to the expense: not viable for resale profit and too costly to justify adding to his personal collection. But it is emblematic of the kind of Christian material culture he remains on the lookout for.

Secondhand stores are enmeshed in an ongoing process of circulation, always sourcing new items and always selling inventory. In turn, the contents of a shop like Adam's are always in flux. When I first visited in December 2022, there were multiple objects depicting the crucifixion of Jesus. There were books, framed prints, and clothing from Masonic orders ("secret societies" being an index for mystery). There were also multiple ex ossibus ("from the bone") relics. One set Adam acquired at a street market in Seville, Spain. The sign next to them read:

Monk Bones

These small reliquaries contain tiny chunks of Sevillian monks! Bones are roughly 16th century, reliquaries are from about 1900. 225 each

He explained that they used to have quite a few more, but all had sold except the three cases that remained. Bone relics are prized among oddity collectors and dealers because of the direct indexicality of death. They are not especially rare, particularly if one is not choosy about which historic figure the bones belonged to, but they tend to sell quickly and at a premium price.[6] A more widely available Catholic death technology that circulates in the secondhand world are last rites (or sick call) kits. These portable objects are kept in homes and include the ritual items needed to serve the Eucharist to someone knocking on heaven's door. Without any prompting from me, Adam named the last rites kits as an example of an object that he has changed his stance toward. He used to source these kits regularly, but because they have become so widely available, he no longer seeks them out. Their ubiquity on the secondhand market has rendered them no longer "weird enough," less capable of lending his store the distinctiveness he desires.

Adam's store is a place where Christian material culture is recontextualized in a way that shifts its valuation. This reflects a kind of secularization process, akin to the pattern of churches and other historically Christian buildings in the United States and western Europe being reworked as museums, event spaces, coffee houses, and nightclubs (e.g., Beekers 2016; Oliphant 2021). Religious materiality is valued in historic and aesthetic registers, but the capacity to serve as an authorized mediator of divine presence is displaced. The devotional value originally sought by collecting, articulating, and displaying bone relics, for example, gives way to an aesthetic value. Unlike examples in which Christian buildings are being preserved as indices of cultural or national heritage (Meyer 2019), the value cultivated in Adam's store is about the indexical range of the oddities marketplace (from strange to macabre).

For Adam, this kind of secularism is a generative condition. The physical, spatial, and relational dimensions of display are one way this is expressed. He does not gather the Christian material culture together in one section of the store, preferring instead to spread these items out. The arrangement and presentation of Christian material culture can be imagined in ways free of traditional expectation, juxtaposed with materials that either magnify or rebut sacredness. On my first visit to Adam's store, I photographed the following display (Figure 17.1), which exemplifies what becomes possible in the secular logic of "oddities."

FIGURE 17.1 Display of Christian material culture inside Adam's store (photo by author)

What do we make of a pile of mass-produced Catholic prayer objects presented directly next to a pile of mammalian penis bones? From an emic Catholic perspective, this may well be interpreted as a polluting act of "matter out of place" (Douglas 1966): a desecration of sacred materiality, or at least a shameful display of sacrilegious taste. Not for Adam. The performative effect of this display, as commodities for sale and as an aesthetic for the store, emerges from the relationality among objects (Starrett 1995). While he does delight in the explicit irreverence, displays like this exceed mere amusement; they express both the expansiveness and the coherence of "oddities" as a material classifier.

Ephemera

In September 2020, two archivists from the University of Dayton's Marian Library published an article in the journal *Catholic Library World* (Cahalan and Harris 2020). They reflected on a particular dilemma: how do they, as library professionals working with sacralized objects, deal with donated items that duplicate existing collections or fall outside their curatorial remit? Their dilemma is an expression of the broader category "sacred waste," where excess, ravaged, or discarded materials become "a kind of leftover for which no proper destination exists" (Stengs

2014: 235; cf. Gould 2018). The Marian archivists have found that they can deal with certain classes of objects easily enough – when Catholic canon law provides an authorized protocol for disposal or when the object can be gifted to a church or school to satisfy a ritual or educational need. Other cases are more confusing. "Paper ephemera can be one of the most complex areas for deaccessioning" (p. 30). Christmas cards, calendars, photographs, scrapbooks, pamphlets, postcards, stamps, newspaper clippings, and prayer/memorial cards pose difficulties because their history of use and sacred status is more uncertain. While the Library's staff has developed a variety of solutions, their accumulation of this material numbers in the tens of thousands and more arrives in bulk "on a weekly basis from donors both well known and anonymous" (p. 31).

The experience of the Marian archivists illustrates some fundamental qualities of the classification "ephemera." By definition, the term indexes items not designed to be materially durable or to endure temporally; "throwaways not thrown away" (Desjardins 2006: 32). Such items are easily lost and easily damaged or destroyed. Perhaps in spite of, perhaps because of, this quality ephemera has been an important class of materials in practices of collection, preservation, curation, and exhibition (Mussell 2011; Brake 2012). For professional and amateur collectors alike, material affordances, such as size and weight, mean that ephemera lends itself to accumulation, mobility, and exchange. Likewise, "ephemera" is an ambivalent category for resellers. On one hand, these materials can be neatly stored and acquired in bulk for modest monetary expense. On the other, an abundance of ephemera can be unruly to catalogue, and the resale value of individual items is often uncertain.

Christian ephemera has abounded in my experience apprenticing as a reseller. I have encountered prayer pamphlets, pilgrimage guidebooks, prayer cards, ritual and membership certificates, Sunday school ledgers, brochures, postcards, calendars, event and program books, flyers, advertisements, bookmarks, display prints, evangelistic tracts, sheet music, hand-written cards, and photographs.

How I encounter these materials in secondhand venues testifies to the uneven valuation of ephemera. Consider the antique mall, where individual booths are rented out to different vendors. This configuration began proliferating in the 1990s when antique shop owners could no longer sustain the overhead of a stand-alone store (Minter 2019). Moving from booth to booth reveals divergent presentations of ephemera. In one booth, individual pieces of ephemera are neatly placed in cellophane slips with cardboard backing and precisely labeling. Here, the vendor has meticulously catalogued the items and has a decided expectation for what each might sell for. In another booth, ephemera sit messily in unorganized piles, and individual pieces are indiscriminately priced the same (Figure 17.2).

I have consistently sourced Christian ephemera of different genres from antique store contexts, but it is at estate sales where the most prolific opportunities have emerged. In early October 2022, I stood in line for the first-day opening of an estate in a northwest Chicago neighborhood. The modest home was packed with

FIGURE 17.2 Mixed ephemera, including Christian prayer cards, at an antique store in Evanston, Illinois (photo by author)

materials. While other buyers made a beeline for jewelry and clothes, I gathered pieces of ephemera. The deceased was a devout Polish Catholic woman, and there were small piles of prayer cards, devotional pamphlets, and other items spread throughout several rooms. While other types of items had been gathered together in one spot, for example, the display of roughly 150 rosaries in the opening room, the ephemera seemed to be untouched from where the deceased (or, perhaps their family members) had left it. When the collection became too much for me to carry, I grabbed a plastic bin and continued adding. The bin was filled to the brim when I brought it to the check-out table, likely nearing 200 individual pieces. The estate sale worker lifted a few pieces and surveyed the bin for about 3 seconds before suggesting a price of $15. The house was buzzing with people, and she expressed zero interest in taking the time to sift through this small mass to separate items of differential value.

In his ethnography of U.S. landfill workers who scavenge unprocessed waste for usable materials, Reno (2009) argues that these workers perform a process of "individuation" (p. 34). That is, they distinguish certain items as "worth the trouble of recovery...assigning something indeterminate an identity that is not set in advance" (p. 34). He observes that individuating is an embodied skill, a learned craft that relies on a multi-sensory assessment of an item's potential value. Much the same is true for encountering undifferentiated masses of Christian ephemera at an estate sale. In my interviews with resellers, they have without exception talked intently about the importance of being able to discern value where others do not. To spot a "hidden gem" when others pass it by, to recognize "flip" potential when others see a hassle not worth the time. In other words, resellers are invested in the skill of individuating. Ephemera poses a particular challenge in this regard. It is abundant, time-consuming to sort, often decontextualized from an original media setting or unmarked (e.g., with a date, a producer, or other signifiers of value in secondhand exchange).

Much of my understanding of how resellers deal with Christian ephemera comes from Mark. Based in a southwestern Chicagoland suburb, Mark is a 40-year-old white man who has been collecting and reselling for five years. He works as an IT consultant for a health insurance company, which pays the bills, but it is not his passion. What Mark loves to do, what he spends most weekends and many weeknights doing, is scavenge secondhand venues for "treasures." Mark is an atheist, but a prominent vein in his sourcing centers on "vintage Catholic and other super cool Christian shit." He is drawn to the artistic beauty of items, to the historical and personal stories they embody, and to their resonance with "curiosities," his unifying category of interest. I was introduced to Mark by a reseller I met at an estate sale. Since we first talked in August 2021, Mark has been an ideal interlocutor. We have attended estate sales together and we text message regularly about the materials we encounter when sourcing. Whenever I have a reselling question, Mark is the first person I ask. In my apprenticeship, he has been a generous mentor.

A December 2021 estate sale prompted a robust conversation about ephemera. The sale was not a home, but a closed Masonic lodge in downtown Evanston (just north of Chicago). It was the kind of sale where everything was up for grabs: if you could detach something from a wall or floor or ceiling and if you could move it, you could buy it. Some people were heading out the door with kitchen equipment, others with ceremonial uniforms. In searching the rooms, I noticed a plastic grocery bag sitting unceremoniously on the floor of an office. It contained 36 pieces of Freemason ephemera, everything from ritual programs to a theatrical play script. A member of the local Masonic chapter was handling payments, and after a quick perusal, he suggested a price of $10 for the bag and a 1923 Bible.

A few weeks later, Mark and I met for an estate sale and talked afterward at a nearby Starbucks for about an hour. I brought along the bag of Masonic ephemera, curious for his take on the materials but also totally unsure of how to approach reselling them. The prospect of creating detailed listings for each item was daunting, but I was also hesitant to list it as a single "lot of 36." Mark flipped through the entire stack, considering each piece in turn. He reflected that "lots are dangerous" because you can easily fail to maximize resale value and you can easily build lots that are too "hectic." The trick was to identify the pieces that are sellable on their own and to group others in relatively small lots that cohere in some way. He pulled aside a few items that were "cool" enough to list individually and suggested a few possible ways to organize the rest into lots. He estimated the pile could fetch about $150 over time. He was right. After 11 weeks, I had sold all of it: 12 sales, 6 individual pieces, and 6 lots of 2–7 items for $140 (after eBay fees and postage).

Mark has helped me learn that the classification "ephemera" is a demanding one for resellers. It requires time to strategically sort and the skill of individuating. But if one has the privilege of both, Christian ephemera has definite resale value given the minimum sourcing cost. There is clearly a market for these materials, which raises the question of how buyers engage with "ephemera." In January 2023, I posted a photograph to Instagram of ~400 pieces of Christian ephemera that I had accumulated, asking other resellers how they handle this kind of mass. Emily – a reseller I have come to know in Syracuse, New York – replied that she has posted large lots with the hashtag "#junkjournal" to attract buyers who create prayer journals comprising mixed Christian ephemera pieces. On at least two occasions, buyers have shared with me that this prayer practice was how they intended to use the items they purchased: early 20th-century Protestant Sunday school cards and Protestant hymnal pages.

Crafting material for stylizing prayer journals is one among many uses that secondhand consumers find for Christian ephemera. Consider a few others. A buyer in Glendale, Arizona, purchased a lot of 30 Protestant Sunday school cards to use as a gratis gift in their upcycling business:

> I am adding them as a "thank you" gift with purchase for items that I am making out of antique buttons, ribbons and trims. A card will be tucked away in the package of the item purchased. I have about 50 of these cards that I purchased from another eBay seller many years ago and was happy to have found more with the ones you sold me ☺

A similar lot of 12 cards was purchased by a buyer in Ferndale, Michigan. They maintain a collection as an aid for Bible reading and also cite the potential value of using the cards as a teaching tool:

It's for my collection of Bible art. I'm reading through the Bible and have been collecting color prints and chrome lithographs as I go. These are really charming and I'm excited to add them to my collection. I don't think I'll frame them but perhaps I'll use them someday to talk about the Bible with my niece and nephew. Thanks so much for offering them for sale!

A buyer in Elmhurst, New York, purchased a lot of 17 Catholic saint cards for devotional use and as part of a sibling relationship:

My sister and I are very devoted to the baby Jesus and St Anthony. In one of the visions the baby Jesus jumped into the arms of St Anthony. Seeing young Jesus run toward the arms of St Theresa of Avila as he did with St Anthony was so so sweet we couldn't resist buying it. It will remain ever so happily with us. I'm not sure if it will stay with me or my sister or we may have joint custody of them. It will remind us to say special prayers to Jesus.

I have sold 13 different sets of Catholic funeral cards, and the interests of buyers vary widely. An oddity reseller was attracted to a lot of five John F. Kennedy funeral cards:

I sell a lot of more macabre or weird antiques here in Seattle. I'll likely be trying to sell them at a flea market.

A buyer in Wilmot, South Dakota, saw them as both gift and family heirloom:

I was both baptized and confirmed in the church earlier this year. I am fortunate to have been married in the church to a wonderful woman over 20 years ago. They are a gift for her as she is still teaching me about the faith. I thought they would be something worth handing down to our children and grandchildren when the time comes. We are interested in the older style as we are 62 and 61. I was glad to have found them as I feel they will help deepen our understanding of the faith. Thanks!

A buyer in Alpena, Michigan, seemed more interested in the cards' connection to death than Catholicism, valuing them for the "imaginative potential of [their] former life" (Gregson and Crewe 2003: 145):

Always was attracted to funeral homes, should have been mortician. Cards love any cards. I try to imagine that person life with the information.

And, a buyer in Pepper Pike, Ohio, wanted a lot of 14 cards as artistic inspiration for a film they are creating:

> I'm working on a film and will use these cards as inspiration for our art direction… It's a small art film about a woman who falls in love with the sound of insects, and wants to marry the sound. There's a scene where she talks to her priest but he tells her he's not able to perform a wedding between a person and a sound. He can only marry people ☺ We're using the cards as inspiration for decoration in his office.

This sample of buyer replies provides a glimpse into the potential ongoing social lives of Christian ephemera. Be it craft, gift, collection, display, devotional aid, or creative inspiration, the material qualities of ephemera are central to the appeal. Some of these same qualities enable them to be gathered and grouped together. If our goal is to better understand the circulation of Christian material culture, then "ephemera" is a classification worth attending to. It helps illuminate vital reseller practices, such as individuation, and the multiple configurations of consumer valuation.

Conclusion

Christian material culture is circulating through secondhand networks at a massive, frankly immeasurable scale. Log onto eBay, Instagram, or Etsy, and you find an incredible range of items up for grabs. The dizzying abundance continues at local thrift stores, where shelves are restocked multiple times daily, and on the estate sale circuit, where hundreds of homes are opened every week to transform personal possessions into negotiable commodities. This chapter has taken up a particular dynamic in this ongoing process: how Christian material culture is classified in resale contexts. The central observation I have sought to develop is that classifying is not a neutral act, but an instrumental part of constructing value.

This analysis has particular resonance for scholarship in material religion. This field emerged in the mid-1990s and has cohered most thoroughly with the performative efficacy of mediation (Engelke 2010): the sensations, technologies, and infrastructures that make religious life possible, sensible, and consequential. This turn has re-conceptualized categories such as "belief" in terms of the forms and processes of mediation, asking how different material and sensory channels structure religious experience, communication, and learning. The organizing conceit is that mediation is constitutive of religious worlds, not merely an incidental byproduct or practical necessity (Meyer 2009; Morgan 2010; Promey 2014). Religious actors use material forms to address the fundamental problems that animate their religious tradition(s), such as authority, belonging, and presence. A key insight is that foundational interests in the critical study of religion – such as "belief," "sociality," "charisma," or "ritual" – do not precede mediation, nor are they products of media. Rather, they are forged, negotiated, and contested through multiple mediating processes.

By taking up the example of secondhand circulation, this chapter highlights an additional point of coherence for material religion. In a landmark collection, Plate (2015) identifies 37 "key terms in material religion." Most of these terms are focused in one of three areas: categories that have been central to the study of religion (e.g., belief, sacred), specific media channels (e.g., smell, sound), or particular practices (e.g., prayer, display). The collection is an ideal introduction to the field, but notably, "circulation" is absent, and there is no comparable term similarly oriented to the ongoing social life of religious materiality.

Some recent scholarship has begun to concentrate on the dynamics of circulation. In addition to classification, Morgan (2017) names circulation as one of the three processes that are vital for understanding religious materiality. Tracing paths of material circulation means tracing the continual movement, exchange, acquisition, and deployment of objects for diverse purposes in diverse contexts. Further, this tracing occurs over time; it does not prioritize the current life stage of an object, but takes a diachronic view, presuming that its "social career" (p. 28) will extend beyond the present to other contexts, other users, other uses. In her historical ethnography of evangelical and Catholic child sponsorship programs, Kaell (2020) explores the circulation of gifts among sponsors, organizations, and children. She argues that this exchange of objects is pivotal for cultivating the affective dimensions of sponsor relationships across space and time. Meyer (2019) examines the secondhand circulation of Christian material culture in the Netherlands. Across three cases – church buildings repurposed as secular venues, ritual objects resold as commodities, and ritual objects redeployed as fodder for artists – she illustrates how these materials are used to proclaim Dutch national heritage.

Alongside this scholarship, this chapter advances the case for circulation as a key term, a term poised to understand the prolific social life of religious materiality. One benefit of circulation is that it presumes contingency: that the use, value, and identity of materiality is transformed as it moves physically, socially, and temporally (cf. Chidester 2000: 378; Callahan 2022). Kendall (2021) observes this in her analysis of Buddhist material culture in museums and markets: "[these objects] wobble in several possible directions, rather than lurching irrevocably in the direction of disenchantment. Shifts between sacred and secular can sometimes be unpredictable and inconsistent" (p. 136). Ultimately, this contingency has much to do with classification, placing materiality in a particular category and framing it in a particular way. To trace the social life of religious materiality, one must pay attention to the multiple and diverse acts of classification that inform its circulation.

Notes

1 See also Shankar (2006) on how classificatory talk about commodities, the "objectification" (p. 298) of objects, circulates as a metaconsumptive practice to construct and communicate status, belonging, and hierarchy in a California Desi community.
2 This chapter emerges from ongoing ethnographic fieldwork in face-to-face and online contexts. The research design includes a range of activities. Thus far, I have conducted

semi-structured interviews with 22 resellers. With several interviewees, I have toured homes and brick-and-mortar secondhand stores to observe collections and inventories. With one interviewee, we have attended estate sales together in order to observe how he sources materials in this context. Online, I trace the circulation of Christian material culture on multiple platforms and observe Instagram live sales that exclusively or heavily feature Christian material culture. Finally, I am apprenticing as a reseller, informed by interviewing and participant observation data. Thus far, I have sourced from 14 estate sales and 47 secondhand venues (28 thrift stores, 16 antique stores, and 3 used book stores). I have sold more than 530 items on eBay and communicated with more than 350 buyers about their purchases.

3 For example, https://news.gallup.com/poll/341963/church-membership-falls-below-majority-first-time.aspx (accessed: March 7, 2023) and https://msana.com/services/u-s-membership-statistics/ (accessed: March 7, 2023)
4 Source: https://relics.es/ (accessed: February 9, 2023)
5 The following details are drawn from multiple visits to Adam's store and a semi-structured interview conducted with him at the store in January 2023.
6 First-, second-, and third-class relics have circulated globally since at least the 4th century, when travelers to the biblical Holy Land began collecting objects associated with the life of Jesus and other scriptural figures (Wharton 2006). For a 21st-century example of how Catholic relics are used for theopolitical performance, see Norget (2021); for an ethnographic example of how relics operate in Eastern Orthodox contexts, see Carroll (2018).

References

Beekers, D. (2016). Sacred Residue. In S. Lanwerd (ed.), *The Urban Sacred: How Religion Makes and Takes Place in Amsterdam, Berlin and London* (pp. 39–41). Berlin: Metropol.

Belk, R. W., M. Wallendorf and J. F. Sherry Jr. (1989). The Sacred and the Profane in Consumer Behavior: Theodicy on the Odyssey. *Journal of Consumer Research*, 16(1): 1–38.

Berry, B. (2022). Glut: Affective Labor and the Burden of Abundance in Secondhand Economies. *Anthropology of Work Review*, 43(1): 26–37.

Bourdieu, P. (1984). *Distinction: A Social Critique of the Judgment of Taste*. Cambridge: Harvard University Press.

Brake, L. (2012). The Longevity of "Ephemera." *Media History*, 18(1): 7–20.

Cahalan, S. B. and K. Harris. (2020). Mary, Undoer of Knots: Unraveling Best Practices for Unwanted Donations and Deaccessioned Collection Items in a Catholic Library. *Catholic Library World*, 91(1): 26–34.

Callahan, R. J. Jr. (2022). Sperm Whale Teeth in Circulation: A Case Study in Material Economics. Constellation. *MAVCOR Journal*, 6(3). doi: 10.22332/mav.con.2022.1.

Campbell, H. (2010). *When Religion Meets New Media*. London: Routledge.

Carroll, T. (2018). Im/Material Objects: Relics, Gestured Signs, and the Substance of the Immaterial. In T. Hutchings and J. McKenzie (eds.), *Materiality and the Study of Religion: The Stuff of the Sacred* (pp. 119–32). London: Routledge.

Chidester, D. (2000). Material Terms for the Study of Religion. *Journal of the American Academy of Religion*, 68(2): 367–79.

Chidester, D. (2014). *Empire of Religion: Imperialism and Comparative Religion*. Chicago: University of Chicago Press.

Desjardins, M. (2006). Ephemeral Culture/eBay Culture: Film Collectibles and Fan Investments. In K. Hillis, M. Petit and N. S. Epley (eds.), *Everyday eBay: Culture, Collecting, and Desire* (pp. 31–44). London: Routledge.

Douglas, M. (1966). *Purity and Danger: An Analysis of Concepts of Pollution and Taboo.* New York: Penguin.

Engelke, M. (2010). Religion and the Media Turn: A Review Essay. *American Ethnologist,* 37(2): 371–79.

Gould, H. (2018). Caring for Sacred Waste: the Disposal of *Butsudan* (Buddhist Altars) in Contemporary Japan. *Japanese Religions,* 43(1–2): 1–24.

Gregson, N. and L. Crewe. (2003). *Second-Hand Cultures.* London: Berg.

Hendershot, H. (2004). *Shaking the World for Jesus: Media and Conservative Evangelical Culture.* Chicago: University of Chicago Press.

Jhally, S. (2006). *The Spectacle of Accumulation: Essays in Media, Culture, and Politics.* Bern: Peter Lang.

Kaell, H. (2020). *Christian Globalism at Home: Child Sponsorship in the United States.* Princeton: Princeton University Press.

Kendall, L. (2021). *Mediums and Magical Things: Statues, Paintings, and Masks in Asian Places.* Berkeley: University of California Press.

McDannell, C. (1995). *Material Christianity: Religion and Popular Culture in America.* New Haven: Yale University Press.

Meyer, B. (2019). Recycling the Christian Past: The Heritagization of Christianity and National Identity in the Netherlands. In R. Buikema, et al. (eds.) *Culture, Citizenship and Human Rights* (pp. 64–88). London: Routledge.

Meyer, B. (ed.) (2009). *Aesthetic Formations: Media, Religion, and the Senses.* New York: Palgrave Macmillan.

Minter, A. (2019). *Secondhand: Travels in the New Global Garage Sale.* London: Bloomsbury.

Moore, R. L. (1994). *Selling God: American Religion in the Marketplace of Culture.* Oxford: Oxford University Press.

Morgan, D. (2017). Material Analysis and the Study of Religion. In T. Hutchings and J. McKenzie (eds.), *Materiality and the Study of Religion: The Stuff of the Sacred* (pp. 14–32). London: Routledge.

Morgan, D. (ed.) (2010). *Religion and Material Culture: The Matter of Belief.* London: Routledge.

Mussell, J. (2011). The Passing of Print: Digitising ephemera and the Ephemerality of the Digital. *Media History,* 18(1): 77–92.

Norget, K. (2021). Bones, Blood, Wax, and Papal Potencies: Neo-Baroque Relics in Mexico. *Material Religion,* 17(3): 355–80.

Oliphant, E. (2021). *The Privilege of Being Banal: Art, Secularism, and Catholicism in Paris.* Chicago: University of Chicago Press.

Parmenter, D. M. (2010). A Fitting Ceremony: Christian Concerns for Bible Disposal. In K. Myrvold (ed.), *The Death of Sacred Texts: Ritual Disposal and Renovation of Texts in World Religions* (pp. 55–69). London: Ashgate.

Plate, S. B. (ed.) (2015). *Key Terms in Material Religion.* London: Bloomsbury.

Primiano, L. N. (2015). Kitsch. In E. M. Mazur and J. Lyden (eds.), *The Routledge Companion to Religion and Popular Culture* (pp. 281–312). London: Routledge.

Promey, S. M. (ed.) (2014). *Sensational Religion: Sensory Cultures in Material Practice.* New Haven: Yale University Press.

Reno, J. (2009). Your Trash Is Someone's Treasure: The Politics of Value at a Michigan Landfill. *Journal of Material Culture,* 14(1): 29–46.

Shankar, S. (2006). Metaconsumptive Practices and the Circulation of Objectifications. *Journal of Material Culture,* 11(3): 293–317.

Starrett, G. (1995). The Political Economy of Religious Commodities in Cairo. *American Anthropologist*, 97(1): 51–68.

Stengs, I. (2014). Sacred Waste. *Material Religion*, 10(2): 235–38.

Strasser, S. (1999). *Waste and Want: A Social History of Trash*. New York: Henry Holt.

Smith, J. Z. (1978). *Map Is Not Territory: Studies in the History of Religions*. Leiden: Brill.

Sullivan, W. F. (2020). *Church State Corporation: Construing Religion in U.S. Law*. Chicago: University of Chicago Press.

Taylor, S. M. and M. Einstein. (2022). Introduction to Special Issue on Religion, Media, and Marketing. *Journal of Religion, Media and Digital Culture*, 11: 1–11.

Van der Veer, P. (2014). *The Modern Spirit of Asia: the Spiritual and the Secular in China and India*. Princeton: Princeton University Press.

Wagner, R. (2012). *Godwired: Religion, Ritual, and Virtual Reality*. London: Routledge.

Wharton, A. J. (2006). *Selling Jerusalem: Relics, Replicas, and Theme Parks*. Chicago: University of Chicago Press.

18

(NOT) MARKETING ATHEISM

A Conversation with Gregory Epstein

Mara Einstein

Atheist, agnostic, secularist, humanist. Religiously indifferent, anti-religious, spiritual but not religious. All ways of describing those who do not practice within the confines of a traditional belief system. Being unaffiliated is not new. What is new is that more people are willing to "confess" their lack of religious attachment.

Statistics tell the story. Today, the religious landscape is incredibly diverse (PRRI, 2021). However, younger age demographics, particularly Gen Z and millennials, are increasingly disaffiliated (Burge, 2023). If this trend continues, Pew Research projects that by 2070, the religiously disaffiliated will approach majority status (Pew Research Center, 2022).

Religious "nones"—those who have no affiliation—on the whole are on the rise and have been for more than a decade. They now represent about a third of the U.S. population (Smith, 2021). A newer phenomenon is the increasing number of religious "dones"—those who were affiliated but left the church, synagogue or mosque. Some of this is fueled by the ex-vangelical movement, an increasingly vocal group, especially online, that is reminiscent of the anti-MLM movement (Editor, 2023).

Within this context, we wanted to explore the marketing of atheism, humanism, and the non-affiliated today, and for that I interviewed Greg M. Epstein. Mr. Epstein is perhaps best known as the author of *Good Without God: What a Billion Nonreligious People Do Believe*. He was also the humanist chaplain at Harvard University, and after more than a decade, he added similar duties at MIT to his resume (Fattal, 2018).

When I sat down to talk to Greg Epstein about marketing atheism, I thought the conversation would hit on the long-running Ron Reagan ads where he says, "Proud atheist. Not afraid to burn in hell." When these ads first aired, they were shocking. How could the son of Ronald Reagan, a president steeped in support from

DOI: 10.4324/9781003342229-25

the religious right, be saying those words? Or the atheist bus ads that proclaimed, "There's probably no God. Now Stop Worrying and Enjoy Your Life."

Or I thought we might go more academic and talk about Elizabeth Dreschers' (2016) work about atheism in America over time, or Ryan Burge's work on religious "nones," or Chris Stedman's *Faitheist* (2012) which tries to bridge the gap between those who do or do not believe in God. I had little doubted that we would talk about the likes of Sam Harris or Christopher Hitchens, as Epstein's book was a response to their screeds about religion and the need to eliminate it.

To my pleasant surprise, the conversation turned out to be far more nuanced. Rather than how is atheism promoted, the question became does atheism—or more broadly humanism or even religion writ large—need to be promoted?[1]

Background

Epstein: I've had a long journey to get to being a humanist chaplain, or being a humanist chaplain at Harvard for 20 years and MIT for five of those. There have been a number of stages in my career.

It starts with being a kid in New York City. Growing up in Flushing, Queens, which was a neighborhood that was so immigrant heavy, and so in the midst of rapid transformation that there were, as far as I understand, anthropologists studying my neighborhood, while I was living there.[2]

Throughout elementary school, I was the only American-born white boy in most of my public-school classes. My mother was a child refugee from Cuba who came to this country by herself with nothing, she was deeply traumatized, but I like to think that she was the less traumatized of my two parents. As for my father, he was born in New York City, but his parents were refugees from Eastern Europe.

I was born in Manhattan, but pretty soon after, we moved to Queens. We were fish swimming in different waters. There was trauma from our immigrant experience, but we looked like what I learned, then, to think of as "normal, American-passing people." Being American, I internalized based on my observations of American culture at a very young age, seemed to me back then to be based on whiteness, who you know, and class, as much as on anything in the nation's founding documents. But as I got a bit older, I came to love the diversity of the new society in which I was being raised.

I became fascinated by what people believed and by different cultures. I could attend my classmate's Buddhist ceremony or pass by the Hindu temple on the way to the park. I attended synagogue, for a Bar Mitzvah. There was a synagogue in Flushing—the Free Synagogue—which had been a grand place with a European-style choir—but was very rundown when I was growing up there. I didn't know much about any of that back then, but I did know that it struck me as inauthentic. The truth is that it was authentic to what it was, but it struck me as inauthentic because I was expecting something different.

My dad had lots of financial challenges and career challenges, but he was a curious and creative person. He died when I was 18, after being sick most of my childhood. The thing that he passed down to me was his collection of religious books which he had amassed mostly before I was born—mysticism from around the world, the Zohar, and the Bhagavad Gita and the works of Carl Jung. Gurdjieff's *The Fourth Way*, Chogyam Trungpa's *Cutting Through Spiritual Materialism*, or the Tao Te Ching. I never really got the chance to talk to him about it, because it was something that he had picked up as an interest in before I was born.

I was so curious about the meaning of life. I pulled those books down from the bookshelf when I was maybe 13 or 14 years old. I would thumb through them and wonder, what is this all about?

When he died, and my mom and I sat at the bedside, it was a couple months before I graduated from high school, and we didn't really know what to do. We were stunned in silence. We recited the 23rd Psalm together because it was something that we both knew, and it seemed appropriate.

When I got to college several months later, I thought I was going to study psychology, but it was very natural to ease into being a religion major. But through the whole course of being a religion major, I don't recall hearing the word humanism.

Discovering humanism wasn't until after I graduated, when I ran into a former teaching fellow. He asked me what I was going to do with my life. I had no idea. He suggested that I might want to visit his secular, humanistic, rabbinical classes.[3] And I did, and I was hooked.

Secular Humanism and Marketing

Epstein: The suburbs of Detroit were the founding place of this organized movement called secular humanistic Judaism. I loved the idea of combining one's philosophy of life, that I had been sort of slowly developing over time, with one's culture and background. Here was this thing that nobody knew anything about. I had never heard of it. Nobody I knew had ever heard of it.

Everybody knows about Christianity, Judaism, Islam, Hinduism. Buddhism has amazing marketing. People like Alan Ginsberg and even more importantly, Gary Snyder, another beat poet. These people were part of marketing of Buddhism. It was marketing and advertising that were a big part of what got me into this professionally. I was like, "Wow, I can do this. I could be a person that helps translate some of these ideas for a new generation that might be receptive to them, if only they could be reached." I very consciously planned out the first years of my career in terms of marketing humanism.

I don't think about it that way now. After all, you don't see much marketing for Christianity, as a whole. You see individual churches do great marketing, brilliant marketing. Denominations can do marketing.

They have different kinds of marketing for Mormonism, or is it the church or is it the Church of Latter-day Saints You can look at the way reformed synagogues are marketing themselves, but you rarely see anybody just saying, Judaism or Christianity. It's something worth noting that we don't stop to think sometimes that humanism, secularism or whatever can't be simply marketed. Do you really see campaigns for Hinduism?

Einstein: I agree. Denominations have had a problem with this. I worked with the Episcopal Church, and they had a good understanding of how to create different levels of a campaign because they had people on staff who had come out of marketing backgrounds. We'd talk about it as similar to the way that TV works—you have NBC—the national network—and then you have the affiliate stations around the country. Those affiliates may or may not be part of NBC corporate. They might be part of, say, Tribune. And so, the local station has to be able to talk about both sides of their identity. They have to talk about the overall umbrella identity (NBC, or Episcopalian), and they have to promote their local identity (WNBC, or St. Lukes.)

Defining the Unaffiliated

Einstein: Let's get into the definitions. What is the difference between humanism and atheism? Or are there other terms that should be discussed?

Epstein: There's a bit of a word salad here. There's humanism, atheism, agnosticism, secularism, free thought, skepticism, and then there's just being none or nothing or non-religious. We're unaffiliated, right? There's no all-powerful Pope in this tradition to give it the one name that everybody needs to call it or shut up.

Atheism is the nervy assertion that the idea of a deity is not real, that it is a human creation. Agnosticism is the also nervy, but perhaps in certain contexts somewhat less nervy, assertion that one cannot know whether the deity is real or was created by people.

Humanism is a term that originated in the European Renaissance to mean essentially that there is more to know in life than the mind of God. About 100 years ago, a group of Unitarian ministers, and then expanding to include others later, noticed that they were each simultaneously beginning to arrive at the idea that they were no longer the same kind of ministers that their predecessors had been. They were realizing that there's textual criticism of the sacred scriptures; there's anthropology, psychology, and so on. They were no longer traditionally theistic. But what were they? And so, the word humanism was something they adopted to mean a positive alternative to traditional religion and theistic belief.

Humanism is another nervy assertion that human beings are the creators of our culture. We have a moral responsibility for ourselves and our actions and that includes responsibility to build a better world. That is what humanism is about. To me, it's about making the life that we have, and the world that we have—which is neither as beautiful or as just or as sensical as we would like—into something better, not just for ourselves, but for those we love and for everyone. We're only human, we're flawed, we're imperfect, we are the product of evolution, and we are responsible for the future of our evolution.

Einstein: This seems to me to be something that should appeal to the religious nones and religious dones. Is there outreach to them? Is there marketing to them? If there is, what does that look like?

Epstein: I personally, and many, many colleagues, have been working very hard for a couple of decades now to try to share the message. I say that with a smile because I'm conscious of the fact that it sounds vaguely like spreading the gospel. But the message that this movement exists is inspiring. People have actively or passively gotten that idea.

There have been organizations created, communities created, congregations created, advertising campaigns, fundraising campaigns, public service campaigns, community service campaigns, working alongside marginalized people in developing countries…there's been all kinds of things like music and art and poetry and storytelling, meditation, mindfulness for developing these concepts and sharing them and making them appealing.

I spent years intensely thinking about how we can get more members and more donations and more participation, and how do we bring in celebrities to do outreach for us, or we spent time making videos that we tried to get go viral and working with politicians.

Now, however, I think that the world has bigger problems than whether young adults affiliate with my movement, or any movement. I'm done with it. I'm not saying this is unique to my tradition. I believe a lot more religious people should be done with it, and by "it," I mean, marketing their traditions.

Let the cards fall where they may. There is a big need for community, we do need to connect with one another on a local level in order to cope with and face the enormous challenges that are upon us and coming our way.

Yet the reason I'm not going back to what I did before is that I'm not convinced that what humanity needs is for people to be competing that hard to try to make this or that kind of community or congregation the more successful one. We're in a lot of trouble with climate and with the direction that tech is heading and [that just shouldn't be our priority].

I've really changed my perspective on what I want to do around humanism. I have come to believe that the thing that has replaced religion, and even secularism or humanism or whatever you want to call it in the minds of young people today, is technology. It's more subtle, more clever and insidious, but in some ways, I have come to see tech as being presented and marketed as what I think of as a new religion. The reason why tech-as-religion is more clever and insidious is because it's a new religion that doesn't call itself a religion or even a worldview or a "lifestance," which is a word we sometimes use to highlight that humanism is *like* a religion in some ways, despite being secular and nontheistic. When you call something religious, that is automatically a turnoff to a lot of people. And even when you call attention to yourself as wanting the allegiance and devotion and faith of the people, you automatically provoke people's innate skepticism. Tech, on the other hand, strikes me as tremendously religious, but it presents itself as morally and socially neutral, and not as anything you need to "join." Nobody is dumb enough to call it a religion or a faith, and therefore people are ironically more ready to offer it their allegiance and devotion; to put their faith in it.

It would be like if a new god emerged on the celestial scene, and said, "I'm going to get everybody to worship me. But the way that I'm going to do it is by pretending I don't exist, and I won't take any credit. I won't expect anybody to praise me. I'm just going to get them to turn their attention to me all of the time. Literally." It would be that that God would immediately outcompete all the other gods because all the other gods want credit. And as you know, if you want to get something done, don't worry about who gets credit.

Co-opting Caring

Einstein: You say tech is the new religion. In my work, I write about the market being the new religion, whether you're following an influencer or a "cult brand." People moved away from traditional faiths, jobs are gigs, and divorce rates are high. Within the context of that social space, corporations have come in to fill the void as the place where people can imbue their beliefs. Brands have answered that question by inserting values into the belief systems of the brands. They don't do it very well and half the time they're lying, so we have everything from purpose washing to woke washing to health washing to greenwashing.

Epstein: Every moral message that you could possibly want has been appropriated and subsumed into this brand management. That is our capitalist society. For example, I wanted to give a talk one time about the idea of adulting, of becoming an adult.

When I get a topic in mind I want to share with my community, I am a voracious researcher. I want to read everything, see everything about it. And I'm walking around one day, and I see these bus ads in Boston, and they say, "You're a grown up," or something like "don't worry, you got this." And I was like, "what is that for?" It turned out it was for a major insurance company. One of the biggest insurance companies in the world had decided that it wanted to create this new brand to appeal to young people, so it created a center. It was out in Brookline of all places—the Center for Adulting, or whatever. So, I went there, and I met the people and I had their pasta and meatball dinner and drank fancy wine and interviewed the young people that worked there.

This one young woman I interviewed was in a rock and roll t-shirt and ripped up jeans. And she's a "wealth manager," it turns out: an employee of the insurance company. I asked her, "tell me about what you're here to do?" And she said, "money is like a community." Another wealth manager in a similar outfit repeated the exact same phrase later in the evening. Money is like a community.

That was a moment for me. It was a big moment in my career. Because it was right when I was starting to think, I need to change what I'm doing. I'd always known that corporations can co-opt humanist messages, but it was then that I saw there wasn't any message that you could come up with—any message that was worth any fucking amount of salt—that some corporation wouldn't absolutely hire 20 people to co-opt.

Take another example. My wife and I used to drive around and look at interesting religious buildings. I would always say, we're going to build one of those for humanists one day. It would cost like $20 million or $30 million, but we're going to do it. I had no idea how to get that money, but I was just so determined.

And right now, if I was all-out determined to build something like that, I know exactly who I would call and I know exactly what I would say, and we would have the fucking checks. But, I would feel terrible about myself. I don't like these people's politics; the policies they stand for and the society they envision just very often doesn't represent what I'm about. The way you acquire that much capital in the first place—to be able to write that kind of philanthropic check—is often by doing things that are not humanistic.

The point is that there is a lot of competitiveness. "My movement has more members than your movement" or "my congregation has more members than your congregation" or whatever, but it's all people trying to hold on for dear life to a shrinking pie. And we're failing to recognize that what's needed to bring people together and make the world better is not about whether we believe the same things. It's about decency and caring for one another and trying to enjoy life together, and building something worthwhile.

But really, I just can't stomach anymore the idea of having my professional value, not to mention my personal value, wrapped up in building some unit of value, some unit of conventional success, that might advance my own narrow community organization or even my "movement," but that wouldn't truly address the complex and systemic and urgent problems that face all of us, as humans, together.

Marketing Examples from the Past

Einstein: Give me the best bit of marketing for humanism you did and the worst thing that you did.

Epstein: I really liked the marketing materials that we put together for a conference I was the lead organizer for in 2007. The idea was to celebrate the 30th anniversary of the humanist chaplaincy at Harvard, the first humanist chaplaincy on any campus, the first humanist chaplaincy in North America.

I had seen, in 2006, a cover story on *Wired Magazine* about the New Atheists. *New Atheism: no heaven, no hell, just science.* And it really blew me away that this thing that I had been studying for years was finally on a magazine cover—like a big magazine cover.

But then I looked at the magazine cover, and it also said, "No Heaven. No Hell. Just Science." I thought, *"That's* what makes it to the cover of the big magazine?" That's not the message that inspires me about humanism. They're either deliberately or by accident getting it totally wrong.

I decided, we're going to do this totally different. Our conference was, "The New Humanism: Diverse, Inclusive, Inspiring." And the speakers were from all over the world, and they represented art and music and international development and philosophy. The idea of combining one's culture with one's secular philosophy of life. It was about service, it was about a youth movement.

We put out a press release that got a lot of controversy because it said that the new atheists were atheist fundamentalists. I never said that, but the press release did. It drew a lot of attention to that conference.

That was our public launch into the world and it ended up being the launch of my public career, as well. I've been part of a lot of large campaigns and outreach efforts since, including a "Good Without God" ad campaign that ran across the New York City and Boston subway systems, and on billboards and buses and even stadiums all across the country (Lee, 2009); there was also a formal campaign to launch humanist communities and congregations nationwide; I founded and chaired "Humanists for Biden," after being asked to do so by leaders in the Biden campaign itself—it was the first time a major American presidential campaign has ever coordinated with the nonreligious community. When we opened our congregation, the Governor of Massachusetts proclaimed it "Humanist Community Day" in the Commonwealth, which was the culmination of a major effort to reach out to him. There have also been big events with celebrities, like the late Carrie Fisher of Star Wars fame. And those are just some of the bigger events that I personally led. Lots of other atheists and humanists have taken on comparable projects, many of which have been tremendously worthwhile. And increasingly, I'm very pleased to say, those projects are more likely to be led by women, or people of color, or both.

In general, as I tried a lot of marketing campaigns, bringing in a lot of allies and a lot of funders, mistakes have abounded. I spent a year raising the money to hire somebody to lead the humanist community project, this idea of spreading humanist communities all across the country, the world—which was more than a little bit grandiose in retrospect—but I spent the year raising money to hire the perfect person to lead the project. We found her and placed the perfect article about her in *The New York Times*. I got a call 36 hours later from the *Times* reporter, the venerable Columbia Journalism School professor Sam Friedman, saying: have you heard? Had I heard what, I asked. Teresa faked her degree. They had to retract the article, and I had to fire her—within 36 hours of announcing her hire.

That's just one. Having to close the congregation that we had started several years earlier, is another. Having to remove all the marketing from it, because we were "The Humanist Chaplaincy at Harvard," and then we were "The Humanist Community at Harvard," and then we were "The Humanist Hub." And now, we're back to being just a humanist chaplaincy again.

Concluding Thoughts

Epstein: Talking about my feelings about all of these experiences, even my own failures—maybe even especially my own failures—is the most fun part of any interview, because few people ask, unless they're being adversarial about it. Our culture prizes a lack of vulnerability. I've read a lot of Brene Brown. I mean, you know, granted Brene Brown is for white people, in the sense that her work probably doesn't do enough to acknowledge systemic racism. But in any case, I like talking about what I fucked up. And I wish other people did too.

Einstein: I actually had this conversation this morning. I was explaining about social media that nobody's life is as perfect as it looks on Facebook, or are they as pissed off as they look on Twitter.

Epstein: I am as pissed off as I look on Twitter!

Einstein: But we're still constantly trying to use them as our ruler to decide whether or not we have matched up to what it is that society thinks that we're supposed to do. Or, everybody thinks that somebody goes onto social media and is automatically perfect by the time they get there, which isn't true. But, they don't have the opportunity to fail, which I think is one of the sort of downsides of social media. Look at someone like Bob Dylan. It's not like Bob Dylan spouted music and was the greatest thing since sliced bread. Nobody wanted to have anything to do with him, and he originally wrote really crappy songs. But it took him some time and then people started to catch on with what he had to say. I mean, think of an artist today that has an opportunity to do that. I don't think they do.

Epstein: I think people sometimes take the opportunity to do it anyway. I'm talking to myself here, because I think that this is something that I need to hear, that you can get caught up in "I've got to look perfect," because I'm already out there. It's always good to able to simply say, "I am I wrong" and "I'm gonna fuck up," again and again. I'm just going to do my thing. It's going to be good enough for me, because that's part of a stage of evolution for me. And you trust that eventually people will get it and like it or you'll evolve it.

It's not like there aren't great artists emerging right now, there are. The existence of social media does not prevent the emergence of great art. I don't think it facilitates it but doesn't prevent it. That will be true for humanist leadership too. Technology will dehumanize far too many of us, but it will also enable those who do get the message and want to do something about it to find one another and to connect. I hope they do.

The number one thing that I should leave you with, about humanism and humanist communities and atheism, is that we have had tremendous success over the last 10 to 20 years. There are a lot of young humanist chaplains and humanist community leaders of all kinds out there, doing all kinds of great stuff and a lot of them are women and again, a lot of them are people of color people from marginalized backgrounds. Many of them are LGBTQ, or non-binary. They're all doing wonderful things: leading projects at universities, or going to Africa and leading development projects in the name of humanism, or working in hospitals taking care of dying patients. They're making art and music in the name of humanism. They're engaging in racial justice campaigns in the name of humanism.

I think that anybody who denies the existence or the vibrancy of the Humanist Movement in this country today because it doesn't happen to look exactly like whatever they think of as a vibrant movement is—to use the most formal academic terminology I can—being either a bit of a dunce or a bit of a jerk, or both. Because it is vibrant. It is healthy. It is growing. Not like hockey stick growing, but growing. It's growing like a plant and I'm curious to see where it will go. But, again, to come back to my ultimate message, I'm really worried about our world, and I think that we've got bigger problems to face together as humans than whether any group is growing or not.

Einstein: This plays off one of the questions: what is the goal of marketing? You've answered this in part. The goal isn't growth; it can't be. That's one of our biggest problems in terms of corporations as well. If we can get off this idea that growth is by default good, we can start moving in, at least, a better direction. Whether you're growing humanism or have to meet quarterly sales goals, the focus on getting bigger creates problems—from anxiety to overconsumption to the environment.

Epstein: We have parts of us that are like flowers. Some of our most beautiful parts grow and then die and need to be replaced in the future. That's okay. I feel good about being part of this forest. And I feel that I'm both part of the forest and I've also been one of the gardeners of the forest. But you know, eventually stuff will grow over me too. But the point is, is the entire forest healthy, is the planet on which the forest is situated healthy? That's the goal. That's what's worthwhile in the end.

For Examples and Resources on Trends in Humanism and Marketing:

Humanists for Biden (2020). YouTube: https://www.youtube.com/watch?v=SRpz86CMnOk

Sarah Levin and Secular Strategies: https://www.secularstrategies.com/. She also writes for The Humanist (https://thehumanist.com/), which has additional resources.

Spectrum Experience (https://www.spectrumexperience.com/index.html) is a marketing firm dedicated to amplifying humanist voices, especially in politics.

Sukivu Hutchinson (https://sikivuhutchinson.com/) is the author of *Humanists in the Hood: Unapologetically Black, Feminist, and Heretical,* among others.

American Humanist Association (https://americanhumanist.org/) is an organization to watch as they have hired their first woman of color as executive director.

Hemant Mehta is the Friendly Atheist and the first atheist influencer. You can find his Substack here: https://friendlyatheist.substack.com/about

Notes

1 This has been edited for brevity.
2 Today, Queens is the most diverse county in the United States.
3 International Institute for Secular Humanist Judaism. See https://iishj.org/

Bibliography

Burge, R. P. (2023). *The Nones*, Second Edition. Minneapolis, MN: Fortress Press.

Drescher, E. (2016). *Choosing Our Religion: The Spiritual Lives of America's Nones.* Oxford: Oxford University Press.

Editor. (2023, January 18). *Who Are the Exvangelicals? Experts on the Exodus from White American Evangelicalism.* ReligionLink. https://www.religionlink.com/source-guides/who-are-the-exvangelicals-experts-on-the-exodus-from-white-american-evangelicalism/

Fattal, I. (2018, May 16). *MIT Now Has a Humanist Chaplain to Help Students with the Ethics of Tech.* The Atlantic. https://www.theatlantic.com/education/archive/2018/05/mit-now-has-a-humanist-chaplain-to-help-students-with-the-ethics-of-tech/560504/

Lee, J. 8. (2009, October 19). *"Good Without God," Atheist Subway Ads Proclaim.* City Room. https://archive.nytimes.com/cityroom.blogs.nytimes.com/2009/10/19/good-without-god-atheist-subway-ads-proclaim/

Pew Research Center. (2022, September 13). *Modeling the Future of Religion in America.* Pew Research Center's Religion & Public Life Project; Pew Research Center. https://www.pewresearch.org/religion/2022/09/13/modeling-the-future-of-religion-in-america/

PRRI. (2021). *American Values Atlas: Religious Affiliation Updates and Trends: White Christian Decline Slows, Unaffiliated Growth Levels Off.* PRRI. https://www.prri.org/spotlight/prri-2021-american-values-atlas-religious-affiliation-updates-and-trends-white-christian-decline-slows-unaffiliated-growth-levels-off/

Smith, G. (2021, December 14). *About Three-in-Ten U.S. Adults Are Now Religiously Unaffiliated.* Pew Research Center's Religion & Public Life Project; Pew Research Center. https://www.pewresearch.org/religion/2021/12/14/about-three-in-ten-u-s-adults-are-now-religiously-unaffiliated/

Stedman, C. (2012). *Faitheist: How an Atheist found Common Ground with the Religious.* Boston, MA: Beacon Press.

INDEX

Printed in the United States
by Baker & Taylor Publisher Services